W9-BFY-068

Praise for John Feinstein's

ONE ON ONE

"Renowned sportswriter John Feinstein returns to the subjects of his early books and shares his stories of running after athletes for interviews and trying to get access to locker rooms.... In his trademark lively prose, Feinstein offers an insider's glimpse of what it's like to cover sports ranging from golf (including Tiger Woods) to college basketball to the Army-Navy football game."
— Molly Driscoll, *Christian Science Monitor*

"Feinstein's gift is his ability to talk to people and to get them to talk to him. He long ago reached celebrity author status, but even before, Feinstein understood how to approach people and, even if they stood on opposite sides of a subject, he could volley with them.... It's a book about Feinstein, who is himself a collection of colorful stories.... He does what few writers can do—take readers to places they couldn't otherwise go. It's a fun trip."
— Ron Green Jr., *Charlotte Observer*

"Some of the most talented and temperamental athletes and coaches in the world have opened up to John Feinstein.... The acclaimed sportswriter's latest book details his conversations over the years with notoriously difficult coaches like Bobby Knight and star athletes like Tiger Woods and John McEnroe."   —NPR's *Fresh Air*

"Feinstein has a rare ability to take his readers inside the intense emotions of his subjects, sharing their hopes, dreams, and tragedies."
— Henry Kisor, *Chicago Sun-Times*

"Feinstein's beat, as it turns out, isn't sports; it's human nature."
— Alex Tresniowski, *People*

"John Feinstein has become sportswriting's John Grisham."
— David Kindred, *Sporting News*

"Stripped down, *One on One* is a reporter's road trip, an engaging journey full of elite athletes and coaches John Feinstein encountered while transforming himself from *Washington Post* political reporter to bestselling sports author.... With his deft, dialogue-driven narrative and knack for describing an interview's atmospherics, Feinstein describes the genesis of each of his year-in-the-life books and the role the 'greats' played in them.... What to a lesser writer could become a boring exercise in point A to point B literary geometry is instead a revealing look beyond the limelight's glare."
— Ross Hemphill, *Winnipeg Free Press*

"Reading Feinstein is to read far more than sports. Great sports books capture the spirit of an era and of a public enamored with the game. Great writers capture the essence of where sports fit in the life-size mural that is life.... Feinstein has succeeded as a sport journalist by going behind the scenes of great athletes and coaches.... Now he has granted readers the type of access he has been afforded. By holding a mirror to his work, he has made his own writing even better."
— Stuart Shiffman, *Bookreporter*

ONE ON ONE

ONE ON ONE

BEHIND THE SCENES WITH THE GREATS IN THE GAME

JOHN FEINSTEIN

BACK BAY BOOKS

LITTLE, BROWN AND COMPANY

New York   Boston   London

Back Bay Books / Little, Brown and Company
Hachette Book Group
237 Park Avenue, New York, NY 10017
littlebrown.com

Originally published in hardcover by Little, Brown and Company, December 2011
First Back Bay paperback edition, December 2012

Back Bay Books is an imprint of Little, Brown and Company. The Back Bay Books name and logo are trademarks of Hachette Book Group, Inc.

The publisher is not responsible for websites (or their content) that are not owned by the publisher.

The Hachette Speakers Bureau provides a wide range of authors for speaking events. To find out more, go to hachettespeakersbureau.com or call (866) 376-6591.

Library of Congress Cataloging-in-Publication Data
Feinstein, John.
    One on one : behind the scenes with the greats in the game / John Feinstein. — 1st ed.
        p. cm.
    ISBN 978-0-316-07904-4 (hc) / 978-0-316-07905-1 (pb)
    1. Athletes—United States—Interviews.   2. Coaches (Athletics)—United States—Interviews.   3. Sports—United States.   4. Success.
I. Title.
    GV697.A1F45 2011
    796.0922—dc23
    [B]   2011026450

10 9 8 7 6 5 4 3 2 1

RRD-C

Printed in the United States of America

*This is for Jane Blythe Feinstein,
whose smile can light up any room.*

Contents

ONE ON ONE

Introduction

THIS IS NOT EXACTLY the book I thought I would write in 2011.

I always thought there might come a point in my life when I would go back and talk to all the people I encountered while researching *A Season on the Brink* twenty-five years ago. I knew exactly where the book would begin and where it would end. I would fill in the blanks in between by talking to the players and coaches I got to know so well in the winter of 1985–86 in Bloomington, Indiana.

But the more I thought about it the more I realized that a *Boys of Summer* book wasn't really what I wanted to do. What made that book unique—besides Roger Kahn's writing—was the bittersweet nature of the story line: young, powerful men twenty years later, stripped of that which made them powerful and dealing with the harsh realities of getting older.

There's really very little that's bittersweet about the characters in *Season on the Brink*. Sure, Bob Knight got fired after twenty-nine years at Indiana, but who among us was surprised to see him self-destruct—and then blame everyone else for his own failings? Most of the other people in the book had gone on to lead successful lives: a handful in basketball, some in law or medicine, while others had gone home to family businesses. If there was one thing Knight always did well as a coach, it was prepare his players for Life After

Basketball. The kids in *A Season on the Brink,* all in their forties now, were a bright group who would find their way in life—probably in ways that were difficult for the old Dodgers of Kahn's book to accomplish. All are college graduates; most knew they probably weren't going to play in the NBA. Only one actually did play in the NBA—Steve Alford, who played for four years before becoming a college coach.

After a lot of thought, I realized how lucky I had been to write the books I'd written. I had come in contact with so many different people from across the spectrum of sports. I hadn't just been in Bob Knight's locker room, I'd been in Mike Krzyzewski's and Jim Valvano's and Larry Brown's locker rooms. I was never in Dean Smith's or John Thompson's, but I'd certainly had plenty of interactions with the two of them too.

I had also been in both locker rooms during an Army-Navy game (a distinction usually reserved, I believe, for those who hold the office of president of the United States). I had spent hours and hours with Tom Watson and Arnold Palmer and Jack Nicklaus and John McEnroe and Ivan Lendl and Pete Sampras and Martina Navratilova and Chris Evert—not to mention Joe Torre and Bobby Cox and Tony LaRussa and Deion Sanders. I even spent an evening once with Tiger Woods. Yup, seriously.

There were others, not nearly as famous but perhaps more fascinating, and at least as admirable: Paul Goydos, Bruce Edwards, Chris Spitler, and Steve Kerr, who is at least semi-famous. And then there were the young men I got to know and like so much while writing *A Civil War* and *The Last Amateurs.* I had dustups around the world with security people, *Pravda,* and the Czechoslovakian secret police. I learned from people like Bob Woodward, David Maraniss, and Tony Kornheiser, and battled with editors, notably George Solomon, who helped launch my career.

So why not go back and talk to all those people?

Going into one's past can be dangerous. You might be disappointed by those you revisit: the way they react to you, what they have become, the stories they don't have to tell. But I was lucky. I found the people I wanted to find and every one of them reacted to my reappearance in their lives exactly as I would have hoped—or in the case of Bob Knight, exactly as I'd expected.

This isn't meant to be a memoir. I hope I'm still a little too young to write one. What it is meant to be is a trip through reporting my first ten books, bringing me—and the reader—up to the present day.

One note about the way the book is written: Clearly, I don't remember word-for-word all the dialogues presented here. A lot of the quotes in the book are verbatim because they come from interviews—old and new—I have conducted over the years. But many of the conversations come from my memory, which is still, I'm happy to report, pretty good. The give-and-take in some cases isn't exactly correct but does accurately depict the gist of what was said. I do not, for example, know exactly how many times Mike Krzyzewski said to me, "Are you out of your f—ing mind?" that fateful night in Lexington, Kentucky, but I do know for certain that was the message he was trying to convey.

I'm happy to report that digging into my past and into my memory bank and old notebooks and tapes was great fun and brought back events I hadn't given any real thought to for a very long time. Seeing people I hadn't seen for years was terrific. Maybe I will do this again sometime down the road. Of course, the chances are good that Bob Knight will react to me then the same way as now.

Which is fine. I wouldn't want him to ever stop being Bob Knight.

1

How It Began

When the semifinal day at the Final Four was still a *day* rather than the long day's journey into night it has now become, the first game tipped off at 3:40 in the afternoon and the second game was over by about eight o'clock. That meant even if you had to write about the second game, you were out of the arena no later than 9:30, if only because Saturday newspaper deadlines dictated you not linger over your story.

The matchups that afternoon were Villanova–Memphis State and St. John's–Georgetown. I had more or less stumbled into the unofficial role of being the *Washington Post*'s Villanova beat writer. The Wildcats were the number eight seed in the Southeast Region, and it didn't appear the basketball committee had given them much respect from the start, since their first-round game had been against ninth-seeded Dayton in the University of Dayton Arena.

Villanova managed to beat Dayton, 50–49. Then, on Sunday, the Wildcats easily beat Michigan while Maryland—triple-teaming future star David Robinson every chance it got—came from behind late to beat Navy. That set up a Villanova-Maryland round of sixteen game in Birmingham the following Friday.

I took the train to Philadelphia on Monday afternoon to spend some time with Coach Rollie Massimino and his players. I hadn't dealt with Rollie much, but thought of him as prickly and difficult. That day he was a delight, telling funny stories and joking about his penchant for unraveling fashionwise during games. His players were bright and outgoing, especially Eddie Pinkney, the starting center, and Gary McLain and Dwayne McClain. The other player who was really helpful was Massimino's son R.C., who was a rarely used walk-on but had great stories about his dad.

Four days later the Wildcats beat Maryland in the regional semifinals—which was a mild surprise to me.

And then it was on to play North Carolina, who had beaten Auburn in the second regional semifinal on Friday night. Massimino had finished all of his postgame media and had walked to press row to scout that game just as Carolina came onto the court. A large chunk of the crowd, dressed in light blue, exploded.

"Hey, Rollie," said Mark Whicker, who worked in those days for the *Philadelphia Daily News* and had graduated from North Carolina. "Take a look: *those* are the Tar Heels."

Whicker and Rollie were good friends, and Rollie waved a hand dismissively at him. "Screw you, schmuck," he said, using one of his favorite words. "We'll see who cheers last on Sunday."

Even though the Tar Heels had lost Michael Jordan and Sam Perkins off their 1984 team, they were still, well, the Tar Heels. They had Brad Daugherty and Kenny Smith and Dave Popson and Steve Hale and, most important, Dean Smith. Back then, people who spent a lot of time around the ACC—myself included—figured if you gave Dean five guys who could walk, he would usually find a way to win. But Villanova pulled the upset, 56–44.

I wrote the next day about Massimino's emotions in the final seconds after Smith had ordered his players not to foul and Massimino got to hug his coaches and his players—including his son—as the final seconds ticked off the clock. "I hope every coach gets to feel what I felt once in his life," he said. "To know you're going to the Final Four is just an unbelievable feeling."

Six days later in Rupp Arena Villanova had pulled away from Memphis State in the final minutes of that first game on semifinal Saturday. Then Georgetown absolutely blew St. John's out of the building in the second game. That made my sidebar easy to write, and I didn't take very long with it, writing about the shock on the St. John's side after being manhandled by a team it had beaten in January. The theme of all the *Post* stories was pretty much the same: Georgetown was one game from a second straight national championship.

As soon as I had filed my second game sidebar, I headed out of the arena and walked several blocks to a nearby Italian restaurant. I can't remember what it was called, but I knew why I was going there: I had been invited to dinner by Bob Knight.

He'd issued the invitation on the phone in February several days after his infamous chair throw. The orange plastic chair had skidded across the court at Indiana's Assembly Hall a few minutes into Indiana's game on a Saturday afternoon against Purdue.

Indiana was in the midst of Knight's most frustrating season as a basketball coach. The previous year the Hoosiers had stunned North Carolina in the Sweet Sixteen. All you need to know about that game is that Dan Dakich spent most of the night guarding Michael Jordan—and Indiana won. Carolina had Jordan, Perkins, Daugherty, and both Smiths, Kenny and Dean. Indiana had Dakich, a freshman guard named Steve Alford, and Uwe Blab. That win had to be one of the high points of Knight's career and one of the low points of Dean Smith's, although he managed to maintain a sense of humor about it.

The next week, when I flew into Seattle for the Final Four, I ran into Dean at the rent-a-car counter. Seeing me, he smiled wanly and said, "I didn't think I'd be renting a car this week. I thought I'd be riding on the team bus."

Indiana lost to Virginia in the regional final after the win over Carolina, but still went into the following season ranked in everyone's preseason top five. Knight was coming off the best summer of his life—or so it appeared—having coached the U.S. Olympic team to the gold medal in Los Angeles. Only later did I find out how upset Knight had been by the Soviet bloc's boycott of those games. More than anything he had wanted to coach his country in the gold medal game against the Soviet Union.

Instead, he got Spain, a team coached by a good friend of his. The U.S. team won by thirty-three and Knight insisted he could not have been more thrilled. That wasn't quite the case: Knight wanted to crush the Soviets and he wanted to do it in the Olympics. Every chance he got when speaking publicly the next couple of years, he took shots at the Soviets and talked about what his team, led by Michael Jordan, David Robinson, and Patrick Ewing, would have done to them given the chance.

But they never got that chance.

The '84–85 season quickly turned into a disaster. Indiana wasn't as good as it had appeared to be in the Carolina game. Knight got frustrated and began feuding with his players. Mike Giomi, the leading rebounder, was thrown off the team for cutting classes. Marty Simmons, after a superb freshman season, put on weight and was benched. Winston Morgan, one of the team's three seniors, got left off the team plane on a trip home from Ohio State because Knight was so angry with him. Even though he had another year of eligibility left, because of an injury, Knight told him he didn't want him back.

In late January, Indiana played at Illinois. Knight couldn't stand Illini coach Lou Henson. He thought he was a cheat, and he didn't respect him as a coach. And so, angry with his team, trying to make a point on national television, he benched four starters—including Alford, who was already an iconic figure in Indiana. He had been Mr. Basketball in the state as a high school senior, Indiana's leading scorer as a freshman, and a part of Knight's Olympic team.

Illinois won the game easily and people began whispering that Knight was losing it, that he was exhausted from coaching all summer and then dealing with a disappointing team.

That's where I came into the picture.

"Go out and see if he'll talk to you," *Post* sports editor George Solomon said to me one morning in February. "He likes you. Maybe he'll talk. If not, stay out there and just write around it."

Knight did like me. I had met him on several occasions, often through Dave Kindred, who had been a columnist at the *Post* and had a good relationship with Knight dating to his days at the *Louisville Courier-Journal*. The first person to actually introduce me to Knight had been Lefty Driesell at a press conference prior to an Indiana-Maryland game in the second round of the 1981 NCAA Tournament.

What really jump-started my relationship with Knight, though, was a piece I wrote two years later in *The Sporting News* about the success his former assistants were having as head coaches. At that point in time, Don DeVoe was winning consistently at Tennessee, Dave Bliss was doing very well at Southern Methodist, Bob Weltlich was having success at Texas, Mike Krzyzewski, who played for Knight at Army and then coached there, was beginning to take off at Duke, and Gerry Gimelstob seemed headed in the right direction at George Washington—having gotten the job back in '81, soon after I met Knight.

Talking to the ex–Knight assistants for the piece was easy. Talking to Knight wasn't so easy. This was during the summer, and every time I called the Indiana basketball office I was told Knight was away either fishing or playing golf or recruiting. I would leave a message and get no call back. I was beginning to think I would have to write the story without Knight.

As luck would have it, the week the piece was due, I was in Chicago on an assignment for the *Post*. Walking into O'Hare Airport, I practically ran smack into Knight, who was walking out of the airport. I reintroduced myself, told him I'd been trying to get him on the phone, and asked if he had a few minutes. More good luck: he did. He was en route to play in a golf tournament and his ride— Digger Phelps—hadn't shown up yet.

The subject was an easy one for Knight, and he talked about how proud he was of all his protégés. I thanked him, wrote the piece, and didn't think about it again until I got a letter from Knight several weeks later. In it, he told me how much he liked the story and how well I had captured what he tried to do as a boss to help his assistants advance their careers. The last line was the most important one: "Anytime I can help you in the future, don't hesitate to call. Let me know anytime you're planning to come to Bloomington."

Coming from Knight, that invitation was a big deal. Dave Kindred had told me that Knight granted regular access to a small handful of reporters. Bob Hammel, his local guy in Bloomington, was a pal, and Kindred, Billy Reed in Louisville, Dave Anderson of the *New York Times,* and David Israel of the *Chicago Tribune* were often granted close-up glimpses of the inner workings of Indiana basketball. All I really wanted was the chance to talk to Knight when I needed to write about him. That appeared to be what he was offering.

That fall, the *Washington Post Sunday Magazine* asked me to do a story on Knight—most of it focusing on his selection as the Olympic coach, something that had surprised some people (including Knight) since he had gotten himself arrested in Puerto Rico in 1979 while coach of the U.S. Pan American team.

Knight was such a good coach that he overcame that incident to get the Olympic job. When I called Indiana sports information director Kit Klingelhoffer, to ask about coming out to spend some time with Knight, he sounded skeptical. "Let me get back to you," he said. The next day he did. "You should have told me you were on the list," he said.

"The list?" I asked.

"Yeah, the list of guys who he'll always talk to. He said come on out whenever you want."

So I did. I flew to Indianapolis on the Monday after Indiana had lost a close game to a Kentucky team that would go on to the Final Four that season. I rented a car and drove to Bloomington in a driving rain—a harbinger, although I didn't know it at the time, of the weather I would see for most of my winter in Indiana. I arrived just before practice began. Klingelhoffer escorted me down to the court and told me to wait in the empty gym. The team was in the locker room having a meeting.

A few minutes later, the players and coaches came onto the court. If Knight knew I was there or cared, he never showed it. I sat and watched practice. When it was over, everyone went back into the locker room and I was alone in the gym again. I waited a few more minutes, then walked across the court to where I knew the coaches dressed in a locker room separate from the players. Maybe, I thought, someone would be in there who could tell me where Knight was and whether he was still planning on talking to me.

Tentatively, I knocked on the door. It was answered almost immediately by Jim Crews, Knight's top assistant. Before I could begin to explain myself, I saw Knight sitting a few feet away in a comfortable armchair. "Jesus Christ, John, where the hell have you been? I thought you wanted to talk."

Welcome to Knightworld.

I ended up spending the evening with Knight, having dinner at his favorite Chinese restaurant, and filling up several hours of tape on my recorder. When he dropped me off at my car, still parked at Assembly Hall, he left me with one last thought.

"There's one thing I don't think people understand about the way I coach," he said. "I coach like I'm still at West Point, like the other team is always going to be more talented. When I get my players to think that way, we're good. When I don't, we're not as good. But I'm always thinking that way."

I covered Indiana in the regional that year when the Hoosiers pulled the monumental upset over North Carolina before the disappointing loss to Virginia. Then I covered the Olympic trials, which were in Bloomington, and the Olympics in Los Angeles. Knight was alternately hot and cold with me as with everyone. At times he would pull me aside, put an arm around me, and explain something to me about a certain player. At other times he would walk right by me as if not seeing me. Kindred explained that was just Knight being Knight, always letting you know that he controlled the relationship. My attitude was simple: as long as I could get in touch with him when I needed to, he was welcome to feel in control.

When George Solomon suggested I go out and talk to Knight not long after the Illinois benchings and the Giomi expulsion from the team, I decided not to call Knight. I called Klingelhoffer and asked for a credential for the following Thursday when Illinois was coming to Bloomington for a rematch.

"You going to try to talk to him?" Kit asked, knowing I probably wasn't coming to write a game story.

"Going to play it by ear," I said. "See what his mood is like."

"Probably smart," he said. "It hasn't been good very often this winter though, I should warn you about that."

I hardly needed warning.

I caught the exact same flight to Indianapolis I had taken in the past en route to Bloomington and drove—again in the rain—down State Road 37 into town. It was mid-afternoon on game day. Since I had gotten to know Knight's assistants a little during the Olympics experience, I figured it couldn't hurt to stop at Assembly Hall before checking into my hotel to see if anyone was around. My best hope was that Indiana would win the game and Knight would be in a good enough mood that he would talk to me afterward.

I knocked on the door of the coaches' locker room, which sits a few yards from the floor. Within seconds the door was opened—by

Knight. He looked at me for a second and then waved me into the room.

"John," he said. "What can I do for you?"

He was alone. He sat down in his armchair, where he had been watching tape. I gingerly sat on the arm of another chair, not sure just how welcome I was, showing up unannounced.

"You show up unannounced to see Dean [Smith] and Mike [Krzyzewski] a lot?" he said, as if reading my mind.

"Only on game days," I said, going for humor.

If he was amused he didn't show it.

"We're a bad basketball team right now, John," he said. With that he launched into an explanation of everything that had gone wrong that winter. I waited a while before I took out a notebook. When I did, he kept on talking. And talking. The coaches began showing up as game time approached. I waited to be dismissed. I hadn't even picked up my credential yet.

"Come on, walk me over to the locker room," Knight said about thirty minutes before game time.

We walked the back hallways of the building to the far side where the players dressed. I could hear the band playing out on the court. Knight nodded to the various security people as we walked down the hall. I followed him into the locker room and found a place in a corner to stand. Knight went through the matchups and explained to his players how sick and tired he was of losing to Illinois. "I don't care how many f—ing All-Americans he [Henson] has out there," he said. "You boys play Indiana basketball tonight the way we coach you to play and we'll win the game."

There was a lot more, but I didn't have my tape recorder with me. It was a miracle I had brought my notebook inside. I trailed Knight when he walked out onto the court, an exercise that would become the norm for me the following season. No one stopped me since I was clearly with him. When Knight went to the bench I went to press row and found Klingelhoffer.

"Where've you been?" he asked. "I thought maybe you weren't coming."

"I've been with Knight since three thirty this afternoon," I said.

Klingelhoffer shook his head as he handed me my credential. "He really *does* like you, I guess," he said.

Illinois won the game easily. Knight got a technical foul and put his foot through a chair before it was over. He refused to shake Henson's hand at the end and didn't come in to talk to the media. I wondered if I should take what I had — which was plenty — or push the envelope a little bit further. I had told Knight that I was hoping to talk to some of the players the following day, and he had said that would be fine. I wondered if it was still fine.

So I went and knocked on the door again to the room I would eventually come to call "the Cave."

Knight was sitting in his chair when assistant coach Kohn Smith opened the door and looked at me as if to say, "Are you nuts?"

"Sorry you flew all the way out here to see that, John," Knight said. "We're ordering food. You hungry?"

I was starving. I hadn't eaten anything since getting off the airplane about nine hours earlier. I sat and listened to Knight talk to the coaches about how they needed to recruit junior college players in order to compete with teams as athletic as Illinois. I listened to him rail some more against Henson. I ate some chicken wings and watched some tape. Klingelhoffer came in and Knight told him to arrange for me to talk to the two captains, Dakich and Blab, the next day. It was 2 a.m. when I called it a night.

I almost felt as if I could fly home the next morning. I had plenty for my story. I stayed and talked to Dakich and Blab, who were brutally honest about how poorly the team had played. Dakich expressed concern. "We're so bad we might drive Coach out of the game," he said. "I've seen him mad, but never like this."

Knight was mad at practice that afternoon. I continued to have complete access: pre-practice talk in the locker room (which wasn't pretty), practice, postpractice talk. Then it was back to the Chinese restaurant for dinner, where Knight talked calmly and philosophically about getting through a season like this one and regrouping to come back next year.

I was on an early morning flight the next day thinking I had enough to write three stories. Indiana was playing Purdue that afternoon. I figured sticking around would be redundant, since I'd seen everything there was to see in the past forty-eight hours. Of course I was completely wrong.

I WAS ACTUALLY SITTING in George Solomon's office writing the Knight story a few hours after I'd left Indiana—it was a quiet place to work on a Saturday afternoon—when someone came in and said, "Your guy Knight just threw a chair."

I walked out into the newsroom just in time to see a replay. I hadn't even bothered to watch the start of the game, figuring I'd wait to see how the first half went and then watch the second. Purdue had jumped to an 11–2 lead, and Knight had gotten into it with referee London Bradley—one of many Big Ten refs he insisted shouldn't be reffing in the Big Ten.

Bradley had teed Knight up. As Purdue's Steve Ross walked to the free-throw line, Knight turned and picked up the orange plastic chair where he had been sitting and sidearmed it across the court. It skittered directly in front of Ross and lost steam just as it reached the far side of the court. What's funny to me all these years later is that if you watch the tape, no one on the Indiana bench moves or shows any kind of emotion—except for a manager who, without missing a beat, grabs another chair and puts it in the spot where the one Knight had thrown had been.

Everyone at IU had seen Knight throw chairs and all sorts of other things, so the sight of him tossing this chair was pretty ho-hum. Not to the rest of the world. Knight was ejected on the spot, and

Indiana president John Ryan was in the Cave a few minutes later. Knight did something at that moment I'm guessing he probably hasn't done five times in his life: he apologized.

Needless to say the lead and the tone of my story had to be changed after the chair throw. There was certainly no defending what Knight had done, and I didn't defend him. In fact, the opening line of the story said this: "Maybe if he had counted to ten he wouldn't have done it."

But of course he didn't count to ten and he did do it. I ended up writing close to three thousand words—many of them coming directly from Knight—about his lost season and the dichotomy of the calm, measured man I'd had dinner with on Friday night and the crazed coach who had tossed a chair about sixteen hours later. The day after the story, my phone rang. It was Knight. I braced myself. About nine times out of ten when the subject of a story calls, it is to complain about something in the piece.

"I just wanted to tell you," Knight said as I readied myself to play defense, "how much it means to me that you went out of your way to tell both sides in that story you wrote. You could have taken me apart after what happened Saturday, like most people are doing, and you didn't do it."

I told Knight that being able to talk to him and to his players and to watch him prepare for the Purdue game—regardless of what had happened—allowed me to write the story that way. I thanked him for the time and the access.

"Anytime," Knight said. "I hope you know that. You're welcome here anytime. Speaking of which, I always go out to dinner on Saturday night at the Final Four with a bunch of my coaches and friends. I don't know what your schedule is, but I'd really like it if you joined us."

I told him if I could get there once I was finished writing, I would. He said he would get me the information on the restaurant they were going to, thanked me again, and we hung up.

It was at that moment the thought first crossed my mind: What if he meant it about me being welcome out there anytime? What if I could have the access I'd had for two days for an entire season? Was I nuts or was there a pretty good book in something like that?

I asked four people what they thought of the idea: Bob Woodward, Tony Kornheiser, David Maraniss, and Lesley Visser. They all thought it had a lot of potential if Knight was actually willing to give me the kind of access I'd had during those two days. The only person who had any doubts was Visser, but it had nothing to do with the book's potential. "Do you really want to spend a winter in Bloomington, Indiana?" she asked.

I was single and had just broken up with someone, so I had no reason *not* to spend a winter in Bloomington. I decided the place to broach the idea to Knight was face-to-face—at the Final Four. I figured I had nothing to lose.

As I WALKED TO the restaurant that night, I was nervous. Even though Knight saying no wouldn't change my life—in fact, him saying yes would potentially change my life far more—I didn't want him to turn me down. I had really come to believe in the idea and I had always wanted to write a book.

In fact, the idea to do a book tracking a college basketball team from the inside dated to my college days. Even though Duke wasn't any good when I was an undergraduate, I had gotten to know both the players and the coaches well by covering the basketball team for the student newspaper, *The Chronicle.* I believed there was a story to be told about what really went on inside locker rooms and practices and huddles.

The idea stayed with me during my early days at the *Post,* but I was convinced you had to have a truly big name coach give you access to his program in order to write a book that a publisher would buy and that the public would want to read.

To me there were only three coaches who fit that profile: Knight, Dean Smith, and Georgetown's John Thompson, who in 1984 had become the first African-American coach to win a national championship. Thompson was brilliant, he was intense, and he was perhaps the most secretive and paranoid person I'd ever met in a business filled with men who were secretive and paranoid. He literally chained the doors to McDonough Gym closed when his team practiced, and he had a bell attached to the door of the reception area leading to the basketball offices so that even when he was in his office, he knew when someone was coming in or going out.

Thompson's desire for secrecy and my desire for storytelling led us to clash early and often. We battled frequently, often screaming at one another outside locker rooms and in hotel lobbies. Once, when I made the mistake of snapping at his academic coordinator/alter ego/best friend, Mary Fenlon, who had more authority than anyone in the program with the *possible* exception of Thompson, he went off on me completely.

On this particular night, I had waited in the hallway for Thompson and Fenlon to make the short walk from the back door of the Capital Centre's home locker room to the interview room. As they came out, I said to Thompson, "John, when you're done in there, I need a minute to ask you a couple of quick follow-ups for the Ewing piece." I'd been working on a feature on Patrick Ewing.

Before Thompson could answer, Fenlon looked at me and said, "He doesn't have time for any of your questions." I never liked Fenlon. I thought she fed Thompson's paranoia and went out of her way to be unpleasant to people. So, when she answered for Thompson, I answered instinctively: "Mary, I don't think I was talking to you. I think I was talking to John."

Now Thompson *did* answer me. Standing up to his full height of 6 foot 10, he loomed over me and screamed, "If you're talking to Mary, you're talking to me. And if you're f—ing with Mary, you're f—ing with me. You want to f— with me?"

Clearly, I didn't want to f— with him. Just as clearly, I wasn't going to let him intimidate me, no matter how intimidated I felt at that moment. He had me by ten inches and probably 150 pounds (I was a lot thinner then than now).

I stood up as straight as I could and remembered something Wil Jones, who had played against Thompson in high school, had once told me: "John loves to intimidate. But he's not so tough. When we played I always told him he was nothing but a pussy jump shooter."

So I looked up at Thompson and said, "Fine, John, you wanna go out back? You want the first swing? From what Wil Jones says I'll have a pretty good shot. And if not, what the hell, you can knock me out and make me a millionaire." (I'd stolen that line from my pal Ken Denlinger, who had once had a similar conversation with Lefty Driesell.)

Thompson's mouth dropped open for a second. Then he started to laugh. He put his arm around me and said, "You know something, motherf—er [that was John's catchall word for everything; it was often a term of endearment], I have to admit something. I respect you. I don't *like* you, but I respect you. I'll give you five minutes when I'm done."

Which he did.

Our relationship got worse before it got better. I used the term "Hoya Paranoia" in a story about Georgetown that I wrote for *The Sporting News* in the spring of 1984, and at the Final Four in Seattle that year, Thompson accused the media of having a "herd mentality" when it came to his team because the "Hoya Paranoia" reference had picked up quite a bit of steam.

Clearly, Thompson was not going to be the guy who gave me complete access to his team for a season. I was lucky to be allowed in the building when Georgetown played.

THAT WASN'T THE CASE with Dean Smith. In spite of my educational background (Duke), I'd always had a good relationship with him. In fact, in 1981 I had written a lengthy two-part series on Smith in the *Post* for which he had given me a lot of interview time and allowed a lot of his close friends to talk with me. For Dean, this was very rare. He hated publicity.

"Write about the players," he would always say when someone asked him for extended interview time. He had even done that when approached by the great Frank Deford for a profile in *Sports Illustrated*. Deford was so good he could write around not having sit-down time with Dean and still be brilliant. I wasn't that good. So in January of 1981, absolutely determined to get Dean to give me some serious time, I drove down to Charlottesville on a Friday afternoon to see him at his hotel—the Boar's Head Inn. North Carolina was playing Virginia the next afternoon.

Rick Brewer—who had been the sports information director at North Carolina since 1975, but had worked in the athletic department since his days as a student in the mid-'60s—had convinced Dean to speak to me that evening and allow me to make my case. So I made the drive from D.C. even though I had to turn around and go right back to cover a game at Maryland the next day.

Dean was trying unsuccessfully to light a fire in the fireplace in his room when Rick and I walked in. Through the years, one thing he and I have shared is a complete inability to figure out anything mechanical or technical. Once, when I was trying to track him down by phone for a story I was working on one Sunday afternoon, I asked Keith Drum, who worked at the *Durham Morning Herald* at the time, if he would give Dean the 800 number at the *Post* and ask him to call me. When Keith handed Dean the number, Dean looked at it and said, "I'm not sure I know how to dial an eight-hundred number." He was serious.

Now he had put out a call for someone on the hotel staff to come to the room to light a fire for him. I would have offered to help, only I probably couldn't have done any better.

"So what do you need?" Dean asked, sitting down.

"You," I answered as he started shaking his head.

I told him I *had* written stories about his players, including one earlier that season on Sam Perkins. I had even driven down to Wilmington to see one of his future players, a kid named Michael Jordan, play that winter. I told him if he didn't talk to me, I was going to write the story anyway, but I also said I knew it would be a lot better if he did talk to me.

He sighed and looked at Rick. "What do you think, Rick?" he asked.

Rick shrugged. "I think if John's going to write the story it *will* be better if you talk to him," he said.

Dean looked at me and shook his head. "I still wish you'd just write about the players," he said.

"I know you do, Dean," I answered.

"Okay. Let me think about it overnight. I'll let you know after the game tomorrow."

"That's fine," I said. "Maybe you can call me, or Rick can call me, because I won't be here. I have to drive back tonight since Maryland plays at noon tomorrow."

He looked puzzled. "You mean you drove down here just to talk to me?" he said.

I nodded.

He smiled. "I wish I'd have known that. I'd have had Rick buy you dinner."

To this day Rick and I still laugh about that line. Because I'd driven to Charlottesville to see Dean, *Rick* should get stuck taking me to dinner. I told him that, as much as I liked Rick and as much as I enjoyed the Aberdeen Barn (a great steakhouse in Charlottesville), my only mission that night was to get him to say yes.

The next day, shortly after Virginia and Ralph Sampson had beaten North Carolina, my phone rang. Hearing Rick's voice, I expected bad news, since I had just seen the end of the game a few minutes earlier.

"Dean says if you can come down the Friday of the North-South doubleheader, you can drive with him to Charlotte and talk then. That'll give you at least two and a half hours."

"That's a start," I said.

Rick laughed. "It's not a start," he said. "It's a miracle."

I really didn't care who was playing the two-day North-South since I wasn't staying for the games. The plan was for me to drive to Charlotte with Dean—who almost never traveled with his team, in large part because he thought the players would be more relaxed without him around, but also because he didn't like to smoke around them—and then drive Dean's car back to Chapel Hill, where I had left my car.

It was a fascinating two and a half hours. Dean talked about how he had always wanted to play the positions where you were in charge as a kid: quarterback, point guard, catcher. He talked about his dad and how proud he had been when he realized years after the fact that he had coached the first integrated high school basketball team in the state of Kansas. He was as open and unguarded as I'd ever seen him. At one point when he was talking about archconservative North Carolina senator Jesse Helms, I asked Dean if he had ever considered running against him. He shook his head.

"I could never get elected in this state," he said. "I'm too liberal."

The highlight of the trip came when we stopped at a gas station. It was February and cold, so the windows were rolled up and Dean was smoking. When he asked if I wanted to stop to get a Coke, I practically screamed, *"Yes, dear God, yes!"* The smoke was killing me. We pulled into a gas station and walked inside. There was an elderly gentleman in red overalls behind the counter. Just as we walked in he spit a large wad of chewing tobacco into a pail next to him.

When he saw Dean, his eyes went wide. Dean noticed and was instantly embarrassed. "Please don't write this—" he started to say just as we heard the man say, *"Oh my God."* Dean was waving him off, trying to get him to stop, when the man added, *"It's Norman Sloan!"*

I'm honestly not sure who laughed harder, Dean, the old guy, or me. As we walked back to the car, Dean said, "You see, I told you I'm not that big a deal around here."

When we got to Charlotte, Dean showed me where the car's registration was after explaining to me for a fourth time that the only reason he drove a BMW was because one of his ex-managers ran a BMW dealership. I laughed when he showed me the registration.

"Dean, if I get pulled over by a cop and I say that Dean Smith gave me his car, what do you think the chances are I'm not going to jail?"

"Yeah, and with your luck, it'll be a State fan," he said.

I was really proud of the story I wrote. I was able to talk to Dean's sister, to lots of his ex-players, and to coaches and friends. The most telling anecdote came from his pastor at the Binkley Baptist Church, Reverend Robert Seymour, who Dean described as one of his closest friends.

Reverend Seymour told me that, shortly after Dean arrived in Chapel Hill as Frank McGuire's assistant coach, he and Dean had gotten into a conversation about segregation. This was 1958 and restaurants in the South were still segregated. The two men agreed it was wrong and decided to try to do something about it. And so, one night that summer, North Carolina assistant basketball coach Dean Smith and an African-American member of the church walked into one of Chapel Hill's best-known restaurants, the Pines, and sat down together at a table.

One can imagine the conversation that went on among the employees and the management that night. They all knew that the man sitting at the table was Frank McGuire's assistant. On the other hand, he wasn't Frank McGuire—he was an assistant. Someone made a decision: dinner was served without anyone saying a word. That night was the beginning of desegregation in Chapel Hill.

"You have to understand," the pastor said to me, "Dean Smith wasn't Dean Smith in 1958. He was an assistant coach. It wasn't out of the question that management might have complained to the university and he might have gotten in serious trouble. But he never hesitated to do it."

When I asked Dean to tell me what he remembered about that night, he looked at me with some anger in his face. "Who told you that story?" he said.

"Reverend Seymour," I said.

"I wish he hadn't."

"Why? That's something you should be proud of."

Dean shook his head. "You should never be proud of doing the right thing," he said. "You should just do it."

I knew he meant it. I can't tell you how much I admired him at that moment. When I interviewed John Thompson, who had been a close friend of Dean's for years, I asked him if he knew the story. "No, I don't," he said. "And I'm not surprised. It's not Dean's way to take bows for anything."

The first part of the story ran the day before the start of the ACC Tournament, which was played in Washington that year. When North Carolina came on the court for its practice session that afternoon, I was standing courtside. Dean walked over to say hello. "I haven't read the paper today," he said. "Am I speaking to you?"

A couple of weeks later, I got the answer, in the form of a note from Dean. Typically, he started by saying he still wished I hadn't done the story. But since I'd done it, he thought I'd been very fair and thorough, although he wished his sister hadn't told me quite so much about his boyhood. I wrote back and thanked him for the note and for the time and his patience. Then I added another sentence: "I think you know how much I admire and respect you. Someday there will come a time for a book to be done on your life. I would love it if you would consider me as the person to write that book."

It was probably pretty audacious for me, at the age of twenty-five, to write that, but I did it anyway. Dean wrote back very graciously and said, "Of course, when the time comes, I would be happy to talk to you about a book. But I hope that I will be coaching for a long time to come."

One year later, North Carolina won the national championship, beating Georgetown and John Thompson in a classic game. Michael Jordan hit the famous winning shot and Fred Brown threw the infamous losing pass. Now Dean had officially done it all: he had won an NCAA title (and been to seven Final Fours), he had won the NIT, and he had won at the Olympics.

Now, I thought, with Jordan and Sam Perkins both coming back, was the time to strike. My plan was to write the book during the '82–83 season and make it a combination biography/story of a season. I had no idea how much access Dean might give me or how much access I would ask for; I just wanted to see if he would agree to a book.

I called him. I told him I knew he was a long way from retiring but, now that he had the national championship monkey off his back and his team had a legitimate chance to perhaps win again the next year, I thought this was the time. I promised I would come down during the summer and get all the long interviews out of the way before school even started. I already had a lot of the background work done because of the *Post* story.

"Let me think about it," he said. "I want to talk to Linnea [his wife] and give it some thought."

That was all I could ask for. He called back within a week. "I seriously thought about it," he said. "I understand why you want to do it now, and I know you'd do a good job. But there are some things I know you're going to want me to be frank about that I'm just not ready to talk about yet. [I'm sure he was talking about his opinions of other coaches.] It's just too soon."

I understood. I was also disappointed. "I really did seriously consider it," he said. "I feel bad about it. Is there anything I can do for you? Maybe get you some tickets?"

I laughed. I didn't need tickets. I told him I hoped someday his answer would be different. It would be twenty-seven years before we would discuss a book again.

THAT LEFT BOB KNIGHT. And when he invited me to the Final Four dinner, the thought crossed my mind that he might — *might* — just go for it. After all, he was inviting me into his inner circle at dinner and he had allowed me a glimpse of day-to-day life inside his team back in February, at a time when things could not have been worse.

Dinner was well under way by the time I arrived. I had hoped to maneuver myself someplace close to Knight, but that option wasn't available. Everyone was in the middle of their entrées when I sat down, and a waitress came and I ordered quickly. I was close enough to Knight that I could hear him explaining that he didn't understand how Lou Carnesecca and Bobby Cremins had won most of the coach-of-the-year awards and John Thompson had been shut out. Somewhere along the line he began addressing comments to me for most of the table to hear.

"You see, it's the writers like you, Feinstein, who just don't understand the game or coaching," he said. "John Thompson had the hardest job in the country this year because everyone picked him to win again and he doesn't have the same team. I know he's got Ewing, but he lost the kid [Michael] Graham, who was a big part of that team, and the other kid, the guard."

"Gene Smith," I said.

"Yeah, him. Ewing finished their defense last year but that kid started it. Now here they are without those two kids about to win a second national championship, and you people are giving all the awards to those other guys."

"Those awards are all voted on during the regular season," I started to say in defense of my brethren.

Knight waved a hand in my direction. "That's bullshit and you know it."

I did...sort of.

At that moment I wondered if his hostility might mean this was a bad night to bring up the book idea. I also wondered if he'd had a few drinks, a notion I would come to learn was laughable. Knight doesn't like to drink. Every so often he will mix a little sangria into lemonade or ginger ale, but that's rare and is usually done more for show than anything else. I would also come to understand that the hostility I had sensed wasn't hostility. It was just Knight showing off for his pals. They knew he liked me, otherwise I wouldn't have been there. But he needed them to know that I was still one of *them*, "you people" as he liked to put it. By next season, when he would go into that routine, I had learned to sit back and enjoy the show. That night, it made me nervous.

When dinner was over and everyone was standing to leave, Knight came over to me and put out his hand. "I'm really glad you could make it," he said.

"I'm sorry I was late," I said.

He waved his hand. "It was no problem, you had to work. As you could see you didn't hold us up any."

I was now beginning to understand—at least a little—that the riff on writers had been just that, a riff. I took a deep breath and decided to dive in. "Have you got a few minutes to talk?" I asked. "I want to ask you about something."

Knight shrugged. "Sure," he said. "Why don't you come back to the hotel with us."

When we got to the hotel, we went straight to Knight's room. We consisted of Knight; Pete Newell, the Hall of Fame coach who Knight traditionally shared a room with at the Final Four; and Mike Krzyzewski. At that point in his career, Krzyzewski was a long way from being the icon he is now. Although he had not been involved in the growth of my relationship with Knight, his name had often come up in conversations I'd had with Knight—since Knight knew I covered the ACC, had graduated from Duke, and was friends with Krzyzewski.

During my visit to Bloomington in February, we had talked at some length about how relieved he was that Krzyzewski seemed to have Duke headed in the right direction. The Blue Devils had made the NCAA Tournament that March for a second straight season, even though Krzyzewski still hadn't gotten beyond the second round.

Knight and Krzyzewski were driving to Bloomington the next day to do a clinic together. Krzyzewski was coming back to the room so they could go over some of the details of the clinic. So the four of us piled into the room. Knight stretched out on one bed, Newell the other. Krzyzewski and I pulled up chairs. I talked to Coach Newell—one of the all-time good men in sports—while Knight and Krzyzewski went over what they were going to do at the clinic. Finally, Knight looked up and said to me, "Okay, John, what can I do for you?"

I had no set speech or pitch. I've never really done that. I just sort of wing it. I think pretty well on my feet and have a good memory, so that makes it easier. I don't remember everything I said, but I remember the basics.

"Next year is going to be an important year for you," I said. "You're going to do a lot of new things. You've recruited the junior college kids, and you're going to play some zone."

"*Might* play some zone," Knight interrupted.

"Okay," I said. "At least you're thinking about it. We've talked about how tough this season was on you. You've never been under five hundred in the Big Ten before."

"I never wanted to see a season end more," Knight added.

"Exactly. Anyway, I know you have a lot of hopes and a lot of fears about next year, and I think there's a hell of a story there."

I paused because I had now come to the punch line. "I've given this a lot of thought, and I think if I came out there and spent the season—you know, just stuck around the way I did for those couple of days in February—that I could maybe write a really good book about what you do, how you do it, and why you do it." (The last line I *had* thought of in advance; Knight talked often about how the public didn't understand *why* he did the things he did.)

Knight looked at me and said, "Have you ever done a book before?"

I shook my head. "No, never. Always wanted to."

"Do you have a publisher for this book?"

I shook my head again. "I didn't think there was any point in talking to a publisher until I had talked to you."

"Probably smart thinking," he said, smiling. "Do you think you can get a publisher?"

"Bob, I have no idea. I've never done this before. But I would think if I told them I had access to Bob Knight for a season, someone would be interested."

"You know I might know a guy in Chicago," he said.

"Well, I might want to call him," I said, having no idea who or what he might be talking about.

"Okay," Knight said. "If you can get a publisher, let me know. If you can't, call me. Maybe I can get you to this guy in Chicago."

I was tempted to jump up and say, *"Really? Seriously? That's it? No negotiations? No ground rules?"*

I didn't think that was the right response. I wanted to get the money issue out of the way though, one way or the other. "Bob, if I get a contract, I don't know how much money it would be for—"

He waved a hand. "I don't need any money. If I get money then the book's not legitimate. If you're going to do it, you're going to do it right."

I'm guessing my mouth dropped open. The fact that he understood that so clearly was remarkable. Krzyzewski was standing up. "Coach, we have to get an early start in the morning."

I had lost track of the time. I looked at my watch. It was close to midnight.

I stood up too. "Bob, thanks for even considering this."

"Let me know what happens," he said.

I shook hands with Coach Newell, and Krzyzewski and I walked out of the room. The instant the door shut, Mike looked at me and said, "Are you out of your f—ing mind?"

"What?"

"You just *volunteered* to spend a season with him? What are you thinking?"

"Look, I know what it's like. I was there in February—"

"*No, you don't.* You haven't got a clue what it's like. You can't. I was with him five seasons."

"So, you spent five seasons with him, why shouldn't I spend one?"

"I spent four so I could go to college, one because I needed a job. You've been to college and you have a job."

I waved a hand at him. "Chances are I won't even get a publisher," I said. "But I *do* want to give it a try."

"In that case, you're crazier than he is," Mike said. "And he's crazy."

Little did I know how prescient those words would turn out to be.

2

No, No, No, No ... and No

As it turned out, my prediction that I wouldn't get a publisher almost proved true. I even had a hard time getting an agent.

Two nights after my conversation with Knight, Villanova won the national championship in one of the most stunning upsets in college basketball history. The Wildcats shot a remarkable 79.3 percent from the field for the game, including going 9 of 10 in the second half of the last college basketball game played without a shot clock. After the game, Rollie Massimino invited me to fly home early the next morning on the Villanova team plane. He also invited my friend Dick "Hoops" Weiss, who was and always will be the dean of Philadelphia basketball writers.

On almost no sleep, we flew into Philly with the team and were actually *in* the parade. Everyone on the plane was loaded onto flatbed trucks at the airport for the trip to City Hall. Since I was there to cover the parade and the scene, I certainly wasn't going to say no. I don't remember anyone screaming my name as we went up Broad Street.

I took the train home after the ceremony at City Hall and after I'd had lunch with Hoops and Dave Zinkoff, the legendary Spectrum public address announcer. I didn't know that day how lucky I was to meet Zinkoff, whose rumbling voice and mannerisms—"*This is the penalty shot!*"—were as much a part of Philadelphia sports history as the Palestra or cheesesteaks. Later that year, on Christmas Day, Zinkoff died. I was glad I had the chance to spend an hour with him.

I was only home briefly because George Solomon always sent me to the hockey playoffs as soon as the Final Four was over. So it wasn't until early May that I went to talk to Sally Jenkins about my book idea. The reason I went to Sally was simple: she was my friend and she was Dan Jenkins's daughter. Dan had worked at *Sports Illustrated* for years, covering college football and golf, and was as funny and talented and brilliant as anyone I had ever read. He and Frank Deford were *SI*'s two signature writers. There was lots of other talent, but everyone else lined up, as far as I was concerned, behind Frank and Dan.

Sally had come to the *Post* at the start of 1985. In fact, she'd taken over the Maryland beat from me, which freed me up to cover national colleges and do stories like the one I'd done on Knight in February. We'd quickly become good friends, and there were two things I knew for sure about her: she could write circles around me and she could drink me under any table where we happened to be sitting.

As soon as I told Sally what had happened with Knight in Lexington, she said, "You have to call Esther right away."

"Esther?"

"My dad's agent. She's the best. Just tell her I told you to call."

So I called the number Sally gave me and, after dropping Sally's name, got put through instantly to Esther Newberg.

I introduced myself and explained that I could get access to Bob Knight for an entire basketball season and that I thought there was a good book to be done based on what I had seen while there just a couple of months earlier and—

Esther cut me off, which I now know she does most of the time when she has either sized up a situation or is bored or both.

"First of all, I represent David Israel," she said. "And I think he's talked to Knight about a book."

"Oh, I didn't know that," I said, deflated. Knight had said nothing about Israel wanting to do a book. "I know David pretty well and this is the first I've heard of it."

"Really?" Esther said. "Well, the other problem you have is no one is going to buy a book by a first-time author about a basketball coach in Indiana. You're wasting your time. Tell Sally hello. I have another call."

The line went dead. "Well," I thought, "that went well." I walked over to Sally's desk.

"How'd it go?" she said brightly.

"The highlight is that she says hello," I reported. Then I told her the rest. Sally rolled her eyes. "That's just Esther being Esther," she said.

While I was mulling over whether to try to find another agent, I figured I better call Israel. Given that he'd known Knight longer and better than I had and that he was a lot more experienced—at least *he* had an agent—I didn't think there was much point in pushing forward if he was trying to do a book, a book that Knight had some- how forgotten to mention to me.

Israel had worked for the *Washington Star,* the *Chicago Tribune,* and the *Los Angeles Herald-Examiner* as a columnist. He'd gone on to work closely with Peter Ueberroth on the 1984 Olympics and was trying (successfully) to make a career in Hollywood as a writer and a producer.

As soon as David heard my voice on the phone he started laugh- ing. "I just hung up with Esther," he said. "She wanted to know who the hell you were."

I would learn through the years that Esther is intensely loyal to her clients. Her first thought when I called that day was that I was somehow poaching on David's territory.

"You don't need to worry about me," David went on. "I've talked to Knight a couple of times about doing a book, but I'm not spending a winter in Bloomington. You want to do it, go ahead. I certainly won't be in your way."

That was a relief. Of course, I still didn't have an agent. I decided to go home and sleep on things for a night and then go see Bob Woodward in the morning. Maybe his agent, even if he didn't represent sports books, would know someone who did. (What I didn't know at the time was that Woodward didn't *have* an agent, largely because he didn't need one.)

Before I could finish my coffee the next morning and head to Woodward's office, the phone rang. It was Esther.

"I'm sorry I was rude yesterday," she said. "I talked to David and I talked to Sally. If you'd still like me to, I'd be happy to take a look at any kind of proposal you have. I'll tell you honestly what I think one way or the other."

A proposal? I'd never thought of that. How in the world did one write a book proposal? Too embarrassed to ask, I thanked her and said I'd be in touch. Then I went to see Woodward to ask him how to write a book proposal.

"Just tell the publisher why this is a book and why you're the person to write it," he said.

"But how long should it be?"

"As long as it needs to be."

Okay, that narrowed it down.

I went home and wrote twenty-two pages. I went through Knight's history and then added some of the details I'd witnessed during my February visit. I concluded by saying Knight would give me complete access to himself and his team for an entire season. After I'd written those words, I wondered if Knight would stick to a deal like that if the book actually were to happen.

I mailed Esther the proposal just before I flew to Paris to cover the French Open. It was my first trip overseas, and I was both excited and nervous about it. I was going to be in Europe for eight weeks: two weeks in Paris, a week of vacation, three weeks in London for the run-up to Wimbledon and then the two-week tournament, a week in Scotland playing golf, and then one week for the British Open at Royal St. George's in the south of England.

I arrived in Paris on a Sunday morning and went straight to bed. I woke up shortly after noon and somehow got myself to Roland Garros, hoping to find a couple of players to talk to so I could write an advance on the tournament scheduled to begin the next day. When I arrived at the player and media entrance armed with the gate pass that was supposed to get me to the press pavilion where I would collect my credentials, I was told it would cost me forty-five francs to get in.

Doing my best to speak French—which wasn't very good—I explained that I was with the media and here to work. The man was sympathetic. In English he said, "I understand. But today is a charity day. Everyone pays to come in. Even the players."

Well if that was the deal, I could hardly argue. I pulled out my money and was handing it over when Chris Evert came strolling by on her way inside to practice.

"Bonjour, Madame Lloyd!" all the security people screamed. (She was married to John Lloyd at the time.)

No one asked her for forty-five francs. I decided against bringing that up.

I managed to find a story that day and arrived the next morning— I didn't have to pay to get in this time—eager to get to work. I found an empty desk in the press room, set up my computer, tossed a rain jacket on top of it, and went out to watch Gabriela Sabatini, who was fifteen and about to become the next glamorous star on the women's circuit.

After Sabatini had won her match, I returned to my computer only to find it wasn't there. Someone was sitting in the seat where I had been writing. I looked around for a second to be sure I hadn't gotten confused. I hadn't. I said to the guy in the seat, "Excuse me, was there a computer and a jacket on this desk when you got here?"

He looked up at me and pointed to a spot on the floor in the corner of the room. My computer and jacket were sitting there.

"This is the room for French journalists," he said in good, accented English. "Your room is downstairs."

"You might have told me that before you threw my stuff on the floor," I said.

"You weren't here, I had to work," he said.

Several ugly American lines about surrender ran through my head, but I passed on them. I picked up my things and found my way downstairs. The room was virtually empty. There were almost no Americans covering the French Open, so I felt pretty lonely as I set up my computer. That night I wrote about Yannick Noah and his godlike status in Paris and walked onto the Bois de Boulogne at about ten o'clock to try to get a cab back to my hotel.

It was raining. There wasn't a cab in sight. The only people around were a few of the famous transvestite hookers who populate the street at night. I began walking in the direction of the nearby square, where I knew there was a Metro stop. I was exhausted and hungry. There's no way to grab a quick lunch in Paris; you have to sit for an hour and I hadn't had time earlier—so when I saw a restaurant right next to the subway stop, I decided to get something to eat.

At any restaurant on the Champs-Élysées, everyone speaks English since a lot of their business comes from American tourists. Not on the outskirts of the city, which is where I was. I recognized the word *entrecôte* (steak) on the menu, but knowing that the portion sizes for meat were about half what they were at home, I wanted a starter.

I looked up and down the menu and finally found something I recognized: *fruits de mer*. Aha—fruit cup! Some nice fruit would be a good appetizer. The maitre d' came to take my order.

Even though my French was limited, my accent was decent. I have a good ear. So, confidently, I ordered the *entrecôte* and then, for my starter, I said, "Fruits de mer, s'il vous plait."

The maitre d' looked at me strangely. "Pour une, monsieur?" he said, holding up one finger.

"Oui," I said, wondering what the big deal was.

"D'accord," the maitre d' said. He shrugged and walked away. A few minutes later the fruits de mer arrived. The plate was so big it barely fit on the table. It was *not* any sort of fruit cup. *Fruits de mer* means *fruits of the sea.* It was a mammoth plate filled with scallops, shrimp, lobster, and anything else that came from the sea—much of which I didn't recognize.

"Fruits de mer, monsieur," the maitre d' said in a tone that I knew meant "you idiot."

I ate what I could, had the *entrecôte*—about five bites, as I'd suspected—and walked back into the rain. "Welcome to Paris, city of great food and romance," I said to myself. There still wasn't a cab in sight.

THINGS IMPROVED OVER THE next few days. Bud Collins got to town on Tuesday, a day later than usual since he had just gotten married.

I had first met Bud in 1980 at the U.S. Open when the *Post* sent me to the last four days of the tournament to back up Barry Lorge, the paper's longtime tennis writer. Bud had been a hero of mine since boyhood. I still remember watching the marathon final of the 1968 U.S. Amateur Championships between Arthur Ashe and Bob Lutz with my dad. Tennis was the only sport Dad was passionate about, and since seeing it on TV was brand new, we both paid rapt attention. Bud seemed to know everything about both players, as well as everyone in the sport. How cool, I can remember thinking then, to be a newspaper guy but also be on TV. No one had ever done it before.

When tennis took off on TV in the Open era, Bud was The Man. At one point, when the networks first got involved in tennis, he was doing Wimbledon for NBC and the Open for CBS. PBS expanded its TV schedule to include most of the summer season in the States, and Bud did that package too. I still remember that when NBC decided to televise the Italian Open (which was a big deal back then), the French Open, and Wimbledon, Bud called it "the old world triple." I dreamed of someday being at the old world triple.

That first weekend in New York in 1980, Lorge introduced me to Bud, who, before I could say anything about how long I had watched him and read him, grabbed my hand and said, "Of course I know who you are. You're one of those talented kids George [Solomon] always seems to hire."

George did, in fact, like to hire young. The saying in the newsroom was that George wanted his reporters young, single, hungry, and cheap. At that point I fit the prototype.

On Friday afternoon, one day after meeting Bud, I was in the press box writing a sidebar on Chris Evert-Lloyd's comeback from a first-set loss to beat Tracy Austin in the semifinals. I got up to get something to drink and happened to walk by the *Boston Globe's* phone, which was in the third row because Bud was smart enough to know that the late-afternoon sun beat right down on the front row, making life down there fairly miserable.

The phone was ringing. Neither Bud nor his *Globe* colleague Lesley Visser was around—they were both outside watching the men's doubles final—so I answered. A voice said, "I'm looking for Bud Collins."

"He's watching a match right now," I said. "Can I give him a message?"

"It's really important I talk to him right now. Tell him it's Abbie Hoffman."

I almost said, "Yeah, right, and I'm Jerry Garcia." Hoffman, who had been a member of the notorious Chicago Seven, had just been released from jail. I had to give the guy credit for originality.

"This is Abbie Hoffman?" I said, my voice no doubt taking on a "yeah, sure," tone.

"Yes, it is. Can you please find him for me?"

Maybe it was because he was so matter of fact about it that I wondered, just for a second, if he might somehow be serious. I put down the phone, walked out onto the porch where people often watched matches, and found Bud.

"There's a guy on the phone claiming he's Abbie Hoffman," I said.

"Oh, really?" Bud said, jumping to his feet. "He must want tickets."

He walked inside, picked up the phone, and said, "Abbie, long time no talk, what have you been up to?"

As it turned out, it *was* Abbie Hoffman and he *did* want tickets. Bud had briefly been the tennis coach at Brandeis University, his alma mater. One of his players had been Abbie Hoffman. They had stayed in touch through the years when Hoffman wasn't in jail.

I saw Bud on occasion the next few years, more often once Lorge left the *Post* to become a columnist at the *San Diego Union-Tribune* and I began to cover more tennis. Now, his arrival in Paris was a godsend. His new wife, Mary Lou, had gone home for a few days after they had honeymooned in Italy, so Bud had some time on his hands to take me under his wing.

On the third night of the French, when I was starting to feel settled a little bit in Paris and at Roland Garros, I went to dinner with Bud and a friend of his named Bob Basche. Basch, as everyone called him, was a very successful sports-marketing guy, but he moonlighted every summer in Paris and London working for NBC, a lot of that work being with Bud rounding up players for various interviews. We went to a very good (surprise) restaurant near the Champs-Élysées and drank a lot of excellent (surprise again) red wine.

After dinner we half walked, half stumbled down the Champs to the Hôtel de Crillon, which was where all the NBC hotshots were staying. We sat down in the elegant Crillon bar and someone—I think it was Basche—suggested we have a round of Armagnac. If you have ever had Armagnac, you know this: it is poison. You drink it, you die, especially if you keep drinking it. Which we did.

At one point Dick Enberg, who was Bud's broadcast partner, stuck his head in the bar, having just come back from dinner with his wife. Someone had apparently told him that Bud and Basch were in the bar. They had failed to tell him the condition that Bud and Basch were in. Enberg took one look at the three of us and fled.

Too late. We had spotted him. Bud leaped from his seat (how exactly he did that I'll never know) screaming, "Monsieur *Enbairg*, Monsieur *Enbairg*, you must join us for a drink!" at the top of his lungs. He chased Enberg down the hall still screaming his name. Enberg, knowing he was beaten, agreed to come back and have *one* drink if he would then be allowed to escape to his room.

I'm honestly not sure how I made it back to my hotel that night. I do remember the doorman at the Crillon looking at me aghast when I asked him if he could get me a cab so I could return to the Hôtel Mercure. That was the media hotel. It was not exactly the Crillon.

I somehow made it to Roland Garros the next morning even though the poison from the Armagnac was still coming out of my pores. I didn't even feel well enough to drink coffee, but when I arrived I went to find Jennifer Proud, the PR person for the Men's International Professional Tennis Council, which ran the men's game at the time.

"I need Mike DePalmer whenever his match is over," I said to Jennifer. DePalmer was a young American who had played for his father at the University of Tennessee. He was playing Joakim Nyström out on court four, which was about as far from the media center as any court on the grounds. Nyström was a Swede and was ranked number six in the world. DePalmer had won the first two sets from him, but Nyström had come back to win the next two. They had been forced to stop because of darkness in the fifth the previous evening at 2-all. I figured, win or lose, DePalmer was worth at least a sidebar.

After talking to Jennifer I stumbled downstairs to the media dining room, which was cool, dark, and empty at that hour. There was a couch in the corner of the room. The matches would resume at eleven. I looked at my watch. It was almost ten. I could lie down for an hour, then walk out to court four to watch the end of the match.

A few minutes later, someone shook me awake. It was Jennifer Proud.

"I can't believe you were sleeping down here the entire time I was looking for you!" she said, genuinely angry.

"What are you talking about?" I said. "I've been here like five minutes."

"Really?" she said. "I've been paging you for half an hour. I finally told poor Mike he could go."

"Go?" I said. "What's he doing here? He has to go play Nyström at eleven."

She was now looking at me as if I was the single dumbest human being on earth. A light finally went off in my head. I looked at my watch. It was 12:45. I had been asleep for almost three hours.

"Oh God," I said, truly embarrassed. "Is the match over?"

"Over?" Jennifer screamed. "It's been over for almost an hour. I made Mike wait here for thirty minutes while I kept paging you."

I had two thoughts: DePalmer had lost — if he'd beaten the number six seed he would have been brought into the interview room. And second, why hadn't Jennifer come looking for me down here during that thirty minutes? I decided not to voice the second thought.

"So he lost."

"*Yes*, he lost and then had to stand around for thirty minutes because I told him the *Washington Post* wanted to talk to him."

Some days it was tough being the *Washington Post*.

I sobered up sometime that afternoon, aided by Bud dragging me to the NBC pavilion for lunch. The woman at the door looked completely horrified when Bud told her I was a guest of Dick Enberg's. Bud loved doing things like that.

It was on the second Tuesday of the French—by now I had pretty much decided I was ready to move to Paris—that I heard back from Esther. She called as I was walking in the door after a relatively tame night out. Esther is nothing else if not direct. She didn't ask how Paris was or if I was enjoying the tennis.

"I like this," she said, referring to the proposal I'd sent her. "I think you have a very good book here. If you'd like me to try to sell it for you, I'd be happy to represent you."

I was happy that she liked it and that she wanted to try and sell it for me. I had very little idea what that meant. "Thank you," I said. "So what happens next?"

"I'll send it out to guys I know who like doing sports books, and we'll see what happens," she said. "I hope the next time I call you it will be with an offer."

I thanked her again and told her my schedule for the next couple of weeks. I finished off my time in Paris by covering one of the great women's finals in history: Chris Evert stunning Martina Navratilova 7–5 in the third set at a point in their careers when neither player really thought Evert could beat Navratilova. I brutally overwrote the match story (I looked it up recently, and the lead made me wince) but was still glad I'd witnessed it. The next day, Mats Wilander shocked Ivan Lendl in the men's final. Wilander had beaten John McEnroe in the semifinals while Lendl had beaten Jimmy Connors, meaning it had now been thirty years since an American man had won in Paris.

After a week's vacation in Vienna and Salzburg—the latter may still be my favorite place in the world—I arrived in London a week before Wimbledon began. It was almost strange hearing English again after more than three weeks in non-English-speaking countries.

The afternoon after I arrived, I had just come back from sightseeing when Esther called again. "Five rejections," she said. "I'm really sorry."

"Wow," I said. "That's not good."

"Jeff Neuman at Macmillan is still on vacation," she added. "He's the one guy I haven't heard back from. So there's still some hope."

I had no idea who Jeff Neuman was, but I was surprised that *no one* would be interested in the notion of having total access to Bob Knight. Esther, who often reads my mind, read my mind.

"They see him as a Midwestern basketball coach," she said. "If he coached the Knicks it would be different. The feeling is, why should anyone care what happens to Indiana's basketball team?"

I was tempted to tell her that if Knight coached the Knicks they would be 30–52 and he might have killed someone by that point. Besides, the book wasn't about Indiana's basketball team. But that wasn't going to change anything.

"Well, thanks for trying," I said, wondering if this was the end of the road and if I should think about other alternatives. Maybe Knight's guy in Chicago?

"Don't give up just yet," she said. "I haven't heard from Jeff and there might be a couple of other guys I can talk to. I still think there's a book here."

We hung up and I went and walked the streets of London for a while. I was discouraged. If I couldn't get an offer for *this* book, what book could I get an offer for? There was no doubt in my mind the book would be good, but how could I prove that to people? I could, I supposed, go to Bloomington and spend the winter, write the book, and *then* try to get a publisher. That, I knew, was craziness. The only good news of the night was that I found a very good Chinese restaurant called The Good Earth. I got takeout—or, as they call it in London, takeaway—went back to the hotel, and ate myself to sleep.

ESTHER CALLED AGAIN TWO days later. I was in much better spirits. I had ridden the train with the great Ted Tinling to Eastbourne, where the women played their annual warm-up tournament, and had a great time. Ted may very well have been the most entertaining person I had ever met. He was best known for having designed Gussie Moran's famous lace-panties dress that had caused such a scandal at Wimbledon in 1949. But he was far more than a dress designer; he was a tennis historian who had known most of the great players and hadn't been a bad player himself.

Ted was 6 foot 5 and completely bald, wore a diamond stud in his left ear, was gay, and had been a spy during World War II. He would say anything to anyone at any time about any subject. He was seventy-five that summer and was working as a consultant for the WTA and Wimbledon, which had finally forgiven him for Moran's dress by making him an honorary member.

After two hours on the train to Eastbourne with Ted, I felt as if I knew more about tennis than I could possibly tell people in ten years of writing on the sport. On Thursday afternoon, I was sitting in the stands with Ted watching Navratilova play, mostly because I was supposed to have dinner with her that night for a pre-Wimbledon story. The weather wasn't great (surprise, bad weather on the English seaside) and there weren't very many people watching the match.

After Navratilova had won the first set 6–1, one man who had been watching sort of lurched out of his seat and wobbled over in our direction.

"I'm leaving!" he screamed in an English accent thickened by quite a bit of afternoon alcohol. "I'm not going to watch that dyke play for one more second! And *you*, Tinling, you f—ing homosexual, you should leave too!"

He glared at Ted, who turned in the direction of a nearby usher. When Ted waved at him, the usher instantly rushed to us.

"Please remove this gentleman right away," Ted said. "He's far too drunk to be allowed to stay."

"I was only joking," the man protested. "I'd like to stay."

"I'm afraid not," Ted said as the usher took his arm. "You know if I was a *practicing* f—ing homosexual and getting something out of it, I really wouldn't mind. But as I'm *not*, I rather resent your comment."

With that, the usher led the man away.

Back then, homosexuality was almost never openly discussed in jockworld. Navratilova was out at that point, and after initially being angry about the story that "revealed" her sexuality, she began to talk willingly and openly about it. Many other female players who everyone in the sport knew to be gay stayed in the closet, at least in part because neither Virginia Slims—the women's tour sponsor—nor the WTA wanted the game getting a reputation as being full of gays.

That night I had dinner with Navratilova, who told the following joke: "Two lesbians are sitting on the couch. One puts her arm around the other and says, 'Let me be frank.' The other says, 'No, dammit, I want to be Frank!'"

If I tell the joke it isn't that funny. When Martina told it, it was fall-down funny.

I WAS BACK IN London on Friday when Esther called again. "Jeff Neuman is offering fifteen thousand," she said.

I could no longer pretend to know what she meant when I clearly didn't know what she meant. So I said, "What exactly does that mean? This is my first book."

Patiently, Esther explained that the fifteen thousand was what's called an advance against royalties. As soon as I signed a contract, I would receive a check for half that amount—minus the agent's 10 percent—and when the book was finished and the manuscript had been accepted by the publisher, I would receive the other half. Later I would learn that larger advances were divided into three payments: one-third on signing, one-third on acceptance, one-third on publication. More recently, some publishers have gone to a *four* payment system in which the author doesn't receive the fourth payment until the publication of the paperback. That's good for the publisher, not so good for the author.

At the moment that wasn't my concern. I was happy to have an offer, but fifteen thousand, assuming I was going to take a leave of absence of about eight months (I was guessing) from the *Post,* was going to mean a considerable pay cut during that period. I think my salary at that point was about $65,000 a year, and that was still considerably more than what Neuman was offering to pay for the book.

Timidly, I asked Esther if there was any way to ask for more—anything—maybe another five thousand to help cover my expenses.

"I can ask," she said. "But you should think about whether you're willing to do it for this much, because this may be it."

Fair enough. The next day, Saturday, I went to Wimbledon for the first time. I made the mistake of taking a taxi, not knowing at that point that the subway wasn't just cheaper, but faster. Still, I was awed walking the empty grounds that day for the first time in my life. There were a few players playing on outside courts and nearby at the practice courts. I walked around with Andrew Sullivan, an Australian colleague of mine who was also making his first trip to Wimbledon. After we'd been just about everywhere, we finally poked our heads into Centre Court and were surprised to find four women playing doubles.

There was no one around, so we sat down about midway up in the stands and took in the place. It reminded me right away of Fenway Park—much smaller than you might imagine it, and all green.

The women were playing with an umpire, linesmen, and ballboys, and score was being kept on the board with the umpire calling out the scores as if a real match were taking place.

"Maybe it's some kind of dry run before Monday," Andrew said quietly.

That seemed to make sense. We watched a few games—the quality of tennis wasn't terrible—and then noticed a lone security guard approaching. Uh-oh, we had violated some Wimbledon rule. I would come to learn that at Wimbledon there are rules for everything, including what bathrooms one can use.

He was, of course, polite. "Very sorry, gents," he said. "Private game."

"Really?" I asked. "Why?"

"Club rule," he said, turning and walking away.

We had actually seen enough, and even though I have battled security people on most continents since then, this certainly wasn't worthy of a battle. We left and I ran into Ted Tinling a few minutes later. He would know what it was we had witnessed on Centre Court.

"Oh yes, it's tradition," he said. "Every year after the last match of the tournament, Centre Court is shut down. No one plays on it until today—the Saturday before Wimbledon begins. Then four female members [unlike Augusta National, Wimbledon *does* have female members] play a doubles match to test the court and make sure it's broken in just a bit before Monday."

"And they play in private?" I asked.

Ted looked at me as if I were crazy. "Private? What are you talking about?"

I told him. He shook his head. "That's *appalling*," he said as only he could. "I'm going to find out about this immediately!"

"Ted, it's no big deal..."

"Yes it *is*. When are these people going to learn to stop acting like they're of some higher breed than everyone else? Ridiculous. This is what they hired me for. To tell them why things like this are outrageous."

I knew there would be no stopping him now. I wondered what, if any, response there would be to Ted's complaint.

I found out Monday. My first Wimbledon was delayed—naturally—by rain. It was one of those Junes in London where it just rained every single day. In fact, it would take five days to complete the first round. During the delay on Monday, I was walking into the cafeteria when I spotted Ted with an attractive middle-age woman.

"Just who I was looking for," Ted said when he saw me. "Barbara, this is the young man I was telling you about."

Barbara was quite charming and very apologetic. "I'm *so* sorry about Saturday," she said. "Ted's told me what happened. You know, I saw the security guard walking up there and started to say something, but didn't. I wish I had."

By now I realized she had been one of the four women playing.

"I promise you if you want to come in and watch next year, there will be no problem at all. If anyone says anything, you just tell them that I said you were *my* guests."

From what I was gathering, dropping her name would probably take care of any problems. I thanked her. As it turned out, she later became someone who would help me with club-related issues on more than one occasion.

That, however, did not solve the issue of what in the world to write on my first day at Wimbledon. "Play was delayed by rain all afternoon" was one solid sentence. The *Post,* having sent me to London, wanted a lead, a sidebar, and notes on matches that, at the moment, weren't being played.

I was sitting at my computer, one of the then brand-new Radio Shacks—you could see about eight lines on your screen and it weighed close to nothing—when I heard a commotion coming from the next room. Wimbledon had built new writing rooms that year for the foreign media, and apparently the Duke of Kent, who was bored like everyone else, had requested a tour of the facility. He was being squired around by Barry Weatherill, the chairman of the club's media committee. Ted (who else?) had introduced me to Weatherill in Paris during the French Open. Weatherill was showing the Duke all the new space and how the walls had been decorated. The Duke didn't appear interested. He kept peering at the computers, sitting mostly unused at that moment, on people's desks. No one was speaking to him because protocol dictates you don't speak to a royal unless he or she speaks to you first.

I had an idea. I grabbed Richard Berens, the club's press officer, who was trailing the Duke and Weatherill at a polite distance, and said, "Would the Duke like to see how one of these computers works?" Remember, this was 1985. The technology was relatively new.

"He might," Berens said. "Let me ask."

A few minutes later, Richard waved me over and I was introduced to the Duke of Kent.

"Your highness," Weatherill said, "this is Mr. John Feinstein from the *Washington Post.*"

I wasn't sure if I was supposed to bow, curtsy, or drop to a knee. I wished Ted was there to tell me what to do. I settled for a handshake, which seemed to be okay with the Duke.

"Aaah yes, the *Washington Post,*" he said. "Woodward, Bernstein, that crowd."

"Yes-sir," I said.

"Are they still employed there?" he asked.

"Woodward is, sir. Bernstein works in television now."

"Television, eh? Went for the money, I suppose."

"Yes-sir."

There was a pregnant pause, everyone looking at me. "I understand you'd like to see how one of these computers works?" I said.

"Oh yes, that would be delightful," he said.

I walked the little group over to my desk. All activity—not that there was much of it—had stopped. There wasn't a lot to tell, but I stretched it out, finishing by showing the Duke how to set up a story that's ready to be sent, then dialing a phone number right there in London, pressing a few buttons, plugging the phone into the computer, and sending.

"And it takes how long for the story to arrive?" the Duke asked.

"If it's working [always a question mark back then], just a few minutes," I said.

"And meanwhile, you can put your feet up and smoke a cigarette, I suppose," the Duke said, clearly amazed by such a thought.

"In theory I could, yes-sir."

"Why, that's *marvelous*," the Duke marveled. He turned to Weatherill and the others. "Ingenious, isn't it, Barry?"

"Absolutely," Weatherill said, just as an announcement came over the PA telling us that officials were hoping to begin play on Centre Court and court number one at 7:30 p.m. Those were the only two courts with tarps—covers as they called them. Play on the outside courts had been called off for the day.

My new best friend the Duke and I shook hands, and he thanked me for the computer lesson. Off he went and I sat down to work. At least I had a sidebar.

JOHN MCENROE AND IVAN Lendl, the top two players in the world, provided me with a lead not long after that—in completely different ways. Sure enough, at 7:30 they were sent out to play their first matches. McEnroe, the defending champion, was on Centre Court as was tradition, playing an oft-injured Aussie named Peter McNamara. Lendl was next door on court one playing American Mel Purcell.

Even after a delay of more than six hours, Centre Court was packed when McEnroe and McNamara walked on court, turned to bow to my pal the Duke in the Royal Box, and began warming up. I was truly thrilled. I had watched Wimbledon on TV from the moment NBC began televising it in the late '60s (then on tape delay) and had dreamed of someday sitting almost exactly where I was sitting, actually covering it.

McEnroe and McNamara played only six games. The court, even though the covers had been on it, was wet and slippery. McNamara, who wore a bulky knee brace, slipped a couple of times. So did McEnroe. Finally, McEnroe told the chair umpire he wanted to speak to the tournament referee, Alan Mills. Out came Mills while the crowd murmured. McEnroe talked, arms waving, pointing at the court, mimicking McNamara's near fall. Mills listened and then spoke to the umpire, and the players began gathering their racquets.

"Ladies and gentlemen, due to wet conditions, play has been called for the day," the umpire announced. There were some scattered boos, but everyone seemed to understand. It was just too dangerous to play on the wet grass.

We walked inside to the media work area and I noticed on a TV monitor that Lendl and Purcell were still playing. I figured Mills hadn't gotten over to court one yet to bring them inside. Pete Alfano, my pal from the *New York Times,* and I lingered by the set for a moment, curious to see if Mills would let them complete the game they were playing or if he would go get them right away.

He did neither. The players finished a game, sat on their chairs during a changeover, and went back on court. Alfano and I looked at each other; they were still playing.

We made our way to court one. It was now well after eight o'clock, but there would be light for at least another ninety minutes. Slipping and sliding often, the two men played on until Lendl won in straight sets—none of them easy, because nothing was ever easy for Lendl at Wimbledon. He shook hands with Purcell just before dark. At least now we had a match to write about, along with McEnroe's unilateral decision to call off play on his court.

We went to the interview room, hoping to get a decent quote or two from Lendl. This wasn't terribly likely. Lendl had grown up in Czechoslovakia but had moved to the United States as an eighteen-year-old tennis phenom. He had been spotted by Wojtek Fibak, a successful Polish player who had moved to Connecticut, and had actually moved in with Fibak and his family while adapting to life in the States.

Lendl is extremely bright, but in the early stages of his career, because of the language issue and because of the overprotective nature of tennis, there were no hints of either that or his somewhat off-the-wall sense of humor. He came across as dour and humorless, even though he was neither. Because I liked McEnroe, my instinct was to dislike Lendl. I remembered being extremely upset when Lendl came from two sets down in Paris in 1984 to beat McEnroe, the one and only time McEnroe made the French Open final.

Most people, myself included, saw that match as a huge break-through for Lendl, who had often had trouble dealing with the kind of mental pressure both McEnroe and Jimmy Connors put on him when they played big matches. He had lost two U.S. Open finals to Connors, and McEnroe always seemed to find a way to beat him when it mattered. The win at the French was the first of eight major titles for Lendl.

"I actually think that match was more important for John than for me," Lendl said to me many years later, sitting in the corner of an Outback Steakhouse that had emptied out while we talked into the night. "If John wins, I think he would have won the Grand Slam that year. He won Wimbledon and the [U.S.] Open, and if he had won Paris he would have gone to Australia [the Australian Open was played then at year's end, not in January as it is now] and probably won there. As it was, in his greatest year he only won two." And, interestingly, never won another major title after that.

Now though, at Wimbledon in 1985, McEnroe was still king and the subject of all sorts of tabloid stories because he was dating

Tatum O'Neal. "John, if you win Wimbledon, will you dedicate the victory to Tatum?" was one press conference question.

McEnroe and every other player, except for Purcell, who was presumably taking a hot shower, were long gone by the time Lendl stalked into the interview room that first night. Stalked is the correct word because he was angry. At Wimbledon, much like the Masters, each player is accompanied to the interview room by a club member who is there (I guess) to ensure that there is a certain measure of decorum in the room.

Before anyone could ask a question, Lendl launched into a tirade. "I can't believe I just walked into locker room and there was no one there," he began. "I find out they let McEnroe go home because he asks, and they just let us go on and play and we could have killed ourselves out there. Nobody told me we had option to stop. This is unbelievable."

Most of us had never seen Lendl like this: angry, passionate, and willing to talk. Pete Alfano asked him if he had talked to Alan Mills.

"Yes!" Lendl screamed. "He tells me if I had asked he would have let us stop. I say, 'How am I supposed to know that? Why don't you come on court and tell us McEnroe stopped?' It's completely ridiculous."

The club member looked pale. I was about to ask Lendl if he was planning any formal protest—it wouldn't do any good, but I wanted to keep him rolling—when Richard Finn jumped in with a question. Finn had been a good junior tennis player and had carved out a nice living as a freelance tennis writer. He was willing to travel just about anywhere on his own dime, so he was often used overseas by *USA Today* and other publications. Frequently he would call newspapers when a player from their town was doing well and offer a story. He also freelanced for a number of tennis magazines. For this Wimbledon, one magazine had assigned him a story on the new racquet Lendl was using that summer. In any other sport a reporter with an assignment like that would have found the player someplace and gotten a few minutes with him one on one to talk about the new racquet. In tennis that's almost impossible to do because there is no access to players at tournaments, other than the interview room, and trying to get an offsite interview with a player is a little bit like trying to get a school from a BCS conference to schedule a home-and-home series with Boise State.

So the interview room was Finn's only shot at Lendl and his new racquet. Thus, while Lendl sat there with steam coming out of his ears, Finn asked him about the new racquet. Alfano and I looked at each other. Was he kidding?

As soon as Lendl finished the answer on the racquet, I jumped in and asked if he planned to follow up on what had just happened. "You bet I will," he said, and then he was off to the races again, demanding to know just who these Wimbledon guys thought they were.

Almost out of a dream I heard Finn's voice again. "Ivan, what's the best thing about the new racquet in terms of your game?"

Back to the racquet. While Lendl was answering, I leaned over to Finn—who was and is a friend—and whispered, "If you ask one more question about that f—ing racquet, I'm going to borrow one from Lendl and shove it right down your throat."

Finn looked at me to see if I was serious. Apparently he knew I was because he asked no more racquet questions. Lendl spent several more minutes accusing the Wimbledon committee of McEnroe favoritism (a remarkable irony given McEnroe's relationship with Wimbledon back then) and most crimes of the twentieth century, practically including the kidnapping of the Lindbergh baby.

As we walked out, Finn wanted to know what the big deal was. "Big deal?" Alfano said. "Ivan Lendl is killing the Wimbledon committee, and you want to know about his racquet? Are you kidding?"

"I've got this story to do..."

"We don't care."

Fortunately, Finn is a good guy. "I can see it from your point of view," he said. "I guess."

All was well. I had all I needed for my first day at Wimbledon: Lendl was the lead, the Duke was the sidebar, McEnroe led the notebook. Not bad for a day when a grand total of three sets plus six games were played before dark.

3

Next Stop, Bloomington

THE RAIN DIDN'T LET up much during that first week at Wimbledon, and the constant delays led to some funny moments in the media room, another of them involving Richard Finn.

One of Finn's clients during that Wimbledon was the paper in Meriden, Connecticut, which was very interested in how one of its local heroes, Bud Schultz, was doing. Schultz was a good story. He was twenty-six and had played Division II tennis at Bates before being talked into trying the tour by friends. Wimbledon was his first major. For perspective: he was born in the same year as John McEnroe, who had already won the last of his seven major titles at that point.

Because it was virtually impossible to talk to the players on the Wimbledon grounds—we were literally threatened with loss of credentials if we did so—Finn had gotten Schultz's hotel phone number. Each night, after Schultz had played another forty-five minutes against Aaron Krickstein before being delayed by rain, Finn would call him from the media room. By Thursday, with the match tied at two sets apiece, everyone in the room was listening to Finn's nightly chats with Schultz.

"Looked like you served pretty well today," Finn would say.

He would listen and take notes and then follow up. Alfano and I (yes, we were instigators) egged Finn on. "Ask him about the point at 2–3, 15–30," we'd say. "That was a great backhand down the line."

The absurdity of filing each night on a tennis match that wouldn't end wasn't lost on anyone in the room—including Finn, who took it all in good humor. "Long as he's in the tournament, I'm getting paid," he said. And he was still in the tournament, even if he hadn't won a match yet.

When Schultz finally won the match in five sets on Friday, we all let out a cheer so Bud could hear us in the background when Finn got him on the phone. "Tell the guys I said thanks," said Schultz, who also understood how comical it all was. He lost in the second round but had one of the great one week/two match runs in tennis history.

It was on Tuesday, during another rain delay, that I met two tennis agents who I ended up becoming friendly with over the years. Up until then, I had thought Donald Dell represented most tennis players on the planet simply because his company, ProServ—which had many of the world's top players—was based in Washington, D.C. IMG, which actually had more top players and was bigger than ProServ, was in Cleveland.

One player ProServ represented was Gabriela Sabatini, who in 1985 was thought to be the Next Thing in women's tennis. She was from Argentina and she was only fifteen, but it was clear that she was going to be a gorgeous woman and that she could play. At the 1984 U.S. Open, because she was seen as a rising star, she was brought into the interview room even after losing to Helena Suková. She was shy and sweet and spoke decent English for a teenager, especially one being asked to talk to a bunch of grown-ups, most of whom spoke no Spanish.

Since the Open was her first tournament as a pro, she would be receiving her first check—for about $8,000, as I remember. Someone asked her what she planned to do with the money.

"I just got a *leetle* dog," she said. "I will buy him a present."

By the following spring, when I went to Paris, Sabatini had grown from about 5'4" to 5'9" and was crushing the ball from the backcourt. She was seeded fourteenth at the French Open, and everyone wanted to write about her. Her agent was Dick Dell, Donald's younger brother. I spent most of the first week of the tournament negotiating with Dick and the WTA for some one-on-one time with Sabatini. This was generally unheard of during a major tournament, but Dell, being Washington-based, was keenly aware of the *Washington Post.*

Finally, after Sabatini had easily won her third-round match, I was told that after she played her next round, *if* she won, I would be given a few minutes alone with her in the players' lounge after she returned from the interview room. Dell would meet me in the hallway outside the interview room door so he could escort me there — since, of course, media weren't supposed to be in the players' lounge.

Fine. Sabatini won and I went to find Dell as ordered. Standing there waiting for her to finish in the interview room, I started thinking how I could try to make her comfortable. Dell had told me that this would be her first one-on-one interview in English and that she had only done one or two in Spanish. Finding common ground with a fifteen-year-old girl would not be easy.

Finally, as Dell was introducing us, I hit on it: the dog. We walked into the players' lounge and found a quiet table in the corner. I congratulated Sabatini on making the quarterfinals. She thanked me.

"So," I said, readying my make-the-kid-comfortable opening question, "Last year at the Open you said you were going to buy your new dog a gift with your prize money. What did you end up buying him?"

Sabatini stared at me, saying nothing. Maybe she hadn't understood me. So I started to ask the question more slowly. "Your dog, you said—"

"The dog died!" she shrieked, bursting into tears. *"He died before I got home! Run over!"*

She was sobbing uncontrollably. People came running: WTA

officials, security people, other players, Dick Dell. What in the world had I done to this child in thirty seconds to cause her to start wailing uncontrollably?

"I'm sorry, I'm sorry," I blubbered, pretty much wanting to cry myself. "I didn't know. She said her dog died..."

"You brought up the dog!" Dick Dell screamed. "Are you crazy?"

"I didn't know, I swear I didn't know..."

Sabatini was calming down. Later she would tell me that she saw a look in my eyes that told her how horrified I was by what had happened. She insisted she was okay, that the interview could continue. It was actually quite brave of her. Needless to say, try as I might, try as she might, the next fifteen minutes were torture. I finally decided to cut my losses, thanked her, apologized for the hundredth time, and fled.

As it turned out, the most interesting quote for that story—which I did finally write just before Sabatini played Chris Evert in the semifinals—came from an agent named Phil de Piccioto, who at the time ran Advantage's women's division and, as such, represented Steffi Graf.

"We think when it's all said and done, Graf will be a better player than Sabatini," de Piccioto said. Graf was also fifteen at the time, but not as glamorous or as highly ranked. Of course, she would go on to win twenty-two major titles to Sabatini's one, so de Piccioto was right. But when he saw the quote in print he was furious with me.

"How could you quote me on that?" he said.

"You said it."

"I know I said it, but I wish you hadn't quoted me."

"Why? Don't you believe it?"

"Of course I believe it. But when Sabatini reads that there's no way I'll ever get her as a client."

I had completely missed that angle. It is one agents are always thinking about: she may not be my client *now*, but someday her contract will be up and maybe I can steal her. Such was life in the agent business.

UNLIKE HIS YOUNGER BROTHER, Donald Dell was anything but soft-spoken or low-key. He was born to be an agent. My first encounter with him had come much earlier at Washington's local tournament, then known as the *Washington Star* International, since the *Star,* which was Washington's afternoon newspaper until it went out of business in 1981, was the title sponsor.

I was covering the *Star* International shortly after returning to the sports staff, following two years of covering cops and courts, first in Washington, D.C., and then in Prince George's County, Maryland. Someday I should write a book about the cast of characters I encountered during my time in Prince George's. Let me put it this way: it was almost impossible to stay off the front page covering that beat.

I had gone back to sports in the summer of '79, even though Bob Woodward, who was then the *Post*'s metro editor and had become my mentor, had strongly counseled me not to do it.

"You have a chance to become a great reporter," Bob said (actually he said *reporder* in his very strong Midwestern accent). "Don't blow it on sports. If you go back there, you'll never be heard from again."

He was, I believe, exaggerating to make a point. Woodward and I had become close while I was researching a story on police corruption in Prince George's County. I think—no, I know—he was *stunned* that someone who had potential as a *reporder* would even consider leaving serious *reporting* for sports. But George Solomon had offered me the job I had dreamed of when I was in college: covering Maryland in football and basketball—and thus the entire ACC—for the *Post.* I couldn't resist.

When I told Woodward what I had decided, he was shocked. "Look, Bob, I'm twenty-three," I said. "I love sports and I know I can do this well. When I'm a little older, if you still want me, I'll come back. But I need to find out if I can do this."

That was when he made the comment about never being heard from again. Which, frankly, pissed me off a little bit. So I made him a bet: my byline would appear on the sports front every day for the first ten days I was back in sports. There was a slight fix involved on my end—Solomon had already told me my first assignment would be covering the *Star* tennis tournament. Unless I wrote *really* badly, that just about guaranteed me seven straight days on the sports front.

Woodward took the bet. The stakes: loser had to go out, buy lunch, and deliver it to the winner in the newsroom.

I wrote a Sunday advance on the *Star* that made the front. I went out to the tournament site on Sunday and tracked down a little-known player named Pat DuPre, who had just made it to the Wimbledon semifinals. That took care of day two. The next seven—tournament play—would be easy. I would worry about the tenth day once the tournament was over.

In those days, Donald Dell *was* the *Washington Star* tournament. Although he didn't have the title of tournament director—his pal John Harris did—he ran the tournament. He represented just about all the top players who showed up to play (often as part of their ProServ deals), he sold most of the sponsorships, *and* he did the color on the weekend telecasts of the event.

Back then, PBS televised the summer circuit, showing one semifinal on Saturday, the final on Sunday. Bud Collins did the play-by-play. Dell did the color.

The way the tournament worked, two quarterfinals were played on Thursday, two more on Friday. The Thursday quarterfinal winners were Corrado Barazzutti, an Italian clay courter (the tournament was played on clay) and Argentina's José Luis Clerc, who would rise to be the number five player in the world. The Friday winners were two Americans: Brian Gottfried and Gene Mayer.

Guess which match PBS wanted for a one o'clock start on Saturday?

There was just one problem: not only had Mayer and Gottfried both played Friday while Clerc and Barazzutti rested, Mayer had played doubles alongside his older brother Sandy until almost midnight. Mayer also had a history of cramping, especially in hot weather, and a one o'clock match in Washington in July was *not* going to be played in cool, nonhumid weather.

So, naturally, the two Americans were on court in 95-degree heat at one o'clock while Collins and Dell (who represented both players) talked about what great guys they were to the TV audience.

The first set was terrific tennis, Gottfried winning a tiebreaker. The second set not so much: Mayer cramped. He could barely hobble to the net to shake hands.

So I went to find Dell. At that point we had never met. Charlie Brotman, who has been the tournament's PR director forever, found Dell and introduced us. I tried to ask the question diplomatically. I said something like, "It seems to me, Donald, you're in a difficult situation because you're wearing so many hats here. You're trying to do what's best for the tournament and what's best for your clients and what's best for TV, and you had to make a decision about which match to play this afternoon..."

He figured out where I was going before I could get to the punch line.

"What is this?" he roared. "Some kind of f—ing Watergate investigation?"

That was really all I needed. Dell knew he had been caught with his hand in too many places, and he didn't like where I was going at all.

"Thanks for your time, Donald," I said.

I turned and walked away.

Brotman knew exactly what was going to happen next, and sure enough, as I sat in the press trailer—which *was* a trailer—writing, I felt a tap on my shoulder. It was Dell.

"Can I talk to you outside for a moment?" he said, giving me a big smile and a friendly tone of voice.

"Sure, Donald."

I then had to listen for at least fifteen minutes while he explained there was absolutely *no* conflict of interest, that he would never want to see a player hurt, that he loved Gene Mayer like a son, that Gene wasn't upset that he had played in the afternoon, and on and on.

Then came the best line of all. "You know, I've always respected your work," he said. "You're not like that guy Tony Kornheiser, who is just trying to nail people."

"Really?" I said. "You've read my coverage of Prince George's cops and courts?"

I used some of his quotes on loving Gene Mayer in the story, but, of course, the "Watergate" quote made it too.

The next morning, when I walked into the backstage area—there were no real locker rooms and no press room—I heard Dell's voice before I'd taken two steps. "You had to do it, didn't you?" he yelled. "You couldn't resist." He was walking straight toward me, pointing his finger in the general direction of my chest. "You guys from the *Post* are all the same."

"Nice to see you too, Donald," I said.

The next day I drove to West Virginia and wrote a story on Frank Cignetti, then the football coach at WVU, who was fighting his way back from cancer. The desk was considering holding it a day, but Cignetti was so open and honest they decided to "strip it" (six column headline) in Tuesday's paper.

That clinched the Woodward bet. I had been prepared to beg the desk to get the story in the paper, but Cignetti made it easy for me. A few days later, without complaint, Woodward walked to the McDonald's on 14th and K Streets that was frequented by most of the hookers in the neighborhood. He had to wait because I like my hamburgers plain or with onions only. He marched with the food back into the newsroom, where I, of course, had the in-house photographer waiting for him.

Woodward signed the photo for me later on. I still have it, framed on the wall of my office. It says, "John, you deserve a break today... Bob Woodward."

The two agents I had met the second day of Wimbledon not named Dell were Peter Lawler and Tom Ross. I had sneaked into the players "tea room"—which was actually the lounge and dining area—with Dewey Blanton, who worked at the time for the Men's Tennis Council. We had walked upstairs and encountered Lawler and Ross, who had been on the balcony that overlooks the outside courts. It was raining again, and even agents know when to come in out of the rain.

"Well, if it isn't the Advantage boys," Blanton said as we got to the top of the stairs.

Both men were young. Lawler was older, taller, about 6 foot 3, with glasses. I would learn later he had been a swimmer at Yale. Ross was closer to my age—mid-20s. I would describe him a few years later in *Hard Courts* as looking like "a slightly overweight Ken doll." In those days he just looked like a Ken doll: sandy hair and a quick smile. He had played tennis at California-Berkeley.

Blanton introduced us. "You looking for a story?" Ross asked.

Oh God, here came a pitch, no doubt, for one of their clients.

"I'm actually just looking to stay dry," I said.

Ross shrugged. "Well the guy from Pony just tipped me that Ann White has a new outfit she's going to wear in her match against [Pam] Shriver that needs to be seen."

I knew the name Ann White but knew almost nothing about her. I was skeptical. "New outfit?"

"Yeah. He said it will be the talk of the tournament."

Since White would be playing Pam Shriver—a semi-local for the

Post since she was from Baltimore—I thought it might not hurt to take a look. I'd probably write something about Shriver anyway.

"What court?" I asked.

"Court two," Ross said.

Court two was Wimbledon's most famous outside court. It was called "the graveyard of champions" because there had been so many upsets there. I hadn't been there yet since no matches had been played on outside courts on Monday. So when the rain finally stopped at about six o'clock, I walked out to court two just in time to see Ann White take off her sweats.

She was wearing a white formfitting Pony bodysuit—as in from head to toe. Let me say this: she had the form to wear the outfit. Ann White was about 6 feet tall with blond hair and what Ted Tinling would call an elegant body. As soon as I saw what White was wearing, I knew I had to find Ted.

I raced across the concourse and told the imperious guard at the tea room door that I was *not* going upstairs to the tea room but to Ted's office, which was a few yards from the entrance. He looked at me suspiciously.

"If you want to walk in there yourself and tell him I need to see him, that's fine with me."

"No media are supposed to be in this building," he said.

Somehow I resisted the urge to say what I was really thinking and instead said, "He's the *media* liaison for the club. He's *supposed* to talk to the media."

The guy glared at me, stared at my badge, and finally moved aside—if only because people lined up behind me to pass his inspection were getting impatient. I raced to Ted's office.

"I need you to come out to court two right away," I said.

Ted looked at me as if I were crazy for a moment, and then followed me out of his office. He still moved pretty well at that point, so it didn't take us long to get back to court two, which was only a few yards from the entrance to the tea room.

As soon as Ted saw White, he gasped. "Oh my God, it's *fabulous!*" he said. "She looks fantastic! Thank goodness she has the body for it. Some players in that thing would look *awful*. A white cat suit—it will be the new thing. The *next* thing will be body paint—no clothes, just body paint!"

I couldn't write fast enough.

Naturally, it started to rain after Shriver and White had split sets. The next day, White was informed by Wimbledon officials that her outfit, although white—which Wimbledon still required—did not conform with their dress code. Of course White—and Pony—got more publicity out of the banning of the cat suit than they would have gotten if Wimbledon had said it was okay.

The only bad news was that my story, which ran in the *International Herald Tribune,* got Ted into trouble. The Wimbledon people weren't at all happy that he approved of the outfit.

"I've been reprimanded," he told me the next day, sipping tea in his office. "They were especially unhappy with the reference to body paint."

"I'm really sorry, Ted," I said.

"Nonsense!" he screamed. "It was an absolute highlight! I'll be forever grateful to you for coming and finding me so that I could see it!"

THE FOLLOWING TUESDAY I finally heard back from Esther. "Jeff will go to seventeen-five," she said. "But that's as good as it's going to get."

I had already decided to say yes even if she had called back and told me Neuman wouldn't move off $15,000. I wanted to do the book. I was convinced it could work. I was a little bit scared about leaving the *Post* for a while and heading off to Bloomington for the winter, but I knew I wanted to do it.

"Tell him I'll take it," I said.

"Before we sign anything, do you want to make sure Knight will go through with this?" she said.

She was right. Faced with the reality of a reporter showing up on his doorstep for an entire season, Knight might have second thoughts.

"Good idea," I said. "I'm not coming home until after the British Open. Can it wait until then?"

"Probably," she said. "But don't waste any time once you get back. I don't want Jeff to get cold feet either."

I suppose I could have tried to call Knight from London, but in those days just getting an outside line to call the U.S. was a major challenge. So I decided to wait.

Boris Becker ended up becoming the youngest man in history to win Wimbledon when he beat Kevin Curren in the final that year. Curren had beaten both McEnroe and Connors to get to the final but couldn't handle the seventeen-year-old Becker, who was spectacular on the court and just as impressive off it. When one of the British tabloid writers asked him after the final if he saw any irony in winning on a court his countrymen had once bombed, Becker didn't even blink.

"I'm not a soldier, I'm a sportsman," he said. "The world is a very different place in 1985, I hope, than it was in 1945."

I went to the British Open after Wimbledon along with Tony Kornheiser, his wife, Karril, and their three-year-old daughter, Elizabeth. We shared an apartment in the town of Deal (the tournament was down the road at Royal St. George's that year) that had no telephone in it. That meant each night after we'd had dinner, Tony and I would walk across the street to a phone booth, where we would usually wait about a hundred rings before an overseas operator picked up and allowed us to call the office to check on our stories.

After the British, I flew home, slept for a day, and then called the Indiana basketball office. Mary Ann Davis was Knight's longtime secretary. In fact, when he went to Texas Tech, she went with him and still works for him today. She told me that Knight was on a fishing trip and that she would pass a message on to him, but that it would probably be a couple of weeks before I heard back from him — he generally didn't return phone calls from vacation.

I reported this news to Esther, who was not happy. "You can't sign the contract without him confirming that he'll do it," she said, correctly. "Jeff is getting a little antsy. I think he's wondering if I sold him something I can't deliver."

This was all new to me, but I understood. Mary Ann had mentioned that Knight was going straight from his fishing trip to Gerald Ford's celebrity golf tournament in Tahoe. I remembered Digger Phelps mentioning that he had played in the event in the past. I called Digger. He was, in fact, going to play in the tournament again.

"I need a favor," I said.

"What is it?" he asked.

"I need you to get a message to Knight when you see him out there, telling him that I need to talk to him as soon as possible."

If it bothered Digger to be asked to play middleman for me, he didn't show it. "Give me a number," he said. "I'll do the best I can."

I was going to be in Stratton Mountain, Vermont, that weekend at a tennis tournament. I gave Digger the number for the hotel and asked him to *please* ask Knight to call me at night since I'd be out all day at the tournament. There were no cell phones, and getting in touch with someone wasn't nearly as easy then as it is now.

"I'll give him the message," Digger said. "I'll walk him to a phone if I can. But I can't promise you he'll call. You know how he is."

Actually I didn't. I would find out soon enough.

I drove to Stratton Mountain, without question one of the most beautiful spots to ever stage a tennis tournament, arriving on Thursday night. I knew that the Ford tournament began on Friday. I heard nothing that day. I even cut short dinner on Friday (tough for me to do) so I could be back in the room in case Knight called. I was thinking if he called and I wasn't there, he might not bother to leave a message.

After watching the semifinals on Saturday — and getting in a fight with a security guard who claimed I couldn't go into the players dining area even when *invited* in there by John McEnroe—I went back to the room and went to bed, feeling discouraged. I figured I had maybe seventy-two hours to find Knight somewhere, somehow, or I would have to admit defeat to Esther and crawl away from the project, probably destined never to write a book.

The phone rang at 2:30 a.m. I know because when the phone rings at that hour and you're asleep, the first thing you do is look at the clock. The second thing you do is you wonder if something is wrong with someone in your family. The phone in the room wasn't next to the bed, so I had to get up and walk over to the kitchen area to pick it up.

The first words I heard were, "John, what can I do for you?"

I was still groggy but I figured out pretty quickly it was Knight. The voice and the tone gave him away, as did the hard Midwestern accent that turns *can* into *cayn*.

"Bob, how are you?" I said, trying to sound cordial. I knew it was two hours earlier where he was, and I knew he knew I was on the East Coast. Neither fact was relevant at that point.

"Did McEnroe win today?"

"Yeah, he plays Lendl in the final tomorrow."

"I really like the way he competes. Do you like him?"

"Yeah, I do. He's actually a good guy. You having fun out there?"

"It's okay. I'm not playing very well."

The next five minutes were devoted to a discussion of Knight's golf game. At one point I wondered if maybe I was just dreaming this whole thing. I looked at the clock again: 2:50. Nope, I wasn't dreaming.

Finally, there was a pause, and I decided it was time to get to the point.

"Listen, the reason I tracked you down is I found a publisher that's willing to do the book we talked about back in Lexington. But I didn't want to sign the contract until I made sure you were okay with putting up with me for an entire season."

There was a pause on the other end of the line. I started to panic. Was this going to be a renegotiation? Or just a flat out no?

"Come on out," he said. "Just promise me you won't be too much of a pain in the ass."

"I promise to *try* not to be a pain in the ass," I said.

"You won't be," he said. "Actually, I think you'll enjoy it. If you have any problems getting set up, call Mary Ann, she'll take care of you."

I think I got "Thanks, Bob" out of my mouth before he hung up, but I'm not sure.

I put the phone down and stared at the clock again. It was official now. I was going to ignore Mike Krzyzewski's advice. I was going to spend a winter with Bob Knight.

4

Back Home Again ... Sort Of

ACTUALLY, IT WASN'T OFFICIAL yet.

After my conversation with Knight, I told Esther we could go ahead and sign the contract. The next step was telling my boss, George Solomon, that I was planning on taking a leave of absence to spend the basketball season in Bloomington.

To say that George and I had a hot-and-cold relationship for twenty-six years—starting with my summer internship in 1977 and ending with his retirement as sports editor in 2003—is a vast understatement. I once joked in a book introduction that George and I worked best together when we weren't working together. These days we see each other once a week at the Red Auerbach lunches—which *do* continue to this day, even though Red died five years ago—and get along wonderfully.

That wasn't always the case. George and I often fought like cats. He loved my work ethic and my level of productivity. He didn't love my big mouth, my involvement in the Newspaper Guild (the writers union at the *Post*), or the fact that I often told him his story ideas were ridiculous. George had been a Redskins beat writer before he became an editor. He understood that the Redskins were the most read and the most important beat at the paper—surpassing even the White House, if you ask a lot of people.

Being from New York, I wasn't much of a Redskins fan. More

important, I found the town's (and George's) obsession with the team ludicrous. But I learned very early on just how important the Redskins were at the *Post*. Even though I was the night police reporter at the time, I was sitting at a desk in sports on the afternoon of the 1978 NFL draft, writing a story on the Washington Diplomats. They were the local soccer team, and I still covered them when I was on the metro staff largely because no one on the sports staff had much interest in doing it.

This was before the draft was on TV, and it began on a Tuesday. As I was writing, Ben Bradlee came striding back to sports. Every story you have ever heard about Bradlee is true: he was (and is) as charismatic, intimidating, and fascinating as any person I've ever met. And he loved the Redskins. Every Sunday, he and his wife, Sally Quinn, sat in the owner's box at RFK Stadium with then Redskins president Edward Bennett Williams, who was both the *Post*'s lawyer and one of Bradlee's closest friends.

"Hey, George," Bradlee yelled. "Who'd we get?"

I had been at the *Post* for less than a year and was, quite literally, the low man on the reporting totem pole—night police and soccer were my beats. I was also very young and already pretty sick of, as the late Maryland football coach Jerry Claiborne once said so eloquently, "reading about nothing but Redskins, Redskins, Redskins every day."

So before George Solomon could answer the question, I turned to Bradlee, who was standing close to my desk, and said, "Gee, Ben, I didn't know the *Post* had a pick in the NFL draft."

Bradlee spun in my direction. (He could spin very fast.) He pointed a finger at me and, eyes narrowing, said in what can only be described as a menacing tone, "Listen, Feinstein, you don't like the Redskins, you can get the hell out of this town right now. You got it?"

Not for one second did I think he was joking. Nor did I even consider a smart-ass answer. "Got it," I said meekly, returning to speculating on the Diplomats' chances that weekend against the Seattle Sounders.

Several years later, after I had returned to sports despite Woodward's advice, George called me into his office. The day turned out to be so important in my life that I remember the date: January 6, 1982. I had been back in sports for two-and-a-half years, and even though George and I battled over space and play and which stories I was going to cover, I was doing well. I had been promoted to cover national colleges in football and basketball, a beat George had created essentially for me because I had outgrown covering Maryland only.

Now, late on a Friday afternoon, George called me into his office and shut the door, which was unusual.

"I've got some good news for you," he said.

The last time he had said that to me had been a couple of years earlier, when he called me in to tell me he had gotten me a raise. I had been thrilled, so thrilled that when I walked back out to the newsroom I told Paul Attner, one of the paper's respected veteran reporters, that George had gotten me a raise.

Attner looked at me skeptically. "I'm not saying you don't deserve a raise, but when did you start working here?"

"It'll be two years next week," I said.

Attner shook his head. "That's a union raise," he said. "George had as much to do with that raise as I did."

Years later, when I would retell the story at Red lunches, George would deny it at first, and then say, "Okay, so maybe it did happen that way."

This time the news was different. I wasn't getting a raise. I was getting something better. "I'm putting you on the Redskins," George said. "You're the best reporter I've got. You deserve it."

I was stunned. George knew how I felt about the Redskins. He knew how much I disliked going to Redskins Park, which I had done on occasion filling in for Attner or David DuPree, who had been the beat writers. One of our first skirmishes had come shortly after my return to sports when he walked over to my desk on a Friday afternoon and said, "You are doing great work on the Maryland beat right now, and I want to reward you."

Another union raise perhaps?

No. He put a media credential for that Sunday's Redskins game on my desk. "Go to the game. Sit in the [press] box. You've earned it. I even got you a parking pass."

"George, thanks," I said. "I appreciate it. But I haven't had a day off in a while and, believe it or not, I've got a date."

He acted as if he hadn't heard me. "Have a good time. It'll be a good game."

"I know it will be, George. Maybe another time. I kind of like this girl."

"Come on, you don't have a date. Who would date you?"

Legitimate question, but I really did have a date. I repeated what I had said earlier.

Finally, he looked me in the eye. "I need a sidebar. I'll see you Sunday."

With that he walked away. I postponed the date and wrote the sidebar in about twenty minutes (I was always fast if nothing else), but I wasn't happy. Unfortunately, in spite of my lack of effort, George decided I was the perfect Redskins sidebar writer. So most Sundays, after covering Maryland on Saturday, I would find myself at a Redskins game, calling Jerry Claiborne from the press box during the game (Claiborne would never talk in the morning because he had to go to church and then look at film before he'd take any calls) so I could write my Maryland follow-up story at halftime and then my sidebar after the game.

No wonder I couldn't get a date.

And now George was telling me he wanted me to give up the national college beat, which I loved, to cover a team I didn't like, spending half my life chasing down stories on the status of the backup left tackle for the following Sunday.

I tried to play nice, which with George was usually a waste of time. I told him I was flattered but I loved covering the colleges—especially hoops—and I was just starting to feel as if I knew enough people to really break some stories. Maybe down the road if he wanted me to cover the Redskins that would be the thing to do, but not right now. (What I wanted to do was yell, "I'm too young to die!")

"Colleges don't matter at this paper," he said, one of the more honest things he ever said to me. "The Redskins matter. You're getting the job every scribe [George loved to call reporters *scribes*] on the paper wants. Congratulations. You've earned it."

"George, seriously, I don't want it."

"This isn't a request, John."

I walked back to my desk dazed. My friend David Maraniss had just succeeded Woodward as metro editor. He had said to me in the past that if I ever wanted to come back to metro and cover Maryland politics—the plum beat in metro, one that had produced many *Post* stars through the years—all I had to do was ask. Ten minutes after leaving George's office, I was in David's office.

"You serious about the offer to cover Maryland politics?" I asked.

"Of course I am."

"When can I start?"

One week later, I was in Annapolis. I never covered the Redskins. And even though a lot happened over the next two years, not all of it good, I never really regretted the decision. I thoroughly enjoyed the political beat. It was a great place to be young and single, and I met a lot of smart, interesting people—on both sides of the political aisle.

But I missed sports. I still hadn't been to Wimbledon or an Olympics, so when George offered me the chance to come back to cover the national colleges again and add the tennis beat, I said yes. I had doubts because I would have gotten to cover the national conventions in 1984 if I stayed in metro, but I had one of those epiphany moments that made the decision clear to me.

I was driving home one night, really wrestling with the decision.

As always, I found myself fiddling with the dial, trying to find a game to listen to on the radio. I finally found WOR in New York, which in those days broadcast the New York Islanders games. I've been an Islanders fan since they came into the league as an expansion team in 1972. The Islanders, at that moment, were the four-time defending Stanley Cup champions, and they were playing the Montreal Canadiens that night. They were up 2–1 with the game winding down when I pulled up to my house.

I kept the engine running so I could listen to the last few minutes. The reception wasn't great, so I leaned down to get my ear close to the radio. The Islanders hung on to win. I shook my fist and got out of the car. I had taken about three steps when I suddenly stopped. What had I just done?

I had stayed in my car, huddled over a radio, so I could barely hear the final minutes of a *November* hockey game. Not a playoff game, a November game. What was the message there? At that moment it was clear to me: anyone who cared about sports that much and had the chance to get paid to write about sports was crazy if he didn't do it.

POLITICS HAD ALWAYS BEEN a passion of mine, but not like sports. I had stuffed envelopes for Bobby Kennedy at his New York headquarters at 81st and Broadway prior to his assassination. I followed elections and election reporting closely as a kid and in college. But I hadn't kept records of every political election the way I kept records on sports. I had my own scoring system for every sport and would often watch one game on TV while listening to another on radio. (I turned down the TV sound.)

That moment in the car crystallized all that for me. I went into the office the next morning and went to see Larry Kramer, the metro editor. Kramer and I had gotten off to a very bad start. He had taken over for my pal Maraniss, and I hadn't been happy about that or the mandate he had brought with him when he took over: no more lengthy takeout feature stories, or, as some in the newsroom called them, "Maraniss thumb-suckers."

Maraniss was — is — a superb writer, as he would go on to prove emphatically by winning a Pulitzer Prize for his coverage of Bill Clinton and by writing one of *the* sports books of this (or any) generation, *When Pride Still Mattered*. He valued good writing and liked to give people on his staff the chance to show off their talent. The list of very good writers who worked for David — and for Bob Woodward before him and for Tom Wilkinson and Len Downie before that — is a lengthy one.

Don Graham, the *Post*'s publisher, someone I admire as much as anyone I've ever known, had decided the thumb-suckers had gone too far. He wanted more "daily" coverage — the fifteen-inch story on the local school board meeting, the eight-inch story on the fatal accident, maybe twenty-four inches on a political debate. That was Kramer's edict when he took over metro, and one of the first things he did was call me in to make it clear that there would be no exceptions to the rule.

"Your boy [Maraniss] is gone," he said then. "You won't be writing any more hundred-inch stories on the Speaker of the House or the majority leader." (I had probably written about a hundred inches *total* on Ben Cardin and Don Robertson, but I got the point he was making.)

Kramer and I — and just about every other editor on the metro staff — battled right through election night in 1982. That night might have been one of the low points of my career. Instead of being assigned to the office to write the lead story on either the Maryland senate or gubernatorial races, I was sent to cover Bob Pascal, the *losing* candidate in the gubernatorial race. The editors were sending me a message.

I sent them one back. My job that night was to call the desk with quotes and color from Pascal's headquarters. Margaret Shapiro and Alison Muscatine would be writing the lead from the office, and the desk would put us in touch if either writer needed it.

Shapiro, whom everyone called "Pooh," was a good friend; Muscatine was not. She had been insulted by the thought of working with a "sportswriter" and had gone out of her way to make my life difficult.

I didn't shirk my duties that night as a reporter. In fact, very high up in the story was a scene I described in which Pascal walked into his hotel suite at 8:00 p.m., the moment the polls closed, and told those of us in the room, "Prepare yourselves for a surprise tonight. We're going to prove a lot of people wrong." At that exact moment, on the TV in the room, NBC was reporting that Governor Harry Hughes would be reelected with 63 percent of the vote. I reported that scene and that moment, but I reported it to Pooh, calling her directly rather than going through the desk.

"John, don't do this," she said. "You've done a great job tonight even though they screwed you. Don't give them an excuse to be mad at you."

"Screw them," I said, even though I knew she was right. I didn't care at that point.

The next morning, after I had taken Pascal to a McDonald's in his bathrobe and slippers for a day-after postmortem story, I went into the office and was immediately called in by Kramer and his deputy, Bob Signer.

"You never checked with the desk last night," Kramer said.

I was tempted to play dumb—"Was I supposed to do that?"—but I knew that wouldn't fly. "That's right, I didn't," I said. "Was there any kind of hole in my reporting?"

"That's not the point and you know it," Kramer said.

"You're right," I said. "I know it. I also know I should have been cowriting that lead last night with Pooh, and you guys know it too. I write and report rings around Alison Muscatine. I'm just not as good at sucking up as she is. Apparently that's more important in this regime than actually doing your job."

Now it was Signer's turn. "Part of doing the job is doing what you're supposed to do. We're all out of patience with you."

"You better not pull this again," Kramer said, standing up to indicate the meeting was over.

I left the office soon after that and went on vacation, as scheduled. While I was away I got a call from Pooh.

"Listen, you're going to have to make some decisions before you get back here," she said.

"Yeah, yeah, they're going to ship me back to night police, right?" I said, unimpressed.

"Worse. Arlington County cops and courts."

"What are you talking about?"

Pooh told me that Kramer and Signer had gone to managing editor Howard Simons to report my insubordination. Simons had told them to do what they wanted with me, and they had decided Arlington County in Virginia, which was the polar opposite of Prince George's County when it came to stories, was a good landing place for me.

"They want you to quit," Pooh said. "I think they're going to give you one last chance in Annapolis. I talked to Howard and told him they'd be sending a bad message by demoting someone who was still doing high-quality work because he didn't get along with his editors. You come back and start arguing with them again, they're going to nail you."

Quitting did cross my mind. In fact, I had been approached during that time by *Sports Illustrated* — a chance I would have jumped at except the job was covering hockey. I liked hockey a lot, but the thought of spending winters flying in and out of Buffalo and Calgary and Vancouver wasn't that appealing.

What's more, in spite of everything, I loved my job and I loved the *Post*. I finally took a deep breath and decided to go back, keep my mouth shut, and just do the best work I could possibly do. Which is what I did throughout the legislative session. When it was over, Kramer and Signer called me in again. "You did a great job," Kramer said. "And I haven't heard one word from anyone about you being anything but cooperative."

That summer I was actually allowed to write long takeouts again. One was on Baltimore mayor William Donald Schaefer, who was going to be reelected with something like 80 percent of the vote. He'd done a remarkable job of revitalizing Baltimore but was, to put it mildly, an eccentric. One of the anecdotes in the story was about his penchant for locking himself in his office and watering his plants for lengthy periods whenever the *Baltimore Sun* criticized him at all. There were several other stories about how sensitive he was to criticism.

On Election Day, I went to the polls early in the morning to gather a few quotes from the mayor after he voted. When he came out he announced that he had, in fact, voted for himself after studying his record. We all asked some rudimentary questions. I asked him if he thought this would be his largest margin of victory in his four elections.

"I'm not speaking to you," Schaefer said.

I thought he was joking. The story I'd written on him (which *had* been a hundred inches long) had basically been a paean to what he'd done as mayor.

"How *dare* you," Schaefer continued, "say I'm sensitive to criticism!"

Everyone cracked up. The mayor did not.

I got called in after Election Day again. This time it was by Howard Simons. The tone had changed in a year. "You've really turned it around," he said. "You've done great work, and I think you're going to get some chances to cover the national elections next year. But I have a question for you: is this what you want to do? My sense is that sports is still your true love."

"I do love sports," I said. "I miss it a lot some days. But I love doing this. Plus, even if I wanted to go back to sports, I don't think George would take me back. He was pretty pissed when I left."

"George is a bigger man than that," Howard said.

I must have given him a look that said, 'Are you kidding me?' because he went on: "If I talk to him, I'm sure he'll take you back— *if* you want that."

I asked him if I could think about it. For one thing, I didn't think it would be fair to have Simons talk to Solomon, convince him to take me back, and then have me turn around and say no thanks. For another, I really was torn. Kramer had called me in after I had talked to Simons to say he really wanted me to stay and would be pushing me in the direction of the national staff if I did.

It was the hockey game that made the decision for me. When I told Kramer what had happened, he looked at me and said, "You're right. Anyone who would care that much about a hockey game on the radio belongs in sports."

A week later, I was standing on the practice field at Holy Cross working on a story on their coach, Rick Carter, who was one of the hot names in the business at the time. Holy Cross's practice field is on top of a mountain, and it was snowing and freezing in mid-November. I could have been in a warm bar in Annapolis, talking to a politician while having a drink.

I was perfectly content to be exactly where I was.

EVEN THOUGH WE HAD continued to fight constantly after my return to sports, I knew George Solomon wasn't going to be thrilled with the notion of me taking a leave of absence. And so, on the day before the U.S. Open started, I flew from New York to Washington (I flew all the time in those days) to have lunch with him. I didn't tell him what it was about, just that we needed to talk.

We went to the Palm—then, as now, *the* power lunch place in

Washington. I laid out for George what had happened and the fact that I would need to take a leave of absence beginning in October and extending until I finished the book—I hoped in time to go to the French Open the following spring.

George shook his head. "No," he said. "You can't do it. I need you. Sorry. Maybe another time."

I looked closely at George to see if perhaps he was kidding. He wasn't. I took a deep breath.

"George, I don't think you understand," I said. "This isn't a request. This is an announcement. I've signed a contract. I'm doing the book. If you won't give me a leave of absence, I'll resign. I don't want to do that, but I've decided I'm going to do this book. I'd much rather be able to stay because I love the *Post,* but if I have to leave, I will."

Now it was his turn to look at me to see if perhaps I was kidding. When he realized I wasn't, he began scrambling.

"Look, you can make several trips to Bloomington—a couple of long ones if you want. Do it that way."

I shook my head. "George, you can't write a book part-time. Knight's not going to call me in advance and say, "Hey, I may throw a chair tomorrow, you better get out here. I have to *be* there."

Now he was angry. "You're making a mistake," he said. "You aren't ready to write a book. You aren't even thirty yet. Stop being in such a rush."

I would have been angry at that remark, except I knew he was making it only to try to get me to back down. So I ignored it. He tried several other angles, including flattery. "You're my best reporter. I can't afford to lose you for an entire basketball season."

"I appreciate that George. But isn't one season better than forever?"

When he finally figured out I wasn't changing my mind, he shook his head. "I'll talk to [Ben] Bradlee. I'll see what I can do."

There really wasn't much for him to do. I knew perfectly well Bradlee would say to him, "Hey, it's your call. He works for you."

I went back to New York to cover the Open. Never once in two weeks did George bring up the book or whether he had talked to Bradlee. I let it go, deciding I would deal with it when I got back to Washington. On the morning of the Open final between Ivan Lendl and John McEnroe, I was sitting in the press box killing time when I heard Bud Collins say, "John, you have a visitor."

No, it wasn't Abbie Hoffman. It was Katharine Graham, the former publisher and chairman of the board of the *Post*. Like just about anyone who had worked at the *Post* for any period of time, I'd met Mrs. Graham on a number of occasions. As a rookie night police reporter, I had been invited to one of her "new people" lunches in her private dining room. I still remember her asking us over dessert to tell her how we thought the paper could be better.

Not surprisingly, there was complete silence. None of us really wanted to tell Katharine Graham how to make her newspaper better, especially since it was pretty damn good anyway.

"Oh, come on, all of you," she said. "I really want to know. That's why I asked. Don't be intimidated."

"Well," I said, "we don't do a very good job in sports with getting things into the paper at night. The deadlines should be more flexible to get game stories into the paper, and we need to get more box scores into the home delivery edition."

Mrs. Graham looked me right in the eye and said, "John, you need to be a little more intimidated."

Gulp. Believe me, I was a lot more afraid of Katharine Graham than of John Thompson.

Now she was standing in the back of the press box talking to Bud when I walked up.

"John," she said. "I just had to come up and see you. I have *loved* your tennis coverage this summer. It's been wonderful."

I knew Mrs. Graham played tennis and was a big fan. It was one of the reasons the paper covered so much tennis. "Thank you, Mrs. Graham, that's so nice of you..."

"The kid's good, Katharine," Bud, always my agent, put in.

"Oh, I know," she said. "And you know what I like best? The way you write about McEnroe. I've always liked him. I know he has that temper, but he's so *passionate*. You've been able to explain him in a different way."

"Well, when he's not losing his mind out there he's actually a good guy," I said.

"*Yes!*" she said. "He *is* a good guy. I couldn't agree more."

A few minutes later she was gone, off to a corporate box to get something to eat before the match began. A few minutes before the 4 p.m. start, Pete Alfano and I went downstairs to our seats in the stands to watch the match. The view from the press box was, generally speaking, terrible, but Ed Fabricius, then the USTA's PR guy, always managed to dig up about a dozen seats near courtside for some of the major media outlets. Pete, being from the *New York Times,* had one of the seats. I had the *Post's* seat. Bud wasn't with us—he sat with Alan King, who had the *best* seats.

The players walked out to start the match. McEnroe was serving. The ball boy tossed him two balls, and he shoved one into the pocket of his shorts as he always did. But as he turned to serve, there was one person who hadn't quite made it to her seat in about the fourth row.

Katharine Graham.

I gasped in terror. McEnroe was staring at Mrs. Graham, bouncing the ball he was going to serve on the strings of his racquet. She had no idea what was going on because she wasn't looking at him.

I grabbed Alfano's arm. "This is it," I said. "I'm done at the *Post* if he yells at her. I just told her what a good guy he is."

Maybe it was because the match hadn't started yet, but McEnroe—whom I'd once heard yell at a woman in Madison Square Garden, "Hey, lady, if you'd lose some weight you might get to your seat on time!"—never said a word. Mrs. Graham took her seat and you could almost feel twenty thousand people (starting with me) breathe a sigh of relief.

Lendl won the match in straight sets, a huge win for him because he had lost three straight Open finals—two to Jimmy Connors and one to McEnroe. Twenty-five years later, Lendl remembered the match almost point-for-point. "That was as big as any match I ever played," he said. "John had me down 5–2 in the first, and I broke him back and won the set. After that, I was in control."

None of us knew it at the time, but McEnroe, who was twenty-six, had just played his last major final.

I flew back to Washington the next morning and went straight to the office. George's greeting was terse. "Go see Bradlee," he said.

When I was waved in, Bradlee was seated behind his desk in his famous pose: chair back, feet up on his desk. He asked if I wanted coffee—the first and only time he ever offered me coffee in his office. I said no thanks.

"George says you want to do a book on Bobby Knight," he said.

"I do," I said. "He's said he'll give me total access and—"

Bradlee waved me off in mid-sentence and sat up in his chair. "John, let me be honest with you. I don't think anyone gives a shit about Bobby Knight anymore. He's yesterday's news."

I knew Bradlee was a sports fan, although more a Redskins fan than anything else. He might very well have been right; maybe the Olympics would prove to be Knight's Last Hurrah.

"Ben, you might be right," I said. "But I think he's still interesting to a lot of people, and if he gives me the kind of access he's promised—"

"What if he changes his mind the first time they lose a tough game?" he said. "What then?"

That thought had occurred to me on a daily basis since July, when Knight had told me to come on out to Bloomington. As mercurial as he was, I knew I would be at risk virtually all season: a bad loss, a disagreement—almost anything could leave me on the outside looking in.

"Good question," I said. "I might be back here before Christmas begging you to take me back."

He looked at me for a moment, then shrugged. "If you want to do it, I won't try to stop you," he said. "I don't think you'll sell five books outside the state of Indiana, but you'll probably sell a few there. Look, if you really want to do it, go with God."

I didn't know whether to thank him or tell him, "Never mind, I think I'll stay here where I'm safe." I thanked him. I was going to Bloomington, and it was time to find an apartment near Assembly Hall.

5

The Honeymoon

THE PLACE I FOUND was less than a half mile away from the parking lot at Assembly Hall in the Dunhill Apartment complex. I got two bedrooms with about six pieces of furniture—a bed, a desk and a chair in the second bedroom, a table and chairs in the kitchen, and a couch in the family room. The cost was $225 a month. That was fine with me.

I arrived in Bloomington in the middle of a driving rainstorm. I also left several months later in a driving rainstorm and endured many others in between. It really didn't snow all that much, but it seemed to rain almost every day.

Knight had told me to make sure I arrived in time to go with him to a speech he was giving that night in Lawrenceville, Illinois. I wasn't sure why it was so important that I be there, but I wanted to get off to a good start so I left my house at three o'clock in the morning to make sure I arrived in time to unpack my car and get to the Cave by five o'clock that afternoon.

I made it with a few minutes to spare. Knight was in the shower, and the only person in the Cave was the one assistant coach I hadn't met: Ron Felling. Jim Crews had left Indiana the previous spring to become the head coach at Evansville. Felling had been a hugely successful high school coach—he'd won four state titles in Illinois—

and had coached, among others, Marty Simmons, who had been at Indiana for two years before transferring to Evansville.

"I'm the reason we're going to Lawrenceville tonight," Felling told me. "That's where I used to coach. Coach is doing this as a favor to me."

One thing I would learn quickly was that no one—I mean *no one*—who worked inside Assembly Hall ever called Knight "Bob." His first name was Coach. This wasn't uncommon in coaching, but it seemed especially true with Knight.

I liked Felling instantly. He had an easy smile and a warm, self-deprecating sense of humor. Perhaps because he was new, he seemed less intimidated by Knight than the other assistants. One of Knight's favorite words on his long list of profanities was *cocksucker*. When he got really angry, everyone became a cocksucker. Whenever he would call Felling a cocksucker—which was often—Felling would laugh, shake his head, and say, "You know, Coach, I'm trying to quit." Knight would try not to laugh or even smile at the response, but more often than not he did.

While Knight was getting dressed (he greeted me by saying, "Good thing you weren't late, we'd have left without you," causing me to resist the urge to say, "Oh God, if only I'd been late"), Felling told me how Knight had courted him to join his staff.

"We've known each other for years," Felling said. "Recruiting, clinics, things like that. He called me about two in the morning, woke me up, and said, 'So are you going to come and coach for me or not?' I said I would so I could go back to sleep."

It turned out we were flying to Lawrenceville on a four-seat plane. I wasn't nearly as bad a flier back then as I am now, but climbing into that little plane with the rain still pelting down, I was not filled with confidence. In fact, I found myself thinking, "What the hell am I doing here? Am I nuts? I should be back at the *Post* getting ready to go out for a drink with my friends *right now*."

The trip was bumpy, to say the least. If Knight was at all nervous, he certainly didn't show it. "You know, John, if it's your time, it's your time," he said.

"Bob, it might be your time," I said. "But it is *not* my time."

During the flight he talked about the ground rules for the book. Actually, the ground *rule* for the book. There was only one.

"Nancy and I are separated," he said, talking about his wife. "I bought a house on the other side of town that I'm going to move into. Right now I'm still at home with [younger son] Patrick because she's down at Duke on the rice diet."

What he didn't mention, which I would learn during the course of the season, was that he had started seeing Karen Edgar, a high school basketball coach from Oklahoma who would eventually become his second wife.

"I don't want the book to be about my personal life. I don't need Patrick and [older son] Tim reading details about their parents getting divorced."

"Do they know?" I asked.

"Sort of," he said.

Actually, Patrick didn't know at that point. He and I would become close during the season—Patrick was a high school freshman, Tim was a sophomore at Stanford—and Patrick told me after his mother came back to town that he thought his parents were going to work things out.

I told Knight I had no problem at all with that ground rule, that I thought it was a more than reasonable request, and that the book I wanted to write was about his relationship with the players and his coaches anyway. I asked if there was anything else.

He shook his head. "No. I want you to see how the program really works, and the way to do that is for you to have access to everything," he said. "I think you're going to really like these kids. They may not be the best basketball players in the world, but they're terrific kids."

We finally landed—somehow—in Lawrenceville. Knight wowed his audience, which was eating the kind of chicken that's usually served at potluck political dinners. He even introduced me toward the end of his talk.

"John Feinstein is a friend of mine," he said. "He works for the *Washington Post* but he's going to spend this season with our team to write a book that I hope will show people just what goes into trying to have a successful basketball team." He paused. "John, stand up so these people can see what a liberal Jew from the East Coast looks like."

I stood up. I had no problem with that introduction. For one thing, it was accurate even though not *all* liberal Jews from the East Coast look like me. For another, that's the nature of jock put-down humor. If I had introduced Knight to someone as a right wing Midwestern WASP, he would have laughed it off or said something like "Damn right I am."

Even though it was my first day with Knight, I felt comfortable, except on the airplane.

THE NEXT FEW WEEKS were, for the most part, enjoyable. Knight waited several days before he introduced me to the team. Maybe he was waiting to be sure he was going to let me stay. I would walk into the locker room with Knight and the four full-time coaches—Felling, Kohn Smith, Joby Wright, and Royce Waltman—and stand in a corner near the door while Knight talked to the team. Most of the time the three graduate assistants—Dan Dakich, Julio Salazar, and Murry Bartow—would stand in the same general area. I had met all the coaches and the other key member of the staff, head trainer Tim Garl, right away.

The players didn't quite know what to make of me, but really weren't that concerned one way or the other about my presence.

Knight was constantly bringing strangers into the locker room—
hunting buddies; pals from Orrville, Ohio, where he'd grown up;
coaches he'd known through the years. Sometimes he introduced
people to the players, sometimes he didn't.

"It was sort of routine for us," Steve Alford told me later. "We just
figured you were another one of Coach's buddies."

After about four days of practice, Knight announced to me as we
were making the afternoon trek across the gym floor from the Cave
to the locker room that today was the day I was going to be introduced to the players.

Knight explained who I was and why I was there and told the
players that, unlike with other media members, I didn't need to go
through the sports information office to talk to them. The players
were a little bit stunned when Knight told them I'd have complete
access for the whole season.

"The only guy who ever had that kind of access on a regular basis
was [Bob] Hammel," Alford said. "And we didn't even really see him
as a reporter. He was Coach's pal and we knew he wouldn't write
anything Coach didn't want him to write."

In fact, the players had two nicknames for Hammel, who was the
sports editor and columnist for the local paper in Bloomington (then
known as the *Herald-Telephone*). One was "the shadow," because he
seemed to go everywhere with Knight. Frequently, while on the
road, Knight would decide to walk back from practice or occasionally from a game when he was angry. He would jump up from his
bus seat and say, "Come on, Hamso," and Hammel would jump up
and follow him off the bus.

The other nickname for Hammel was "Pravda," because the players considered him the official Bob Knight news service. Hammel
knew almost everything about the team but rarely reported much of
it. He was a very solid, professional newspaperman, but he had figured out early on that being in a position to report some of what

went on in the Indiana basketball program by keeping Knight happy was better than being able to report none of what went on by making Knight angry.

Plus, he genuinely liked Knight. Even after Knight had thrown the chair, Hammel had defended him. Looking back on that column, he was genuinely chagrinned. "I realized that it read like a legal brief," he said. "I acted as if Bob was my client rather than my subject."

My nickname among the players as the season went on was "the invisible man." That came from Alford, who was the player I became closest to. That made sense: Alford was the team's best player and the captain. He was also the subject of more Knight tirades than anyone, in part because Knight knew he needed Alford to be a great player for the team to be good, but also because Knight knew Alford could take it.

After graduating, Alford actually cowrote a book called *Playing for Knight*. The chapter on his junior year was called "The Invisible Man." I considered that high praise. He often referred to me as being in a room doing my "invisible act."

That was exactly what I wanted. I wanted to be there without being there, and as the days passed, it became easier. The assistant coaches were thrilled by my presence for one reason: it meant they had a chance to go home for dinner. Knight has never been good at being alone, even for short periods of time, which is one reason why he always had people hanging out with him before and after games. He needed an audience.

I was a brand new audience. Knight liked to go out to dinner somewhere just about every night. Usually that meant one or more of the assistant coaches had to go with him. Felling was the prime candidate because he was divorced. Once I arrived though, I stepped into that role. It made sense for me because Knight was expansive and talkative at dinner. Plus, I certainly didn't have anything better to do back at the Dunhill Apartments.

I was also occasionally helpful to him during that period in his role as a single dad. Patrick was a freshman at Bloomington North High School and often needed to be picked up shortly after class or—once his high school basketball season began—shortly after practice. One day I volunteered to do the pickup. After that, I did it often. I didn't mind at all. For one thing, I liked Patrick, who was bright, outgoing, and funny. For another, after I'd been there awhile, a thirty minute break from hearing yet again about the shortcomings of Alford, Daryl Thomas, and the two junior college transfers, Andre Harris and Todd Jadlow, was not a bad thing.

To this day, Patrick Knight jokingly refers to me as his old babysitter. The summer after *A Season on the Brink* came out, I ran into Patrick, who was playing in a summer league tournament in Princeton, New Jersey.

"My dad still mad at you?" he asked.

"Of course," I said.

"I wouldn't worry about it," he said. "You know how he is. The important thing is I still like you."

Actually, that meant a lot to me. I liked Patrick Knight then and I like him now.

His father and I spent a lot of time together prior to the beginning of the season. If we weren't going out to dinner, we were often in his car driving to a speaking engagement somewhere in Indiana. Once Knight decides he likes a line, he tends to repeat it. And so I was routinely introduced as "my Eastern liberal Jewish friend."

One of the things I figured out early on about Knight was that he wasn't nearly as funny as he believed himself to be. I was never able to articulate my feelings about that until my friend Dave Kindred described it perfectly: "The sound of Bob Knight's life is uncomfortable laughter."

Yes. Exactly. Knight will often say something he thinks is funny that just isn't. People know he's trying to be funny so they try to laugh—and it is uncomfortable. Knight liked to joke with

African-Americans about race, with Jews about being Jewish, and with women, the few he allowed into his life, about women. He often joked with his former center Steve Downing, who had become an assistant athletic director, about how lazy black guys were. Downing, who loves Knight and is devoted to Knight, would laugh and wave it off.

I felt the same way about the Jewish cracks. I'm a believer that if you can't laugh at yourself, you have issues. One of my all-time favorite jokes is one my mother told me years ago: Jewish mother is on the beach with her infant. A giant wave washes the baby out to sea. She looks up at the sky and says, "Oh God, Oh God, if you'll only spare my child, I'll be eternally grateful." Another wave washes in and there's the baby completely unharmed. She looks back up at the sky and says, "He had a hat!"

Like most people, Knight loved that joke. There was only one time where I thought he stepped over the line with me when it came to that sort of humor. It was after practice one afternoon and Knight had walked to one end of the court with Kohn Smith, Royce Waltman, and Joby Wright. I was at the other end of the court being regaled by Ron Felling with one of his never-ending stories. As Felling was talking, Knight called his name. Felling didn't hear him. Finally, I said, "Hey, Ron, I think Bob is calling you."

Felling turned around to see Knight waving him over. I honestly don't remember what it was he wanted. Chances are good he was going to ask Felling why in the world Alford couldn't do a better job of fighting through screens. When Felling and I walked up, Knight had decided the reason for the ten- or fifteen-second delay in Felling's arrival was me, since Felling had been talking to me when Knight had tried to get his attention.

"You know, John," Knight said. "There are times when I'm not sure that Hitler wasn't right about you people."

I froze. This was about three weeks into my Bloomington sojourn, and one thing I had figured out quickly was that Knight did not like anyone arguing with him when other people were around. Earlier that week, Al McGuire had been in town to do a preseason interview with Knight for NBC. As was usually the case when an important friend visited, Knight gathered a group for dinner. Somehow the subject of the 1971 Penn team came up during the conversation.

"One of the most unbelievable games I think I've ever seen was when Villanova demolished them in the regional final that year," Knight said. "They were 28–1 going into that game and Villanova beat them by forty."

Without thinking I said, "They were 28–0 going into the game, Bob. Villanova was their only loss."

Knight stared at me for a second as if shocked I had said anything. "John, I was at the goddamn game," he said. "I was scouting for [Ohio State coach] Fred Taylor. You think I don't remember their record?"

"If you think they were 28–1 going in, you don't," I said.

Knight was now officially pissed off. "I know you have a good memory," he said. "I know you think you have the greatest f—ing memory in the history of the world. But you've got this one wrong."

"How much?" I asked.

"What?"

"How much do you want to bet?" I said. "A thousand dollars?"

McGuire was trying to change the subject. I wasn't having any of it. Looking back, I was acting like a jerk. But at that moment I was going to *prove* I was right.

"I'm not taking that kind of money from you," Knight said. "I'll bet you a hundred."

We agreed. There was no internet in those days, so Knight dispatched Bob Hammel to call his office and have someone look it up. When Hammel returned to the table a few minutes later, he was pale.

"Well?" Knight asked.

"Um, Bob, Penn was 28–0 going into that game."

Knight turned bright red. Pointing his finger at me he said, "I don't ever want to hear about your f—ing memory again."

He wasn't upset about the hundred dollars—which I never tried to collect and he never offered to pay—he was upset that he'd been proven wrong in front of his friends, and especially in front of Al, who could have cared less one way or the other.

There had been other moments in which I had started to argue with Knight about something and realized I simply couldn't do it in front of people, especially in front of his coaches. Now, though, he had crossed a line I considered uncrossable. Several answers ran through my head while Knight was yelling at Felling about something. But I knew—*knew*—if I challenged him in front of his coaches he would have to win. And I knew once I started I wasn't going to back down. I reminded myself what my goal in being there was: get through the season with my access intact and write the book.

So I shut up.

That night, Knight and I were again in the car en route to a speech, and it was just the two of us.

"I gotta say something to you," I finally said. "Because if I don't I won't be able to sleep tonight."

"What is it?" he asked.

"I think you know I have no problem with you making jokes about me being Jewish or liberal or whatever," I said.

"In fact, you're really good about it," Knight said.

"I think so," I went on. "But I gotta tell you, Bob. Hitler wasn't funny. Not on any level."

There was dead silence in the car for what felt like five minutes. It was probably no more than thirty seconds—maybe less.

"You know what I hate more than anything?" Knight finally said.

Oh God, I thought. He's going to lecture me on being ungrateful and drop me off by the side of the road in the middle of nowhere.

"What's that?" I asked.

"When I say something stupid," he said.

It was the closest I ever heard Bob Knight come to saying I'm sorry, to me or to anybody.

We drove in silence for a good long while after that. He introduced me that night as "a friend of mine who works for the *Washington Post* and is a great writer."

As time went by I began to understand what Mike Krzyzewski had been talking about that night in Lexington. As the start of the season drew closer, Knight became more uptight and more impatient, with everyone. I hadn't become a target for his anger — yet.

On the day after the team's first exhibition game, Knight completely lost it with Daryl Thomas, the team's starting center. I ended up using that Sunday afternoon as the starting point for *A Season on the Brink* because it provided such a clear illustration of what it was like to play for Knight. One thing I did *not* do in the book was repeat the word Knight called Thomas fourteen times during a three minute tirade. Hint: it rhymes with *bunt*. I used a slightly less offensive word in its place and used it four times instead of fourteen. That was pretty typical. My editor, Jeff Neuman, and I decided during the editing of the book to leave that word out completely; to take a tirade in which any profanity was repeated, say fourteen times, and use perhaps three or four to make the point; and to write *f*— on occasions when Knight used his favorite word repeatedly.

Knight loves that word. He once made a video describing all the ways to use it. "You can use it to express surprise, as in 'Well I'll be f—ed!' Or to express admiration: 'What a f—ing great guy he is!' Or anger..."

You get the idea.

That's why I found it so remarkable when Knight's objection to the book was my use of his profanity. When Royce Waltman called shortly after I had sent Knight an advance copy and said, "This is your official phone call, Coach is really pissed," I wasn't surprised. One thing I had figured out long before I left Bloomington was that Knight was going to find *something* to not like about the book. I didn't know what it was going to be, but I never for one minute expected to get a phone call saying "You did a great job."

That's not Knight. Reminding people that they have not done as well as he had hoped is one way he maintains control of his relationships. That's also why he has gone long periods not talking to people such as Mike Krzyzewski and Steve Alford (among others). Everything has to be done by Knight's rules.

The best description of Knight I ever heard came from another of his former assistants. He and Knight were having an argument. It was a classic Knight double standard: he had continued to recruit a player who had made a verbal commitment to this former assistant. If another coach had done that to the ex-assistant, Knight would have hammered the guy for it. Rather than defend what he had done, Knight began screaming about how the ex-assistant never would have been anything in basketball if not for him. Which may have been true. It also entirely missed the point. To this day the ex-assistant doesn't want to put his name on the story, not because it would affect his career at this point (he's not even in coaching anymore), but because he still cares about Knight's feelings. But at that point, really angry, he just said, "Coach, you know what your problem is? You treat your enemies better than you treat your friends."

Knight's friends constantly have to live up to a standard of loyalty that is almost impossible to maintain. Knight was angry with Krzyzewski—although I'm sure he would claim different—because Krzyzewski's Duke team beat Knight's Indiana team in the 1992 Final Four. He was furious with Alford because Alford refused to skip his father's summer camp (which he had worked since he was a kid) to come play a cameo role in the movie *Blue Chips,* on which Knight was an advisor to Nick Nolte.

And he was mad at me for leaving a fraction of his profanity in *A Season on the Brink.*

When Waltman said to me that Coach was pissed off because I'd left his profanity in the book, this is exactly what I said: "No, seriously, Royce, what's he really pissed about?"

It literally took me a couple of minutes to believe Waltman wasn't joking, that this wasn't some kind of not funny Knight joke or prank. Nope, it was the profanity. I had *promised* Coach I would leave it out of the book.

No, I hadn't. We *had* discussed it. It came up one night at dinner when Knight had been especially profane—if that was possible—in practice, and I joked that the book might be the first sports book in history to have to be wrapped in brown paper.

Knight laughed. "You aren't going to leave all my profanity in, are you?"

"No, I'm not," I said. "For one thing, I don't want the book to be longer than *War and Peace.* But you understand I have to leave some of it in for it to have credibility. If I write a book about you without the word *fuck,* it would be like writing a book about you without the word *basketball.* It wouldn't be taken seriously. People would just say, 'Knight let Feinstein in the locker room and he wrote him a love letter.'"

"I get that," Knight said.

Except in the end he didn't get it. Or chose not to get it. I have never honestly been sure why he decided to be angry about the profanity that showed up in the book. Not only did I take most of it out, but how many people reading that book didn't know Knight used profanity? He was proud of it, liked to make a point of using it in public, and could certainly be seen and heard using it during games. Bob Knight says *fuck* a lot is film-at-eleven news?

To this day I believe Knight thought, in spite of all our talks, that I *would* write him a love letter, that the book would read as if

Hammel had written it. The irony, of course, is that the book did exactly what Knight hoped it would do when he granted me access: it showed that there were methods to the madness. Everyone had seen and heard the cartoon character side of Knight. What people asked all the time was "Why do the players put up with it? Why are they so loyal to him when they graduate?" The book provided answers—firsthand because I was right there.

When ESPN made the book into a movie in 2001, they went the cartoon route with the script. Except for one fictional scene with Alford—there were plenty of those in the movie—the entire movie was the crazed Knight: throwing chairs and screaming at officials and players and the president of Indiana and assistant coaches and anyone else who happened to wander into the path of Brian Dennehy, who played Knight about as well as he could be played, given the quality of the script and the directing.

I had done some work for ESPN, but we had gone through an ugly divorce shortly before the movie was made. As a result, Mark Shapiro, who was in charge of making the movie, had ordered that I not see a script until and unless I agreed to come back to work for ESPN—on his terms. He even dispatched two people, Len DeLuca and Vince Doria, to fly to Washington to try to make a new deal with me—part of which involved having me fly to Winnipeg where the movie was being shot to try to doctor the script, and part of which involved me helping with the promotion of the movie.

I was willing to do that, but not to give in to Shapiro's continuing professional coercion on other issues. Actually DeLuca and Doria signed off on the deal I offered, and then Shapiro said no to it. So I never went to Winnipeg. I did however see the script because someone working on the movie sent it to me. I could not believe how bad it was.

I never thought *Season on the Brink* was a good candidate to be turned into a movie. For one thing, it didn't really have a "movie" ending. That 1985–86 season ended with an absolute thud: a blowout loss at Michigan with the Big Ten title on the line and an upset loss to fourteenth-seeded Cleveland State in the first round of the NCAA Tournament. It didn't hurt the book, but it meant there was no real ending to the movie, unless you could somehow spin it forward to the next season, when Indiana won the national title.

But the movie didn't have to be terrible. If I had been given the chance to doctor the script, I would have added two scenes from the book. The first came after Indiana lost its first two Big Ten games, both at home, to Michigan and Michigan State. In mid-tirade during a review of the Michigan State tape, Knight suddenly stopped the tape.

"You know, boys," he said. "I tell you all the time that you can't be good basketball players if you're selfish people. You don't really understand what I'm saying when I say that, do you? I'm not talking about helping on defense or passing the ball, it's more than that. I'm talking about Winston [Morgan] seeing Stew [Robinson] lose his man and not thinking for an instant, 'Oh, that's Stew's guy,' but scrambling over to pick the guy up. You boys never do that. You only worry about yourselves."

He paused, standing in front of the screen in the pitch-dark locker room. "Let me ask you boys a question. On Thanksgiving Day, Dr. Rink [team doctor Larry] and his wife had you all over for Thanksgiving dinner. Mrs. Rink shopped for you, cooked, cleaned up after you left. All so you could have a nice Thanksgiving. Any of you in here who called her, wrote her, or sent her flowers to say thank you raise your hand."

Not a hand went up. "Exactly what I thought," Knight said. "This is what I'm talking about. As long as you are selfish people, you will never be good basketball players."

He turned and walked out. As all the coaches followed him and I followed them, Kohn Smith turned to me and said, "Now *that* was coaching."

Coincidence or not, Indiana won its next seven games.

The second scene was in a Bob Evans restaurant. Knight was approached by a young boy named Garland Loper (I think he was thirteen at the time) who wanted to know if he could bring his father and older brother over to meet Knight. A bit baffled, Knight said of course. Garland explained that his father and brother were deaf and mute and he spoke for them. Would that be okay? Knight nodded.

Garland brought his dad and brother over and they signed to him and he spoke to Knight. It was normal stuff: we love IU, we're proud of the way you play and represent the university and our state. Knight was blown away by Garland Loper. He invited the family to a game and brought the three Lopers into the locker room beforehand. There, he had Garland speak to the team on behalf of his family. It was a remarkable scene to witness. When Garland was finished, as was always Knight's custom when visitors came, each player stood up, shook hands with the Lopers, and introduced himself. After they had left, Knight said to the players, "I don't ever want to hear how hard your lives are."

That was his pregame talk that night.

It is *that* side of Knight that people hadn't seen before the book. If you had added those two scenes to the movie, it would have at least been — as Mary Tyler Moore used to say — not awful.

There were a lot of emotional moments during the season, also some cringe-worthy moments. Knight grew fond of telling people after the book came out that he had gotten tired of me by the time the season ended. I found that interesting since he called me a couple of times while I was writing and asked me to come out to Bloomington to play golf. I said no thanks, in part because I had a tight deadline, but also because — being honest — I had gotten pretty tired of Knight. Even those who are most loyal to him will tell you that being around him on a daily basis wears you out. That was what Krzyzewski had been talking about.

We'd had two battles, for lack of a better word, during the season. The first had come in Minneapolis, the morning after a bad loss at Iowa. It had ended that seven-game winning streak and had been a blowout from the start. Knight was upset about being blown out, but also about losing to George Raveling—who had been one of his assistants on the Olympic team but had somehow become another name on Knight's bad guy list. I don't even remember George's specific crime other than the usual: he had started winning games against Knight.

The team had flown through a snowstorm from Iowa City to Minneapolis and, even though it was two o'clock in the morning, Knight made everyone watch tape for about ninety minutes. He was still, to put it gently, cranky at breakfast the next morning when Sid Hartman, the long-time *Minneapolis Star Tribune* columnist and another of Knight's confidant/pals, walked in. Knight, as he often did when upset, ignored Hartman. Sid understood. As we were walking out of the breakfast room, Sid turned to me and said, "So what are you going to do all day in the snow here?"

I shrugged and said, in what I thought was a self-deprecating way, "Just do what I do every day: follow Knight around."

Almost fifteen years later, when Knight got himself fired for grabbing a kid who walked by him and said, "Hey, what's up, Knight?" I thought back to that morning in Minneapolis. Knight was walking a couple of steps ahead of us, going on about how awful Daryl Thomas had been the night before, when he heard my comment. He stopped, whirled, and pointed his finger at me.

"Don't you ever call me Knight," he said, his face red. "You call me Coach, you call me Bob, you call me Coach Knight, but you don't call me Knight!"

"Bob, I wasn't calling you anything," I said, somewhat stunned but also understanding in the back of my mind that this was a reaction to exhaustion and a bad loss. "I was making fun of myself..."

"I don't give a goddamn what the f— you were doing. I'm a lot older than you and one hell of a lot more important than you in the game of basketball, so you show me some respect!"

I hadn't realized that our places in the basketball pantheon had ever been at issue. What I really *wanted* to say at that moment was "It's not *my* fault the team played poorly last night." But a little voice in my head was saying what it had said to me on several other occasions: finish the season. We were almost in the home stretch—this was the end of January.

"I'll see you at practice," I said and turned and walked off before saying anything I'd regret. I went for a walk in the snow before it was time to leave the hotel for practice. I really had to give myself a talking to at that moment. One thing was for sure: Krzyzewski had been right. I'd had no idea what I was getting into. It wasn't just being screamed at for referring to *Coach* as *Knight,* it was the constant anger at everyone and everything. The good news was I was seeing Knight up close and personal day after day, morning, noon, and night. The bad news was that I was seeing Knight up close and personal day after day, morning, noon, and night.

"Every minute you're with him you're on the brink of a disaster," I said to myself as I plowed through a snowy park near the hotel. That was when I pulled up short and knew I had a title for the book: *A Season on the Brink.*

Knight and I didn't speak to each other the rest of that day or the next day. I just showed up the way I always did: for practice, for coach and player meetings, for walkthrough, for meals, and for the game. Hammel, who was very supportive of me throughout the year, was nervous: "They lose this game he might not let you back on the plane."

I shrugged. At that point I honestly believed I was connected enough with the other people on the team—coaches, trainers, doctors, and players—that I would be able to finish the book even if Knight threw me out. I knew it wouldn't be ideal, but I thought I was far enough along and had enough material that the thought didn't panic me the way it might have in November.

What's more, it was a game Indiana should win with ease. Several Minnesota players had been arrested the week before during a trip to Wisconsin and were thrown off the team. Coach Jim Dutcher had been fired and the Gophers had been forced to add several football players to fill out their roster. All of which made Knight very uptight before the game.

He was right. Indiana could have lost the game. Minnesota played inspired basketball, fueled by a loud crowd in creaky old Williams Arena—one of two buildings in the Big Ten (the other being at Purdue) where the benches and press row are actually below court level. As it turned out, the two schools were ahead of their time. In 2009 the NCAA began setting up Final Four venues the same way—the better to sell more high-priced courtside seats so the money people could look over the heads of the teams on one side and the media on the other.

Down by five at halftime, Knight went ballistic in the locker room. "This is the same shit as last year," he railed. "Anytime things get a little bit tough, you guys wilt."

Inspired by that talking-to, Indiana proceeded to fall behind by eleven. Knight called time-out and pretty much threatened to leave all the *players* off the plane home if they didn't get their act together. That got their attention. They rallied and won and all of us got to fly back to Bloomington.

The next afternoon, when practice was over, Knight walked over and sat down next to me. I was prepared for a lecture on showing respect for one's elders. What I got was entirely different.

"How long have you been at the *Post* now?" he asked.

"Eight years," I answered.

"So since you got out of college."

"Yes."

"That's pretty unusual, isn't it?"

"Yeah, I was lucky..."

"No, you weren't, John. Look, here's one thing I know about you: you're a smart sumbitch [Knight never said *son of a bitch*, he always said *sumbitch*]. You know you're smart and you know you wouldn't have done the things you've done if you weren't smart.

"But let me give you some advice from someone who's also pretty smart and is a lot older and more experienced than you are: you don't have to prove you're the smartest guy in every room you walk into. Not everyone needs to know that about you. Let them figure it out by reading what you write."

I had no idea what any of this had to do with what had happened in Minneapolis on Friday. I also knew that Knight was right. I had always felt—and still do—the need to be right (the Penn bet was a good example), which is a way of proving how smart I am. I had—and still have—a bad habit of interrupting people when I think I know what they're going to say next and I'm ready to respond. I wish I could say that since that talk I've never acted that way, but since that talk I *have* tried to cool my act, to listen more, especially when smart people are talking, and to not try to prove I know more than everyone around me, whether it is at a dinner table or in an interview room.

In fact, I almost never ask questions in interview rooms. My old friend and mentor Dave Kindred pointed out to me years ago that if you get a good answer in an interview room, everyone else has it too. If you wait and ask your question—and get a good answer—either in private or in a small group, the answer is either yours alone or yours and a handful of others'.

I told Knight I understood what he was saying and that I thought he was right. The irony of Knight telling someone they didn't have to always prove themselves—as smarter, tougher, meaner, whatever—wasn't lost on me, but I knew that what he was saying about me was still right. Twenty-five years later I'm still not cured, but I'm at least in recovery.

Although we never addressed what had happened in Minneapolis, that conversation ended our "dispute." He and I were back at the Ground Round that night eating buffalo wings while the assistant coaches, exhausted by the forty-eight hours in Iowa and Minnesota, got to go home and get some rest.

————

OUR SECOND "FALLING OUT" occurred a month later, just prior to Indiana's last home weekend of the season, which was again against Minnesota and Iowa. The specter of the Gophers and Hawkeyes always seemed to cause trouble for me one way or the other.

Throughout the season, I had been the subject of a fair bit of media attention. Needless to say, the notion that Bob Knight was giving a reporter complete access to his program surprised a lot of people. Actually the best line came from Dean Smith, who seriously couldn't believe what I was telling him.

"He lets you into the locker room before and after practice?"

"Yes."

"Team meetings?"

"Yes."

"Coaches' meetings?"

"Yes."

"You travel *with* the team?"

"Yes."

"And you're in the locker room before games and at halftime?"

"Yes."

"Where do you sit during the games?"

"On the bench."

"On the *bench?* He lets you listen to him during time-outs?"

"Sometimes I make substitutions."

Dean looked long and hard at me at that moment to be sure I was kidding.

"But the rest of it, sitting on the bench and everything, is true?"

"Yes."

He shook his head in amazement. "I wouldn't let my mother into my locker room," he said.

"Why not, Dean? You don't even curse."

"No, but I do get angry."

There had been a number of stories written about my access and the book I intended to write. Most people found it harder to believe that Knight had no control over the content than that I was making substitutions. It was another coach, Jim Valvano, who simply would *not* believe it.

"He's going to tell you he has to have control," Valvano said. "He's an even worse control freak than the rest of us are. No way you write everything you see and hear in that book."

Nothing I said could convince Valvano I was going to write an honest book.

Sometime in mid-February I got a phone call from Mark Heisler of the *Los Angeles Times*. Heisler wrote a basketball notes column once a week, and he wanted to lead the column with a few paragraphs about my season with Knight. That was fine with me. Jeff Neuman had told me not to get too excited about the publicity I was getting. "It doesn't mean anything until the book comes out," he said. "In fact, I would low-key it as much as possible."

I had followed his advice. I told no stories about the tantrums I had witnessed, or the touching moments I had also witnessed. I stayed generic. What I told Heisler was pretty much what I had told the other guys who had written about the book: "I think Bob was willing to do it because he thinks an honest book, written by an outsider, will show what his program is really all about. I think he's hoping it will give people a better understanding of what he does and why he does it."

Pretty mundane stuff. Heisler quoted me accurately. It was the headline that caused the trouble: "Knight Hopes Book Will Change His Image."

Remember this was pre-internet, but someone Knight knew in Los Angeles sent Knight the clip, thinking he'd like the story. I'm not sure he ever read it. I wasn't there—as I recall I had gone on a Patrick Knight pickup run—when he opened the envelope that had the story in it, but the assistant coaches were. They told me later that when he read the headline, he went ballistic.

Knight loves to say that he doesn't care what people think of him, *especially* people in the media. He once proudly told David Israel for a piece in *Playboy* that on his tombstone he wanted the following inscription: "He Never Cared What Anybody Thought."

Of course, nothing could be further from the truth. Everyone cares what people think about them, and Knight is no different—except he may care more. The angriest I think I saw him get all year—and that takes in a lot of ground—was after Indiana lost a very good game at Louisville, which would go on to win the national championship. It was exam week at IU and Knight told Kit Klingel-hoffer, his sports information director (SID), that he wasn't going to go into the media room because he wanted to get back to Blooming-ton as fast as possible.

Knight *could* have gone in while the players showered and dressed, but he opted not to, knowing that needing to get the players back home so they would be rested for their tests would be an acceptable excuse for not talking to the media. The only problem was that the reason he didn't come in never reached the media. Even though Klingelhoffer told the Louisville people Knight wasn't com-ing in because of exams, the media was simply told, "Coach Knight isn't coming in." Given Knight's propensity through the years for blowing the media off, the assumption was made that Knight was pouting about the loss. In fact, he was quite happy with the way his team had played.

He was *not* happy the next day when he picked up the *Indianapo-lis Star* and saw that he had "refused" to speak to the media. Klingel-hoffer was summoned. "Why the hell am I getting attacked by these people for not coming in when I had a goddamn good reason for not coming in?" he shouted.

There was nothing Klingelhoffer could say. He had done as he was told but the message hadn't been passed on. When he tried to explain that to Knight, he was cut off and subjected to a speech about how this was *his* fault. Knight was so angry that he kicked a telephone sitting on the floor with his bare foot and then began hopping around, screaming in pain, demanding that everyone get out of the Cave and leave him alone. Everyone gladly did so — because the sight of Knight screaming and waving his arms while trying to balance on one foot was making it almost impossible for any of us to keep a straight face.

On the day that Knight got his hands on Heisler's story, I came back to the Cave shortly before practice and knocked on the door. Knight had actually given me a set of keys to get into the building and into the Cave, but I always knocked first rather than use my key. Kohn Smith opened the door and, before he moved aside to let me in, said softly, "Be ready."

Now prepared for something but not knowing exactly what, I walked into the room and saw Knight sitting in his chair with a newspaper in his hands. "You better have a goddamn good explanation for this, John," Knight said, waving the newspaper at me.

Naturally, I had no idea what he was talking about. "For what, Bob?" I answered.

Knight held the paper up and read the headline aloud. "Where the hell do you come off telling someone — *anyone* — that I'm letting you do this goddamn book because I want a better image?" he said. "When the hell have I ever said anything along those lines to you? Tell me one time."

"Bob, I never said anything like that," I said. "If that's in the story I was misquoted, but I can't believe Mark would misquote me. Can I see the story?"

Knight threw the newspaper at my feet. I picked it up and looked through the story quickly, just in case Heisler *had* somehow misquoted me, and to see if there was even a line from *Heisler* about Knight's image. There was nothing. He had quoted me accurately and in context. Somehow the headline writer had come up with the line about image.

"Bob, there's nothing in this story about your image," I said. "Someone wrote a bad headline."

"I don't want to hear any f—ing excuses. This is *your* fault."

"How is it my fault?" I asked instinctively, which was probably a mistake.

"It's your fault because if you hadn't talked to that sumbitch he wouldn't have had a story, and then the goddamn headline never would have been written."

Okay, now I knew why it was my fault.

"Bob, I've been talking to the media all season, and I've said the same thing in every story. You've even been quoted in some of the stories. I'm sorry the headline got written that way."

"Yeah, well, that doesn't really do any goddamn good right about now, does it?"

No, it didn't.

I had already let the argument stretch longer than I should have, given the presence of the assistant coaches. Knight stalked off to the bathroom. Smith, Royce Waltman, and Joby Wright stood there silently, shaking their heads as if to say, "This is going to be a long day." Ron Felling, as always, managed to find the humor in the situation. "Well," he said, "at least he's stopped talking about Alford for a few minutes."

Knight had been railing about Alford's inadequacies since Sunday (this was now Tuesday) after Indiana had been routed at Purdue in a game that was over by the second TV time-out. Alford had saved the first meeting between the two teams, an overtime win for Indiana in Bloomington, but he had been blanketed by Purdue's quick guards in the game on Sunday and simply couldn't get any decent looks at the basket. Knight had spent most of the last forty-eight hours ranting, saying at one point, "We will never be any good until Alford is no longer on this team."

Now Alford was off the hook, at least for a little while. On the other hand, Knight—who didn't care what people thought about him—was so upset that he was about as angry during the first hour of practice as I'd seen him all year. No doubt the Purdue loss and the team's need to win two home games that week to ensure an NCAA Tournament bid were part of it. But I was part of it too, because I had talked to that sumbitch.

The thought that I should just leave practice so Knight would have one less visible thing to be angry about crossed my mind after about thirty minutes. But I was torn. I had tried to show Knight respect at all times during the season, but I didn't want him to think he could intimidate me. I knew that was how he liked to operate: he believed that if you intimidated people, you controlled them. If I left practice because I had been yelled at it might appear I was intimidated.

It was Tim Garl, the head trainer, who helped me make my decision. "Hey, come on in the back for a second," he said while the team was shooting free throws. "I need to show you something."

I walked back to the training room with Tim. He came right to the point. "I think you need to take the rest of the day off," he said. "Go home. You're like red to a bull for him right now. If anything at all happens that you should know, we'll let you know about it."

I wasn't really worried about missing anything. There were only about thirty or forty minutes left anyway.

"I know that, Tim, but if I leave it makes him think I'm intimidated because he yelled at me."

Garl laughed. "You've been here almost five months," he said. "He knows you aren't intimidated by him by now. Believe me. You need to take one for the team today. You may not owe this to him, but you owe this to the players."

He was right. Knight went off on the players often enough without me adding to their misery. "Okay," I said. "But if anything happens..."

Garl held up a hand. "I promise," he said.

I went home angry because I didn't think I had done anything wrong. There was a part of me that wanted to pack my bags, write a note to Knight saying, "See you down the road, asshole," and get the hell out of town. I knew that finding out what was going on inside the team for what little was left of the season wouldn't be difficult. By that point I was friends with the assistants, with Garl and his assistant, Steve Dayton, and with most of the players. Then again, it wouldn't be the same as me being there firsthand and I knew it. I had to remind myself one more time: the goal is to get to the end of the season and write a good book, *not* to let your ego or your temper get in the way.

I cooled off considerably when Felling called to thank me for leaving and to tell me that Knight had, in fact, calmed down after I had left. He asked me if I wanted to go out to dinner, but I thanked him and said no. An evening at home after all those nights out with Knight would be a nice change of pace.

"I'll be there for walkthrough in the morning," I said. "If he doesn't want me there, he's going to have to tell me to leave."

"I understand," Felling said. "We're all with you. We'll help any way we can."

I appreciated that, but I also knew this was strictly between Knight and me. No one was going to intervene, and I didn't want anyone to intervene. I had seen what happened when Knight was upset with a person and someone else dared to speak up on his behalf.

Knight didn't say a word to me on game day. Indiana struggled against Minnesota again, but won the game. I just went about my business as if nothing had happened. The only thing I did that was different was ride to the pregame meal with the assistants instead of with Knight. Indiana won again on Sunday against Iowa to unofficially wrap up an NCAA berth. The Hoosiers were 20–6 at that point. There was one week left in the regular season.

I was in the locker room talking to some of the players when Kohn Smith pulled me aside and said, "Coach wants to see you."

My first thought was, "Well, if he throws me out now, I got through two more key games this week." I walked across the court to the Cave. Knight had just come out of the shower and was sitting in his chair in a towel. As usual, he began the conversation without any sort of greeting.

"I've been pretty goddamn pissed off at you the last few days," he said as soon as the door closed.

"I noticed."

"I came this close to telling you to get the f— out of here about five times," he said. "If you hadn't left practice when you did on Tuesday, I don't know what I would have done."

I actually didn't think he would have done anything, but he wanted me to know that he had noticed that I had felt the need to leave.

"That was Garl's idea," I said, knowing the answer was a little bit risky but, since we were alone, not caring as much as I would have if the other coaches had been in the room. If I was going out, I'd go out swinging.

"Garl's a smart man," Knight said.

I waited to see where this was going. Knight launched into a lengthy doth-protest-too-much speech about how little he cared about his image or what anyone thought about him, which was why it pissed him off so much when anyone *thought* he cared about his image.

I kept listening. "I decided to let you stay," he said. "And let me tell you why. First of all, I thought you showed guts just showing up these last few days, knowing I might tell you to get the f— out at any minute. Second, I know you've rooted like hell for this team. And third, even though you're a f—up sometimes, I like you."

"Thanks, Bob," I said. "I like you too."

I wasn't sure at that moment if I meant that, but it was the right thing to say. And I *had* rooted like hell for the team. I liked the players a lot and I certainly could appreciate what they had gone through to be 20–6 at that moment.

"Okay," he said. "Do me a favor and go tell the coaches to come on back in here. How about if we go to Zagreb's tonight to celebrate beating the Hawkeyes?"

That sounded good to me. Little Zagreb's was one of those really good steakhouses with sawdust on the floor. I went and found the coaches, who were back in the locker room.

"Well?" Felling asked.

"He likes me," I said. "And I've rooted like hell for the team."

"We like you too," Felling said.

That was nice to hear. We all walked back into the Cave.

"Fellas," Knight said, "Feinstein lives to fight another day."

More important, I lived to *report* another day.

6

Moving On . . . and Not Moving On

THE REST OF THE season passed without incident, at least without incidents involving me. Indiana played superbly at Michigan State after the Iowa game, setting up a rematch with Michigan for the Big Ten title. There was no tournament back then and winning the Big Ten—especially the idea of somehow stealing it from Michigan—was a big deal for Knight.

Unfortunately, it was also a big deal for Michigan, which took control of the game at the start and turned it into a blowout before halftime. Knight ranted at the players afterward for lacking toughness, but he had to be happy with the way they had bounced back from their 7–11 Big Ten record of a year earlier to finish 13–5 and in second place. When the NCAA field came out the next day, Indiana was the number three seed in the East behind top-seeded Duke and two seed Syracuse. Knight loved the draw. He was convinced that Syracuse wasn't that good and, at that point in time, losing in the regional final to Mike Krzyzewski would be about as close to an acceptable loss as was possible.

"At least if we lose to Duke, one of the good guys will make the Final Four," he told the coaches on Sunday night.

Knight expected a difficult first-round game from Cleveland State because the Vikings were quick and they pressed—much the same way Iowa pressed. Even in the win at home against Iowa, Indiana had struggled against that sort of quick, full court pressure. Repeatedly he told the players to expect a difficult game. And yet I felt as if he was already thinking, in the back of his mind, about Syracuse in the round of sixteen.

As it turned out, neither Indiana nor Syracuse got that far. Indiana was sent to Syracuse to play in the Carrier Dome. Syracuse was playing a home-court first-round game against Brown, and then was scheduled to play the Navy-Tulsa winner in the second round. Indiana would play the second afternoon game on Friday, right after St. Joseph's played Richmond. The assistant coaches sat and watched that game on press row, having already made arrangements to get game tapes from the losers on the winners in order to prepare for a second-round game Sunday.

Because the NCAA had strict rules about the number of people who could sit on the bench, I watched the game from press row. I was still in the locker room before the game and, as soon as the half ended, I raced across to join the team to walk into the locker room. I did the same at game's end.

The NCAA now has rules that basically make it impossible for any media member to have this kind of access during an NCAA Tournament game. I have been told by people I know at the NCAA that I am directly responsible for two NCAA rules: the first is on locker room access. Now the rule says that if any media member is allowed in the locker room prior to the official open–locker room period after the game, *all* media members must be allowed in.

Clearly, that wouldn't work for someone writing a book like mine, which is what the NCAA wants. This has come up as an issue twice in books I've done since *Season on the Brink*. The first was in 1997 when I was working on my book on ACC basketball. Knowing that the NCAA had changed the rule, I didn't apply for media credentials at any of the early-round sites. This was at the suggestion of Terry Holland, who was the basketball committee chairman that year.

"If you don't have a media credential, then I would think the rule on opening the locker room wouldn't apply," he said.

So I got the coaches—except for Dean Smith, who still wasn't letting his mother or me into his locker room—to put me on their "official party" lists. That meant I would walk in with the team, be given a lapel pin that allowed me in the locker room and onto the bench area (the NCAA had extended the bench area to two rows by then to accommodate more managers and assistant coaches) but not into media areas. That was fine with me. I needed to be with the teams I had been given that sort of access to all season.

Good plan. Except that the late Dave Cawood, whom I had done battle with frequently in my role as president of the Basketball Writers Association (USBWA) a few years earlier (Cawood didn't want the media to have even one little bit more access than we already had), saw my name on the official party lists and wrote me a letter saying that, as a media member, I couldn't be on any official party list. "Who are you," I asked, "to say who can and can't be on official party lists? That's strictly up to the schools." Cawood said, "Fine, but the open–locker room media rules will apply if you're in the locker room," and he would make sure all media members in attendance knew that any locker room I was in was open to all of them.

I called Holland and asked him to intervene, especially since he had said if I wasn't on a media list, I wouldn't be considered media.

Holland and I have known each other and liked each other (at least I like him) since he first got to Virginia in 1974, when I was an undergraduate at Duke, and he returned my call on a story I was working on for the student newspaper. Terry didn't want to get in the middle of a fight between Cawood and me. He said the media was Dave's bailiwick, and he would defer to Dave. So I had to give in and get media credentials. If you think I ever forgave Cawood, you're wrong.

Three years later, when I was working on my Patriot League book, I was smarter. Plus, Cawood had "left" the NCAA. I applied for a media credential in Buffalo, where Lafayette, the league champion, was being sent to play. Then I got the Lafayette people to add me to their official party list on the official practice day, twenty-four hours before their game against Temple. By the time Jim Marchiony, who had taken Cawood's job, figured out that I was in the locker room, it was too late; the game was over and, since Lafayette had lost, I didn't have to worry about a second-round game.

The other NCAA rule I am told I'm responsible for is one that now makes it a violation for a coach to take a member of the media on a recruiting visit. When I was researching my second book, *A Season Inside,* I went on home visits with a number of coaches, including Gary Williams, Paul Evans, and Dale Brown. The Brown visit was one of the greatest experiences I've ever had. Dale was visiting a kid named Chris Jent—I also went with Williams when he visited Jent—and he spent the night regaling the Jent family with stories about his world travels, which included, I think, a hunt he went on in search of Sasquatch. Or maybe it was to see the Dalai Lama. I'm not certain. I was ready to sign with LSU and Brown. Jent signed with Ohio State and Williams.

Soon after *A Season Inside* came out I got a call from a guy I knew on the NCAA enforcement staff. "Congratulations," he said. "We now have *two* Feinstein rules." He then explained to me that it was now considered an "unfair advantage" to take a media member on a home visit because it might imply to the recruit that he would get more media coverage by playing for that coach and school.

"What if I went with *every* coach who visited a kid?" I asked.

"Good question," the guy said.

Maybe someday I'll test it, if only to upset my friends in Indianapolis.

ON THIS DAY IN Syracuse, no one tried to stop me from getting into the Indiana locker room—until after the game.

Indiana lost, 83–79. Cleveland State jumped to a 4–0 lead and Indiana never caught up. I still remember Knight's line at halftime: "I ought to fire all of us."

The game really wasn't close. Indiana made some consolation buckets late, but Cleveland State was in control. I was sitting next to Jackie MacMullan of the *Boston Globe*. Late in the game when it was apparent Indiana wasn't going to rally, Jackie leaned over to me and said, "I'm so sorry. I know how much time you've put into this book."

Her implication was that a book about a season that ended with a first-round loss to Cleveland State in the NCAA Tournament probably wasn't going to have too many buyers. I could understand why she'd think that, but I honestly believed by then that the book I had was going to be very good regardless of how Indiana's season ended. I just didn't think anyone had ever had the sort of access Knight had given me.

At that moment, I wasn't thinking about how the loss might affect the book. I was thinking of the players. As Knight had correctly pointed out, I *had* rooted like hell for the team, because I liked and admired the players so much and because I had come to consider the assistant coaches friends.

When the game ended, I walked with Knight to the interview room. He had to wait briefly while Cleveland State coach Kevin Mackey was finishing up. Mackey's life would go off the rails four years later when he was arrested coming out of a crack house and charged with possession of cocaine and DWI. At that moment though, he was riding high, explaining to the media how, while an assistant coach at Boston College, he had come up with the novel idea that recruiting the inner city was the way to go. Knight looked at me and said, "Is he f—ing kidding?"

Those were the last words he spoke to me that day. He handled the press conference calmly, lecturing the media only briefly on how many of them hadn't understood how good Cleveland State was. He walked out of the room and headed directly to the bus. I walked back to the locker room to try to see people before they left. I was staying behind because the *Post* had asked me to cover Navy for the weekend while I was in Syracuse. Thinking that Indiana would be playing two games — I guess I was one of those media members who underestimated how good Cleveland State was — I had agreed. I knew I wouldn't miss much on the plane trip back. And if I did miss anything, it would be reported to me, so I wasn't that concerned. But I knew the players were leaving on spring break, and I probably wouldn't see them again before I left town, which would now be early the next week since the season was over.

What I didn't know when I walked back down the hall was that Knight had left instructions with security not to let the media into the locker room. The NCAA has rules about postgame media access, but Knight didn't care and no one from the NCAA was going to tell him at that moment that he had to open his locker room. So when I tried to walk back inside, a security guard stopped me.

"No media allowed," he said.

"Look, I'm with the team," I said.

"Your badge says media," he said correctly. "No media."

"Okay, then. Can you just walk inside and find one of the coaches, they'll explain to you —"

"Hey, pal, I said get lost, now get lost."

Now I was pissed. The guy had gone from doing his job to being a bully. "Look, *pal*," I said, "I need to get in there. I know you're just following orders, but I'm asking you to find someone who knows what's going on —"

The guy put out his arm as if to shove me. I took a step back. Things were about to get ugly. At that moment, Brian Sloan (son of Hall of Fame coach Jerry), who was a redshirt freshman that year, came out of the locker room and saw what was happening.

"Hey," he said to the guard. "Leave him alone. He's with us."

The guard looked at Sloan — clearly a player at 6'7", dressed neatly in a suit — and then at me.

"His badge says media."

"He's with us," Sloan repeated. "Let him in."

The guard stepped back. "Thanks, Brian," I said, shaking hands.

"See you on the bus," Sloan said, not knowing I wasn't making the trip back.

I didn't take time to explain, just thanked him again and walked inside. I didn't have the chance to say much except to shake people's hands and thank them. I told Alford I would call him at home over the weekend, and we made tentative plans for me to stop in New Castle, his hometown, on my drive east the next week. As I watched the players empty the locker room, I felt a profound sense of sadness because I was certain I would never feel this close to a group of athletes again. I was looking forward to getting home and to the return of some normalcy in my life, but I knew I'd miss the friends I had made the previous few months.

Once everyone had left, I walked down the hall to the media room, grabbed something to eat, and sat down at a table with several writers. It felt strange not being with the team. When I walked back onto the court, Navy and Tulsa were warming up. I spotted Navy coach Paul Evans and walked over to say hello.

"Well, you survived," Evans said, knowing my time with Knight and Indiana had ended a couple of hours earlier.

He was right. I had survived. Now all I had to do was write the book.

I FLEW BACK TO Indianapolis late Sunday night and made the drive down SR-37 one more time. I had my car packed and ready to go by mid-morning on Monday. The players had scattered for spring break, but I knew the coaches were in town, and I had heard that Knight had them in looking at tape of the Cleveland State game most of the weekend. He had also told the players that they would be practicing once they returned from spring break until the day of the national championship game. The NCAA would change the rule allowing teams to practice until the tournament was over soon after *Season on the Brink* mentioned Knight's postseason practices.

I made the short drive back to Assembly Hall one last time and walked into the Cave to find Knight alone and on the phone with Gene Pingatore, Daryl Thomas's high school coach. He was telling him in no uncertain terms that Daryl was the biggest pussy he'd ever coached and as far as he was concerned there really wasn't any reason for him to come back to Indiana for his senior year. I felt like I was walking out at almost the same moment that I had walked in.

Knight hung up the phone and looked at me expectantly. "What can I do for you, John?" he said.

"First, I wanted to give you your keys back," I said, handing them to him. "Second, I just wanted to say thank you for putting up with me all season."

"That it?"

I shrugged. "That's pretty much it."

"Don't f— this thing up, John. Don't piss me off."

"I will do my best not to f— it up, Bob. If I do f— it up, it's my fault. You gave me plenty to work with."

"Daryl Thomas is a pussy, you know."

The season was over. I probably should have stood up for Daryl Thomas at that moment. To this day I feel bad that I didn't. I had a long drive ahead of me.

"Yeah, I know," I said.

Knight picked up the phone and started dialing a number. That was his way of saying good-bye.

Later, when the book came out, Knight would claim to people that his last words to me were, "Don't let the door hit you on the ass on your way out." It's one of his favorite expressions. He tends to use it when telling stories. I never actually heard him say it to anyone. He didn't say it that day either.

I stopped, as planned, in New Castle to see Alford. We had

dinner at a Perkins Pancake House, something I couldn't help but remember when a Perkins waitress was included among the list of Tiger Woods's many liaisons at the end of 2009. I asked Alford if he ever regretted choosing Indiana at those moments when Knight was railing on him.

He laughed. "I think my dad is still a few ahead of Coach when it comes to throwing me out of practice," he said. "Coach gets on me because he knows I can take it. Doesn't mean it doesn't piss me off sometimes, but I can handle it."

He looked at me. "What about you? Are *you* sorry you picked Indiana?"

I laughed. "I'll let you know when the book comes out.

WRITING A BOOK TURNED out to be a lot easier than I had imagined it might be. The reason was simple: I had so much material to work with that sitting down at my computer each day was something I actually looked forward to doing. I had driven to my parents' house on Shelter Island right after the Final Four in Dallas, where I had seen Knight—he wore a "Go Duke" button the entire weekend—and had spent some time with him. Even though the team had turned itself around after the disastrous '85 season and had gone 21–8, he was still haunted by the two losses that had ended the season. He had left instructions with the coaches to continue practicing the team through the weekend. I learned later that he had observed earlier postseason practices from a chair, arms folded, commenting occasionally on why a particular play or bad shot or missed screen or box out was the reason for the losses to Cleveland State and Michigan.

I asked Knight if he was going to go to the coaches' annual dinner on Sunday night, where Krzyzewski was being honored as national coach of the year. He shook his head.

"I don't think I want to be in a room with all those coaches," he said.

"Why not? A lot of them are your friends."

"John, we're just not very good right now."

As always, that was the bottom line for Knight.

Being on Shelter Island in April and May was something I always used to look forward to as a vacation once basketball season was over. I loved the solitude of the island during the offseason. Most years, I would sleep in, go pick up the newspapers, and after reading them thoroughly, go have lunch with Bob DeStefano, the golf pro at Gardiner's Bay Country Club, the (then) unpretentious little club where I had learned the game as a teenager and worked for seven summers in the pro shop.

Back then the clubhouse was open for lunch on weekdays in April, and Bob and I would sit at a corner table and talk for a couple of hours. If the weather was nice I'd hit some balls and play nine holes of golf. If not, I'd go home and read, make myself dinner, and then watch baseball or the hockey playoffs on TV. I was about as content as you could possibly be.

My schedule wasn't all that different in April of 1986. I woke up earlier to go get the papers. Once they had been read, I would sit down for a couple of hours to review what I had written the day before. Everyone who writes develops habits, especially in terms of when they write. Like everyone else, I've read about writers who wait until all is quiet in their home and write until the wee hours. Others are up before dawn to kick-start their writing day.

Perhaps because I spent so many years working at a newspaper, I do most of my writing in the afternoon. Although I covered games at night for years—and still do on occasion—most of my writing when I was young was done in the office after lunch. So it probably wasn't surprising when that became my habit for writing the book.

As I did when on vacation, I'd have lunch with Bob. But instead of relaxing all afternoon, I sat at my computer, which was still the tiny Radio Shack Tandy that had so impressed the Duke of Kent the previous summer. My parents' house wasn't very big: it was one floor with four bedrooms, one of which had been the garage when my dad bought the house in 1960. I set my computer up on the dining room table—it ran strictly on batteries, so it didn't really matter where I sat it—so I could have a breathtaking view of the water.

I usually wrote for four or five hours. I never set goals in terms of how many words I should write on a given day, I just wrote until I felt tired. I learned quickly that if I forced myself to keep going when tired, what I wrote at the end of the day was usually so poorly written I would end up tossing it the next day anyway. One thing helped me from the beginning: I had read somewhere that Ernest Hemingway always tried to stop writing mid-thought. He didn't try to get to the end of a chapter or a story line. That way, when he began again the next day, it was easier to get started. Right from the beginning, I did that—sometimes stopping in mid-sentence. This did two things: it made starting each day a little easier, and it gave me at least one thing in common with Hemingway. Actually two: I also like cats.

The writing went faster than I could have dreamed. When you have done your job as a reporter, writing is easy. The only issue was what to leave out. After I had written about thirty thousand words, I sent them to Jeff Neuman. I didn't want to write the whole book and have him say, "Oh God, this is awful, start again." He called me after he had read what I'd sent him and said, "Just keep doing what you're doing."

That was very comforting.

Every afternoon, when I finished writing, I would walk down to the beach in front of the house and walk west, toward the setting sun. I could only go about a mile before I reached a point where I would have to walk up to the road to get around a patch of water. So I'd walk to that point, sit, and watch the sun until it was almost down, then walk home and fix dinner. It was pretty close to perfect. I felt like a real writer—whatever that means.

I finished the book in seven weeks. When I wrote the final words late on a May afternoon, I felt exhilarated, a little sad, and a lot nervous. I walked down the beach that night saying to myself over and over, "You wrote a book!" Of course it wasn't official until Jeff finished editing, but still, I'd done it. The last thing I had written was the dedication, which was to my parents: "To Mom and Dad...and that's nonnegotiable." That was my father's term when he was done with an argument.

The question now was how the book would be received. The editing was relatively painless. Jeff and I wrestled over some things, including how many times we should actually use the word *fuck*. He wanted less, I wanted more. We met halfway and probably got it about right. The funny thing is, with all the talk about how angry Knight was about my leaving in his profanity, there's not *that* much of it in the book.

That summer Larry Kramer, my old metro editor and former antagonist, offered me a job. He had become the editor of the *San Francisco Examiner,* and he was looking for a columnist. I was interested, in part because I wanted to be a columnist, but also because I liked San Francisco. I flew to San Francisco and spent a couple of days with Kramer and his editors, and met with Will Hearst, the paper's publisher. Kramer offered me the column and a considerable raise from what I was making at the *Post.*

Because of his past relationship with the *Post,* Kramer had called both George Solomon and Ben Bradlee before contacting me. When I came back from San Francisco, George called me into his office and asked me if Kramer had offered me a job, and if so what had he offered. I told him.

"Bullshit!" he screamed. "No way he offered you that much. You're a liar!"

I suggested that George call Kramer while I was sitting there, tell him I was in the office, and ask him how much he had offered. George glared at me for a moment.

"I'll get back to you," he said.

About a week later he did—offering me a $5,000 raise over lunch while giving me the speech about how lucky I was to be working at the *Post*. I didn't disagree with him. Even nine years after my first day as a summer intern, I still found it remarkable that the words "*Washington Post* Staff Writer" appeared under my name. But the *Examiner's* offer was a *lot* of money—especially since I wasn't counting on the book, which was about a month from being published at that moment, making me a dollar more than the $17,500 advance. Plus, I was a little hurt that, knowing what I had been offered by Kramer, George was offering me so much less.

"Is that the best you can do?" I asked George.

"Best I can do," he said. "I took it to Bradlee."

"Well if that's the way you guys feel, maybe I should go to San Francisco," I said.

Again, the glare.

"Give me a few more days," he said.

"I told Kramer I'd give him an answer by the end of the World Series," I said. I was getting ready to leave to cover the baseball playoffs.

"Okay," George said. "I'll get you an answer by then."

I headed off to the playoffs, starting in Boston for the first two games of the Red Sox–Angels American League Championship, then going to New York to pick up game three of the National League Championship between my beloved Mets and the Astros. On the morning of game five, which had been delayed a day by rain, I got a call from Jeff Neuman.

"It's a book," he said simply.

That meant he had gotten the first copies of the actual book— not a manuscript, not a galley proof, the actual book. "I've got two copies I can give you," he said. "I'll be at the game this afternoon. I can bring them to you there."

And so, about an hour before game time, Jeff and I stood on a Shea Stadium ramp and he handed me two copies of *A Season on the Brink.* It's a cliché, but next to the births of my three children, being handed those books was the most spine-tingling moment of my life.

"Congratulations," Jeff said, clearly getting the fact that I was very emotional. "Now I hope the Mets can get you a win today."

He left me standing there staring at the book cover, Knight looking as if he is trying to glare a hole through the camera. I looked at my name on the jacket and didn't move for a few minutes. Finally, I walked back up the ramp to the press box level. I saw Dave Kindred, who was someone who knew Knight about as well as anyone. Kindred had left the *Post* several years earlier to take a job in Atlanta. He'd been offered a lot more money and the *Post* refused to match the offer. Does that sound familiar?

I held the books out for him to see.

Kindred smiled and said, "Congratulations."

I was planning to keep one book and give the other to my parents. But I really wanted to know what Dave thought of it. And I knew he would be flying to Houston the next day. "If I give you one, you think you might want to read some of it on the plane tomorrow?" I said.

"I'd love to," he said.

The Mets won that day, on a Gary Carter single in the eleventh inning, to take a 3–2 lead in the series. The next day I, along with Richard Justice, who was the *Post*'s number one baseball writer (Tom Boswell was the baseball columnist and I was sort of the rover, thus my bouncing from series to series), caught an early flight to Houston for game six. We went straight from the airport to the Astrodome because the game was scheduled to start at two o'clock. One of the first people I saw was Kindred.

"I didn't read this on the plane," he said, handing it back to me.

"Oh," I said, a bit baffled. Before I could ask why not, he said, "I started it last night at the hotel. I stayed up all night reading it. You should be very proud of what you've done. This is a great book."

I can't begin to tell you how I felt at that moment. There's no one I respect more in my profession than Kindred. Plus, he had known Knight for years, and I also knew if he didn't feel that way he wouldn't have said it. He would have said, "Nice job," or, "There's some really good stuff in here." Or he might have told me where he thought I'd gone wrong.

"Really?" I said.

"Really," he said. "It's not good, it's great."

I was still glowing when the game started. Of course, the next few hours were torture as the Astros jumped to a 3–0 lead on Bob Ojeda in the first inning and Bob Knepper shut the Mets down for eight innings. At one point, completely frustrated, I turned to Justice and said, "You're on your own for game seven. If you think I'm going to sit here and watch Mike Scott scuff the ball all night, you're nuts."

Justice laughed. Scott had already beaten the Mets twice in the series, and the Mets were convinced he was scuffing the ball. Since they were convinced, I was convinced.

Fortunately, Scott never got to (allegedly) scuff any more baseballs. The Mets rallied for three runs in the ninth inning and ended up winning one of baseball's all-time classic games, 7–6 in sixteen innings. Roger McDowell pitched five brilliant shutout innings in relief, and Jesse Orosco barely hung on, loading the bases in the sixteenth before getting the final out more than five hours after the game had started.

The Red Sox had come back from down 3–1 in their series and one out from elimination in the ninth inning of game five to beat the Angels. The World Series started in New York, and the Red Sox promptly won the first two games. Off to Boston we went. When I came upstairs to the press box after batting practice prior to game three, George Solomon was waiting for me. He had flown to Boston to schmooze people for a couple of days. He had also come with an offer for me. We walked to the back of the press box, which was then on the roof of what was a one-deck stadium, one of the great views in all of baseball.

George laid out the deal for me. For all intents and purposes, the *Post* had matched the *Chronicle*'s offer. In addition, I would get to write one column a week. As soon as George made the offer, I knew I was going to accept it. But he'd been such a jerk about everything, starting with the "you're a liar" comment in his office, I wasn't just going to say, "I accept," standing on the roof of Fenway Park.

"That's a really nice offer, George," I said. "I'll let you know as soon as the Series is over."

"*What!*" George said. "Really nice offer? Are you kidding me? That's more money than I offered Kindred [five years earlier] and you're not fit to carry Kindred's typewriter!"

I didn't disagree with that, even though Kindred hadn't carried a typewriter for a good long while. (Tony Kornheiser likes to tell people that when he worked at the *New York Times* he was often told he wasn't fit to carry Red Smith's typewriter. "In fact, toward the end of Red's career, when Red and I covered events together, I actually *did* carry his typewriter," Tony said. "So fit or not, I carried Red Smith's typewriter.")

"I'll let you know as soon as we're back in Washington," I said. "I don't want to make a snap decision standing here."

George ranted for several more minutes. Richard Justice said later that when he walked past us, he couldn't imagine what George was so angry about. "I thought maybe he was trying to get you to cover the Redskins again," he said.

The Series, as most people remember, turned into another one of the all-time classics, highlighted by the historic game six. After the Red Sox went up 5–3 in the tenth inning, I was resigned to the fact that they were going to win. Then, with two outs, came the remarkable Mets rally: Gary Carter's single, Kevin Mitchell's pinch-hit single, Ray Knight's single to make it 5–4. Bob Stanley then wild-pitched Mitchell across the plate (some think Rich Gedman should have been charged with a passed ball) and Knight to second. It was 5–5. People forget that the score was *tied* at that moment. Even if Bill Buckner had fielded Mookie Wilson's roller cleanly, the game would simply have gone to the eleventh inning. Buckner did *not* lose the World Series for the Red Sox, a fact many, many people forget.

Years later, when I brought up that night to Esther Newberg, one of those crazy Red Sox fans who thinks anyone who has ever worn a Yankees uniform should burn in hell, I asked her what the score was when Buckner booted the ball.

"I don't know," she said. "It was either 5–4 or 6–5."

"No," I said, "it was 5–5. The game was already tied. You need to stop blaming the whole thing on Buckner."

She looked at me with genuine hatred in her eyes. "No, I don't," she said. "I don't care what the score was. It's his fault."

Okay, fine.

As soon as the game ended, I raced to the Mets clubhouse. Keith Hernandez was sitting in front of his locker as he always did postgame, smoking a cigarette and drinking a beer.

"Thank God Buckner booted that ball," he said. "After I made the second out I came back in here, and I was so depressed I went into [manager] Davey's [Johnson] office and took a beer out of his fridge. I was dehydrated so I drank it in about ten seconds and opened another one. I'm watching on TV, not even really paying attention when Gary and Kevin got their hits. I opened a third one. Ray gets his hit. I'm still not thinking that clearly, so I finish the third one. Stanley comes in and throws the wild pitch.

"That's when it hit me: *the score's tied and I just drank three beers. I'm buzzed.* I was sitting there frozen, trying to figure out how I'd go out and play first base when Mookie hit the ball." He pulled on his cigarette. "Holy shit. How lucky did I just get?"

I ran down the hallway to the tiny Red Sox locker room. You could still see signs of plastic that had been put up to cover the lockers in anticipation of a champagne celebration that never took place.

Buckner was repeating his story for probably the third or fourth time. I stood and listened as new wave after new wave of reporters came at him. He never blinked or complained or said, "Hey, I've already answered that five times."

He took the blame, said he should have made the play. It was about as classy a display as I've ever seen from someone who would become a pariah in Boston for years. Overjoyed Mets fan that I was, I walked out of that clubhouse feeling sick for Bill Buckner. I wrote my story on the two first basemen and how different their lives might have been had Buckner fielded the ball. I had no idea just *how* different.

Two nights later, after an all-day rain pushed game seven back twenty-four hours, the Mets won the World Series, rallying from 3–0 down in the sixth inning (another thing Red Sox fans forget when they rant against Buckner) to win. I flew back to Washington the next morning and told George I was staying at the *Post*.

"Smart decision" was all he said.

I didn't disagree.

7

Book Two

THE FIRST SMALL CLUE that *Season on the Brink* wasn't going to be what the folks at Macmillan had envisioned—a nice little regional book that might sell close to twenty thousand copies—came in a couple of pre-publication reviews. The first came from Kirkus, a service that specializes in writing short, synopsis-like reviews of books, mostly to give booksellers an idea of what the title is about and some sense of whether they think it is worth ordering a lot, a little, or none at all. The review was the kind of rave you dream about: never been a book like this; gives a view of Bob Knight you never would have imagined.... Perfect. Still, just one review.

The official publication date for the book was November 15, but it began arriving in stores on November 1. The first printing was exactly the same as my advance: 17,500—books instead of dollars. Jeff Neuman told me almost right away that orders for the book were strong, so strong in fact that they were going back to print another 5,000. Gee, that's nice, I thought, still hoping all this was going to lead to a second book contract.

Macmillan had scheduled a two-day book tour for me in Indiana: one day in Indianapolis doing media there and the next day in Bloomington doing a couple of book signings, appearing on the one local TV station, and doing a couple print interviews—including one with Mike Leonard, a local columnist who had written a piece about me when I first got to town a year earlier. Hammel had already written his column, having been sent an advance copy, saying the book had some insights into the program, but that I had betrayed Knight by leaving his profanity in the book. I wasn't surprised or even disappointed. Given a choice between Knight and me, Hammel had to choose Knight. I was a little hurt when I called Hammel to try to talk to him and he said, "I'm just telling you this right now: you better not come around here anymore."

Why not? Was Knight going to show up somewhere and start a fight? Or send someone else to start one? I told Hammel I'd take my chances.

By the time I got to Indiana for my "tour," the book was starting to get national attention. Knight still hadn't said anything publicly about it—that would come later—but people were saying and writing that no outsider had ever written a book as inside as this one. When one reviewer called it "the *Ball Four* of college basketball," I shook my fist happily. To be compared to my all-time favorite sports book was about as good as it could possibly get as far as I was concerned.

Promoting a book was a whole new world to me. At my first TV stop, one of the hosts began screaming at me almost before I had walked in the door: "Didn't you bring a copy of the book? I only have *one* and I need one for my nephew."

I actually did have a copy out in the car, but I certainly wasn't giving her one for her nephew. I've always found it remarkable the entitlement people feel to free books. In fact, I try to make it a point to go out and buy books written by friends because I know how much it bothers me to be asked for freebies. There's one writer I've known for years who has never once written a word about any of my books but still comes up to me every time I have a book out and says something like, "Hey, I haven't gotten your new book yet and I've got a coast-to-coast flight next week. How about getting your publisher to get moving and send me one."

But this was a complete stranger who already *had* a book. She then told me she had read the book, which I would learn later is unusual. Most TV and radio types love to start interviews by saying, "So, tell us what your new book is about." Or they'll say, "Your publisher sent me a copy, but I haven't had time to look at it." Great. If you got a free book sent to your doorstep and didn't read it, why should anyone else bother to go out and *buy* it?

Someday I am going to write a book about book tours. Then I'm going to refuse to go on a book tour to promote it.

My not having a book for the nephew of the local host put her in a bad mood. The interview didn't go terribly well either.

"Have you ever met Coach Knight?" was her opening question.

I was kind of stunned. She had said she'd read the book.

"Well, yes," I said. "I spent an entire season with him."

"But did he know you were there?"

Okay, I couldn't answer that one with a straight face. "Well, I weigh close to two hundred pounds," I said. "I think it would have been hard for me to stay invisible the whole time."

She glared at me.

"So why should people buy your book?"

That one was easy. I went into a lengthy answer about the access I'd had, told a couple of stories, and made sure I used the rest of the time I knew I had left to keep talking so she wouldn't get a chance to ask me if I knew that Bob Knight's first name really was Coach. I was learning on the job.

It wasn't until I got to Bloomington that it *really* hit me that something I had never expected or planned for was happening. My first book signing that day was at a bookstore right near the Indiana campus called T.I.S. I parked my rental car across the street from the store and saw a line of people down the block. I groaned: what in the heck was going on at the store today that would draw this sort of crowd? How was I going to get anyone to even notice I was there if some celebrity was also doing a book signing? I was early; maybe the other signing had already started and would be over by the time mine began at two o'clock.

When I walked into the store, the manager was waiting for me at the front door.

"Like the crowd?" he asked.

"Who's it for?" I answered.

He looked at me for a moment as if trying to figure out if I was kidding. "They're here for you," he said. "We ordered a thousand books. I hope it'll be enough."

I was truly amazed. Those people were all waiting for *me?* One thousand books? At one store? Whoa.

I was supposed to sign from two to four. I had been worried that I would spend a lot of that time looking around for something to do. That wasn't a problem. I stayed until 5:45 and left then only because I had another signing to do at six o'clock at a Walden's in a nearby mall. The notion of stopping to get something to eat in between signings went up in smoke. My hand was ringing with pain when I left, but I certainly wasn't complaining.

When I saw the line outside the Walden's, I wasn't surprised. In fact, when the manager at the first store had cut off the line, he had told people I would be at Walden's, and many had said they were going to go there. I signed books at Walden's until they closed at nine o'clock. I probably signed close to two thousand books that day.

Two things happened during the Walden's signing that made me feel very good. Because of Hammel's column, the word was out in Bloomington and around the state that Knight wasn't happy with the book. I was surprised when I looked up and saw Todd Meier standing in line. Todd was a backup forward who had overcome numerous injuries to become a real contributor to the team. He was a Wisconsin kid, as friendly and as down-to-earth as you might expect someone from a small town in Wisconsin to be. There were TV cameras there doing a story on the sensation the book was starting to cause, and as soon as I saw Todd I was concerned he might get in trouble if word got back to Knight that he had shown up at my book signing.

"I'm really glad to see you, Todd," I said when he got close to me. "But are you sure this is a good idea?"

Todd smiled. "What's Coach going to do, yell at me?"

He had a point.

A few minutes later an attractive young woman handed me a book. As I opened it to sign it, she said, "There's a note for you in the back."

Baffled, I turned to the back of the book. "When you're done, I'm at the other end of the mall in the ice cream shop—Steve."

I looked at the young woman and just mouthed "Alford?" so no one could hear me.

She nodded.

When I finally signed the last book and thanked everyone, I walked to the other end of the mall. Alford was alone, sipping on a soda.

"So look who's a big star," he said, laughing.

"You know Meier came down and stood in line with all those people watching and TV cameras rolling," I said.

"Meier's not very bright," Alford said. "What do you think coach would do to me if I showed up on TV having you sign that book?"

I laughed. "Has he brought it up to you guys?"

Alford nodded. "Oh yeah. Said he made the worst mistake of his life letting you in and none of us should read the book."

"I sent copies for all you guys to [Tim] Garl," I said. "He called and told me it would be an NCAA violation if he gave them to you."

"I heard," Steve said. "Someone brought a copy on the plane the other day. We took the jacket off so Coach wouldn't recognize it and passed it around."

A few months later at the Final Four's Sunday press conference, someone asked Alford if he had read the book. With Knight sitting right next to him, Steve said with a straight face, "No, I haven't."

"Come on," the reporter said. "You really haven't read it?"

Alford glanced at Knight and said, "I didn't need to read it. I lived it."

After Indiana had won the national championship, I called Alford to congratulate him. I told him he'd done a good job with his answer when the book question had come up. "No way was I going to tell the truth," he said, laughing. "I still had one more game to play."

Indiana won that last game, beating Syracuse in New Orleans to win the national championship on a Keith Smart jumper from the corner with five seconds left. My feelings from that night are hard to describe: I was thrilled for the players, knowing firsthand what they'd gone through to get to that moment. On the other hand, I was pretty worn out from all that had gone on in the months leading to the Final Four.

After my "official" phone call from Royce Waltman, I sat down and wrote Knight a letter. I told him I truly found it hard to believe that seeing his profanity in the book had made him feel betrayed. I reminded him of our "shorter than *War and Peace*" conversation and told him that, in fact, I had probably left out at least 80 to 90 percent of the profanity I actually had on tape. And then I wrote this: "The book, I believe, does everything you and I set out to do. It shows people what it is *really* like inside your program; it shows why the players not only put up with you, but come away admiring and respecting you; it gives people a firsthand understanding of *why* you do the things you do."

I believed that then, I believe that now. I think Knight knows it's true, and I know — because people have told me — that he's received hundreds of letters from people who read the book telling him just that. It didn't matter. Knight had decided I was a villain because I hadn't written a G-rated book about someone whose language was decidedly X-rated.

His second move — the first was to have Waltman call me — was to call Mike Krzyzewski and tell him the whole thing was his fault.

In Knightworld, he never would have given me access if Krzyzewski had not spoken up on my behalf. The fact that Knight had agreed to do the book without so much as even saying, "Mike, what do you think?" on the night I'd proposed the idea didn't matter. The irony, as I pointed out to Krzyzewski, was that he'd tried to talk *me* out of the book.

Krzyzewski was completely caught in the middle. On one side, he had his college coach and professional mentor telling him that he had been betrayed and it was *his* fault. On the other side, he had someone he trusted telling him his mentor hadn't been betrayed on any level.

We sat down and talked about it after Duke had played an early-season game in the Meadowlands against Alabama. "I have no choice here," he said to me. "I have to side with Knight. I don't know what happened between you guys, I wasn't there. But he's basically given me an ultimatum: I can be his friend or your friend, but not both."

I was hurt if only because I thought Krzyzewski should know me well enough to know that betrayal wasn't my M.O.

"Let me ask you a question," I said. "Do you think after six months there I didn't know just about everything there was to know about his divorce, about his relationship with his wife and his two sons and the woman he's dating?"

"You probably did."

"Other than one sentence in which I report that he filed for divorce, which was a matter of public record and had been in the newspapers [and was the way Pat Knight found out his father was leaving his mother for good], is there one word in the book about his personal life?"

"I haven't read the book."

"So you haven't read the book, but you're prepared to judge it based on what Knight—who also says he hasn't read the book beyond Chapter One—has told you about it?"

"Yes."

I looked at Krzyzewski, not knowing what to say next. We were in a small, bare room right next to his team's locker room, which he had used for his postgame session with the media. The only other person in the room was Mickie, Mike's wife. I looked at Mickie, who shrugged as if to say, "I can't help you right now."

"Okay, Mike," I said. "I'll see you later. Nice win."

I walked out of the room. Mickie followed me. "Listen to me," she said. "One of Mike's great strengths is his loyalty. I've already told him he's misplacing it here. I understand why it's tough for him, and I think you do too. You have to give him some time. He'll figure it out."

As it turned out she was right. Krzyzewski never called me to say "I've changed my mind" or "You were right all along," but as time went on, it became apparent that he knew I hadn't betrayed Knight. Later that season, I was at Duke doing a Sunday story on Tommy Amaker, who was from Fairfax, Virginia, and thus a local kid for the *Washington Post*. I was sitting in the locker room alone with Amaker after practice when Krzyzewski walked in to get something.

"If you've got time, come by the office when you're finished with Tommy," he said.

I did. He started talking about the game the previous day against North Carolina—a close loss. "Paul Houseman missed two calls that killed us," he said, talking about one of the ACC's better officials. "The second time he ran by the bench and said, 'If I missed that one, Mike, I'll buy you a Coke.' When the game was over, I went back, watched the tape right away, and sent someone down to the refs' locker room to tell Houseman he owed me a f—ing Coke."

We both laughed. The tension broke. A lot more would happen over the next few years between Knight and Krzyzewski. None of which, I'm happy to report, had anything to do with *A Season on the Brink.*

———

THE FIRST INDIANA GAME I attended that season was at Notre Dame. By then (late November) Knight had told enough people that he was angry about the book that the story was starting to pick up some steam. Gary Nuhn, an old friend from the *Dayton Daily News,* wrote a column about it that day and predicted that Knight would try his bully act on me after the game.

He didn't. He did, however, send Hammel to me before the game carrying the letter that I had sent him. "Bob said to tell you he wouldn't read this," Hammel said, handing it back to me.

"Very mature of him," I said.

"I wouldn't come around Bloomington very much in the future if I were you," he said, repeating what he had said on the phone.

I liked Hammel a lot. He is an extraordinarily decent man. But at that moment I felt sorry for him.

"Bob, when did you become Knight's personal messenger?" I asked.

He didn't answer that one.

The one funny moment of the evening came when Joe Hillman, who had been a redshirt the previous year, walked over to inbound right in front of my seat. "Oh boy," Joe said, looking at me and smiling. "Here we go."

We didn't go anywhere. George Solomon and I had discussed how to deal with any potential postgame problems. I wasn't going to ask any questions in Knight's press conference because that could be seen as baiting him. If Knight did what he had done to *Sports Illustrated*'s Curry Kirkpatrick a few years ago and refused to answer questions unless I left the room, I was going to say, "Bob, with all due respect, I'm credentialed to be in here. If you want to make *me* the story by not answering questions from the rest of the guys about the game your team just won, that's your prerogative."

None of that happened. In fact, every time I showed up at a game that season, Knight never said a word about my presence. The only real incident occurred when my friend Kit Klingelhoffer claimed he didn't have room for me in the building when I requested a credential for the Iowa-Indiana game in Assembly Hall.

"Kit, don't do this," I said. "I know you're under orders from Knight, but you need to talk him off this ledge. All he's doing is making himself look bad and selling *more* books." (This was February and the book had now hit number one on the bestseller list.)

"It's not Knight," he said. "It's me. I haven't got room for you."

"Well then *you* are making Knight look bad. Look, you don't even have to give me a seat on press row. I'll watch the game in the press room if you guys want your pound of flesh that way. But don't create a national incident."

The fact that Kit wouldn't budge made it clear he wasn't making the call. He wasn't going to tell Knight he was making a mistake and neither was anyone else at Indiana—including President John Ryan, who wouldn't take a phone call from George Solomon.

So instead of going to Bloomington that day, I went to Chapel Hill to see North Carolina play Clemson in a game with first place in the ACC at stake. When Dean Smith walked into his postgame press conference and saw me, he smiled. "John, you know you are *always* welcome at the University of North Carolina," he said.

The entire room cracked up.

Before I flew down to Chapel Hill that day, I taped an interview with Ahmad Rashad that was to air at halftime of the Indiana-Iowa game. Rashad reported that I had been denied a credential to the game and then said, "John, Coach Knight has called you a pimp and he's called you a whore, what's your response?"

I answered instinctively. "Well, Ahmad, I wish he'd make up his mind so I'd know how to dress in the morning."

Dan Dakich told me later that even *Knight* acknowledged that was a pretty good line. I have used that story and that line as my opening anecdote when speaking publically for most of the last twenty-five years.

My being "banned" *did* become a national story as I had

predicted. Marv Albert and Bucky Waters discussed it at halftime of the first game of the NBC doubleheader that day, and Al McGuire brought it up during the Indiana-Iowa game. Bucky stood up for me as did Billy Packer on CBS. Al, always the diplomat, said, "I just hate to see the two of them fighting like this."

After Keith Smart hit the shot to win the title for Indiana, Alford found me amid the chaos on the floor and gave me a hug.

"Careful," I said. "There could be cameras around."

"No more games to play," he said, laughing.

THE QUESTION FOR ME once basketball season was over was what next? I was now a "hot" property in publishing, and Esther was all over me for another idea. "Something basketball," she said. "Anything basketball."

"But I thought basketball books didn't sell."

"Shut up, John."

I actually came up with two ideas: One was to spend the following season traveling far and wide and writing about the game from different levels—coaches and players after the Holy Grail of the Final Four; players who were in it strictly for the love of the game; referees and anyone and everyone involved in college basketball. Publishers loved that idea. But I wanted a two-book contract, since I knew at that moment I was dealing from strength. My second idea was to go back and talk to the players and coaches from Duke's 1978 team, which had lost the national championship game to Kentucky after finishing tied for last in the ACC a year earlier.

Everyone had expected that team—whose top ten players were underclassmen—to come back and win at least one national championship the next couple of years, but it never happened. There were a lot of reasons why, and I knew most of them since I'd been in school when Bill Foster had put that team together in what was one of the most overlooked rebuilding jobs in the game's history.

A lot of publishers weren't thrilled with the Duke idea. In fact, only Peter Gethers at Random House was willing to make a legitimate two-book offer. Jeff Neuman had left Macmillan, and I'm honestly not sure if they even made an offer. But I had known Peter through Esther, so I was perfectly happy to sign with him. The money was considerably higher than $17,500, which would lead, inevitably, to yet another conflict with my boss at the *Washington Post*, George Solomon.

I HAD KNOWN THAT the success of *A Season on the Brink* was going to change my life and my relationship with the *Post*. In one sense I was very fortunate to have a role model in Bob Woodward. That's not to imply that the success of the book put me anywhere close to Woodward in any way, shape, or form, but it did give me an idea of how to deal with sudden success.

In 1982, on the tenth anniversary of the Watergate break-in, Woodward and Carl Bernstein had been interviewed by Ted Koppel on *Nightline*. Bernstein had left the *Post* not long after the publication of *All the President's Men* and had tried his hand at television and celebrity. Woodward stayed at the *Post* and eventually became metro editor. He kept producing best-selling books, even after his partnership (though not his friendship) dissolved with Bernstein. Not surprisingly, Bernstein did most of the talking throughout the interview with Koppel.

At the end, Koppel asked the two men what Watergate had meant to each of them personally. Bernstein went through a lengthy answer about how it had restored his faith in the Constitution, how it had proved the importance of the media acting in its role as the fourth estate, and the importance of never giving up on a story.

Woodward said nothing. Koppel finally turned to him and said, "And you, Mr. Woodward?"

Bob smiled, shook his head, and said, "Well, it was a great learning experience as a *reporder*."

I laughed out loud. By then I had worked for Woodward and considered him a friend. The answer was classic Woodward: asked what breaking the single most important story in the history of journalism meant to him personally, his answer was that it was a great learning experience as a reporter.

To this day, Woodward is still trying to get better. The very best reporters are always asking questions, and Bob still does that. I knew my life was different after *Brink.* I'd been promoted to columnist and I had more money than I'd ever dreamed of having. But I wanted very much to keep learning and growing as a reporter—if Bob Woodward still had things to learn, God knows I did—and not feel somehow satisfied because I'd been lucky enough to write a bestseller.

One of the nicest compliments anyone ever paid me was meant at least half in jest. When Sandy Bailey, who was an assistant sports editor at the *Post,* was asked by someone doing a story on me if the success of the book had changed me, she said, "Unfortunately, not at all."

I'd also gotten very good advice from Len Downie, who was then the *Post's* managing editor: "I don't think you're going to change because of this," he said. "But what you better understand is that this *will* change the way people look at you."

One person who looked at me differently was George Solomon. George, as mentioned before, liked his reporters young and hungry. As far as George was concerned, the minute the book hit the bestseller list, I ceased being hungry. Or more important, I stopped being someone he felt he could control. The fact that the new dynamic probably wasn't going to work first became apparent in January. With the book about to go to number one on the bestseller list, Macmillan wanted me to do a more extensive book tour.

I had plenty of vacation time, but didn't want to bolt on George in the middle of the basketball season. I went in and explained the situation and told him I needed five days—Monday through Friday—

for the tour. I would cover games on the weekend leading into that week and leading out, and leave him with two midweek features that I'd write before I left. Grudgingly, he agreed. I also suggested he send someone to cover Indiana at Iowa that Thursday, the one big midweek game I wouldn't be able to cover.

"We don't need it," George said. "I don't need to cover a game to promote your book."

"George, I don't need the book promoted. They're ranked one and four."

"Forget it," he said. "Pass."

That was fine with me. On Wednesday I was in Indianapolis, preparing for a long day of interviews and appearances, when the phone rang. It was George.

"I decided you were right," he said. "We should cover Indiana-Iowa."

"Good," I said. "Who are you going to send?"

"You," he answered. "You're already out there."

"George, I'm out here promoting the book." I looked at my schedule. "I have *fourteen* commitments tomorrow. The first is at six thirty a.m. and the last is at nine p.m. No way can I make it to Iowa City."

"Can't you just tell them you need to cover a game?"

"*No.* This has been set for weeks now. That's why I told you I need these five days off."

"Come on, it's not that big a deal."

"*Yes,* George, it is a big deal."

"So you're refusing to go?"

I sighed. This was classic George. "George, I'm not *refusing.* I *can't.*"

"Great. Thanks for nothing."

Looking back, I probably should have gone in to George at the end of that basketball season, when the new book contracts had been signed, and told him that it was time for me to leave the *Post.* I didn't want to do that though because I loved daily journalism—

still do—and loved being a part of the newspaper. There were few things I enjoyed more than walking through the newsroom for a cup of coffee while working on a story and bumping into someone from the metro staff or national staff and talking to them about what was going on in the real world.

I thought I could make my new double life—author/daily journalist—work. As it turned out, I was wrong.

8

Starting All Over

THE FIRST THING I did to begin work on my second book was sit down and make a list of people I thought would be good stories during the 1987–88 basketball season: coaches, players, even referees. There were three coaches I knew would be part of the book: Dean Smith, Jim Valvano, and Mike Krzyzewski.

During my winter in Indiana I had been teased early and often by Knight—and later everyone else as they got to know me—about being "an ACC guy." Although I consider myself a basketball guy, there's no arguing that my reporting roots are in the ACC. I started covering ACC basketball as a Duke sophomore, and even though Duke wasn't very good at the time (a notion people under forty find difficult to grasp), I loved the electricity of the conference, the rivalries, the packed gyms. I also loved the fact that you could see three games on a weekend in the Research Triangle, hopping from Duke to North Carolina to North Carolina State. To me, there was nothing better than a weekend that started in Carmichael Auditorium on Saturday afternoon, then moved to Cameron Indoor Stadium in the evening, and over to Reynolds Coliseum on Sunday afternoon.

The day I enrolled at Duke as a freshman, the basketball coach was Bucky Waters. Ten days later he resigned—he claims to this day it had nothing to do with my presence on campus—and was replaced on October 18 by Neill McGeachy. The reason the date is significant is that basketball practice began on October 15. It began with athletic director Carl James looking for a coach and a letter to the editor in the student newspaper, written by starting center Bob Fleischer, wondering just what in the world James was up to and if he planned to have anyone coach the team during the season.

James did have a plan: he was trying to hire Adolph Rupp. Seriously. Rupp had been forced into retirement by Kentucky a year earlier and still wanted to coach. James offered him the job and Rupp was ready to take it. In fact, a press conference was scheduled. But Rupp's business partner died suddenly and Rupp pulled out, leaving James with a press conference to introduce a new coach and no coach to introduce.

So James called McGeachy in that morning—minutes before the press conference—and offered him a one-year contract. McGeachy was willing to accept it as long as he wasn't labeled an "interim" coach. Interim or not, McGeachy was fired after going 10–16, including a game in Chapel Hill that Duke lost in overtime after leading by eight points with seventeen seconds left. This was with no three-point shot.

Bill Foster was hired a month after the season ended and began a rebuilding program that would land Duke in the Final Four in his fourth season, which happened to be the year after I graduated. During my four years in college, Duke had a combined record in ACC play of 10–42 and an overall record of 50–56. In those days, when Duke players dreamed of making the Final Four, they were talking about the final four of the ACC Tournament. Duke never won an ACC Tournament game while I was in college.

Duke being lousy actually benefitted me as a reporter. North Carolina and North Carolina State were the power schools in the state during those years. State, led by David Thompson, won the national championship in 1974. North Carolina, coached by Dean Smith, was good every year. In 1977, my senior year, the Tar Heels lost the national championship game to Marquette.

Because Duke was bad, the local newspapers often didn't bother to staff their games on the road. That was a boon to me. I had started covering basketball on a regular basis as a sophomore and had gotten to know a number of the writers, most notably Keith Drum of the *Durham Morning Herald* and Bob Heller of the *Greensboro Daily News*—Bob having preceded me at the *Chronicle* by several years.

Keith and Bob both took an interest in me and were willing to hook me up with their bosses to set up stringing assignments. "Stringers" were often used by newspapers in the old days to contribute to stories written by staff writers—gathering a few extra quotes to feed to a writer or doing research to add to longer stories. If a stringer was lucky, he would occasionally be allowed to write a story himself.

Keith and Bob got me assigned to write stories for their papers. Sometimes this involved doing a sidebar on a Duke game when the game merited a second story. Sometimes I covered high school games and, more and more often as I grew as a reporter, I'd be asked to write a game story *and* a sidebar when their papers didn't cover Duke on the road. By the time I was a senior, I was also stringing for the *Winston-Salem Journal,* the *Charlotte Observer,* and the Associated Press. Generally speaking, I was paid $25 a story; $40 if I did a sidebar. The AP paid me $10 at Duke home games, $25 if a ranked team (always the visitor in those days) was playing, in which case I had to write an "alternate" lead—one that had a feature angle rather than the straight "Jim Spanarkel scored twenty-six points and added seven assists last night to lead Duke to a 79–71 victory over East Carolina..."

By the end of my sophomore year, there was no doubt in my mind that I wanted to work at a newspaper when I graduated. In fact, I had plotted my future fairly specifically: I would get a job at a paper in North Carolina with the intention of working at the *Washington Post* by the time I was thirty. My parents had moved to Washington when I was a senior in high school and I had fallen in love with reading the *Post*—especially the sports section. I loved Shirley Povich, who was technically retired but still wrote columns, and Ken Denlinger, who eventually succeeded Povich as the number one columnist. I thought Leonard Shapiro, who covered the Redskins, did an amazing job of bringing a team and a season to life. I loved the style section and reading about national politics in the A-section. Fortunately, you could buy the *Post* every day in the student union, and I never missed it.

For all intents and purposes, my major at Duke was the *Chronicle,* because that's where I did most of the learning that would take me where I wanted to go when I graduated. Technically, my major was history and I had a number of professors—notably the great Bill Scott—I really enjoyed, but there wasn't any doubt during my last two years about what I wanted to do.

The *Chronicle* was an amazing place. It was completely student run, and the tradition was for the older kids to teach the younger ones.

By the time I was a senior, I was essentially a full-time newspaper reporter. By then my friend and former roommate David Arneke was editing something called the *Carolina Financial Times,* so I wrote features for him. I was the *Chronicle's New York Times* stringer—which really *was* stringing work, feeding quotes to the paper for use in lengthy pieces—and I was assistant managing editor and sports editor of the *Chronicle,* in addition to doing all the stories I was doing for the various local papers.

On one Duke road trip to West Virginia and Duquesne, I wrote game stories for Durham, Charlotte, Greensboro, and Winston-Salem—in addition to the *Chronicle.* I had to drive back roads from Washington to Morgantown because the interstate had been closed by a snowstorm, and I almost got stuck after a tractor-trailer had overturned and blocked the road. It took about ninety minutes before police could clear a path for cars to get by, and I was almost out of gas—and heat—by the time we got clear.

This was in the middle of the energy crisis, and the heat in WVU Coliseum that night was set at 58 degrees. As soon as the game ended—West Virginia won—the heat was turned off. I went to the locker rooms to get quotes and then headed back to the media room to write. I could see my breath as I walked across the court to get back to where my typewriter was waiting for me. I guess all the local guys had gone back to their offices to write, because there were only two people in the room (and, I think, in the building): Tom Mickle, the Duke sports information director, and me.

I sat at my typewriter writing as fast as my frozen fingers would allow, and Mick stood there with his coat on, taking off his gloves each time I handed him a page so he could feed it into the telecopier, which transmitted back to the newspapers at the lightning-fast rate of six minutes per page. By the time we walked out of the building shortly after midnight, the parking lot was pitch-black and there wasn't a soul in sight. You want to talk about having good friends, I never had a better one than Tom Mickle.

I even managed to get a byline in the *Washington Post*. I had gotten into the habit of cold-calling sports editors at big-time newspapers to offer them stories with local angles. I had tried to sell George Solomon story ideas a couple of times with no luck. Finally, I took a shot at a game story: North Carolina was playing at Wake Forest and both were ranked in the top ten. I had gotten Solomon's direct phone number from Mark Asher, the paper's Maryland beat writer, so I was able to get through to him. I offered the story.

"What time's the game?" George said.

"Nine o'clock."

"Okay, fine. If you can get me fourteen inches with quotes by eleven thirty, we'll take it."

I swallowed hard. That would give me thirty minutes—maybe—from game's end to get the story to the paper.

"So do you want to do it?" George said while I was doing the math in my head.

"Absolutely," I said.

"Good. O. D. Wilson is the night editor. I'll let him know to expect a story from you."

I needed a strategy to get this done and I *had* to get it done. I was applying for a summer internship at the *Post* and I was dying to get it. I knew, from Asher, that sports would take two interns and one would be a woman. There were usually about three thousand applicants in all for twenty total spots. Long odds. This was a way to perhaps set myself apart from the other applicants in Solomon's mind.

I called Bruce Herman, the sports information director at Wake Forest, and explained the situation to him. One of the great things about the ACC in those days was the quality of the SIDs. Not only were they good at what they did, they were willing to help *anyone*—whether that person was working for the Duke student newspaper or the *Washington Post.* Bruce offered to have one of his student assistants standing by so I could hand them each page—I would need three—to be taken directly to the telecopier as soon as I finished each one.

That would help. Keith Drum offered to feed me some quick quotes from one locker room. Carolina won a close game that ended on the stroke of eleven o'clock. I spent the ten minute cooling-off period before the coaches came out of the locker rooms writing the first five inches and handing them to Bruce's assistant. Then I raced under the stands at the old Winston-Salem Coliseum and listened to Dean Smith for exactly three minutes. I sprinted back to the press table and wrote the second page in another five minutes. By then, Drum was there with player quotes. I handed the third page to the student assistant at 11:27.

Damn! The last page was going to be three or four minutes late by the time it got through the telecopier. I raced to a phone and called O. D. Wilson. "Mr. Wilson," I said, completely breathless. "The last page is on its way. I'm sorry it's a couple of minutes late..."

"Late?" O.D. said. "We've got until midnight. You're in great shape. Good show down there."

I would learn later that "good show" was the best compliment you could get from O.D.

Of course the story wasn't in the first edition of the paper that came to Durham, since that deadline was at seven o'clock. But it was in the home edition that my parents got at their house. They were not sports section readers. So I called my mother.

"Mom, I'm looking for a story in today's sports section of the *Post* — can you take a look for it?"

"What story is it?" she asked.

"It's on the North Carolina–Wake Forest game," I said. "It'll be somewhere inside the section."

"Let me find sports," she said.

A moment later she was back on the phone. "Here it is," she said. "'North Carolina Hangs On to Beat Wake.' Is that it?"

My heart was pounding. "Yeah, that's it," I said, trying to sound casual. "Can you tell me who wrote the story?"

There was a pause and then a gasp. "Johnny!" was all she said.

I'm not sure I've had a better moment as a reporter. I told her the whole story. "You owe your friend Keith big-time," she said.

She was right. I did. Still do.

I called Solomon that day, ostensibly to thank him for giving me the chance to write the game story, but in truth fishing for compliments. "O.D. said you did really well," he said. "Handled it like a pro. Stay in touch."

At that point in my life, if Cybil Shepherd had said "stay in touch" to me, it wouldn't have been as big a deal as George Solomon saying it.

About a month later, I was home for spring break. The Eastern Regionals of the NCAA Tournament were being played at Maryland and I had convinced the sports editor of the *Chicago Sun-Times* to let me cover the regional for him since Notre Dame was playing North Carolina in the round of sixteen. The other game would match Virginia Military Institute (yes, VMI) and Kentucky.

On the morning of the Sweet Sixteen games, Mark Asher called my parents' house. When I got on the phone, he said simply, "Congratulations, you got it."

I was stunned. Was he *really* talking about the internship?

"You mean..."

"Yup. George just told me. It's you and a girl from Marquette. He's going to be at the games tonight. Introduce yourself. But do *not* tell him you know anything. Let him tell you."

"But you're sure?"

"Yeah. He remembered the Wake game and he asked Kenny [Denlinger] to read four or five applications he had whittled it down to. Kenny liked yours the best. I think that clinched it."

Years later, when Denlinger became a close friend, I asked him if he remembered reading the applications. He did. "You had some story in there about officiating in the ACC," he said. "I noticed you had quotes from all the coaches. I thought that was impressive that someone from a student newspaper could get all those guys on the phone.

"Of course, when I walked back into George's office I couldn't remember your name. So I just said, 'I like the kid from Duke.'"

Doing the referees story had exposed me to the intense nature of coaching in the ACC for the first time. The big issue on the table back then was whether to go from two referees to three. So I decided to try to call every coach in the league to see what they thought. Most weren't that difficult to track down—Drum had told me that NC State coach Norman Sloan always had lunch in his office, and if I called then he would probably answer the phone himself since the secretary was out. He was right.

The only two coaches I couldn't get to call me back were Dean Smith and Lefty Driesell. The secretaries took messages but told me that Coach was very busy and didn't know when he'd be able to call back. Finally, I decided they weren't going to call back unless I gave them an incentive.

I called Smith and said to the secretary, "I'm sorry to bug you again, but I'm on deadline and I've talked to all the other coaches and I really want to give Coach Smith a chance to respond to what Coach Driesell and Coach Sloan said about him." (Driesell, Sloan, and Smith were the power axis in the league at that point.) She promised to let Coach know. Within twenty-four hours, Dean called back.

By then I actually *had* talked to Lefty and did have some quotes from him I could bounce off Dean. The reason I had talked to Lefty was I had pulled the same trick on him, telling the secretary I wanted to give him a chance to respond to what Coach Smith had said. Within *five minutes,* Lefty called back. "What'd Dean say about me?" he asked.

I hadn't expected a call back so quickly. Semi-panicked, I said, "Coach, to be honest, I haven't talked to him yet. But I figured if I mentioned him you'd call back."

Lefty laughed. "Oh really?" he said. "That's pretty smart for a Duke guy." Lefty, of course, went to Duke.

I asked him how he felt about three officials. "I'm against it," he said.

"Why?" I asked.

"Because if we have three officials, when we play Dean it'll be eight against five instead of seven against five."

That is *still* one of the great quotes of all time.

And perhaps most important, it caught Denlinger's eye.

THE FIRST TIME I met Dean Smith was on his forty-fifth birthday. I remember it because Duke played at North Carolina that afternoon. I was a college junior and had grown accustomed to seeing the Tar Heels beat the Blue Devils, so Carolina's 91–71 victory in Chapel Hill was hardly a shock.

The shock came when I timidly introduced myself to the great man in the locker room after the game. I was writing a story on the remarkable emergence of Tate Armstrong as a star in the ACC that year. With no three-point shot and no shot clock, Tate was routinely scoring thirty-plus points every night. I didn't think—and I was, of course, completely unbiased—that he was getting enough credit and, after Tate had scored thirty-six against Carolina in spite of being double- and triple-teamed most of the day, was hoping Dean would give me a couple of quotes to back up my premise.

So I walked over to where he was standing in the corner of the locker room and waited for him to finish talking to another writer. When I introduced myself the very first thing he said was, "Oh yes, of course. I read your column last month on what Bill should do to build his program. I thought you were very fair to us, especially for someone from Duke."

Little did I know that line was to become a recurring theme in our relationship for more than thirty years. At that moment though, I was completely stunned. Dean Smith knew *my* name? He had read something I had written in the *Chronicle*? I would find out later that the Carolina basketball office subscribed to every major newspaper in the country, every paper in the state of North Carolina, *and* all the student newspapers in the ACC. One assistant coach—in those days it was Roy Williams—was assigned to look through all the papers for any story that might in some way be significant to North Carolina. He would clip those stories, put them in a folder, and Dean would read them on airplanes.

That was why he had read the column I had written a few weeks earlier, which said that if Bill Foster needed a role model upon which to build his program, he need look no farther than down Route 15-501 to Chapel Hill and Carmichael Auditorium. The column hadn't just been fair to Smith and Carolina, it had been gushy to the point that Foster had kidded me about it: "I always thought it was Naismith who invented basketball," he said, "not Dean Smith."

Dean hadn't invented it, but he had come pretty close to perfecting it as far as I could see. Every time I stepped inside Carmichael Auditorium, which was where Carolina played until the Dean Dome opened in 1986, I thought, "This is the way college basketball should be." The building was packed—Cameron was half empty for most games back then—the students were clearly having fun, and the team was always very good. There was no doubt that Dean controlled everything. In fact, that afternoon, when a profane cheer had sprung up briefly early in the game after a couple of calls went against Carolina, Dean walked to the PA mike, grabbed it, and said very firmly, "We don't do that here. We win with class. Stop it."

They stopped. And they won.

So now, after recovering from my initial shock, I asked Dean my question about Tate Armstrong. He talked for about five minutes without stopping. Most of what he said was about how proud he was of Walter Davis and what a great senior leader Mitch Kupchak was. I walked away still wondering exactly what he thought about Tate.

That was Dean. His mind worked so fast and went in so many different directions that he could take a question about a poor shooting night in a Final Four game and somehow come out on the other end talking about Larry Brown becoming a father again in his mid-50s.

I always liked Dean, and obviously respected him greatly. The "Duke thing" was always a part of our relationship because Dean refused to let it go. Most of the time I didn't mind—it was delivered with good humor. Once, when I met him in a hotel lobby while wearing jeans, he shook his head and said, "You Duke guys don't like to dress up do you?"

"Dean, we're just driving over to a shootaround," I said.

"You're right," he answered. "Considering where you went to college, I'm surprised you're not wearing sandals."

Once, he offered to buy me a jacket and tie if I couldn't afford one. This was shortly after I started working at the *Post*.

"Don't they pay you very much there?" he asked.

"Actually they don't," I said. (I was making $238.25 a week before taxes as a first year reporter.) "But that's not why I don't have a jacket and tie."

"Well, I can't buy clothes for my players," he said. "But I could buy you clothes — especially since you went to Duke."

There was only one time when it became a real issue, and it turned into one of the two serious disagreements we had through the years.

IN 1995, DURING THE brief period that I was doing some work for ESPN (I never worked for the network full-time, thank God), I reported that Rasheed Wallace, then a sophomore, was a virtual lock to turn pro at the end of the season and, in fact, was being pushed hard by Smith and his staff just to stay in his classes until the end of the semester. My source was someone very well connected at Carolina, someone who had spoken directly to Dean about how frustrated he was with Wallace — who was a great talent, but a handful then as he was throughout his long NBA career.

The Carolina people went nuts about the story. Wallace and his mother categorically denied it. Rasheed, his mother said, was going to stay four years. Wallace said I was trying to have my "fifteen seconds of fame" by reporting the story. If nothing else, he probably needed to stay in college to study famous Andy Warhol quotes more closely.

In any event, the North Carolina media spent a lot more time reporting the Wallace denials and what a bad guy I was than reporting the initial story. Which was fine. But then someone asked Dean about it, and his initial answer was, "Well, we all know that John went to Duke..."

Now *that* made me angry. Dean knew me better than that. He also knew I had the story right even though I certainly didn't expect him to confirm it. In fact, he was very careful to say, "As far as I know, Rasheed plans to be back here next year." He then went off on a Dean tangent about what a fine young man Rasheed was.

I was going to call Dean about the Duke crack, but Carolina was coming to play Maryland that week anyway. I decided to talk to Dean about it in person. I almost always saw him before games at Cole Field House because he would walk into the tunnel leading from the locker rooms to the floor to do his pregame radio show. I would make sure to find him.

As it turned out, he found me. I was talking to my friend Doug Doughty from the *Roanoke Times* when someone walked up from behind and tapped me on the shoulder. I turned around and saw Dean standing there. Before I could say anything, he said, "I owe you an apology."

I answered instinctively. "You're damn right you do." Then I felt badly because here was Dean throwing out an olive branch and I was being disrespectful. "I'm sorry, Dean, I'm overreacting," I said. "But I couldn't believe you said my going to Duke had anything to do with the story. Of all people you know better than that."

"You're right," he said. "I was defending one of my players, and sometimes when I do that I say things I shouldn't."

"You know the media down there is killing me," I said. "They love the idea of painting me as 'a Duke guy,' and you opened the door for that."

He nodded. "I know. Is there anything I can do to help?"

I thought for a second. "Well, since you made the comment publicly, it would help if you apologized publicly."

He never hesitated. "I'll do it after the game. In my press conference. Win or lose."

"If you did, that would be great."

He put out his hand. "Done. And I *am* sorry. I hope Rasheed comes back and proves your story wrong, but I know you didn't report it for any reason other than the fact that someone told you it was true."

"That's exactly right."

Maryland won that night. I sat in the back of Dean's press

conference and listened while he talked about the game. After a while it became apparent that, in the wake of the loss, he had forgotten our pregame conversation. I got up and quietly walked out the back door. Maybe, I thought, another time.

I was picking up final statistics when Jim O'Connell of the AP, one of my good friends in the business, walked out of the interview room. "Hey, John," he said, "Dean says he needs you to come back inside."

I followed O'Connell back into the room. Dean was standing there smiling.

"John, you left before you got your apology," he said.

"Dean, um, I thought you'd forgotten."

"No, I didn't," he said. "A promise is a promise. I wanted to tell everyone here I was wrong to say John's reporting on Rasheed had anything to do with where he went to college. It didn't. We think Rasheed will be back, but that's not the point here. John, I'm sorry."

"Thank you, Dean."

"And I know you pull for *all* the ACC teams in the NCAA Tournament."

Now everyone was laughing. "Absolutely, Dean."

I MET MIKE KRZYZEWSKI and Jim Valvano on the same day, at the same moment.

During my senior year, Duke played a game in Madison Square Garden against Connecticut. To show you how different times were back then, Duke-UConn was the preliminary game that night. The feature game was Fordham-Rutgers. Yes, seriously.

On the day before the game I flew to New York with Bill Foster, Tate Armstrong, and Tom Mickle. Bill and Tate were going to make a number of media appearances, and Bill was scheduled to speak at the weekly coaches luncheon at Mama Leone's.

The lunches were a longtime New York tradition. Every Tuesday, all the local college basketball coaches and the media would get together at Mama Leone's. After everyone ate, each coach would get up and talk for a few minutes about his team and upcoming games. Then everyone would stand around and gab for a while. It made for a very fraternal feeling in an era when relationships between the media and coaches were completely different from what they are now, when getting a one-on-one interview with a big-time coach can be more difficult than getting invited to the Oval Office to have a sit-down with the president.

As he did whenever he spoke in public, Jim Valvano, then in his second year as the coach at Iona, stole the show. This was no small feat. Foster was a very good speaker and Lou Carnesecca of St. John's was a great storyteller. No one was in Valvano's class.

"When I first got the job at Iona I was *so* excited," Valvano said that day. "I was at a party and I kept introducing myself to everyone there, saying, 'I'm Jim Valvano, Iona College, great to meet you.

"Finally this one woman looks at me like I'm crazy and says, 'Young man, aren't you a little young to *own* your own college?'"

Valvano had played for Foster at Rutgers in the late 1960s. He was one of two coaches there that day who I remembered seeing play in college. The other was Krzyzewski, who had played at Army under Bob Knight and was now in his second season as the coach at his alma mater. Valvano was loud and funny; back then, Krzyzewski was neither.

They both came over as soon as the lunch was over to say hello to Foster, along with Tom Penders, who was then the coach at Columbia. We had walked in a little bit late because our flight had been delayed, so Valvano raced over as soon as the lunch was over to see his old coach and to introduce him to his two friends. They were three fresh-faced young coaches: Penders, the oldest at thirty-two; Valvano a year younger; and Krzyzewski a year younger than Valvano, a couple months shy of turning thirty. To put that in a little bit of perspective, think about how gaga everyone went at the 2010 Final Four when baby-faced Brad Stevens took Butler to the final. Stevens was thirty-three. Of course, at that moment, none of the three coaches was thinking about coaching in the Final Four.

Foster introduced Tate, Mickle, and me and told them that I did a good Dean Smith imitation. In truth, I did an *okay* Dean imitation. Years later, during a conversation with Dean and his longtime SID, Rick Brewer, Dean said to me, "I hear you do me pretty well."

"I'm okay," I said. "But Rick's better."

Dean turned to Brewer, who instantly turned forty-eight shades of red. "Rick," he said, "do *you* do me?"

Brewer was flustered for a moment and then said, "Coach, *everyone* does you."

That was certainly true in North Carolina; almost everyone imitated Dean's nasally Kansas twang, complete with all of his clichés about senior leadership and how fortunate Carolina would be to beat anyone they were playing. As Lefty Driesell once put it, "Dean Smith's the only man in the history of coaching to win eight hundred games [879 to be exact] and be the underdog in every one of them."

Now the three young coaches were looking at me expectantly. "It's not that good," I said.

"Come on," Valvano said. "Don't be shy. The three of us *combined* will never win as many games as Dean's won."

I thought about that line on the night Krzyzewski won his 880th game. Certainly none of us standing there on that December afternoon thought Valvano's line was off target. "When Jimmy said it," Krzyzewski said thirty-four years later, "it made absolute sense." As it turned out Penders won 650 games and Valvano 346—and a national championship—before he stopped coaching at the age of forty-four, three years before he died of cancer. That means, if you add in Krzyzewski's 900, the three of them had won 1,896 games combined. Back then they had combined to win about 100.

Urged on by Valvano, I did the imitation—talking about seniors and points per possession and how proud I was of all the doctors and lawyers I'd coached.

"That's pretty good," Krzyzewski said. "Now if you can do Jimmy, I'll really be impressed."

"No one can do Jimmy," Foster said, accurately.

After I got to the *Post,* I stayed in touch with Valvano, Krzyzewski, and Penders—who by then had gotten the job at Fordham. As a young reporter, I liked the fact that they would call me back right away. The first time I called Krzyzewski I reminded him that I was the guy he had met with Bill Foster who did the Dean Smith imitation. He remembered.

It was only after Valvano and Krzyzewski both moved to North Carolina in 1980 that I got to know them well. Both took over for coaches—Foster at Duke and Norman Sloan at North Carolina State—who had been very successful but had been frustrated by Smith's godlike status in North Carolina. Sloan used to get so frustrated with Smith that he would call Driesell, who he saw as an anti-Dean soul mate, and start the conversation by saying, "Do you know what that goddamn Dean just did?!"

"After a while," Driesell said, "I thought that was his full name, 'that goddamn Dean.'"

Valvano and Krzyzewski both vowed not to be bothered by the aura coming out of Chapel Hill, but both *did* find it difficult to deal with at times. Valvano was one of the world's great storytellers. Whether all his stories were true no one knew for sure, but when he told them they *sounded* true. One he especially liked was about the first haircut he got after getting to NC State: "I go to the campus barbershop. The old barber has been there for a hundred years or something. He says to me, 'You the guy replaced old Norman?' I say,

'Yes, I am.' He says, 'Well, I sure hope you have more luck than old Norman did.' I look at him and I say, 'Wait a second. Didn't Norman Sloan win a national championship? Didn't he go 27–0 one season?' Guy looks at me without missing a beat and says, 'Yeah, I guess he did. But just think what old Dean Smith would have done with that team.'"

Krzyzewski and Dean clashed publicly in 1984 after a game in Cameron that Duke could have won—but didn't. Dean never liked going to play at Duke. Unlike most people, he never found the students funny. That game was actually one of their better performances. A week earlier, when Maryland had been in town, they'd gone over the line, taunting the Terrapins' Herman Veal, who had been charged with sexual assault, by throwing panties at him and chanting R-A-P-E. Terry Sanford, the university president, had written an open letter to the students in the *Chronicle* that week that basically said, "Not funny. We're classier than this."

When Carolina came into the building, they were considerably better. Before the game, the Blue Devil mascot presented Dean with a dozen roses. (He wasn't amused. By contrast, when NC State's Lorenzo Charles was charged with stealing pizzas from a Domino's delivery truck, Valvano *signed* for the dozen pizzas Duke students had delivered to his bench just prior to tipoff and handed them out to the crowd.) When Carolina ran onto the court the students held up signs that said, "Welcome honored guests." They also chanted "We beg to differ" when they didn't like a call, rather than using the profane and worn-out "bullshit" chant heard so often in gyms to this day. And when Carolina was shooting free throws, instead of waving their arms behind the basket, they held up signs that said "Please miss."

All of that, combined with a great Carolina team that included Michael Jordan, Sam Perkins, Brad Daugherty, and Kenny Smith taking on a young Duke team coming of age—Johnny Dawkins, Mark Alarie, Jay Bilas, David Henderson, Tommy Amaker—made for an electric game and atmosphere. At one point, when the official scorer didn't see one of his subs and failed to hit the horn, Dean stormed down, accused him of cheating, and hit the horn *himself*. Krzyzewski demanded that the refs tee him up. They didn't. Carolina ended up winning a tight, tense game, and Krzyzewski got teed up in the waning seconds (the game had been decided), screaming at the refs that they had stolen the game from his team.

Two things happened afterward, one well chronicled since then, the other not. Krzyzewski made his infamous double standard comment, claiming that ACC referees gave Dean preferential treatment. When Dean heard about it, he was furious. He got even angrier after I called the other six coaches in the league to see if they agreed with Krzyzewski. Four of them weren't going anywhere near the argument. "Mike and Dean are both just trying to protect their players," Bobby Cremins, who was at Georgia Tech at the time, said. "I don't blame either one of them."

Bill Foster of Clemson (who was known as Clem-Foster in the league when the other Bill Foster was at Duke) and Lefty Driesell both sided with Krzyzewski. "I don't think they do it on purpose," Clem-Foster said. "But referees are human. They *think* Carolina's better, so they ref the games that way."

Lefty repeated his "eight against five" line (by now there were three officials working games) and said he knew how Krzyzewski felt.

Dean was so upset when he read the story that he called Foster, called Lefty, and called me. "Did Mike tell you to write that story?" he asked.

"Come on, Dean, don't be ridiculous. It's all anyone in the league is talking about. If the other six coaches had all said Mike was completely wrong, I'd have written that. I had no way of knowing what they would say when I called."

Dean was already angry with me that week because of the other postgame moment. Someone had asked him what he thought of the Duke students' performance. He waved it off dismissively. "The schedule says we have to come over here once a year," he said. "We do it, hope we get a win the way we did tonight, and go back to Chapel Hill."

I was standing near the door with Keith Drum while Dean talked. As he walked out he turned to me and said accusingly, "*You* think they're funny."

I did think they were funny—not always, but certainly that night. "I'm sorry, Dean," I said. "They *were* funny tonight."

He walked out shaking his head, clearly not happy with me, or anyone else who had ever been associated with Duke.

That game jump-started the Duke-Carolina rivalry, which had been languishing for years because Carolina had been dominating the series. Duke hadn't won a game in Chapel Hill in almost twenty years, and the Tar Heels had won eight of eleven in Cameron. Carolina won the regular season rematch in Chapel Hill, but needed an off-balance jumper at the buzzer by Matt Doherty to tie (Krzyzewski maintains to this day that Doherty walked on the play) and then win the game in double overtime. A week later they met again, in the ACC Tournament semifinals. This time, Duke hung on and won, in what turned out to be Michael Jordan's last ACC game.

During Krzyzewski's first three years at Duke, there had been one member of the North Carolina media who had consistently defended him: Keith Drum. Keith wasn't your typical sportswriter. He *really* knew and understood basketball, so much so that in the early '90s he made a unique job switch, going from reporter to NBA scout. He's now been a scout—first with the Portland Trail Blazers, now with the Sacramento Kings—for twenty years. Drum saw in Krzyzewski what others didn't: a young coach who had a plan and knew what he was doing. They became friends, and Krzyzewski would often ask Drum what he thought about his team and individual players because he respected his understanding of the game. He still does that today whenever Keith, who still lives in Chapel Hill, goes to watch his team practice.

Keith had gone to North Carolina. There are lots and lots of Carolina graduates covering sports in the state. UNC has a great journalism school, and many of those who graduate from it stay in the state, often for life. Most — not all — are unabashed Carolina loyalists. Drummer wasn't. He respected Smith and Carolina but, unlike a lot of his colleagues, didn't live and die with the fortunes of the Tar Heels.

That bothered Dean. Remember, Dean read *everything* written that involved his team or his rivals, and he knew that Drum had consistently written that, given time, Krzyzewski would bring Duke back and challenge North Carolina. Moments after Krzyzewski's and Duke's breakthrough win in the ACC Tournament, Dean stood outside his locker room smoking his postgame cigarette. (For the record, Dean gave up smoking in 1987 after a series of nosebleeds led his doctor to tell him he *had* to stop. He still chews Nicorette constantly and admits the cravings have never gone away.) When Keith and I came down the steps leading from the floor to the locker room area, Dean spotted us. He made a beeline for Keith, his hand extended.

"Congratulations," he said. "Your team played very well. I'm sure you're very happy."

Classic Dean. He had to make the point to Keith that he *knew* he liked Krzyzewski. You see, it was okay for me to like Krzyzewski because I was a *Duke* guy. But for a *Carolina* guy to like Krzyzewski was some kind of betrayal. That's one thing about the ACC, especially in those days when it was a smaller league: everyone was into labels. Dean always said I was okay for a Duke guy. Lefty Driesell often said Drum was okay for a Carolina guy.

ACC politics were so intense that when Gene Corrigan retired as commissioner in 1997, almost everyone in the league believed the right person to succeed him was Tom Mickle. According to Corrigan and everyone else involved, Mickle blew away the search committee with his vision for the league and the plans he said he would follow through on as commissioner.

The committee chose John Swofford.

Why? Because Corrigan was Duke class of '52 and Mickle was Duke class of '72. League politics simply wouldn't allow one Duke graduate to follow another as commissioner. Swofford is a graduate of North Carolina.

"Absolutely ridiculous decision," Maryland coach Gary Williams said years later. "Tom Mickle was as smart as anyone in college athletics. Who cares where he went to school? He would have been the best guy for the league. But that's not how the league works."

Duke's win in Greensboro in '84, on the day when Drum's "team" played so well, changed the dynamic of the Duke-Carolina rivalry and the entire league. Smith was 8–1 against Krzyzewski up until that day. His program certainly didn't slip afterward, but Krzyzewski's continued to improve. The last twenty-nine times the two met, Dean won sixteen times, Krzyzewski thirteen.

LOOKING BACK, THE IRONY of Dean and Mike is that almost everyone believed Valvano would be Dean's great rival. In his third season at NC State, Valvano won the national championship, matching the one Dean had won a year earlier, but in many ways surpassing it because no one had given that State team even a second thought. Just making the NCAA Tournament seemed like a long shot as the ACC Tournament began.

State pulled three upsets that weekend in Atlanta, beating Wake Forest by one, Carolina in overtime, and Virginia in the final minute. Carolina and Virginia were both considered serious Final Four contenders. State was a great story, but that was about it.

On that same weekend, Duke wrapped up an 11–17 season by losing 109–66 to Virginia in the first round of the tournament.

Think about that score: Duke lost by 43 at the end of Krzyzewski's third season. That made him 38–47, and he had yet to win an ACC Tournament game. The previous season had ended almost as badly— an 88–53 ACC Tournament loss to Wake Forest in the dreaded 9:30 game on the tournament's first night.

By the end of that game it was closing in on midnight and there were no more than three thousand people left in the Greensboro Coliseum. Twice in the last minute, veteran ACC referee Lenny Wirtz called fouls on Wake Forest walk-ons who Coach Carl Tacy had mercifully put into the game. As Wirtz stood in front of the press table while free throws were being shot, Bill Brill (Duke '54, who *was* a Duke loyalist) reached across the table and grabbed Wirtz's arm.

"If you blow that whistle one more time," Brill said, "I swear to God I will take it and shove it right down your throat."

Wirtz, who had known Brill for years, got it. There were no whistles in the final seconds.

The Virginia game a year later was a lot worse. For one thing, the Omni, Atlanta's then NBA arena, was packed because Duke-Virginia was the first game of the evening doubleheader and people from all eight schools wanted to see Virginia's Ralph Sampson, who was about to become a three-time national player of the year for Virginia.

Jay Bilas, who was a 6'8" Duke freshman, was assigned to guard the 7'4" Sampson. He knew he had no chance to stop him but had to do everything he could to try to contain him. Bilas tried to get his body into Sampson, to push him off the block and do anything possible to keep from being overwhelmed. Sampson didn't like being played physically, and he especially didn't like some kid trying to play him physically. He got angry and so did his coach, Terry Holland, who thought Bilas was trying to hurt Sampson.

Years later, Bilas could look back on the game and laugh. "I wasn't trying to hurt him," he said. "I was trying not to get completely humiliated."

Duke got completely humiliated. Holland left his starters in long after the outcome had been decided. Then, in the postgame interview, he expressed his frustration with Bilas—and indirectly, Krzyzewski—for what he thought was dirty play. When Krzyzewski came in and was asked about Holland's comments, you could almost see the steam coming out of his ears.

"We just got beat 109–66 and he's complaining about dirty play?" he said. "I've got a six-eight freshman hanging on for dear life trying to guard the national player of the year, and he's complaining about dirty play?" He stopped and shook his head. "Unbelievable."

A few minutes later, when Krzyzewski walked back to his locker room, he crossed paths with Holland, who was standing outside his own locker room talking to several writers.

"That was bullshit, Terry," Krzyzewski yelled. "You went out of your way to humiliate my team and *then* you complain about dirty play? That's bullshit."

Holland just looked at Krzyzewski as if he was from another planet. Both men were doing the same thing: standing up for their players.

Twenty-eight years later, Krzyzewski remembered that night vividly.

"It was an important night in my career and my life," he said as he sat in the stands at Georgetown Prep (a Jesuit school in the Washington, D.C., suburbs), watching a kid named Rasheed Sulaimon, who was a junior from a Houston high school, play in a post-Christmas tournament. "That team defined everything that wasn't about being a team. We had older kids who were jealous of the younger kids, and younger kids who weren't ready to be the team's leaders—even though Johnny [Dawkins] tried.

"I wasn't a good enough coach then to figure out how to get them to play together, to work together, to compete together. That failure on my part was reflected in the whole season [11–17] and in that night.

"We weren't very good to start with, and then they left their starters in the game until the end so we got humiliated. When I was walking into the hotel that night, none of our fans would look at me. They all turned away from me. They were embarrassed. A lot of that night was about hate: I hated what my team had become that season, I hated my opponent, and I hated the fans."

After the Duke-Virginia game ended, I stayed at the Omni for the last game of the day between Maryland and Georgia Tech. Late in the second half of a game that ended up going to overtime, Bobby Dwyer, who had been on Krzyzewski's staff at Army and had followed him to Duke, showed up on press row. I was sitting with Drum when Dwyer grabbed an empty seat—a lot of the North Carolina writers were writing in the press room at that point in the evening—and told Drum and me that he needed our help.

"You guys need to come to our hotel," he said. "You've got to get Mike out of there. Mickie is in the room crying, convinced they're getting fired. No one will even look him in the eye. He's bouncing off the walls. He needs someone from outside the team to get him out of there."

Keith and I both had to write when the game was over—and it went to overtime, so it took a while.

"Are you sure he isn't going to try and sleep?" I asked as we piled into Dwyer's car at about 1 a.m.

"No way," Dwyer said.

It was pouring down rain by then. We drove to Duke's hotel on the outskirts of Atlanta. Krzyzewski, Tom Mickle, and his assistant SID Johnny Moore were waiting in the lobby. We went from there to a nearby Denny's. As soon as we sat down, the waitress brought everyone a glass of water.

Moore picked up his glass and held it up as if to give a toast. "Here's to forgetting tonight," he said.

Krzyzewski picked up his glass. "Here's to *never* f—ing forgetting tonight" was his return toast.

I've written and told that story often in the past because, to me, it defines Krzyzewski. He knew he had failed as a coach that year. He made no excuses for it. He didn't blame it on having to play four freshmen or on his seniors wanting no part of the freshmen. That was *his* fault. Sure, he was mad at Holland, but the fact that his team was lousy wasn't Holland's fault.

"I've always been a believer that anger can be a very good thing if you channel it the right way," he said that day at Georgetown Prep. "I was really angry that night—more at myself than anyone, but also at where we were. I still thought I was a good coach, but I knew I had to do a lot better job than I'd been doing."

That may explain why he instantly shot Dwyer down when he brought up the fact that Tom Sheehey, who had made a verbal commitment to Virginia, might still be open to being recruited by Duke.

"No," Krzyzewski said before the words were out of Dwyer's mouth. "First of all, we don't do that. We'll kick Virginia's ass the right way, not that way. Plus, if we can't win with these kids [the freshmen] and Tommy Amaker [who was an incoming freshman] then we *should* get fired."

When Krzyzewski first arrived at Duke, Drum and I had jokingly started to call him "the captain" as a takeoff on Knight's insistence on being called "the general"—even though Knight had never risen above the rank of private during his brief stint in the Army while he was coaching at West Point. Krzyzewski had left the Army in 1974 as a captain, so Keith and I started calling him captain. To this day, when Krzyzewski calls me on the phone he always starts out by saying, "Fein, it's the captain." (At Duke everyone called me "Fein" since there were about a million guys named John who worked at the *Chronicle* and that's what he heard people call me when he first got there.)

And, almost without fail, that night in the Denny's will come up at some point in almost every season. Krzyzewski and Maryland's Gary Williams are among a very small handful of coaches I consider friends. On the night that each won his first national championship, the first thing said on the court as the nets were coming down was a reference to how long I'd known them and how far they had come to get to that moment.

"Long way from Fort Myer," Gary said in Atlanta in 2002, almost twenty-four years after I first covered his teams at American when they played their games in the tiny Army-base gym at Fort Myer in Arlington, Virginia.

Eleven years earlier, when Krzyzewski won his first national title in Indianapolis, he grabbed my hand when I offered it in congratulations and said, "We've come a long way from Denny's, haven't we?"

Yes, he certainly had. And like Gary, he remembered that I'd been around long before he was a star. Which is why I laughed when Mike's longtime right-hand man, Mike Cragg, was shocked when I told him I'd be riding the bus with the team to Greensboro on the night Krzyzewski would win his 880th game. Cragg has worked with Krzyzewski for twenty-five years, first as Duke's SID and now as his chief fundraiser and non-basketball confidant.

"You're talking to him *by phone* on the bus, right?" Cragg said that afternoon.

"No, I'm talking to him from the next seat on the bus," I said. It had been Krzyzewski's idea: ride the bus, talk during the ride, and finish up in the locker room while he was killing time before the game.

"I don't believe it," Cragg said. "He never lets anyone not connected with the team on the bus. And no one sits next to him *ever* except Mickie."

To me riding the bus was no big deal. I've done it with numerous teams in various sports through the years. Often it is the perfect time to talk to a coach, because there's not much else for him to do during the ride.

"Well, I'm riding the bus," I said, sort of enjoying Cragg's dismay.

"I still don't get it," Cragg said.

"I do," I said. "I was in the f—ing Denny's."

9

V. and Other Characters

I WAS NEVER IN a Denny's with Jim Valvano, but I was frequently in his office at three or four o'clock in the morning.

Like almost every coach I have ever met, he couldn't sleep after games. There would be too much adrenaline pumping to just go home, put up his feet, and go to sleep. A lot of coaches use that time and pent-up energy to watch tape. Valvano didn't watch tape. When NC State played at home in Reynolds Coliseum, he would do all his postgame interviews and then head for his office. Pizza, beer, and wine would be ordered, and Valvano would hold court. His assistant coaches were always there and so were various friends. Often I would show up for games at State, not so much to see the game as to hang out in Valvano's office afterward.

Most nights, Valvano's wife, Pam, would call sometime after midnight to ask when he was coming home. Jim would promise her it would be soon, pick up another slice of pizza, and resume telling stories. Most were hilariously funny. My favorite was the one about the barber. But there were many, many others. Such as the one about the dog:

"First year here we lose twice to Carolina—get blown out in both games," he said. "After the second game, an old State alum in a red jacket comes up to me and he says, 'Now, coach, I know you're a Yankee so you don't really understand yet about our rivalries down here, but we can *not* be losing to the Tar Heels this way.'

"I tell him I really *do* understand and next year, gosh darn it, we are going to do a *lot* better against the Tar Heels. He shakes his head and says, 'No, coach, you really don't get it. You see, if you lose at home to the Tar Heels next year, we're going to have to kill your dog.'

"I look at him. He's not smiling. So I say, 'I get the message, but I do have to tell you I don't *have* a dog.'

"Now he smiles and he says, 'Don't you worry about that.'

"Next morning I go out to get the newspaper. On my stoop is a basket with a blanket on it. I look under the blanket and—you guessed it—the cutest little puppy you've ever seen is in the basket. There's a note tied around his neck. It says, 'Don't get too attached.'"

Valvano told that story in public. He never did tell the Dean/barber story in public. It had a bit of an edge to it, revealing that there were times that he chafed just as Krzyzewski and other ACC coaches did over Dean's godlike status. This frustration was best summed up once by Lefty Driesell after his Maryland team had won a truly dreadful game, 40–36, over Krzyzewski's second Duke team. Lefty had opted to hold the ball—there was no shot clock—during most of the second half, and his players had reacted angrily to that decision.

"We should have killed that team," said Adrian Branch, who was a freshman at the time. "No way should we have held the ball against them. We kept the game close." Many of his teammates expressed similar sentiments. I, of course, quoted them in the next day's newspaper. A couple of days later at practice someone asked Lefty about his players' comments.

"Where'd you see that?" Lefty asked. (I wasn't at practice that day because I was still in North Carolina working, naturally, on a Dean Smith story. Michael Wilbon was there and he was the one who asked the first question and later told me the story.)

"It was in John Feinstein's story."

"Fahnsteen, Fahnsteen, I'm sick of that name, Fahnsteen," Lefty said. "All them years, Dean comes into Cole Field House, holds the ball, holds the ball, holds the ball. Evabody says, 'Dean's great, Dean's a genius, Dean's *God!*' Aah hold the ball *one* game, evabody says, 'Lefty's a dog!'"

He was, of course, right. Dean *was* a great coach and, especially in North Carolina, people *did* think he was God. Which leads back to a Krzyzewski recruiting story. He was making a home visit during his first season to a kid named Mark Acres, a 6'11" Californian who was good enough to later play in the NBA.

"It was one of those visits where, as a coach, you know almost right away it isn't working," Krzyzewski said. "It's something in your gut. You know you aren't getting the kid. But you still have to go through the ritual, make the pitch, tell him everything, and see if by some chance you strike a chord. The entire evening his mom never said a word. So finally I turned to her and said, 'Mrs. Acres, is there anything at all you'd like to know about Duke? About our program? About how Mark might fit in with us?'

"She shook her head and said, 'No, I don't need to ask any questions. The only thing that's important is that Mark go to college someplace where he can be close to God.'"

At that point Krzyzewski figured he had nothing to lose. "Well, you know, if Mark comes to Duke, God will be coaching ten miles down the road in Chapel Hill, so you might want to give us some serious thought."

Acres went to Oral Roberts.

A lot of Valvano's stories weren't repeatable in a public forum. One he *did* tell in public was about the year the NCAA changed recruiting rules and took coaches off the road for the entire month of August. "I came home and announced to my wife, 'I'm going to be home for the entire month of August.' She said, 'Great! I want to have sex twenty-five times,' I looked at her and said, 'Put me down for two.'"

The stories always stretched well into the night. Eventually people began to trickle out. The pizza was gone, the wine and beer mostly gone. I would linger. The best times with Valvano always came after he stopped performing. Sooner or later—usually later—it would be just him and me and he would turn serious. He would lie down on his office couch and talk about how confused he was about his life.

"All I ever wanted to do was cut the nets down, win a national championship," he would say. "When I did clinics at summer camps, at the end I would make the kids pick me up on their shoulders so I could cut down the nets. Then I won the national championship when I was thirty-seven years old. All of a sudden I had *done* coaching. Maybe I could win it again, but it would *never* feel the way it felt that first time. It couldn't.

"So now I'm looking for the next thing. What do I want to be when I grow up? Do I want to be Dean Smith? No. Do I want to be on TV? I'm good at it, but is there that much to it? I mean really— do I want to spend my life breaking down defenses and talking about how great every coach in the world is? I don't think so. Do I want to get paid to be funny? I already get paid to be funny when I speak. I mean sometimes I wonder what the hell is real in my life—besides my family.

"Is there anything real about coaching? Selling yourself to kids, glad-handing alumni, talking to the media? What's real about it? I'll tell you what's real: the forty minutes during a game. That's real. You win, you lose. There's no talking your way out of an *L*. An *L* is an *L* and a *W* is a *W*. Period. Doesn't matter what the refs did or didn't do or anything else."

He worried because he knew he wasn't spending enough time with his three daughters. He was always running—giving speeches, trying to host a variety show in Los Angeles, hosting an awful sports bloopers show, doing the CBS *Morning* show in New York on Mondays, starting a company that sold blue jeans. He flirted with the

NBA and took the job as athletic director at State because he was bored just coaching.

He took risks on players he probably shouldn't have taken. He kept winning—reaching the Elite Eight in 1985 and 1986 after the national championship in 1983—but spent less and less time making sure his players were going to class and staying out of trouble. In 1986 he walked into the sparkling new Dean E. Smith Center (aka the Dean Dome) in Chapel Hill and looked up in awe at all the banners hanging from the rafters.

There were national championship banners (1957 and 1982) and there were banners for Final Fours and for making the NCAA Tournament. There were banners for ACC championships—tournament and regular season—and NIT championship banners, plus banners for *playing* in the NIT. There were also banners for players' numbers that hadn't necessarily been retired but were "honored." There were even banners for years when Carolina had *tied* for an ACC regular season championship. Those banners said "ACC Champions" in bold letters across the top. At the bottom, in much smaller letters, they said "tie."

"Look at all those banners," Valvano said. "You know what I'm going to do? I'm going to get a banner for the last two seasons that says, 'National Champions.' Then at the bottom I'll just put 'almost.'"

In 1987, after finishing sixth in the ACC in the regular season, NC State beat Duke, Wake Forest (in double overtime), and Carolina, which had been 14–0 in conference play, to win the ACC Tournament. A year later, the Wolfpack finished second in the conference, although it was upset in the first round of the NCAA Tournament by Murray State.

Valvano was still riding high during those years, still looking for the Next Thing but making a lot of money during the search. Then came the book—or, more specifically, the book jacket. In January of 1989 a story broke that a forthcoming book on State and Valvano would, according to the jacket, reveal all sorts of improprieties within the program and paint a picture of a program running amok. *Sports Illustrated* had the manuscript and was preparing to publish an excerpt.

The source for most of the information in the book was a former State manager. As soon as I heard about the book, I knew it was tainted. The reason? I had received a call about a year earlier from someone who said he had a close friend who had "serious dirt" on Jim Valvano and NC State. To be completely honest, I wasn't happy to get the phone call. I liked Jim Valvano—a lot. He'd been good to me. The last thing I would want to do was write a story that would bring grief to him.

But as a reporter I had to hear the guy out and find out if he, or his friend and his so-called "dirt," were credible. If I didn't do that, I wouldn't be doing my job. So I started asking questions. What I got was that the guy's friend had been a manager at State. He knew all the players and had information detailing multiple rules violations that had taken place. I sighed and told the guy I would have to meet his friend in person.

"Before you do that," the guy said, "we have to agree on payment."

"Payment?"

"He wants to be paid for this information. He's handing you a gold mine."

I had no idea what the guy was handing me, but I knew neither I nor the *Post* was going to be handing him any money. I know that checkbook journalism is practiced in the tabloid world all the time and that TV and radio stations pay athletes and coaches and managers to appear on their air all the time. But if you are trying to write the truth and be fair—a practice I know many people believe doesn't exist—you can't pay sources. If you pay a source it can easily lead them to stretch the truth or flat out make things up to keep the money coming. I know there have been important stories broken through checkbook journalism, but the places where I've worked simply don't practice it. Plus, it is a Pandora's box. You pay one source, others will (correctly) demand they be paid too. People have an absolute right to not tell their stories or be sources of information. But if they choose to be sources or to tell their stories, you have to do everything you can to be sure the information is given voluntarily and with as little axe to grind as possible.

I've only been asked directly for money on one other occasion. That was when I was working on my first baseball book and asked Barry Bonds, then in his final year in Pittsburgh, if we could talk at some point during the 1992 season.

"You paying?" he asked.

"No," I said.

"Well, if you're not paying, I'm not talking. And if you put my name in the book, I'll sue you."

I wasn't surprised that Bonds was saying no or that he was being a jerk about it. The only other person who had turned me down that year was Danny Jackson, who was pitching for the Cubs. When I asked Jackson during spring training if we might talk at some point during the season, he shook his head and said, "I don't talk to people for books."

"Really?" I said. "How many times have you been *asked* to talk to people for books?"

I probably should have just let the Bonds thing go and walked away, but I couldn't resist asking Barry one more question.

"So when you just did that interview outside with ESPN [we were standing in front of his locker], did they pay you for it?"

"No. But that's different. They aren't being paid to write a book."

"You're right. They're being paid to interview you on television."

Bonds muttered a profanity and walked away. When I told Jim Leyland, who was then the Pirates manager, the story, he shrugged. "You might ask him the same thing tomorrow and he could give you an hour," he said. "That's just Barry."

I never did test that theory.

That day on the phone, I told the guy that under no circumstances would his friend get paid for information. "Then we'll go someplace else," he said. "You'll be sorry."

When I read the book I *was* sorry—it seemed that someone had actually paid the guy. Peter Golenbock, the author, has written many very good books in a long, distinguished career. This wasn't one of them. There were so many simple factual errors—including his saying that Thanksgiving fell on a Friday, just to give you one example—that the book had little credibility. Plus, I'm convinced Golenbock or his publisher paid for the bulk of the information.

Tainted or not, the book brought Valvano down at NC State. The NCAA came to town to investigate the program, and the local newspapers ran wild with the story. It was a confusing story for me to deal with: on the one hand, it was pretty clear that Jim, in his search for the Next Thing, had stopped paying enough attention to his program. He'd given the assistant coaches too much responsibility and taken far too many marginal kids who had, in many cases, gotten themselves into trouble. The NCAA did find State guilty of enough violations that it was banned from postseason play in 1990, but didn't find it guilty of the most serious charges made in the book.

Still, it was enough to force Valvano to resign at NC State after the 1990 season. It was a sad ending to what had started out as one of the more joyous runs in coaching history.

The fall of Valvano was difficult for me because I felt caught in the middle. I didn't want to come across as a Valvano apologist, acting as if nothing at all had gone wrong in his program. I knew, from being around, that he *had* lost interest at times and had been distracted by the hundred different things he was doing while looking for the Next Thing. But I also considered him a friend, one of the smartest people I knew, and someone whom I had given advice to at times and, at least as often, taken advice from.

Valvano's reaction when I told him I was going to do *Season on the Brink* was to the point: "Don't tell me the guy has a good side.

He's an arrogant bully. You want to know why we hear so much about his good deeds? Because he makes sure we hear about them. He's got his handful of media guys—like you—who make sure every time he walks a little old lady across the street the world knows about it. That way, the next day, when he runs another little old lady over because he's mad that practice went badly, it's okay because he helped the other one out. A lot of coaches visit sick kids in hospitals, you know. We just don't bring camera crews with us when we do."

When Knight turned on me after the book was published, Valvano never said, "I told you so." In fact, he read the book and liked it, even though overall he thought it was too kind to Knight. "You showed guys like me that there *is* another side to him," he said. "I still don't like him, but I understand him a little better now."

Every year, the National Sportscasters and Sportswriters Association gives out awards—two national awards and then local awards across the country. I won the local award while at the *Post* several times, but unless I missed it, I don't think I've ever been nominated for the national award. For a long time, Frank Deford—deservedly—won the national award every year. In the spring of 1987 I was on vacation when I got a late night phone call from Valvano, who had been at the ceremony because he had received an award for cooperating with the media—or something like that.

"I thought you should know what Deford just said in his acceptance speech," Jim said. "He said he was honored to win the award but that it should go to the person who made the most impact on sportswriting in a given year and that there was no question that *Season on the Brink* made more impact than anything else last year. I know you're a big fan of his, so I thought you'd want to know."

I did want to know. I was thrilled that Deford would say that about me.

"Oh, one other thing," Jim added. "Knight's still an asshole."

As usual I was laughing at the end of a conversation with Valvano. The point of the story is this: Valvano went to a pay phone in an airport on his way to a flight to make that call. No one else ever called to tell me what Deford had said.

So there I was in 1990 caught in this conundrum. I tried to be fair — to both sides — and probably got it wrong. Jim had gotten defensive near the end. He thought a lot of the media in North Carolina, particularly on the news side, was out to get him, a theory shared by Mike Krzyzewski.

"Remember a lot of those guys, especially the news guys and editorial guys, were Carolina guys," Krzyzewski said twenty years after it had all come down. "The sports guys at least knew Jimmy, knew me, were in a position to judge us as people, not just as a Duke guy or a State guy. The news people saw Jimmy as a threat to Dean and Carolina. This was their chance to take him down — and they did."

In his last press conference after State lost in the ACC Tournament that year, Jim sounded almost Nixonian to me. Instead of saying, yes, he'd made mistakes, he kept citing statistics to prove all was well inside his program. When I said and wrote that, Jim was genuinely angry.

"How can you possibly compare me to Richard Nixon?" he said. "You know me better than that."

"How can you stand up there and say you didn't do anything wrong? How many times did we talk in your office at three in the morning about looking for the Next Thing? About how you wished you could still be as driven as Dean and Krzyzewski?"

We argued at length. He was angry and, according to Jim, so was his wife, Pam, who felt I had betrayed their friendship. I understood. One of the tough things about journalism is that when you do it for a long time, no matter how much you try to stay at arm's length, there are always going to be people you like and people you dislike. Some will become your friends, because we're all human.

I taught a journalism class at Duke for three years. The first question I asked on the first day of the semester was always the same: What is objective journalism? After the students gave their answers I'd tell them they were all wrong; there's no such thing. None of us is objective. We all have biases that we grew up with or that develop through the years. The key is understanding that you're biased and trying as hard as you can to put those biases aside and be fair.

Looking back, I think I may have tried too hard to put aside my bias—and my friendship—with Valvano. If it all happened again now, I'd probably say something like, "Look, I've known Jim Valvano for years. He's a friend. I have a bias in this. I think he may have made mistakes in his job like we all do, but I also think there are people out to get him. And the kid who started all this was looking to make a buck."

Back then I said a lot of that, but called him Nixonian.

Jim went to work for ESPN and ABC after leaving NC State. He was great at it—as you might expect—but I knew, even though we didn't have our post-midnight chats anymore, that he was still searching. I missed listening to him talk. What I heard on TV was smart and clever, but it was TV talk.

In the summer of 1992 I was sitting at my computer with *SportsCenter* on in the background. I was getting ready to go downstairs and start the grill to make dinner. Bob Ley was anchoring that night and, as he was about to close the show, I saw a picture of Valvano pop onto the screen. I moved my hand away from the off button.

I don't remember his exact words, but paraphrasing, this is what he said: "There is no way to deliver this news except to do it directly—the way Jim Valvano would want us to do it. Jim has been diagnosed with cancer."

In 1992 cancer was no longer an automatic death sentence, but it was still, as it is today, a very frightening word to hear. I honestly don't remember who I called, but it didn't take very long to find out that it was serious. Valvano was being treated at Duke Hospital, and no one I talked to ever said, "They caught it early; they think he'll be okay."

In fact, Valvano's description of how he learned he had cancer was chilling. He had been experiencing serious back pain and went in for tests. The doctor showed him a scan of his back.

"It's all black," Valvano said to the doctor.

"That's right," the doctor answered. "The black is where the cancer is."

It had spread throughout his entire back.

As it turned out, Valvano had nine months to live. Tragically, it was *then* and only then that he found the Next Thing. Cancer was the Next Thing. Valvano knew as soon as he saw the pictures of his back that he was going to die. He knew research and research dollars wouldn't save his life. But they could save other lives. That's where the idea for what became the V Foundation came from. He enlisted the support of ESPN, which he knew had the money and the power to aid the cause, and of his friends—most of them coaches—starting with Mike Krzyzewski.

Since his death a lot of myths have grown around Valvano. One is that he was close friends with Dick Vitale. He wasn't. They were colleagues, and Vitale was genuinely torn apart by Valvano's death and has worked night and day since his death to raise money for the V Foundation. But they were never close.

The other myth is that Krzyzewski and Valvano were longtime friends. They weren't. "Until Jimmy stopped coaching we were more rivals than we were friends," Krzyzewski said. "Remember, we coached against each other in New York [Iona and Army played every year] and then when we came to the ACC at the same time. We socialized with our wives at ACC meetings on occasion, but not very often. I think we respected each other as coaches, but it didn't go any further than that until he left NC State."

Once they were no longer rivals in recruiting or on the court, Krzyzewski and Valvano did become friends. Krzyzewski believed Valvano had been railroaded out of State, and Valvano appreciated the support. But they only became close after Valvano got sick. He was going to Duke Hospital on a regular basis for treatment, and whenever he went, he called Krzyzewski, who would walk from his office on one end of the Duke campus to the hospital at the other end to spend time with him. As the stays became longer and more frequent, so did the time the two men spent together.

"It got to the point where we could talk about anything, we could say anything to one another," Krzyzewski said. "We almost never talked about basketball, but we talked about everything else there was to talk about. Jimmy was very smart and very honest. We talked to each other in ways that you can't talk to your parents or your wife or even your brother. It became something remarkable in my life and, I'd like to think, in his."

When Valvano was honored at the first ESPY Awards in March of 1993, Mike and Mickie Krzyzewski flew to New York with Jim and Pam Valvano. "Jim was in the bathroom sick the whole flight," Krzyzewski said. "By that point he could barely walk. I was convinced there was no way he was going to be able to make it through his speech that night."

Of course Valvano did make it through—memorably. He talked that night for eleven minutes and fifteen seconds. He talked about Krzyzewski: "What you need to know is that he is ten times a better person than he is a coach—and we all know how great a coach he is." He talked about the three things his parents had urged him to do every day of life: laugh, think, and cry. He talked about the need for more funding for cancer research and about what it felt like to be dying and, in a moment that still gives you chills even if you've seen it a hundred times, said, "Cancer cannot rob me of my mind, it cannot rob me of my heart, it cannot rob me of my soul. Those three things will live on forever."

When some fool in the production truck actually turned on the blinking light to let Valvano know his time was up, Valvano pointed at the blinking light and said, "Can you believe this? I've got tumors running through my entire body and someone is trying to give me the blinking light to get off?" He then saluted the light with an eloquent Italian profanity and gesture. Everyone watching was laughing and crying at that moment.

As soon as Valvano finished, everyone in the audience leaped to his or her feet—one person, Krzyzewski, jumping onstage to help Valvano down. "He had told me he knew the speech would exhaust him so much he wouldn't be able to get down the steps on his own. He said, 'When I finish, come get me because I don't want to fall on my face.'"

I watched that moment with tears in my eyes because it was apparent Jim was very near the end. Three days later, Jim and I talked for what would be the last time. After his resignation at NC State, I had written a column saying, as I have often said, that when coaches take credit for success, they have to take the blame for failures.

A year before the ESPYs speech, in February of 1992, we were both working at a game in St. Petersburg, in the building now known as Tropicana Field. Jim was doing TV. I was doing radio. We hadn't seen each other in a while. Jim had suggested we walk back under the stands. This was about ninety minutes before tipoff. No one was around.

He was angry. He couldn't understand how I could—his word—attack him the way I had. I was his friend. Plus, I knew that a lot of the book was inaccurate, so he wanted to know how I could lend it credence the way I had.

I reminded him that I had pointed out how inaccurate the book was on more than one occasion. I also told him that he knew there were a lot of things we had talked about in private through the years that I had never written or repeated and never would write or repeat. That wasn't good enough. He had *needed* me there, and I hadn't been there.

"Jim, do you really think if I had come out and said you were blameless in the whole thing it would have made any difference?" I said. "People would have just said I was one of your apologists. The things I *did* write in your defense would have been meaningless."

"It would have made a difference," Valvano said, "to *me*."

Ouch.

Even though I still believed I had done what I had to do, I felt terrible. I had that sick feeling you get in the pit of your stomach when, deep down, you know the other guy is right. Valvano clearly felt betrayed. We shook hands. I wondered if we'd ever talk to each other again.

We did. We saw each other at games after that and Jim was always cordial. But it wasn't the same. Then came the news of his illness. I wrote him and told him how horrible I felt hearing the news and how no matter what had happened between us I would always consider him a friend. He wrote back saying that meant a lot and he felt the same way.

I've written before about the last time I saw him. It was in Chapel Hill, the final Sunday of the 1993 regular season. Jim was doing Duke-Carolina for ABC. By then people knew how sick he was, and the security around the TV-announce location at midcourt was almost presidential. I was walking to my seat, hoping to at least be able to wave hello to Jim as I went by. He spotted me and waved me toward him.

"John, come over here for a second," he said. "I need to talk to you."

I took about one step in Jim's direction and was shoved backward by a security guard. I've had bad experiences with security guards around the world, but never more so than in Chapel Hill. Once, when I walked over before a game to say hello to Dean Smith, one of them started pushing me away until Dean saw what was going on and waved the guard off. Rather than just let me go as he had been instructed to do, the guard—who had to be a hundred—said, "You're lucky Coach Smith was here."

To which I replied—always calm when confronted—"You're lucky I didn't knock you into the fifth row."

Like I said, security guards and I have never done terribly well together. Tony Kornheiser has suggested for years that I write a book strictly on my run-ins with security people. "*That* book I'll read," he likes to say.

Now, as the guard and I started to square off, I heard Jim say, "Hey, do me a favor, pal, and leave my friend alone."

Unlike the guy with Dean, this one simply stepped aside. Valvano waved me to an empty seat next to him, the one where I knew the floor director would be sitting once the telecast began. Brent Musburger, who was doing play-by-play, was on a headset talking, I presume, to the truck.

"I was hoping you'd be here," Jim said. "I don't know when I'll get to see you again."

"How are you feeling?" I asked.

He laughed. "Look at me. How do you think I feel?"

He was hauntingly thin, and when I looked into his eyes they had none of the spark I had always seen.

"I owe you an apology," he said.

"No, you don't."

"Yes, I do. I was mad at you because I wanted you to be my apologist and that's never been who you are. In fact, what you did was really an act of friendship. You wouldn't let me off the hook. I could have used more of that."

He had his hand on my arm as he spoke. I remember thinking I wasn't going to see him again. I was trying to think of something to say, but nothing brilliant was coming into my mind. I wished we could be back in his office at three o'clock in the morning so he could explain to me again why perestroika was a work of genius or why he loved listening to Red Barber call Yankee games when he was a teenager.

"It means a lot to me that you would say that," I finally said.

"I'm glad I got the chance."

I hugged him and could feel just how frail he was. He must have seen something in my eyes because he said, "Pretty scary, isn't it?"

"There are about a zillion people pulling for you."

"I know," he said.

I gave his shoulder a final gentle squeeze and stood up just as the floor director arrived.

That was the last time I saw Jim alive. He died on April 28 in Duke Hospital—eight weeks after the ESPYs speech. His family was there and so was Mike Krzyzewski. I was teaching at Duke at the time, and I heard the news on the radio while driving into campus. I went straight to the basketball office. When I arrived, Krzyzewski was there.

"It's good for Jim that it's over, believe me," he said, his eyes dry and clear but red. "No one will ever know what he went through to give that speech in New York."

A little less than two years after Valvano died, Krzyzewski found himself in Duke Hospital, the place where Valvano had been treated and had died. Krzyzewski had had back surgery in the summer of 1994 and had tried to come back too soon. On the morning of a road trip to Georgia Tech, Mickie Krzyzewski looked at her husband, who was pale and weak and barely able to stand up to get out of his chair at the kitchen table, and said quietly, "If you get on the plane today and don't go to the hospital right now and find out what's wrong, I'm leaving you."

Krzyzewski knew she was serious. He skipped the plane trip and went to the hospital, where the doctors ran tests to find out what was wrong.

"I was convinced I had cancer," he said. "All I could think about was Jimmy. There was just too much that was the same: He had back problems, I had back problems. He was forty-six when he was diagnosed, I was forty-six. He had three daughters, I had three daughters. I knew it was cancer. I was convinced I was going to die too."

It wasn't cancer. Krzyzewski had simply pushed himself too hard too soon, believing the old Army mantra of mind over matter. Tell yourself your body can do something and it will do it. Only his body was in complete collapse. He was exhausted, burned out—pick your phrase. The doctors told him he shouldn't coach again that season, which made him feel as if he had failed his team.

"In the Army, if the leader has to leave his unit, he's failed," he said. "I had left my unit. I had failed it."

He went to athletic director Tom Butters and offered to resign. Butters told him he wasn't resigning—he was going to return when he was healthy and take his program back to the top. Which is what he did.

Almost eighteen years after Valvano's death, after the V Foundation has raised more than $70 million for cancer research, Krzyzewski's voice still gets very soft when he talks about Valvano.

"People always talked about how he let his program at NC State go after the national championship," he said. "Let me tell you something. The program he built with the V Foundation was as great a job of coaching as anyone has ever done. Look at the legacy he left behind."

Part of that legacy is the work Krzyzewski has done to help raise that money. To Krzyzewski, doing that sort of thing isn't heroic in any way. "To those who much is given, much is expected," he says, referencing the Bible (Luke 12:48). "I've been given a lot."

WORKING ON *A SEASON INSIDE,* surrounded by those guys, was a very different experience than working on *A Season on the Brink.* Day to day it was a lot more fun, if not quite as mesmerizing.

Every week I would sit down with the college basketball schedule and decide where to go. I had put together my "list" of major characters before the season, so a lot of what I did was built around them.

But if a game or a player popped up who intrigued me, I just got on a plane and went to see them.

The way that season went may have been best defined by a trip I made in late January. On a Wednesday morning, I flew to Knoxville to have lunch with Tennessee coach Don DeVoe. DeVoe, a very good coach and very good guy, was fighting to keep his job that season. About once a month I'd fly to Knoxville on a game day, meet DeVoe for lunch at a place that had spectacular banana pudding, and then stick around for the game that night.

On this trip I was supposed to go from Knoxville to Tulsa and then to Tucson and back to Pittsburgh. I was going to interview Oral Roberts—yes, *the* Oral Roberts—in Tulsa and then go to Tucson to see Steve Kerr, who to this day is one of the most remarkable people I've ever encountered, before flying on a Sunday night red-eye to see Paul Evans, then the coach at Pittsburgh, on Monday before his team played Providence that night.

On Thursday morning I flew from Knoxville to Memphis, en route to Tulsa. From the airport, I called Dave Pritchett, who was an assistant coach at Oral Roberts University. I wanted to make certain I was still all set to talk to Mr. Roberts.

"We've got a problem," Pritchett said.

I had first known Pritchett when he was Lefty Driesell's top assistant at Maryland. He was as Runyonesque a character as there was in college basketball, famous for his recruiting escapades. Dave swears he had one day on the recruiting road during which he rented five cars. Whenever he got to the airport to leave on a trip, he routinely parked his car at the curb right in front of the terminal.

"I always knew where they would tow it to," he said. "It was cheaper than paying for parking and saved me a lot of time when I was running to get my flight."

Dave had some health problems that forced him out of coaching for a while in the early '80s, but he never stopped recruiting. Once, he and I and Ken Denlinger took one of those hotel vans to an airport. Dave got out of the van and gave the driver a twenty-dollar bill.

"I think the tip is included in the fee," Denlinger told Pritchett.

"Doesn't matter," Dave answered. "You always give a guy a big bill. You never know when a recruit might be watching."

Dave had gotten back into coaching when Ken Trickey had hired him at Oral Roberts. The school built by and named for the TV evangelist played pretty good basketball. Trickey and Pritchett both told me that Roberts was a big fan who often came into the locker room and gave pregame pep talks.

"There was one about Ulysses S. Grant talking to his men before a big battle," Pritchett said. "According to Oral [Pritchett always called everyone he ever met by his first name *or* by a nickname: Dean Smith was "The Music Man" because he was too good for words] Grant told his men they were outnumbered, they had to begin the battle in the dark, and the Confederates were lying in wait for them. He told them all that and then he said, 'And so I have but one word for you: *attack, attack, attack!*' Oral gave this whole speech and he's screaming 'attack' and all our guys are looking at each other saying, 'Who is this Grant guy?'"

I had asked Trickey and Pritchett if Roberts would talk to me about hoops. Absolutely, I was told. So I was en route when I called Pritchett that morning.

"What's the problem?" I asked.

"Oral's gone up into the tower."

"He's done *what?*"

"There's this giant tower on campus and Oral's gone up there, and he says if we don't raise ten million dollars God is going to take him home from there."

"So I guess he isn't going to be talking to me today at lunchtime."

"I'm really sorry."

I had never had an interview canceled before because someone had gone up in a tower to raise ten million dollars or have God take him home. It was, if nothing else, a unique excuse. I hung up the phone and wondered what to do next. There was no point in going to Tulsa. I was supposed to fly from there the next day to spend time with Kerr that night. I was staying in Tucson through Sunday to see Arizona play UCLA.

I called Keith Drum and told him what had happened.

"Well, I'm about to fly to El Paso to see UTEP play Brigham Young," he said. "Why don't you fly there and then go to Tucson out of there tomorrow?"

Brigham Young was undefeated. Texas–El Paso was the school that had won the most important game in college basketball history in 1966 when it was Texas Western. Don Haskins, the coach then, was still the coach. Why not? I managed to change my flights—it was a lot easier back then—to fly from Memphis to Dallas and on to El Paso. I called the SID at UTEP, who said he'd be glad to get me in that night.

It was a great game. BYU was led by Michael Smith and UTEP by Tim Hardaway. BYU won late. I learned that Haskins always wore a clip-on tie so he could take it off as soon as the game started. BYU was fun to watch and Michael Smith was one of those guys you liked right away. BYU was going to New Mexico to play Saturday in the famed Pit—the building where Valvano had won his national championship in 1983.

I decided to change my plans again. Instead of hanging out in Tucson on Saturday, I'd catch a plane to Albuquerque in the morning, see BYU play New Mexico in the afternoon, and then fly back. I'd still have plenty of time with Kerr on Friday night, Saturday at breakfast, and Sunday after the game before I caught my red-eye flight to Pittsburgh.

It all worked perfectly. BYU won another great game in the Pit, and I flew to Pittsburgh after Arizona-UCLA on Sunday, arriving at seven in the morning. I slept for several hours and then saw Pitt's Jerome Lane shatter a backboard during the game that night. In six days I had seen five games in five cities and had been on nine airplane flights. Those really *were* the days.

THERE WAS NO ONE I enjoyed more during that season than Steve Kerr. As has often happened in my career, I blundered into him. Actually I blundered into him as the result of blundering into another story.

During the 1984 Olympics in Los Angeles, I had picked up a daily update while riding from the gymnastics venue back to the main press center one morning and had spotted a small item that said, "Blatnick wrestles for gold tonight."

It meant nothing to me, but I read the item. It said that Jeff Blatnick, a Greco-Roman wrestler in the superheavyweight class, would wrestle that night for the gold medal, having come back from a bout with cancer, specifically non-Hodgkin's lymphoma. He'd had his spleen and his appendix removed as part of his treatment.

I knew nothing about Greco-Roman wrestling. But I knew coming back from non-Hodgkin's lymphoma to wrestle for an Olympic gold medal was probably a pretty good story.

I was en route back to the media center to get something to eat before heading out to boxing when I read the item. As soon as I got there, I found George Solomon and told him I wanted to go to Anaheim (the wrestling venue) that night because there might be a story in Blatnick.

"You're off tonight," George said. "You need a break. The story's a four-inch bleeder at best. Go get a good dinner."

George was never into what he called "tearjerkers" or "bleeders." But jeez, it was the Olympics, which, when you get down to it, is *always* about tearjerkers. I told George I was going to go. Maybe I'd get a decent second-day feature out of it. Fine, George said, you're on your own. I'm not promising you any space. It was the Olympics.

I would have plenty of time to go out to dinner when the Games were over.

After I'd finished my boxing story, I got on a bus headed for Anaheim. The first two things I noticed were that I knew no one on the bus and that no one was speaking English. Greco-Roman wrestling was popular in Europe, completely unheard of and unthought about in the United States.

Somehow the bus driver got lost—took the wrong exit off I-5 and ended up driving in circles through Anaheim. We were, I can promise you, a long way from Disneyland and from the old Anaheim Arena, where the wrestling was being held. Great, I thought, I'm going to end up riding this bus for three hours and not even get to see Blatnick wrestle. Finally, one of the writers who had been to the arena before figured out where we needed to go and we arrived minutes before the evening program was to start. Blatnick, in the superheavyweight category, was wrestling last. I had plenty of time.

Before Blatnick wrestled, I realized those on my bus had been a harbinger in terms of the media contingent. There was only one other writer representing a U.S. paper in the building, someone from the *Los Angeles Times,* which had at least one staffer at every venue. Because of that, Butch Henry, who was in charge of the media for the wrestling venue, greeted me as if I were a long-lost brother. Butch was then the sports information director at Arizona and, like a lot of college SIDs, was working as a volunteer for the U.S. Olympic Committee. He had been assigned to Anaheim and was basically losing his mind since almost no American media outlet, other than the *Times,* had any interest in his sport.

"I was hoping the Blatnick story would get some people's attention," Butch said.

"It did," I said. "From me."

"He's a great guy," Butch said. "You should meet his parents too. I'll make sure you get to all of them afterward."

That would be helpful. Generally speaking, getting to any athlete one on one at the Olympics was close to impossible. The biggest stars were brought to an interview room and others were asked to voluntarily go to what is called a "mixed zone," where the athletes stand on one side of a railing and the media stands on the other, somewhat liked caged animals. It's demeaning and rarely helpful, since it usually ends up with shouted questions, like when reporters yell at the president as he waves, shakes his head, and gets into a limousine.

I called George to check in. "If the guy wins you might get ten inches," he said. "But don't count on it."

I wasn't counting on anything. I just wanted Blatnick to win, give me some wonderful quotes and anecdotes, and let me write a second day story that — based on what I'd already seen in the arena — no one else would have. The problem, at least according to Butch, was that he wasn't likely to win. The wrestling competition had been watered down in a lot of weight classes because of the Soviet/Eastern Bloc boycott, but the best superheavyweight in the world, Sweden's Thomas Johansson, was there and was Blatnick's opponent in the final. He outweighed him by thirty pounds — 270 to 240 — which is a big deal in Greco-Roman wrestling.

Somehow, Blatnick won. He took Johansson down in the second period and then hung on for dear life in the third. Unbeknownst to me, ABC decided to switch over to the match at the start of the third period. The announcers quickly explained Blatnick's story and, at 10:30 on the East Coast, the entire country suddenly knew who Jeff Blatnick was and what he was trying to do.

When the match ended, with the crowd going crazy, ABC interviewed Blatnick. With tears running down his face, Blatnick delivered the line that became his signature: "I'm a happy dude." Remember, this was 1984, before anyone really said *dude*. Blatnick cried again during the playing of the anthem at the end of the medal ceremony. As soon as it was over, Butch came over and said quietly, "Follow me. Don't say anything, just walk right behind me."

He led me to a hallway that was marked restricted, nodding at the security guard as if they were old friends. We walked the length of the hallway to an area marked, "Drug-testing. Competitors and officials only."

Standing there were Blatnick's parents. Jeff was inside doing his mandatory postmatch drug test. Butch introduced me as if I were Bob Woodward, Edward R. Murrow, and Ernest Hemingway rolled into one. Both had been crying and both were eager to talk. It turned out they had not only dealt with Jeff's cancer but had lost their younger son, Mike, in a car accident. I wrote as fast as I possibly could while they talked.

After several minutes, Jeff came out of the drug-testing room. He still had the medal looped around his neck. He didn't say a word, just walked over and enveloped his parents in hugs. Then he took his medal off and put it around his mother's neck. "This is for you," he said. "And for Mike."

I still get chills thinking about that moment. Butch had walked away so Jeff's parents introduced me. Jeff could not have been friendlier. The only reason we didn't talk longer was because it occurred to me that it was after eleven o'clock in the East and the deadline for the paper's main edition—home delivery—was midnight. I thanked the Blatnicks, got a number for Jeff in the athletes' village in case I needed it, and raced back to press row to call George. I was prepared to launch into a speech pleading for more space when he answered.

"Where the hell have you been?" he said.

"Talking to Blatnick and his parents," I said.

"Good. Start writing."

"I am but I really need more space…"

"Write as much as you want. Just write fast."

"What?"

"They switched to it on TV. Everyone saw it. [Len] Downie saw it. They want it for A-1."

"A-1?"

"Yes. Now stop saying I told you so and write."

I wrote. And wrote. My lead was direct: "America cried with Jeff Blatnick last night."

Then I let the story tell itself. It ran at the top of A-1 with a huge picture of Blatnick on his knees after the clock had hit zero with tears running down his face.

All of which was great. What was greater was reading the *Los Angeles Times* lead the next morning: "Americans earned three more wrestling medals last night in Anaheim, including a gold from super-heavyweight Jeff Blatnick."

Oh my God! The only lead I can think of that missed the point by a wider margin than that one was an AP lead on a soccer game in South America that read (I'm making up names here): "Jose Olivero scored on a header in the fifty-seventh minute last night to give Alamos a 1–0 victory over Laredo in a game marred by the pregame deaths of twenty-two people during a riot outside the stadium."

That one was a lot worse. But this was pretty bad.

The next day Blatnick was brought to the media center and was interviewed en masse. He had officially become a star. But I had gotten him one on one and already written the story, thanks to Butch Henry.

Four months later, I encountered Butch again. I was in Albuquerque to cover a Georgetown–New Mexico game. Georgetown was the defending national champion and George sent me to New Mexico on my way to Hawaii to cover Maryland in the annual Rainbow Classic. I couldn't complain about the assignment, even if John Thompson and I weren't exactly on speaking terms at that moment. This was the season after my infamous "Hoya Paranoia" story.

I got to Albuquerque on Friday. Because the Georgetown game had been a late add-on to New Mexico's schedule (I still don't know why Thompson wanted to play out there, but knowing him it was probably an easy way to spend a couple of days in Las Vegas, a place he loves more than life itself), the Lobos were actually playing Arizona on Friday and then Georgetown on Saturday.

With nothing else to do, I went to see Arizona–New Mexico on Friday night. Naturally, Butch was there with Arizona, which was in the early throes of rebuilding under new coach Lute Olson. We talked about Blatnick, and I thanked him again for making me a hero for a night at the *Post*. Butch laughed and said, "You know, there's a kid on our team who may be a more amazing story than Blatnick."

I found that hard to believe.

"His name's Steve Kerr," Butch said. "He's a sophomore, our sixth man right now. Lute took him at the last possible second two summers ago. He'd had no scholarship offers at all, and we had one open scholarship."

Okay, that was a nice story, but hardly in Blatnick's class.

"The thing is, his father was president of the American University in Beirut. Steve actually spent a lot of his boyhood in the Middle East. Last January, his dad was assassinated."

Now Butch had my attention. "Assassinated?"

He nodded. "Two days after Steve's dad was killed we played Arizona State. There was a moment of silence before the game. Steve played because his mom told him there was nothing his dad enjoyed more than watching him play. He came into the game six or seven minutes in, and the first time he touched the ball he had an open three."

"Let me guess..."

"Drained it. There wasn't a dry eye in the house. We won the game going away."

I was convinced. I was also surprised the story hadn't gotten any national attention. New Mexico won a close game that night — surprisingly close because this was before Olson had rebuilt the Wildcats into a national power — and Butch had Scott Thompson, Olson's top assistant, take me back to meet Kerr. I don't think he was thrilled to meet me, not a few minutes after a tough loss. But he couldn't have been nicer. I liked him right away. He had one of those dry, self-deprecating senses of humor. When he was talking about his recruitment—or, more accurately, nonrecruitment—he talked about his quickness.

"I'm deceptively quick, actually," he said. "When people first see me they think I'm a step slow. In truth, I'm *two* steps slow."

He talked about his father and his death and the hours and days and weeks and months following his death. "Anytime I play I think about him," he said. "Because the truth is, if not for him, I wouldn't be playing at Arizona."

It turned out there had been some confusion about whether Arizona was going to offer Steve a scholarship. Lute Olson and his wife, Bobbi, had gone to a summer league game in Los Angeles to look at underclassmen, and Olson had been intrigued by Steve's shooting range. When he told his wife that he was interested in the pale, skinny jump shooter with the shock of Tom Sawyer hair, her response—according to Olson years later—was "Oh no, Lute, you can't be serious."

He was serious enough to contact Kerr. At that point, Steve was planning on going to Cal State–Fullerton, where he had accepted a last-second scholarship. A chance to play in the Pac-10 had seemed like a dream come true, but when the Kerrs heard nothing from Arizona for several weeks, it looked like he was going to end up at Fullerton—until Malcolm Kerr intervened.

"He called Lute," Steve said. "He asked him what the deal was, why they hadn't called back at all. Lute said he had thought I was going to Fullerton. My dad told him I really wanted to go to Arizona. Lute said, 'Well then, we'd love to have him.' The truth is my dad recruited them more than they recruited me."

As luck—bad for Steve, good for me—would have it, he tore up his knee playing in the World Championship in Spain in the summer of 1986. Initially the doctors told him he might not play again, the damage was that serious. But he went on a strenuous rehab program after his surgery and red-shirted that winter. As a result, he was a fifth year senior in 1987–88 on what had now become a very good Arizona team.

By then, Steve was an icon in Tucson. He had made himself into a very good player—a solid point guard who became a big-time threat when the three-point rule became a part of the college game. But it was more than that. Everyone there knew his story and the community came to see him as an adopted son. He responded by showing up at every charity event there was and going to schools to read to kids and encourage them to learn to read themselves.

Whenever Steve made a shot in McKale Arena, the announcer would scream, *"STEVE KERRRRRRR!"* Without fail, 12,400 people would yell back, *"STEVE KERRRRRR!"* It became both a tradition and one of the most spine-tingling moments in college basketball, even after you'd heard it dozens of times.

Arizona had been occasionally good in basketball, but never great. It had never reached a Final Four. But the team Olson had put together by Kerr's senior year—with Steve and Craig McMillan in the backcourt and Sean Elliott and Tom Tolbert up front—was clearly going to be a national contender. They started the season by winning the Great Alaska Shootout, which back then always had a great field, and then went to Iowa, where Olson had once been a hero, to play a Tom Davis–coached team that had reached the Elite Eight a year earlier.

My lead in the *Washington Post* the day after that game said this: "Vice President George Bush came to Iowa today to campaign for president. He might as well have been invisible. Why? Because Lute Olson, the prodigal son, had returned to Iowa."

Okay, overwritten and maybe I enjoyed it a little too much given my political biases. But it really wasn't far off. There were—without question—more camera crews chronicling Olson's walk back onto the court at Carver-Hawkeye Arena than anything Bush did in the state that day.

Which was fine with me. I was there to see Kerr. I had lunch with him after the team's shootaround that morning. We talked for several hours. At one point, Olson walked by our table and shook his head disapprovingly.

"Don't keep him too much longer, John," he said. "We do have a game to play tonight."

"We do?" Kerr said. "I'd completely forgotten."

Even Lute laughed at that one. Later he told me if it had been anyone but Kerr, he'd have been apoplectic about one of his players spending time with a reporter a few hours before a difficult road game.

"I knew Steve could handle it," he said. "Steve can handle most things."

Kerr's sense of humor did get him into a little bit of trouble later that month. After Arizona had beaten Duke to win its own post-Christmas tournament (the Wildcats also won in Olson's return to Iowa, meaning they ended up doing a lot better in the state than Bush would do), Kerr was on a postgame radio show in Tucson. The host asked him if he and his teammates had made any New Year's resolutions—no doubt expecting Kerr to say they had all resolved to make it to the Final Four.

That just wasn't Steve.

"Yes, we have," he said, sounding quite serious. "We're all very determined to help Coach Olson overcome his heroin addiction. We really want to help him deal with it."

One could almost imagine Arizona fans driving home from the game swerving into trees at that moment. "As soon as I said it I knew I'd gone too far," Kerr said later. "I mean even then Lute was God in Tucson. It wasn't a good place to go for a joke."

Olson forgave Kerr for the same reason he had let him talk to me on the day of the Iowa game: it was Steve. "I was mad at him when he said it," he said. "But I have trouble staying mad at him."

Arizona made it to the Final Four that season. I'd flown from East Rutherford on Saturday to Seattle on Sunday to see the Wildcats play North Carolina for the last spot in Kansas City. Duke, Oklahoma, and Kansas were already in. It was the first time all season I'd seen Kerr nervous.

"I can't believe this is really it," he said before the game. "We're either going to the Final Four or we're not. Period."

I had another of my "Dean encounters" that day. When I walked into the Kingdome a couple of hours before tipoff, he was standing outside his locker room. He had quit smoking by then but was working the Nicorette hard.

"Didn't you go to see Duke yesterday?" he (of course) asked me.

"I did. Then I flew here. That was a nice win you guys had on Friday."

"Except that [senior Steve] Bucknall got hurt. I'm not sure we've got anyone else who can guard Sean Elliott."

"Oh, come on, Dean. Bucknall will play, you know that."

"Only if the trainers and doctors say he's okay."

"They will. I know you want to leave doubt in Arizona's mind, but he'll start."

"Don't be so sure."

"I'm sure. In fact, I'll bet you he starts."

Dean smiled. "Okay, I'll bet you a dollar."

Knowing how competitive he was, I nodded and said, "But you can't not start him the first two minutes just to win the bet."

Sure enough, when the lineups were introduced, Bucknall started. I looked across the court at Dean. Seeing me, he reached in his pocket and held up a dollar bill. He paid me too — even after Arizona won the game.

In the movies, Arizona would have won the national title and Kerr would have dedicated the championship to his father. In real life, he shot two for eleven against Oklahoma and blamed himself for his team's loss.

Even though Kerr was drafted in the second round that spring by the Phoenix Suns, I didn't expect him to play very long in the NBA, and I don't think he did either. He went from Phoenix to Cleveland to Orlando—always in a limited role as a shooter off the bench but, nonetheless, in the NBA. Then, prior to the 1996 season, he signed with the Chicago Bulls.

Most people know the rest of the story: Michael Jordan, after starting a fight with him in his first practice, became Kerr's biggest supporter. In 1997, with game six of the Finals on the line, Jordan reversed the ball to an open Kerr, who drained the three pointer that clinched the title. It was at that point that I called Steve and said, "*Now* your life is a movie."

I had really believed for years his story was worthy of a movie, but, like with *A Season on the Brink* a few years later, it lacked an ending. Now that it had an ending, Steve didn't want to do it.

"I just can't picture my life story up on a movie screen," he said.

"Most of it was in a book," I answered.

"I know," he said. "But it's different."

He was right, and I certainly wasn't going to push him. It was, after all, *his* life.

Kerr ended up with five NBA championship rings—three in Chicago with Jordan, two more in San Antonio with David Robinson and Tim Duncan.

"Right place, right time," he likes to say.

Perhaps. But Kerr played a major role, in the locker room and on the court, in all those titles. And I can't think of anyone who deserved good things more than—as they still say in Tucson whenever he's back there—*STEVE KERRRRRRR!*

10

Junior and Friends

As much as I have always loved college basketball, and as much as I now enjoy covering golf, the truth is, the sport I dreamed about covering when I was young was tennis.

Part of that, no doubt, had to do with my parents. Tennis was the one sport they both truly enjoyed. My parents were the antijocks. Music and the performing arts were their great loves. My mom, Bernice, got her PhD in music history, played and taught the piano, and taught music history at Columbia and George Washington University. My dad—Martin—grew up in Brooklyn in the shadow of Ebbets Field. Just as I would do with sports as a boy, he rode the subway often to pursue his passion: classical music. He would pay the nickel fare to get into Manhattan to go to the Metropolitan Opera House or Carnegie Hall. As a teenager he sold librettos at the Opera House so he could get into all the operas for free.

When he got out of the Army in 1945, he refused to listen to his family's pleas to go to work with his uncles in the garment district, and instead he pursued a job—any job—in the performing arts. He finally landed one as an assistant public relations director with Sol Hurok, the Russian impresario. He stayed there twenty-seven years before becoming the first executive director of the John F. Kennedy Center in Washington. Later, he was the director of the National Symphony Orchestra and the Washington Opera.

As a kid, my parents' involvement in the arts world was something I rolled my eyes at most of the time. The fact that their West Side apartment was often filled with artists such as Isaac Stern (my dad's best friend), Rudolph Nureyev and Margot Fonteyn, Vladimir Horowitz, and Marian Anderson hardly impressed me. Why couldn't it have been Tom Seaver, Willis Reed, Brad Park, or Joe Namath?

I still remember a night in 1971 when my (then) beloved New York Rangers were playing the Chicago Blackhawks in a critical game five of a Stanley Cup semifinal series. My parents were throwing a party for Marian Anderson, the great singer, who had retired by then but had remained a close friend of my dad's. Deep into overtime, Bobby Hull scored off a faceoff to give the Blackhawks the game and a 3–2 series lead. I was furious. I began screaming at the TV, throwing pillows around the room in complete frustration. I was, um, loud.

My father burst into the room. "What the hell is going on in here?" he demanded.

"Goddamn Bobby Hull just scored and the Rangers lost," I said, as if that would completely explain my behavior.

I guess, to some degree, it did. "Well, keep it down, will you? Miss Anderson is singing!"

To him Marian Anderson singing was somehow more important than Bobby Hull scoring.

My parents often took me to the ballet, to the opera, to concerts when I was a kid. In fact, I remember my mother forcing me to go to Marian Anderson's farewell concert at Carnegie Hall when I was eight years old. "It's an historic day," she said. "You can miss one ball game." I'm forever grateful to her for that.

Once, my dad took my younger brother, Bobby, and me to a dress rehearsal of *Aida*. If you love opera you love *Aida*. If you are ten or eleven years old and you want to go home to watch a baseball game, you hate *Aida*. That goes double for the final scene, when Aida and Radames are sealed in the tomb and sing of their love to each other as they wait to die. They sing. And sing. And sing.

As we walked out, my dad, riding high on the performance the way I might be riding high after a Final Four game, asked my brother what he had enjoyed most about the opera. Bobby was about seven at the time. "When they died," he answered.

Looking back now, I realize how fortunate I was to be exposed to all that my parents exposed me to. I still love the ballet and I enjoy some—if not all—opera. There are few things in life I enjoy more than the theater. I can remember vividly the night it first really clicked with me.

I was twelve. My parents were insistent that I see *Hamlet,* which was being put on by the Old Vic, the forerunner to the Royal Shakespeare Company, at City Center on 55th Street in Manhattan. I went alone—I was too embarrassed to ask any of my friends if they wanted to go see *Hamlet*—and sat on the aisle in the tenth row. If I was spoiled as a kid in any way, it was in the seats I got for the theater because of my dad.

I went from wondering how long the damn play was going to take to screaming "bravo!"—I'd learned that from my dad too—when the final curtain came down. I was transfixed by the play and by Richard Pasco, who played Hamlet. When Horatio whispered, "Good night, sweet prince," I can remember feeling as if the entire audience took a deep breath. I was crying. The next time I would feel that exhilarated was when the Jets beat the Colts in Super Bowl III.

I went home and went to bed. My parents hadn't gotten home yet. Sometime after midnight, my dad came into my room and woke me up.

"What did you think of *Hamlet*?" he asked.

"Dad, it was the most amazing thing I've ever been to," I said. "The guy who played Hamlet is the greatest actor I've ever seen in my life. He was incredible!"

"Well," Dad said. "He's in the living room right now. Would you like to meet him?"

Understand, famous people from the performing arts were in my parents' house throughout my childhood. I came home one night while I was in college and walked in to find Victor Borge sitting at the piano making up songs while my parents and Jason Robards sang along with him. My brother and I routinely played basketball in the driveway with Richard Cragun, the brilliant dancer for the Stuttgart Ballet.

But this was a big deal. Richard Pasco was in the living room? I jumped out of bed and padded into the living room in my pajamas. Pasco was sitting in a chair that I'm looking at right now, drinking coffee. His wife, Barbara Leigh-Hunt, was on the couch next to my mother. If Tom Seaver had been sitting there I *might* have been more excited. I began gushing to Mr. Pasco about how brilliant he had been. I did have one question though: When Laertes's poisonous sword cuts him on the arm, how did he make it look as if his arm was suddenly spurting blood?

Pasco laughed. "Red toothpaste," he said. "You notice when he cuts me, I reach"—he demonstrated—"with my left hand to the spot where I've been stabbed? I have red toothpaste in that hand. I quickly spread it on the white shirt I'm wearing so it appears the blood is spurting out of my arm."

Wow. How cool. I was rattling on about the entire performance when my mother broke in. "You know, John," she said, "Mrs. Pasco played Ophelia tonight."

Barbara Leigh-Hunt was a very beautiful woman. I had barely noticed she was in the room. "Oh yeah," I said. "You were fine."

My parents loved telling that story.

It was that same year that I first really fell in love with opera, or one opera specifically. It was Tchaikovsky's *The Queen of Spades* (*Pique Dame* in Russian), which was being performed by the Bolshoi Opera in Montreal. My father was sent there by Mr. Hurok to hear the Bolshoi's repertory, since the company was supposed to come to New York for their American debut the following year. The trip was canceled because of politics, and it wasn't until 1975, when my dad convinced the Russian government to send the Bolshoi to the Kennedy Center, that they finally appeared in the United States.

That night in Montreal I went with my father. As always he told me the story before we got to the theater, since I wouldn't understand the words, which were being sung in Russian. I didn't need to understand the words. The music was completely overpowering. By the middle of the second act I was entranced. At the beginning of the third act, Hermann, the protagonist—hardly a hero—is singing on the dark stage. He is being stalked at that moment by the ghost of the Queen of Spades, whom he killed in act two. As he sings, she creeps up behind him, singing too. Just before the ghost reached for Hermann, I jumped out of my seat and yelled, *"Watch out!"*

My dad pulled me back in the seat. "John," he hissed, "it isn't real. It's just an excuse to sing."

It felt real to me at that moment.

More often than not, it was my mom who took me to games when I was young. Dad had given up on baseball completely when the Dodgers left Brooklyn. He still had a passing interest in basketball—he'd gone to City College during the school's glory days—so every once in a while he'd grudgingly take me to a basketball game. I never got to go to New York Giants games because it was impossible to get tickets, and in the old blackout days, I would listen to the home games on radio, which is why Marty Glickman, then the Giants' play-by-play man on radio, was one of my early heroes. It was only later that I learned Glickman had been an Olympic sprinter and had been replaced on the U.S. 4×100 relay at the 1936 Games by Olympic Committee chairman Avery Brundage, who didn't want to offend Hitler by having a Jew running for the U.S. team.

By the time I was about ten, I could get to games on my own on the subway. Looking at my own children now, I understand why my parents weren't that thrilled with me riding the subway by myself, but it was a different time then and I knew the subway system cold before I was twelve. I can still remember the ticket prices every-where: Shea Stadium was $1.30 for general admission, and Yankee Stadium was $1.50. Yankee Stadium was a better buy though because it only had three decks and you were a lot closer to the field. With a student GO Card you could get into Madison Square Garden for Ranger games for $3 and Knicks games for $2. That went up as the teams got better, but not that much. I could buy a standing-room ticket to any Jets game—they went on sale every Monday at the Jets offices at 57th Street and Madison Avenue—for $3.

That was easily the best bargain because, inevitably, there were no-shows in the downstairs box seats, and since the standing room was right behind those sections, we could usually sneak into good seats by the time the ushers got bored in the second quarter.

The other fairly easy sneak-down was at the Garden for college basketball doubleheaders. In those days, Manhattan and NYU hosted doubleheaders, usually on Thursdays (tough for me because it was a school night) but also occasionally on weekends. The build-ing was typically about half full, and if you found a section with a friendly usher—not easy in the Garden—you could sneak at least into the orange section, which was one up from courtside.

The one sport my dad was always willing to go see with me was tennis. He had come to the sport late as a player but loved it. He didn't play especially well, but the people he played with regularly were all at about his level, so their matches were always competitive. I would frequently go to watch and then hit some balls with my dad when the grownups were finished.

My first exposure to the pro game was technically not the pro game. Tennis wasn't an "open" sport until 1968, and those who had declared themselves to be pros were banned from the four major championships until then. The top "amateurs" were all paid under the table. When my parents took me to the Meadow Club in Southamp-ton for the annual summer stop on the amateur circuit that led to the U.S. Championships at Forest Hills, I saw Roy Emerson and Fred Stolle and John Newcombe and Dennis Ralston and Chuck McKinley and Charlie Pasarell play. I still remember being thrilled when a young American named Jerry Cromwell stunned Emerson in, I think, 1966. I remember the score was 9–7, 6–3 in a round of sixteen match. Cromwell went on to become a successful doubles player, but that might have been his highlight in singles.

My parents took me to tennis all the time, including at Forest Hills, every year. It was an easy subway ride from Manhattan and then a quick walk through the leafy neighborhood. They also took me to see the "pros" when they came to Madison Square Garden: Rod Laver, Ken Rosewall, Pancho Gonzales, and Lew Hoad were the big stars. Aussies dominated the sport in those days. When Arthur Ashe won the first U.S. Open in 1968, he was the first American to win the U.S. title since 1955.

Tennis was my connection to my parents—especially my dad. He would actually sit and watch tennis with me on TV once it started to become a TV sport. One of my early thrills was visiting my uncle Peter and aunt Vivian in Boston one summer and going with them to Longwood to see the U.S. Pro final between Laver and Tony Roche, another up-and-coming Aussie. The match was great. What was *really* great though was seeing Bud Collins in person for the first time; he was wearing the brightest pair of multicolored pants I'd ever seen.

I followed tennis closely just as I followed the four major team sports. I rooted for the Americans: Ashe, Clark Graebner, McKinley, Ralston, Gene Scott. Later it was Jimmy Connors and then John McEnroe, both of whom I got to know early in my career. I had a huge crush on Chris Evert when she first came on the scene in 1971, making the Open semifinals at the age of sixteen. She was a little bit older than I was and I thought she was *it*. I remember when she was awash in publicity during that '71 Open saying something like, "It's wonderful all these things people are saying about me. I just wish *someone* would say I'm sexy."

Somewhere in Manhattan I was jumping up and down saying, "Me, me, me!"

Throughout college, I read Barry Lorge in the *Washington Post* on tennis. I thought his writing was brilliant, his descriptions of the matches and the players and the settings remarkable. I fantasized about someday *being* Lorge, traveling the world to all the great tennis venues and writing about them. The one thing I didn't know about Lorge, who died way too young in 2006 at the age of sixty-two after a long fight with cancer, was that the writing he made look so easy was incredibly hard for him.

No one wrestled with a computer like Lorge — nicknamed "Bear" by Bud because he looked like a large, though extremely gentle, bear. The stories about how long it took him to write are still legendary. The first time I covered Wimbledon, in 1985, Bud convinced me to stay at Dolphin Square, the apartment/hotel complex where he had stayed forever. Lorge, who by then was working for the *San Diego Union,* also stayed there every year. One morning I set out for Wimbledon at about 8:30, walked out the entrance to the hotel, and bumped smack into Lorge: he was *just* getting back from Wimbledon, having worked most of the night. He was, as far as I know, the only writer in history to blow a deadline with an eight-hour time difference in his favor.

I first worked with Lorge during the 1980 U.S. Open — the one where I went and got Bud to take a phone call from Abbie Hoffman — and he went out of his way to help me at every turn. He let me write the men's semifinals on Saturday (he covered the women's final), which meant I got to sit practically on the court during a McEnroe-Connors classic that ended with McEnroe winning 7–6 in the fifth set after he and Connors almost went nose-to-nose at one point in the fourth set. He also suggested I try to follow McEnroe back to the locker room after McEnroe had beaten Bjorn Borg in the final in five sets the next day.

"You never know with John, you might get lucky," Lorge said. "You're fast enough that you don't need to get started writing right away, why don't you take a shot?"

The U.S. Open used to be the only tennis tournament that allowed media in the locker room. (Now there are none, one of many reasons tennis is virtually a dead sport in this country.) So I trailed McEnroe and a few of his friends back there after his press conference. The friends couldn't go in the locker room. I could. Borg was long gone, having gone straight to his car from the awards ceremony. There were two people in the locker room: McEnroe and me.

McEnroe looked at me as if to say, "Who the hell are you?" I told him. He was unimpressed but sat down in front of his locker. I knew exactly what I wanted to ask him: the crowd had been completely pro-Borg, pulling for a Swede against a New Yorker *in* New York. Someone had asked John about that in his press conference, and he had just said it was disappointing and left it at that. I suspected there was more to it.

I stood with my back to the lockers and tried to look casual. "Listen, John, there's one question I wanted to ask you..." He wasn't looking at me but was pulling racquets out of his bag. I pushed onward. "I grew up in New York..."

Now he stopped. "Oh yeah, where?"

"Manhattan. West Side."

He went back to his racquets.

"I was wondering, as someone who grew up here, what went through your mind at the end of the fourth set when it seemed as if most of the stadium was on its feet cheering for Borg?"

He looked up at me. "Most?" he said. "How about all?"

I'd been trying to make the question softer.

"To be honest," he said, "it sucked. Can you imagine *anyone* in

Sweden rooting against Borg? I mean *anyone* in the entire country? I know we're different, and I know some people don't like me because of the way I behave..."

And he was off. I'm not sure he took a breath the next five minutes. I didn't even need to ask follow-up questions. He asked and answered them himself.

"How did I get myself together in the fifth set?" he asked himself. "It wasn't easy. But I told myself you are *not* losing another five-setter to Borg [who had won their classic Wimbledon final earlier that summer, 8–6 in the fifth]. At the beginning of the set I felt like my whole body was going to fall off. Holding serve at the beginning was big. It gave me a chance to catch my breath..."

When he was finished, I thanked him and we shook hands. I was surprised when he said, "What's your name again?" only because I didn't think who I was would interest him. I told him, thanked him, and ran back across the almost empty grounds to the press box. When the elevator—built in about 1890, I think—finally got me back upstairs, I walked to the *Post* seats, where Lorge was listening to his tape of the postmatch press conference.

"Any luck?" he asked, pulling off his headphones for a moment.

"A lot of it," I said.

"Tell the desk," he said. "Maybe they can give you some extra space."

My sidebar was supposed to be twenty inches long. The desk thought they could give me twenty-four. I wrote forty. They used it all and moved the sidebar from inside to the front, twinning it with Lorge's lead. That night had two long-term implications in my life: one good, one not so good.

The not so good happened when I got back to the *Post* late the next morning. I was, as they say in the newsroom, taking bows for the McEnroe story. A number of people were standing around talking about how great it was that I'd gotten him one on one and that he'd talked so candidly (McEnroe talking candidly is hardly a big deal; he *always* talks candidly). As the discussion went on, Tony Kornheiser joined the group.

Tony had come to the *Post* that spring. His arrival was a big deal to me because I loved reading him in the *New York Times*. We'd quickly become friends—more of a big brother/little brother relationship than anything else. We were both insecure smart-ass New Yorkers. Tony had covered a lot of tennis at the *Times* and knew most of the top players, including McEnroe.

"So you got Junior to talk to you, huh?" he said, walking up. McEnroe's nickname was "Junior" because his full name is John Patrick McEnroe Jr. and because when he first came on tour he was younger than almost all the other players.

"Yeah, I got lucky," I said.

"You didn't get lucky," Tony said. "He talked to you because you're the *same* person. It was Junior talking to Junior."

Okay, so we're both from New York, we're both left-handed, and we both have fairly quick tempers. Other than that...

The nickname stuck instantly. Back then I didn't mind it that much because I was still one of the youngest guys at the *Post*. I didn't especially like it when I got older and guys at the paper younger than me who didn't even know *why* I had the nickname used it. And I really can't stand it when a complete stranger comes up and uses it. I try to be polite, but I'm not great at it:

"Hey, it's John Junior Feinstein."

"It's John. What's your name?"

On the other hand, I've been called worse—by a lot of people.

The better outcome of my McEnroe encounter was that it was the beginning of a relationship with John. I wouldn't call it a friendship, but we certainly were friendly. More important, he almost always cooperated with me when I asked him for time. He and I did a long sit-down interview during the French Open in 1985, when I first began covering tennis regularly that summer. That was the story that Katharine Graham liked so much.

Early in my season with Bob Knight—late October—I got a call from George Solomon. McEnroe and Borg were playing an exhibition in St. Louis on Friday night. Borg had walked away from tennis in 1981 after losing both the Wimbledon and U.S. Open finals to McEnroe, but he had come back to play a series of big-bucks exhibitions with McEnroe as part of what was called the "McEnroe Over America Tour."

Borg had never said very much to the media when he was playing, and once he retired from playing in real tournaments, he had pretty much stopped talking altogether. One of the things he liked about playing McEnroe on "his" tour was that John did all the media stuff. Borg just showed up and played.

George wanted me to go to St. Louis and see if I could get Borg to talk. "Maybe your pal McEnroe will help you," he said.

I was willing (and able) to go because Indiana had an early practice Friday and wasn't scrimmaging until Saturday afternoon. That left me a window to catch a flight to St. Louis after practice and get back before the scrimmage Saturday. The only downside was that one of the coaches would have to be available to take Knight to dinner on Friday. When I told Knight I was going to St. Louis to see McEnroe and Borg, he thought it was a good idea.

He repeated what he had said that summer during our postmidnight phone conversation when I was in Stratton Mountain.

"I like McEnroe. I really like the way he competes."

That Knight and McEnroe would be kindred spirits made perfect sense.

The match was in the old Kiel Auditorium, which still exists to this day, even though the building's main tenant, the St. Louis Hawks, left for Atlanta forty years ago. As is always the case with these exhibitions, the two players split the first two sets and then played the third set for real—McEnroe winning. McEnroe was brought into some kind of makeshift interview room afterward. Since he hadn't been playing real tennis, he was relaxed, funny, and charming. When he finished, he walked over to me and said, "What in the world are you doing here?"

I told him I was spending the winter in Bloomington working on a book on Bob Knight. McEnroe looked at me for a moment and then said, "Bobby Knight? Isn't he kind of crazy?"

If he recognized the irony in that comment, he didn't give it away.

I told him I had come over, to be honest, to see if there was any way Borg would talk to me.

"Part of our deal is I do all the media stuff," John said.

"I know," I said.

He got it — McEnroe always gets it.

"Follow me," he said.

We walked around the building to a small locker room. Borg was in there getting into his street clothes. "Bjorn, I need you to do me a favor," John said. "This is John Feinstein. He works for the *Washington Post*. He's a friend of mine. Can you give him just a couple of minutes?"

Borg shrugged. "Sure," he said.

As different as they were, McEnroe and Borg were always friends. Part of it was the mutual respect that came with playing their sport at the absolute highest level. Part of it was each wishing he could be a little more like the other: Borg admired McEnroe's unbridled passion; McEnroe wished he could stay as controlled as Borg did in the most tense moments. I think they also shared a mutual dislike of Jimmy Connors. As often as McEnroe and Connors are linked as tennis "bad boys," they are completely different people.

McEnroe went to shower while Borg and I sat down to talk. I can't remember a single word he said that night. I asked him about how much he missed competing (not much, apparently) and being at Wimbledon and Paris every year (same thing). We talked about his friendship with McEnroe. In the end, John saved the story by talking about Borg. I was able to set the two of them in the tiny locker room in the ancient building on a rainy night in St. Louis. George stripped it in the Sunday paper in large part because there were Borg quotes — boring as they might have been — in the piece. Thanks to McEnroe, I was able to return triumphantly to Bloomington.

"How's your boy McEnroe?" Knight asked when I got back.

"He likes the way you compete," I answered.

11

Hard Times and *Hard Courts*

FOR SIX YEARS, BEGINNING in the summer of 1985, I covered tennis on a regular basis. I covered it for the *Post* for four years and then for *Tennis World, Tennis Magazine,* and the *National Sports Daily,* which I worked for during its brief sixteen-month lifespan in 1990 and 1991.

A Season Inside sold well, but not nearly as well as *A Season on the Brink.* If *Season Inside* had been my first book, I would have been thrilled with the sales numbers. But I'd been completely spoiled by *Brink* and was disappointed the second book hadn't sold as well as the first. My third book, *Forever's Team,* sold a lot less than the first two had, but that had been expected. As Esther put it, "That was the book you got to do as a reward for *Season on the Brink.*"

I enjoyed doing *Forever's Team* greatly, because it gave me a chance to go back and see old friends from college. The book got very good reviews. But I had now used up my freebie. If I wanted to continue to make a living as an author, the next book had to be what Esther called "a big book."

Tennis made perfect sense. By 1989 I knew most of the important people in the sport well, both on and off the court. I didn't get along with all of them—especially a lot of the agents—but I knew them all. Tennis was still hugely popular, but McEnroe and Connors were both well past their peak and there was concern about when the next American men's star was going to come along. I can remember Arthur Ashe, as early as 1985 when he was still the U.S. Davis Cup captain, standing on the top of a bleacher at the French Open saying, "So where's the next McEnroe? The next Connors? I don't see them anywhere."

Ashe's words proved prescient a year later when no American man made it past the quarterfinals at the U.S. Open for the first time in the Open era. In fact, the only quarterfinalist was Tim Wilkison, who had the tournament of his life to get to the round of eight. McEnroe looked completely lost going down in the first round to Paul Annacone following a lengthy sabbatical earlier in the year. After losing to Brad Gilbert in the first round of what was then the season-ending tournament in Madison Square Garden, he told his childhood pal Mary Carillo that if he couldn't beat Brad Gilbert, he shouldn't be playing tennis.

"We were driving uptown in Manhattan and he was just screaming," Carillo said. "'If I can't beat Brad F—ing Gilbert, I shouldn't be playing.'"

So he didn't play for the next six months.

Connors was playing but was about to turn thirty-four when the Open started. He lost his third round match to Todd Witsken, a rookie on tour from Indiana whose highest singles ranking would be forty-three. It was the first time since 1973 that Connors hadn't at least reached the semis at the Open.

That left Ivan Lendl and Miloslav Mecir to play in the final. Midway through the second set of Lendl's straight-set rout, fans began streaming out of Louis Armstrong Stadium. Ed Fabricius, who was the USTA's publicity director at the time, was standing just outside the stadium as the third set began. "It looked as if there had been a bomb scare," he said. "People were running for the exits."

It was after that Open that *Sports Illustrated* ran its infamous cover photo of Lendl with the caption: "The Champion Nobody Cares About."

Years later, Lendl admitted that cover bothered him. "I just don't know what I did to deserve that," he said. "I worked hard to get better at my game. I never went crazy on court like John and Jimmy did sometimes. My English got better as time went on. They don't want to like me, okay fine. But I thought that was over the line."

No one was more guilty of being unfair to Lendl than me. I was like the guys at *SI*. Of course, I recognized that he was a superb player—Lendl ended up winning eight majors, as many as Connors and one more than McEnroe. He grew into a tenacious competitor, one who was never out of a match no matter how far down he was. After ducking Wimbledon early in his career because he wasn't comfortable playing on grass, he realized his mistake and worked tirelessly to become a good enough volleyer that he could win Wimbledon. He made the final twice, losing to Boris Becker in 1986 and to Pat Cash in 1987. In 1990, he made one last all-out attempt to fill the one hole in his tennis resume, skipping the entire clay court season—including the French Open, which he had won three times—to work on grass and prepare for Wimbledon. He still lost, in the semifinals to Stefan Edberg. By then I felt bad for him because I knew how hard he'd worked to win that year.

"Actually the match with Stefan didn't bother me that much," he said. "I didn't play poorly. He was just too good that day. I did everything I could to win Wimbledon [Lendl always said *Veembladon*] that year, and it wasn't quite good enough. I have no regrets."

My relationship with Lendl bottomed in the summer of 1986 when I wrote a column saying I thought it was ridiculous for then Vice President George Bush (a big tennis fan and Lendl friend) to try to push Congress to waive the five year waiting period for citizenship so Lendl could play in the Davis Cup for the United States. I wasn't really being critical of Lendl as much as I was being critical of those who thought the Davis Cup was so important that the country's laws should be ignored to try and win it. Lendl didn't see it that way.

He was in Washington playing in what had been the *Washington Star* International and now had some other corporate name on it. It was still known to all of us at the *Post* as "The Donald Dell Open." Lendl won a taut three-set semifinal from Connors during which he got so angry at one point that he slammed his racquet to the ground—which was very un-Lendl-like.

In his postmatch press conference, someone asked Lendl what had happened to cause the racquet slam. He shrugged. "I just figured that no matter what I do out there, John Feinstein's going to rip me for it," he said. "So I slammed my racquet."

That got a laugh. When Lendl was finished he walked over to me, pointing his finger at my chest. "I don't deserve the shit you write about me," he yelled.

Since we were in public, I wasn't going to get into an argument. I just said, "I'm sorry you feel that way, Ivan." He glared at me and stalked away.

What Lendl didn't know at that moment was that our relationship was about to change because of something that had happened to me a couple of weeks earlier in Czechoslovakia.

AFTER WIMBLEDON THAT YEAR, the *Post* had sent me to the first Goodwill Games, in Moscow. From there I went to Prague to cover the Federation Cup—the women's version of the Davis Cup—an event that was being covered by American newspapers for one reason: it would be the first time that Martina Navratilova would be returning to Czechoslovakia since she had defected in 1973. She was now an American citizen, having waited the five years, and would be teaming up with Chris Evert on the U.S. team.

I got myself into trouble on that trip—first in Moscow, then in Prague.

The Goodwill Games—created by Ted Turner after the Soviet

boycott in Los Angeles to try and get U.S. and Eastern Bloc athletes competing against one another again — was one of the great adventures of my life. A group of us had flown from Wimbledon to Moscow. We arrived on Monday afternoon, checked into the massive Hotel Moscow, which was across the street from Red Square, and went straight to the track-and-field venue.

As it turned out, Sergey Bubka broke the world record in the pole vault that night. Bubka was breaking the world record about once a month in those days, and doing it in front of his fellow Russians — or Soviets, back then — was a very big deal. Rather than go to Bubka's press conference, Dave Kindred and I walked through the stands to the track to talk to the two American vaulters, Earl Bell and Mike Tully. Our sense was Bell and Tully could give us a better idea what made Bubka so great than Bubka could speaking through a Russian translator.

Two things were surprising that night. First, after two weeks at Wimbledon, where approaching an athlete without written permission from fourteen people could result in you being put to death, it was refreshing to just be able to walk up to two people and introduce yourself.

"Nice to be in a free country," I cracked to Kindred as we walked across the track unimpeded.

"At Wimbledon we'd be in jail by now," Kindred said.

"At least," I answered.

Tully and Bell were both friendly and outgoing. But they didn't give us what we were looking for — or at least what we were expecting — on Bubka, our second surprise of the night.

"He's beaten the system," Bell said. "He's figured it out. Or his doctors have figured it out. No way you can be that good that often if you aren't getting help."

Kindred and I were both wide-eyed. Bell was standing there casually calling a guy who had just broken a world record a cheat. I think I must have said something clever like, "Really? Seriously?" Bell shrugged and waved Tully, who was gathering up his equipment, over to us.

"Hey, Mike, what's the key to Sergey's success?" he said.

Tully made a gesture with his hand as if he was releasing a syringe into someone's arm. "He's juicing," he said. "Has to be."

"But drug testing?" I said.

They both laughed. "Their scientists are always ahead of the testers," Bell said. "He's masking it. No doubt about it."

Kindred and I looked at each other. We had thought we had a pretty good first-day story when Bubka had broken the record. We now had something we hadn't bargained on getting. We raced back up to the interview room wondering if there was some way to ask Bubka privately about what Bell and Tully had said. We knew we weren't going to ask it in an open press conference — in part because we'd give the story away, but also because it would be rude to bring something like that up in front of an adoring crowd. When we got upstairs, Bubka was being led away by security people. There was no way to get close to him.

So we wrote. The next day, all hell broke loose. The Soviet government and Bubka were furious — not with Tully and Bell, or with Kindred for that matter, but with me. Why? Kindred's story was almost identical to mine, but it appeared in the *Atlanta Journal-Constitution*. The *Journal-Constitution* wasn't delivered each morning to the Soviet embassy in Washington. The *Post* was. In fact, the embassy, on 16th Street, backed up to the *Post* building, on 15th Street. From George Solomon's window, you could see the back of the embassy.

So I was the bad guy, not Kindred. Bubka denounced me and denounced the *Post* and said there was no truth at all to what Tully and Bell had said. The Soviet sports bureau did the same. Oh well, I figured, at least someone was reading my stuff.

A couple of days later Ben Johnson absolutely destroyed Carl

Lewis in the 100-meter dash. Once again, because the Soviets had essentially given us free rein, Kindred and I were able to walk right up to Lewis within a couple of minutes of the race ending to talk to him. We were standing in the tunnel a few yards from the finish line. Lewis made Tully and Bell sound gentle when he talked about Johnson.

"He's cheating," Lewis said. "There's no doubt about it. Look at him. You think that body's real? No way."

Kindred and I looked at each other walking away and had the same reaction: Tully and Bell's accusations had an absolute ring of truth to them. They weren't said with any malice, more matter-of-fact. Actually, both guys made a point of saying how much they liked Bubka personally. Lewis sounded to us like he was whining. He'd gotten his butt kicked, he wasn't used to it, and he couldn't take it. So he called Johnson a cheating steroid user.

As it turned out, Johnson *was* a cheating steroid user who was stripped of his gold medal when he tested positive at the Seoul Olympics after again beating Lewis. I was in the stadium for that race too, and it was about as electric an Olympic moment as I've ever witnessed. Too bad it wasn't real.

And Bubka? He went on to break the world record in the pole vault thirty-five times, he won an Olympic gold medal in 1992, and he never tested positive for anything. My gut feelings are usually pretty accurate. They weren't in Moscow.

After Lewis finished ripping Johnson I wrote a story that began, "The first Goodwill Games are rapidly becoming the Ill-Will Games." I went on to quote Lewis on Johnson and made it pretty clear that I was skeptical. I described Johnson's race in glowing terms. The Soviets, already on alert for anything I wrote, went completely crazy over the "Ill-Will Games" line. They put out all sorts of statements about the fellowship among the athletes and how hard they and the people from Turner Broadcasting had worked to make the Games a success for all. The funny thing was, I was making fun of Lewis and other whining American athletes—not the Soviets—in the Johnson/ Lewis piece.

A few days later, when I was introduced to Ted Turner, he looked at me and said, "So you're the guy the Sovietskies are so pissed off at."

Yup, I was the guy.

A couple of days after the Lewis/Johnson story, *Pravda* wrote a long story on what a huge success the Goodwill Games had been. There were only two bad guys, they said, in the entire scope of the Games. One was Secretary of State George Shultz, who had refused to sign off on letting American boxers who were in the armed forces participate in the Games. The other was me.

Gary Lee, who was then the *Post*'s Moscow correspondent, translated the story for me. Sitting in the *Post*'s Moscow bureau he started reading the section about me aloud. First, he read the Russian, then he translated. Midway through the first sentence, he burst out laughing.

"What is it?" I asked.

"They called you fat," he said.

The actual line was this: "Who is this dull, unoriginal, and roundish journalist who breathes the dark, long-lost breath of the Cold War?"

Pretty good writing, I must admit. When Steve Woodward of *USA Today* decided to do a notebook item on *Pravda* ripping me, he asked me if I wanted to comment. "Sure," I said. "Dull and unoriginal, maybe, but roundish is hitting above the belt."

Aside from being attacked by *Pravda* and the Soviet government, I had a great time in Moscow. Most of the people could not have been nicer, and as I said, the access we had to the athletes was terrific. Most nights, after we had all finished writing, the American writers would gather in the Hotel Moscow, where we were all staying, for late-night drinks. Frequently, at about two or three o'clock in the morning, we would walk across the street to Red Square to watch the changing of the guard at Lenin's Tomb. The guards were changed every hour of every day. What was cool about it in the middle of the night is that you could hear the new guards coming before you actually saw them. You could hear their heels clicking on the cobblestones just before they rounded the corner to the main portion of the square, where they very formally took over for those who had been on guard beforehand.

One morning, when there were no events going on, Dave Kindred, Tom Callahan (who was working for *Time* magazine at the time), Bud Shaw (who was also with the *Journal-Constitution,* for whom this was a big event since Turner was based in Atlanta), and I decided we wanted to go see Lenin. We'd seen the long lines waiting to go through the tomb during the daytime, so we checked with the concierge at the hotel to find out how long we might have to wait.

"One moment," the concierge said.

A minute later he was back with a very attractive young woman who worked for Intourist, which was the agency that had made all the travel plans for the international media. The young woman walked us across the street to a spot in the line about two hundred yards from the entrance to the tomb, which was maybe a five-minute wait to the front door. She spoke in Russian to several people and a moment later said to us, "Join the line there."

We did as we were told. No one said anything except for one man, who was clearly French, and furious. This was during a time when U.S. relations with France were not wonderful. Earlier that year, when the U.S. had asked the French government for clearance to send planes through their airspace en route to Libya, the French had said no.

The Frenchman began yelling at the four of us in clear, accented English: "How dare you cut into the line this way? Who do you think you are? We have been waiting in line almost two hours and you cut the line this way? It is outrageous!"

Before any of us could start to explain we were just doing what we'd been told to do, Callahan jumped in. Tom has a temper and he is very quick on his feet. He looked right at the man and said, "You know, we *wanted* to go to the end of the line. We were *going* to go to the end of the line, but we just couldn't do it. You know why? Because we were just *so* tired after our planes had to fly *all the way around France* to get to Libya that we just couldn't do it!"

Clearly a lot of the Russians in line spoke English because they all started laughing. The Frenchman glared at Callahan for a moment and said nothing. A few minutes later, after being instructed to keep our hands at our sides and not talk while in the tomb, we were inside. Lenin was inside a glass case, dressed in a dark suit, lying propped up on a pillow. Ted Turner would later say that he thought Lenin looked pretty good when he saw him, "but a little bit pale."

The whole thing was actually quite eerie. Still, it was something you had to do at least once if you were in Moscow.

From Moscow I went to Prague, which is one of the most beautiful cities I have ever been to in my life. I didn't figure to get into any trouble there covering the Federation Cup and Martina Navratilova's return to Czechoslovakia. I had done a long interview with Martina during the Eastbourne Tournament for a Sunday feature that would run the day before the event began. The only real story after that would be how the Czech fans reacted when Navratilova was introduced as part of the American team.

The answer to that question came quickly: the minute the Americans marched into the stadium, almost everyone was on their feet cheering. When Martina was introduced, the cheers were overwhelming. It was a neat scene.

The first few days in Prague were like a vacation. The weather was perfect, we were all staying at a beautiful hotel right on the river, and there wasn't that much work to do after the opening ceremonies. We did a lot of sightseeing, going to, among other places, a Holocaust museum that was absolutely heartbreaking, and the second oldest temple in Europe. It was one of the few times in my life that I felt intensely proud to be Jewish.

My reverie was interrupted by a phone call from George Solomon. The Capitals, Washington's hockey team, had just signed a player named Michal Pivonka. This was significant to me, in George's mind, because Pivonka had defected from Czechoslovakia in order to sign with the Caps.

"See what you can find out about the guy since you're there," George said.

"George, this isn't like the Caps just signed a free agent who'd been playing for the Flyers. I can't just call the general manager and get a scouting report."

"Poke around," George said.

Poke around. I was behind the Iron Curtain. You didn't just "poke around."

Still, I figured I'd give it a shot and when I got nowhere I could honestly tell George I'd tried. I found a number for the Czech Hockey Federation. I even found someone there who spoke English. I don't remember word-for-word what he said, but it was something like this: "Pivonka is a minor prospect. We are not concerned that he is gone. If he chooses to leave his family and his country that is his choice. It is not our problem."

Maybe it was his tone that got to me. What I knew for sure was that it was unlikely that an NHL team would go to the trouble of signing a defector to a five-year contract if they didn't think he was a pretty good prospect. That afternoon, while watching the United States easily win its second match of the Fed Cup, I asked one of the Eastern Bloc reporters I had become friendly with if he knew much about Pivonka. Greg was from Poland, but he spoke enough Czech to get around easily and he covered hockey. We had met because a lot of Eastern Bloc reporters covered the major tennis tournaments.

"He was going to be a big star," Greg said when I brought up Pivonka. "His defecting is very bad for their national team."

That was what I had guessed. Pivonka was twenty and had already played for the national team. He would go on to play in the NHL for thirteen years as a very solid two-way center who retired having scored 599 career points.

"How far away are we from Kladno?" I asked, knowing that was Pivonka's hometown.

"It's not at all far from Prague. About twenty-five miles west. You can drive there in under thirty minutes."

Of course I didn't have a car. Nor did Greg. There weren't all that many people in Czechoslovakia who had a car. Reading my mind, Greg said, "We could get there by bribing a cab driver to take us. If we give him twenty dollars U.S. he'll do it."

One thing I had learned in my brief period behind the Iron Curtain was that people craved American money. Regardless of the exchange rate, you could make a deal for almost anything very cheap if you paid in American money. In restaurants, if you tipped in American money you could get almost anything you wanted.

"Do you think you can ask around and find out where his family lives?" I said. "Or see if we can maybe find his coach?"

We agreed to meet early the next day at the media center. I was now officially intrigued by the story. I told two people—Lesley Visser, who was then with the *Boston Globe,* and Mark McDonald of the *Dallas Morning News*—what I was doing. "If I'm not back by lunchtime, call the embassy," I joked.

The next morning Greg said he had not found out where the Pivonkas lived but he *had* learned the name of the factory where his mother worked. We walked several blocks from the media center, because we thought there was a good chance that area was being watched, and flagged down a cab. Greg leaned into the window with the twenty-dollar bill I'd given him, talked to the cabbie for a moment, and said, "Get in."

We jumped in. It was searingly hot and the cab wasn't air-conditioned. "Does he know where the factory is?" I asked.

"No, but we can ask when we get there."

Which is exactly what we did. Kladno was a steel-factory town of about a hundred thousand people. I remember my first thought as we drove the streets was "What a depressing place this must be in winter."

On the third try the cabbie found someone who had heard of the factory we were looking for. As it turned out we were no more than five minutes away. We pulled up to a building that looked exactly the way you would expect a factory in a small town behind the Iron Curtain to look: forbidding. We agreed that having someone who only spoke English showing up at the entrance wasn't a great idea, so I waited outside while Greg went in to see if he could find Mrs. Pivonka.

I paced up and down in the heat while the cabbie, who I had given another twenty dollars so he would wait for us, sat nearby with the engine idling. Ten minutes went by, then fifteen. It felt like a couple of hours. Finally, I saw Greg come out accompanied by a short, attractive blonde woman who appeared to be in her early or mid-40s.

"John Feinstein, this is Magdalena Pivonka," he said.

There was something about Magdalena Pivonka I liked right away. She had light-blue eyes and a shy smile. Her handshake was warm and she looked me right in the eye when she said in English, "You are from Washington—where my son has gone?"

"Yes, I am," I said. "I would like to know more about him—and you."

She nodded in assent and the three of us got in the cab. She gave the cabbie instructions and we pulled up a few minutes later to a drab, three-story building with peeling paint that stretched the length of the block. The Pivonkas lived on the second floor. The apartment consisted of three main rooms—a small living room and two bedrooms, as well as a bathroom. When we walked inside, Magdalena Pivonka picked up a pair of sunglasses sitting on the chest by the door. Her eyes clouded. "This is all I have left of my son," she said.

She offered us coffee, which we accepted. I remembered the scene in *All the President's Men* when Dustin Hoffman, in the role of Carl Bernstein, gratefully accepts a cup of coffee offered by the sister of a reluctant potential source. If someone offers coffee, as a reporter you accept—even if you don't drink coffee. Of course, almost everyone who has been in journalism for more than fifteen minutes drinks coffee.

Greg and I sat on the couch, and Magdalena, who had asked me to call her by her first name, sat on one of the two chairs in the small living room. She told me that her husband was out of town for the weekend and that her daughter, Michal's younger sister, was at school. She then began explaining that the plan for Michal to defect had started taking shape not long after the Capitals drafted him at the age of eighteen, more than two years earlier. She spoke in English at times, at other times she switched to Czech and Greg interpreted. About ten minutes in, I knew I had a front-page story. This was one time George had been right: poking around had been the thing to do.

About forty minutes went by and we were beginning to wind down. Suddenly, there was a sharp knock on the door. Magdalena Pivonka looked surprised. It was too early for her daughter to be home and she had keys anyway. She had made more coffee, so she put down her cup and walked to the door. I heard her talking to someone for a moment and then a hard-looking man in a dark suit stepped into the apartment. I saw Greg stiffen as he continued to talk to Magdalena.

"What's up?" I said quietly.

"He's Czech KGB," Greg whispered. He looked quite scared.

I was just as terrified. But my first thought was that I had to deal from strength: I was an American and, fortunately, two people back at the tennis center knew where I was and would note my absence if it was extended. The cold war—as *Pravda* had pointed out ten days earlier—was over.

The KGB agent was now in the apartment and had walked over to me. Greg stood up. I didn't. This guy clearly wasn't here as a friend. He ignored Greg and pointed a finger at me. *"Vashington Post?"* he said.

"Yes," I said, hoping my voice was calm.

"Pity," the man said. "Your papers please."

"And who might you be?" I asked, still not moving.

He flashed some kind of ID and called himself something that didn't include the letters *KGB*.

"You are not authorized to be here," he said. "Papers, please."

I stood up and reached into my pocket for my passport and the visa I'd been issued by the Czech embassy in Washington before my trip. As I handed them to him, I said, "I didn't realize one needed authorization to talk to people here. I've been told ever since I arrived that Czechoslovakia is as free a country as mine."

I wasn't making that up. One difference between the Soviet Union back then and Czechoslovakia was that the Russians made no pretenses about who they were and how their country was run. The Czechs were different—they told us constantly how "free" their country had become.

My new friend took a lot of time looking at my passport and visa. Whether he was trying to find something wrong or just trying to ratchet up the tension, I'm not sure. I sat back down. Greg was still standing. Magdalena Pivonka was still standing at the open door. As the agent was *still* looking my papers over, a second man came to the door and walked into the apartment—uninvited. He spoke briefly to Magdalena and then to the agent who had my papers. It was clear to me he was in charge because, even in Czech, I could tell the first guy's tone was deferential.

Finally, he turned to me and said in very good English, "Who authorized you to speak to this woman?"

I'd been thinking of a story while I sat waiting. Now I launched it. "I spoke to [the Czech Hockey Federation official whose name I still remembered back then] to ask him about Mrs. Pivonka's son, since he is now going to play in the city where I live. He told me that Mr. Pivonka was an unimportant player and his departure didn't matter here. I didn't think it would be a problem for me to come here and talk to his family."

The only part of what I'd said that was a lie was the last sentence. Obviously I knew it was a problem for me to come here. I just hadn't realized how *big* a problem.

The two agents went back to talking. They still hadn't said a word to Greg. The boss agent pulled up the chair Magdalena had been sitting in so he could get close to me. "Your visa allows you only to be in Prague," he said. "You have violated it by coming here. I can arrest you for this. You will tell me the truth in this or I will arrest you— and him." He pointed at Greg.

"I've told you the truth," I said. "There wasn't anything sinister going on here. I just asked Mrs. Pivonka about her son and what his future in hockey might be."

We fenced that way for a while. He kept repeating that he had the right to arrest me; I kept insisting I didn't see what I'd done wrong. The other three people in the room were spectators.

By my watch, the "interrogation" went on for about two hours. After about the fortieth time I was threatened with arrest, I said, "Look, if I'm *not* under arrest, I'm leaving. I have work to do. If I am under arrest, I would like to contact the American embassy."

The two agents walked into a corner to talk. I looked at Greg. "You okay?" I said.

He nodded. Magdalena actually came and asked if I wanted more coffee, which reminded me that I desperately needed to go to the bathroom. I thanked her, offered her my seat on the couch, and got up to go to the bathroom. The boss agent jumped at me.

"Where are you going?"

"The bathroom."

He nodded and waved me in that direction. When I came out he told Greg and I that we were free to go *but* not only was I not to leave Prague during the rest of my stay, I was to go only to the tennis center, the media center, and my hotel.

"Is that what my visa says?" I asked.

"It is what I am telling you."

I didn't argue because it was pointless. He was trying to prove he was still in charge and somehow intimidate me. I had felt intimidated early but not now. Now I was angry—though still a bit scared. Mostly I was worried about what the agents might do to Magdalena. I was more worried when we walked to the door and they instructed her to go with them.

"Where are you taking her?" I asked.

"Back to her job," the boss agent said.

The two of us were standing in the doorway. He wasn't very big but he had about the hardest eyes I've ever seen. "If you do anything to her, I'll find out," I said. "I will let my government know what happened here."

"Do you threaten me with this?" the agent said.

"No," I said. "I tell you this as fact."

We exchanged brief glares. We all walked down the hallway and back down the steps we'd come up three hours earlier. Remarkably, our cab driver hadn't deserted us. He was waiting at the end of the block where he had dropped us off. As the agents and Magdalena got into the car, I asked Greg what he thought they were going to do to her.

"They will ask her many questions," he said. "They will make her feel fear. But I don't think they will arrest her. In spite of what the Hockey Federation claims, her son is a hero here."

It was mid-afternoon by the time I got back to the media center.

Visser and McDonald had told the rest of the American media where I'd gone, and they had started to worry about me. I told them what had happened and someone said, "You need to write what happened and get it sent to the *Post* as soon as possible. Who knows, they may try to confiscate your computer."

They were right. I sat down and wrote every single detail I had, including all the quotes from Magdalena Pivonka. It wasn't a story per se, I was just trying to get it all on paper and in the hands of my editors at home. It might have been the first blog, now that I think about it. Sending was complicated. An operator in the media center had to hook you up to a special phone connection and dial the call for you. In the story, I said at the top: "George, I'm going to call you soon. Assume when we talk we're being listened to." We had all figured from day one in both the Soviet Union and Czechoslovakia that the phones were tapped in the media centers and the hotels. It hadn't really mattered to me until now.

A short while later, when I knew George would probably be in the office — the time difference was six hours — I called.

"Did you read what I sent you?" I asked.

"Yes," he said. "People back here [that would probably mean Ben Bradlee and Len Downie] want you to contact the embassy. If they recommend you should come home, come home right away."

"Okay," I said. "If they do that though, maybe I should go to Paris. The Tour de France ends there on Sunday. I could cover that."

"Don't do that, John."

"Why not? I mean, if I have to leave here..."

"John, don't do that. We still have diplomatic relations with France."

It might have been George's best line. It helped break the tension I was feeling. As soon as I hung up, I called the American embassy. I explained to whoever answered the phone that I was an American journalist in Czechoslovakia covering the Federation Cup and that I'd run into a problem with my visa. I was put through immediately to a man named Sam Westgate, who said he was the embassy's second secretary.

I started to tell Westgate what had happened, but he cut me off. "We should have this conversation in person," he said. "We're not far from where you are. Why don't you come over here tonight and we'll talk."

He was saying the phones were tapped. I finished my routine tennis story for the day, attaching a note saying I was going to the embassy that night. I took a cab and was greeted at the gate by a young marine who told me I was expected. I walked inside, and Westgate took me into a packed room where loud music was being played.

"We have a party every Friday night for our people and people from the other Western embassies," he said.

We sat at the bar, and he offered me a beer and introduced me to an attaché from the Canadian embassy.

"Tell me what happened," he said.

When I finished the story he sipped the beer for a moment, thinking.

"Okay, first of all, the next couple of days you don't go anywhere by yourself," he said. "Make sure the other Americans know the story, and don't go for any walks or even to breakfast alone."

"Do I need to get out of the country before Monday?" I said.

He shook his head. "No, you don't want to do that," he said. "That will tell them that they got to you. They know you're here to cover the tennis and it ends Sunday. In fact, they know what flight you're booked on Monday morning. You stay and I'll meet you at the airport. There will be trouble there, I guarantee it."

"Trouble?"

"What they'll probably do is try to make you miss your flight. They'll stamp your exit visa, you'll miss the flight, and you'll be stuck in the airport until Tuesday morning because your flight [on Lufthansa] is the only one out of here to Frankfurt every day. That'll be your punishment—spending twenty-four hours stuck in the airport."

Remembering the dinginess of the airport when we'd landed, I certainly wasn't looking forward to that. My face must have registered something because Westgate said, "Don't worry. I'll get you on your flight."

I asked him if he thought I had been followed to Kladno.

"Absolutely," he said.

"But why?" I asked. "Why would they even think to follow me?"

The Canadian answered the question. "After what happened to you in Moscow [I had told them that part of the story], I guarantee you were followed the minute you landed here. In fact, someone's probably in trouble because you got to Mrs. Pivonka and spent time with her. They screwed up."

"Which is all the more reason why they'll mess with you Monday," Westgate said. "They can't arrest you; there's nothing to charge you with. But they can make you pretty miserable."

The next morning at the tennis center, I told everyone in the American group what was going on. The next two days were without incident. The United States easily won the championship, and all of us got on a bus at seven o'clock Monday morning to go to the airport. Sure enough, almost as soon as we arrived, there was trouble. I was pulled out of line at passport control. There was a problem, I was told, with my visa. I was taken to a supervisor who told me to wait and then got on a phone while I stood and waited.

As if by magic, Westgate appeared. He had been looking for me on the passport control line and had been told that I had been taken out of the line. He walked *into* the booth where the guy was on the phone. Apparently the two men knew each other, because they began speaking quite animatedly. After a few minutes it appeared a standoff was developing. Westgate stopped talking and folded his arms. The Czech official said nothing for a moment, then picked up a stamp and stamped both my passport and visa. Westgate literally grabbed both of them off his desk and came out of the booth.

"Come on," he said. "If we run you can still make it."

The flight was due to leave at 9:10. It was exactly 9:00.

The only thing I was carrying on board was my computer and some Czech crystal I had bought for my mother and my girlfriend. Westgate grabbed one of the bags with the crystal and I grabbed the other.

"What happened in there?" I said as we ran down the hallway toward passport control.

"To make a long story short, I told him that if you missed the flight we would consider it a diplomatic incident," he said. "I told him there wasn't a thing wrong with your visa and he knew it. He said you'd violated the visa by going to Kladno."

"He knew?" I said.

Westgate gave me an "are you kidding me?" look.

Passport control was empty by now. There weren't a lot of international flights outgoing from Prague. We got through and sprinted—as best we could with the crystal banging against our legs—through the long, curving hallway. Naturally, the plane was at the far end of the terminal.

We finally got to the gate. There was no jetway. I showed my ticket to the agent, who shook his head and said something to Westgate in Czech.

"What'd he say?" I asked.

"That you won't make it," Westgate told him. "The stairs are still there. Run for it."

I took the bag of crystal from him and tried to say thank you. He was waving me out the door. I could see a flight attendant in the doorway as I ran toward the stairs. I made the stairs and, completely out of breath, made it onto the plane.

"Don't worry," the flight attendant said. "We were waiting for you."

I was baffled. Then I saw Martina Navratilova, who was sitting in the first row. "The guys [the other Americans] told me what was happening," she said. "I asked the pilots to stall a few minutes."

If anyone understood dealing with the Czech government, it was Martina. "Thank you," I said, which was about all I *could* say at that moment. I made my way back to my seat to a round of applause from my colleagues.

"Well," Mark McDonald said as I put on my seat belt. "That's one you can tell your grandchildren about someday."

12

Around the World and Beyond

WHICH BRINGS ME BACK to Ivan Lendl.

After I finally got home from Prague, I wrote a piece in the Outlook section of the *Post* detailing some of my adventures and misadventures behind the Iron Curtain. News didn't travel the way it does now, but by the time the U.S. Open rolled around, most people in tennis had heard about my being detained by the Czech KGB and my mad dash through the airport.

Including Lendl.

After he played his first-round match in that year's Open, I went to the interview room and sat in the back. I hadn't seen him since the "I don't deserve the shit you write about me" speech, and I figured I should show up just so he knew I hadn't been bothered by the incident.

Lendl didn't say much during the press conference, and I wasn't paying much attention when he got up to leave. Most of the time players entered and exited the interview room in the bowels of Louis Armstrong Stadium through a door that was next to the podium. There was also a door in the back of the room, but players almost never used it because it led to a public hallway, meaning one would have to fight through a crowded hallway en route to the locker room. Most players would walk out the front door and stop in the CBS production area either to do an interview or to grab some of the CBS food.

I was talking to Pete Alfano in the back of the room when suddenly I became aware of Lendl standing over me. As always, his agent, Jerry Solomon (who later married Nancy Kerrigan), was right behind him along with a couple of USTA types. When I saw Lendl I prepared for another confrontation.

"So I hear you have a message for me from back home," Lendl said, a huge smile on his face.

At first I missed the joke completely. "A message?" I said.

"From my friends in the Czech KGB. I hear you spent some time with them." Now I got it. "Yeah, friendly guys," I said. "We had a lot of laughs together."

Lendl was cracking up. "Yeah, they are very funny guys," he said. "Funny like a heart attack. At least you were interviewing hockey player's mother—doing something worthwhile, not wasting your time on tennis."

Lendl loves hockey; in fact, for a while he was part-owner of the Hartford Whalers.

"You've got that right," I said.

"Someday we should talk about hockey," he said. "I'll teach you a few things."

"Anytime, Ivan."

At that moment he did something that truly surprised me. He leaned down, put a hand on my shoulder, and said quietly, "Was it okay? Were you scared?"

"To death," I said.

He stood up and smiled. "You're smarter than I thought you were." With that he and his little entourage marched out.

From that day forward my relationship with Lendl changed. In 1990 he not only cooperated with me when I was working on *Hard Courts,* but he also almost got me arrested in Australia—one of the world's friendliest countries.

I was in Sydney the week before the Australian Open began

The mentor and me.... Were we really ever that young? (*John Terhune*)

Bob Knight with my former babysittee, Patrick Knight, during their days at Texas Tech. (*Texas Tech Athletics*)

Damon Bailey did everything ever asked of him. Problem was, in spite of what Knight said in 1986, he wasn't superhuman, just very good. *(IU Athletics)*

Dean Smith (with Michael Jordan and Charles Scott). His story is the book I wish I'd gotten to write. *(Hugh Morton / UNC Athletics)*

Mike Krzyzewski has come a long way from the Denny's. *(Duke Athletics)*

Steve Kerr was a lot more talented than he ever gave himself credit for. I still think his life story is a movie. If Rudy's life was a movie, Kerr's is definitely a movie. (*Courtesy Steve Kerr*)

Kevin Houston played only one season with the three-point shot. If he'd played four, he might be the all-time leading scorer in NCAA history. (*Army Athletic Communications*)

Ivan Lendl. Who would have thought he'd become one of my favorite people in sports? *(MSG Sports)*

Mary Carillo was always one of my favorite people in sports. She's a reporter at heart—which is why she had to leave ESPN. *(Courtesy of Nat Welch/HBO)*

Andrew Thompson and me shortly after the 1995 Army-Navy game. This is still the only photo in my office of me with an athlete. *(Phil Hoffmann)*

David Duval is the only golfer I've ever heard quote Tennessee Williams and Ayn Rand. *(Sam Greenwood)*

Paul Goydos has brought a lot of sunshine into my life over the past eighteen years. *(Sam Greenwood)*

because I had learned enough about tennis by then to know that you don't try to set up lengthy, sit-down interviews during a major championship. So I had set up a number of interviews during the warm-up event in Sydney—including one with Lendl.

He wasn't playing in the tournament, but he was practicing at the tournament site, getting on court with his coach, Tony Roche, early every morning and beating the midday heat of Australian summer, which is right at its height in January. Lendl told me to meet him in the locker room one morning at ten o'clock to talk after he'd worked out and taken a shower.

That was fine except for the constant nagging fact that, by then, there was no tennis tournament in the world, no matter how minor, that granted the media access to the locker room. Play didn't begin until eleven o'clock, but I knew even at ten there would be an issue. "No problem," Lendl said. "I'll just leave your name with the guy at the door."

Lendl is about as efficient as anyone I've ever met, so I had no doubt that he would take care of me. He did. It didn't matter. "No media in here, mate," the guy on the door, one of the few unpleasant people I encountered during a month in Australia, said as he fingered my media credential.

"I understand that," I said, without telling him how ridiculous it was for a fourth-rate tournament to have *any* rules on media access. "But I believe Ivan Lendl left my name with you or with someone so that I could get in there to see him before play begins."

I was doing my most polite "I know you're just doing your job but..." routine. Before the guy could answer, a *second* unpleasant guard came up. I had now encountered, I'm guessing, half of the unpleasant people in Australia. "Yes, Mr. Lendl did try to leave your name with us," he said. "Even if he *was* playing in the tournament, which he's not, he wouldn't be in charge of the rules. Now be on your way."

After the obligatory glares back and forth, I left, planning to go into the media room and start screaming at ATP Tour officials about why their stupid rules were making it impossible for me to do my job and someone better damn well walk me in there because Lendl was expecting me. It turned out, though, that there was a back door to the locker room. As I rounded a corner, a couple of players were coming out, heading for practice courts. Before the door closed, I grabbed it and walked inside. Lendl was sitting in a chair reading the newspaper.

"Where the hell have you been?" he said. I was about three minutes late thanks to my pals on the front door.

"Put it this way," I said, "the Czech secret police have nothing on the guys on the front door."

He laughed and I told him what had happened. Then we had a long talk during which he told me he was going to skip the French Open that year in order to do everything he could to prepare for Wimbledon. He also told a joke about how stupid Democrats were.

"I'm a Democrat," I said.

"Who did you vote for in '88?"

"Dukakis."

"In that case you are not Democrat, you are communist."

"Well, Ivan, if anyone would know a communist, I guess it would be you."

To know Lendl is to like him. His sense of humor, as he would tell you himself, is off-the-wall, but—our different politics aside—he has a good heart. And he forgave me for all the shit I had written about him. I've had people stay mad at me for a lot longer than Lendl did for writing things far milder than I wrote about him. I once called him, among other things, a choking dog.

When we were finished, Lendl said to me, "Come on, you can walk me out to my car and meet Tony [Roche]."

He stood up and started walking toward the front door.

"Ivan, how about we go through the back door?"

"Oh no," he said. "I want to make sure these guys know you were in here."

Okay, I *should* have just said, "That's fine, I'll go out the back and meet you," but there was part of me that wanted them to know too.

So I followed him out the door into the hallway and up to where my two friends were standing at the front of the building. Lendl is at least as much of a troublemaker as I am.

"Thanks for being so nice to my friend," Lendl said as we were about to go past the guards. "We had great two hour talk in there."

The two men turned and saw me.

"Hey, how did you get in here? You're not authorized to be here. You're under arrest!"

"Really?" I said. "You're rent-a-cops."

I started to walk past them, but one of them grabbed me.

"Hey," Lendl said, turning serious. "Let him go."

I honestly don't know if they would have let me go or not. At that moment Larry Scott, who had played at Harvard and then briefly on tour (he's now commissioner of the new Pac-12) and was then an ATP Tour vice president, walked up and saw the scuffle.

"Hey, fellas, let him go," he said. "He's with a player, he can be inside the building."

"That's not the rule," one of them said.

"Yes, it is," Scott said. "I'm with the ATP Tour. Let him go *now*."

Lendl now had a huge grin on his face, loving, no doubt, the havoc he had wreaked.

"Is that really the rule?" I asked as we walked away from the (still) angry guards.

"It is now," Scott said.

"Why don't we do this again tomorrow," Lendl said. "Same time, same place."

"Ivan," I said. "I'd rather vote Republican."

As it turned out, that Australian Open was the last of Lendl's eight major championship wins. It was also the tournament in which John McEnroe got himself defaulted in midmatch for saying to longtime umpiring supervisor Ken Farrar, "Just go f— your mother."

Farrar, who was walking off the court at that moment after trying to mediate a dispute between McEnroe and chair umpire Gerry Armstrong, said later, "When he said it, I thought I'd heard wrong. I'd dealt with John for years and he'd never come close to saying anything like that. I walked back to Gerry and said, 'Did he say what I think he said?' He just nodded. At that point, I had no choice."

McEnroe had won his first three matches in the tournament so easily people were starting to say he was going to win a major for the first time since 1984. Then he got into a tough match with Mikael Pernfors, a very good player who had been a French Open finalist in 1986, and you could almost see him melting down as the match went on.

That month in Australia was also the beginning of my friendship with Pete Sampras. I had actually been introduced to Sampras a month earlier in Florida when I had gone down to spend some time with Jim Courier.

Courier was nineteen, Sampras was eighteen. I liked Courier because he was completely different than the other two rising Americans of that time, Andre Agassi and Michael Chang. The latter two were already stars. Agassi had been to the U.S. Open semifinals two years in a row and the French Open semis in 1988. In 1989 Chang had become the first American in thirty-four years to win the French Open.

Agassi had an entourage before everyone had an entourage. In later years I would joke that Agassi's entourage consisted of his agent; his agent's assistant; two shoe reps; a racquet stringer; a masseuse; his coach, Nick Bollettieri; Nick's assistant; his personal trainer; and his religious guru—whom he once fired after losing a match to David Wheaton in Stratton Mountain. Oh, and his brother, who as far as I could tell was being paid to be his brother. Agassi was an image back then and little more, thus the famous "image is everything" commercial.

Chang didn't really care about his image. But he hated doing interviews, and on the rare occasions that he did one, almost all his answers came back to his relationship with Jesus Christ. In fact, after winning in Paris, he told the media he had won because he had a better relationship with Jesus than Stefan Edberg, the losing finalist. When someone asked him how he could possibly *know* that he had a better relationship with Jesus than Edberg, Chang shrugged and said, "Because I do."

On days he played matches, Chang wouldn't talk to anyone in the media one on one. He did his press conference and bolted. One day at Wimbledon, Tommy Bonk of the *Los Angeles Times* and I waited for Chang to come off a practice court a few days before the tournament began. When we asked Chang if he could talk to us for a couple of minutes, he shook his head and said, "I don't talk on practice days."

Unlike me, Bonk is one of the more patient people to ever work in journalism. But at that moment he'd pretty much had it with Chang's sanctimony and consistent unwillingness to cooperate even a little bit. "Let me see if I have this straight," he said as Chang started to walk away. "You won't talk on days you play, you won't talk on days you practice. Exactly when *will* you talk?"

Chang never answered that question. He wasn't talking on a practice day.

When I told that story to Peter Lawler, whose company, Advantage International, represented Chang at the time, he shrugged and said, "Don't worry about Chang. He'll never win another major."

As it turned out Lawler was right about that. But he was wrong about Jim Courier.

Courier was a kid from Dade City, Florida, whose favorite sport was baseball. For years, you almost never saw him without his beloved Cincinnati Reds cap on. He had a little bit of a Huck Finn look to him: reddish-blond hair and freckles and a knack for looking you right in the eye when you talked to him, even when he was a teenager.

When I was beginning my research for *Hard Courts* in the summer of 1989, I was looking for young American players who might be part of the book. I was doing that in part because of Arthur Ashe's 1985 comment about "where is the next McEnroe, where is the next Connors?" I was also doing it because players like Lendl and Mats Wilander, even while ranked number one and number two in the world, had talked about how important it was for the sport to have Americans competing for major titles.

"It's just a fact," Lendl had said at the U.S. Open in 1986 after beating the last American in the field, Tim Wilkison, in the quarter-finals. "Most of the TV money is in the U.S. Lots of sponsors and the most people. You need Americans competing."

By the summer of '89, Agassi had emerged as a star and Chang had won the French Open. Chang apparently only spoke on February 29 and Agassi already had a posse that was pretty much impenetrable. Plus, I didn't have much desire to penetrate the posse. The thought of buddying up to Agassi's brother made me slightly sick to my stomach. There was something completely phony about Agassi that I didn't like. People who know him now say that he's done a complete one-eighty. There's no doubt that he's done wonderful work for charity along with his wife, Steffi Graf, and I admire that. Hell, I admire him for marrying Graf. But as a young player he reminded me a little of a young Tiger Woods. Everything he said was calculated; everything he did was with one thing in mind: how will this affect my ability to make money.

After losing badly in the first round at Wimbledon in 1987, he ducked the tournament for the next three years. He had all sorts of excuses: he needed a rest after the grueling clay court season, he didn't want to wear all white (and upset his sponsors, I guess) as was required at Wimbledon, and the best one of all—*Wimbledon isn't that big a deal.*

In the spring of 1990, Agassi and McEnroe played an exhibition in Washington. As with McEnroe and Borg (and almost all exhibitions), they agreed to split the first two sets and then play for real in the third. Agassi won. After the match, Harold Solomon, the onetime French Open finalist who was the event promoter, came down on court to "interview" the two players. Agassi was no doubt surprised when in the midst of the "great to have you here, Andre" spiel, Solomon said, "So, Andre, when are we going to see you at Wimbledon again?"

There was a long pause. Then Agassi said, "Okay, let me put it to the fans. How many of you think Wimbledon is that big a deal, think it's *the* most important tournament?"

Many, if not most, in the crowd clapped and cheered to indicate that they thought Wimbledon was, in fact, the most important event in tennis.

Undaunted, Agassi plowed ahead. "Okay now, how many of you *for America* think the *U.S. Open* is the most important event?" He began waving his arms wildly to get the fans going. Many, if not most, responded. Rah-rah, U.S.A. I was standing with McEnroe at that moment, and he turned to me and said, "Did he really just do that?" Without waiting for an answer, he said, "That may be the single most absurd thing I've ever seen."

He was absolutely right.

So neither Agassi nor Chang would be my young American storyline. The previous June, Courier, whacking forehands from all over the court, had upset Agassi at the French. That was when I decided I wanted to try to work with Courier. That was when my friend

Lawler told me I was wasting my time, that Courier was a nice player but nothing special. I didn't care. I wanted Courier.

At the U.S. Open (*for America!*) that fall, I also decided I wanted Pete Sampras. He had just turned eighteen and a lot of tennis people thought *he* was the Next One. Unlike Agassi, Chang, and Courier, he played serve-and-volley, which was becoming a lost art even then in tennis. He beat Wilander late one night in the second round of the tournament, and I was sold. As it turned out, even though I didn't intend it that way, Courier was my door to Sampras.

Early in December, I flew to Florida to spend an evening with Courier, getting what I call the "tell me your life story" interview out of the way before everyone headed to Australia to start the season. Courier and Sampras were practicing together at Nick Bollettieri's academy in Bradenton and sharing a condo. When I went to meet Courier, Sampras was there. The three of us sat and talked for a while, and I asked Pete if he'd be willing to take part in the book too.

"I'd love to," he said. "It sounds like fun."

As tough as it is to cover tennis—because of the access issues and the dominance of the agents—I enjoyed a lot of the people I spent time with in 1990. Some were non-stars like Elise Burgin, Shaun Stafford, Glenn Layendecker, and Bud Schultz, who I latched onto because I remembered his five-day victory at Wimbledon five years earlier.

Others were the big names like Lendl and McEnroe and Connors and Boris Becker, in addition to Graf, Navratilova, Monica Seles, and Zina Garrison, who emerged that year by upsetting Seles and reaching the Wimbledon final. Chris Evert had retired at the end of 1989 but was still a major factor in the game, doing TV for NBC and being an unofficial mentor to, as she was introduced in Rome, "the future of the game," Jennifer Capriati.

No pressure there for a fourteen-year-old kid, huh?

Capriati's arrival on tour was considered only slightly more important than the discovery of fire. The buildup to her debut in Boca Raton, at what my friend Sally Jenkins called "the Virginia Slims of Capriati," was almost Super Bowl–like. I knew Capriati and her family were going to be an important part of the book one way or the other, so I set up a meeting with her father, Stefano.

This was one of those rare cases where an agent was helpful. I couldn't help but like John Evert, not because he was Chris's younger brother, but because he was one of the few agents I'd met who didn't take himself seriously. When I started calling him "Colonel Parker" (Elvis reference for those born after 1977), he not only didn't mind, he took to calling me and saying, "Hey, it's the Colonel."

He set up a breakfast meeting for me with Stefano—just the two of us, no babysitting. I explained to Stefano what I was doing, that I was chronicling a year in the sport, that I was working with a number of players, and that I would love for Jennifer to be part of it.

Capriati asked me if I was paying any of the players involved, clearly wanting to know if *he* would get paid for cooperating. I explained I didn't work that way, but that I understood that in Italy, where he had grown up, it was not uncommon to pay sources. We went back and forth for a while before he shook his head.

"I am planning to write my own book on how I did this," he said. (Yes, he said, "how *I* did this." Jennifer, apparently, was along for the ride. Shades of Earl Woods circa 1996.) "If I like what you write, maybe I will let you write the book for me."

I took a deep breath, both to choose my next words carefully and to make sure I didn't start to laugh. This was during the Virginia Slims of Capriati and his daughter had won *one* professional tennis match at that moment. And yet here sat her father telling me with a straight face that he was going to do a book on how *he* had created Jennifer.

Oy vey.

"Well I wish you the best with it," I finally said. "I think, to be honest, you're getting ahead of yourself, but that's your call, not mine."

At that moment Bud Collins walked into the hotel restaurant where we were sitting. "*Stay*fano," Bud said, always using an Italian accent because he liked to speak Italian and, in fact, had a very good accent. "*Complimenti!*" he added, referring to Jennifer's win the day before.

"Grazie," Capriati said. Then he looked back at me. "Maybe I let *him* write the book."

"Be my guest."

CAPRIATI ACTUALLY MADE IT to the final that first week before losing to Gabriela Sabatini. She was a big strong kid, still a month away from turning fourteen. *Sports Illustrated* put her on the cover the following week. She had an infectious enthusiasm and was still innocent enough to say things like, "Wow, playing Martina will be so cool. I mean, she's like a *lege*." (That would be *legend*.)

After she won her opening match at the VSOC in Boca, Ted Tinling sat in the back of the interview room with a huge grin on his face. "Well, now I can die," he said. "I've seen all the great ones: Lenglen, Connolly, Mrs. King, Virginia, Margaret, Bueno, Chrissy, Martina, Miss Graf, and Seles. She [Capriati] is *wonderful*. Spectacular. I absolutely love her."

Sadly, Ted wasn't kidding about dying. He clearly wasn't well and hadn't been for a while. Walking had become a challenge for him. He had trouble breathing if he had to walk more than ten or twenty yards to get anywhere (he'd had respiratory problems his entire life and, just shy of eighty, they were finally catching up to him). But he was still very much Ted. If someone asked him how he was feeling, his answer was always the same: "Dying, thank you!" In Australia,

Wendy Turnbull, who had once been ranked in the top ten, was doing TV for Channel 7, which televised virtually every tennis match played in Australia from the warm-up tournaments through the Australian Open. Ted didn't think much of Turnbull's work and told people just that.

Early one morning, Turnbull stormed into the media room looking for Ted. "I understand, Ted, that you've been quite critical of my commentary," she said.

"Of course I have," Ted said. "It's *awful*. Commentary for the *blind!* I don't need you to tell me someone hit a crosscourt backhand, I need you to tell me *why* they hit it or *why* they can't hit it. I need you to tell me what it *feels* like to be out there trying to return Steffi's forehand because you've been out there trying to do it in the past. That's why you've been hired, because you're Miss Turnbull. I'm almost dead and I can sit there and tell you when I see a crosscourt backhand."

Turnbull was clearly unprepared for that answer. She turned on her heel and walked out of the room.

Ted, being Ted, didn't worry about whether his advice was wanted or not and had jumped into Wimbledon's stiff-necked boardroom with the enthusiasm of a twenty-five-year-old. Among other things, he insisted that the club stop treating the American media like second-class citizens. He was the person most responsible for the club finally building a decent-size writing room for us. He also told the members it was outrageous—one of his favorite words—that the club traditionally invited a member of the English media to its morning meeting but never anyone from overseas. Grudgingly, the club finally began inviting us occasionally to sit in on the meetings.

I was first invited to a meeting one morning in 1986. I think I had about three glasses of sherry at eight o'clock in the morning (talk about commentary for the *blind*) when Barry Weatherill, the chairman of the media committee, asked me if "everything is all right with you chaps." The correct answer, or so I'd been told, was "Oh yes, Barry, quite well. Thank you so much." Then you asked for more sherry.

As usual, I flunked the etiquette test. After saying something about how much we appreciated all the club did, I launched into a list of complaints: press conferences were cut much too short, why did we have *zero* access to the tea room when the English media was allowed in there at any time, and thanks for the new writing room, but did anyone notice there wasn't a single bathroom on that floor or anywhere in the same zip code (postal code in Great Britain)?

The bathroom issue seriously concerned them. Something, they agreed, must be done. But the access issues...well, this was Wimbledon. When I talked about our need to get more access to the players, Weatherill—a genuinely nice man—turned to Ted and said, "Surely, Ted, you can't agree with any of this."

"I only agree with *all of it!*" Ted, who hadn't had any sherry and didn't need it, yelled. "*Of course* there should be more access. These players aren't the bloody *royal family*. The media should be allowed into the locker rooms too!"

That set off a round of serious choking on the sherry as it went down. I was trying not to laugh. This had clearly been a setup. Ted knew I'd bring up access and when I did he pounced.

By the end of that day—seriously—the American media had tea room access, although we had to go and request a pass as opposed to the Brits, who had one with them at all times, and Richard Berens, who ran the media room, had pointed out a secret, off-limits bathroom to me in the club offices.

"Use it whenever you want," he whispered. "Anyone gives you a hard time, tell them I authorized it."

Sure enough, one day in the middle of a match, I raced from my seat at Centre Court to the secret bathroom, which was only a few steps from the court and remarkably convenient.

As I was getting rid of all the coffee I'd had in the morning—when you drink coffee in England it is *very* strong because they don't make that much of it—I heard a voice behind me say, "You there, who authorized you to be in here?"

It was one of the security guards.

"Richard Berens," I said.

"I don't believe you. No member of the media is allowed in here."

"I am."

"No, you're not, come with me *right now.*"

"Not a good idea."

He was now standing *right* behind me. He grabbed my arm and spun me around.

An even worse idea.

"How dare you!" he screamed.

"How dare I?" I said. "How about how dare you! What, are you crazy?"

The fact that I was also laughing at the sight of his spotless uniform no longer being spotless probably didn't help.

"You come with me right now!" he screamed even louder, his face quite red.

"Okay if I zip up?"

"Now!" he screamed as I zipped up.

He took me down to Berens's office ranting about how I had claimed that Berens had authorized me to use the super-secret bathroom.

"That's right," Berens said.

"But, but, that's an off-limits area. *Strictly* off-limits."

"Unless someone in authority says it's not," Berens said. "I'm in authority. When you were told I had given permission you should have come and seen me before..."

He nodded his head toward the guard's pants. The guard stormed off in a fury.

"John, I'm terribly sorry about this," Berens said.

"Oh no, Richard, please don't apologize. I'll tell that story forever."

"I imagine you will."

Of course the great Dan Jenkins beat me to it. Told the story by his daughter, my friend Sally, he repeated it almost word-for-word in his book *You Gotta Play Hurt*.

The book is fiction. Dan's depiction of the incident is not.

13

Dream Season

TED TINLING DIDN'T LIVE to see *Hard Courts* published. He was hospitalized shortly after Capriati's debut and died early in May 1990 after his doctors had let him briefly leave the hospital to attend a reunion of his old bowling team. Ted had also been a champion bowler once upon a time.

I dedicated *Hard Courts* to Ted and to Bud Collins, both of whom had taught me more about the game and covering the game than anyone. The book sold extremely well, getting as high as number four on the *New York Times* bestseller list and staying on the list for four months.

Some of the reviews were very good. Others weren't as good, especially those from "serious" tennis fans who were appalled by my views on how poorly the game was being run and how spoiled and difficult to deal with many of the players were. Agassi and Chang, both fan favorites, didn't fare very well in the book. Neither did most agents—or anyone in tennis management.

One reviewer in *Time* magazine really let me have it, saying I simply didn't understand the beauty of the game (oh, please). In fact, he said, if you really want to read a book in which the author appreciates the wonders of the sport and the genius of the players, you should read Bud Collins's autobiography, *My Life with the Pros.* (For the record, Bud wanted to call it *What a Sweet Racquet,* but his publishers, showing all the imagination of an NCAA bureaucrat, turned him down.)

I had, of course, read Bud's book and loved it. There were two major differences between the books: Much of Bud's story was about his early days in the game in the '50s and '60s and into the '70s, before big money and agents had taken it over. Back then, someone like Bud had total access to the players, and the players were a lot easier to deal with because no one was treating them like royalty at the age of fourteen—or, in the case of Jennifer Capriati, at the age of nine, when her father started making deals on her behalf.

The second difference, to be honest, was the difference in our personalities. Bud, much like my mother, can find the good in anyone. Dick Enberg, his longtime colleague at NBC, once said to him, "I just don't know how you find it in yourself to love a sport this much when it has so many bad people in it." Dick isn't exactly a guy who is hard on people either.

I think I find the good in people, but I recognize the bad. I also, like my mother, can't stand phonies. That's why I wasn't kind to Agassi or Chang. It is also why I haven't exactly been best friends with Tiger Woods through the years.

The *Time* review did do one thing that looked as if it was going to help the book. Someone at *Nightline* read the review and thought it would be fun during U.S. Open week to do a tennis segment and have Bud and me—whose views were so completely different—come on and argue about tennis: he who saw beauty versus he who saw phonies. Someone called and asked if I would do the show.

You bet.

Then they called Bud, who also said yes.

Network talk shows, whether they be "news" shows like *Nightline* or the morning shows like *Today,* tend to do what they call pre-interviews. At best, they are a complete waste of time. At worst, they can cause serious problems. Twice during the 1991 U.S. Open, pre-interviews created major issues for me.

The first happened when *Nightline* talked to Bud prior to our joint appearance. Wanting to set up the adversarial relationship between Bud and me, the pre-interviewer kept asking him about things in my book.

"Feinstein says appearance fees are a pox that's killing the game."

"He's one hundred percent right."

"He also says that agents have far too much control and can't be trusted to tell you the correct time of day."

"Couldn't agree more."

"He's pretty tough on Jennifer Capriati's father and on Andre Agassi."

"He should be."

Exasperated, the interviewer finally said, "Well, what *do* you disagree with Feinstein on?"

"I like the Red Sox. He likes the Mets."

Shortly thereafter I got another call. Our appearance had been canceled. "We thought you and Mr. Collins disagreed on the sport, but you seem to agree on everything," the guy said.

"Did you happen to read the book dedication?" I said. "Who do you think taught me most of this stuff in the first place?"

As soon as I hung up the phone I stormed over to Bud. "Couldn't you have faked it?" I said. "Couldn't you have just said you think Agassi's the greatest guy who ever lived?"

I thought I was going to get another *Nightline* shot the next week. This was the year Jimmy Connors made his final melodramatic run to the semifinals at the age of thirty-nine, winning one five-set match after another. Connors had been one of tennis's first real bad boys in the '70s—along with Ilie Nastase—and had been wildly unpopular with tennis fans. Until John McEnroe came along. Then Connors became the loveable old man, the guy who had grown up, gotten married, had kids, the whole thing.

The image change made the McEnroe family crazy. "Jimmy has done things that make John look like Little Lord Fauntleroy," John

McEnroe Sr. said to me once. "This notion that he's the good guy and John's the bad guy is a joke."

Connors and McEnroe simply didn't like each other. The one time they agreed to play Davis Cup together—in the 1984 finals against Sweden—they refused to speak all week and both played lousy because most of their animosity was directed at each other rather than at the Swedes.

Now Connors was in his glory one last time and everyone was falling all over themselves to capture the moment. After Connors had come from behind to beat Aaron Krickstein in the fourth round on Labor Day afternoon, I got another call from *Nightline*. They again wanted to do a Friday tennis segment—*if* Connors won his quarterfinal against Paul Haarhuis. When he did, the booker called and said, "Okay, we're on."

Then he wanted to do another pre-interview. One of his questions was this: Why are people so in love with Jimmy Connors at this point?

I can tell you my answer almost word-for-word. "What he's doing by still winning at thirty-nine is defying mortality. You're not supposed to be able to play at this level at his age. Who among us can't identify with defying mortality?"

The guy thanked me and said he'd call me Friday to confirm that the segment was going to go forward. I was going to be on with Arthur Ashe, who had beaten Connors in the 1975 Wimbledon final and then spent many years as Davis Cup captain trying to convince Connors to play Davis Cup more often. Arthur was not only a friend, he was (and is) the one and only person I have ever used a blurb from on a book. He had offered it after reading *Hard Courts*, and I had, of course, taken him up on it.

Perfect.

Friday afternoon, during the men's doubles final, I got a call. For years I remembered this guy's name, but now I've forgotten it. "Hey, John," he said. "Really sorry to have to tell you, but you didn't make the cut."

I looked at the phone. "Cut? What cut?"

"Oh, we always have several candidates for the show. We decided to go with Ashe and Robert Lipsyte."

I looked at the phone again, still disbelieving. I know Bob Lipsyte well, like him, and have always enjoyed his work. At the time he was a highly-respected columnist at the *New York Times*. He lives on Shelter Island and we sometimes run into each other there. Although I knew he had covered a good deal of tennis during his first incarnation at the *Times* (he had just returned after leaving for a while), I couldn't remember seeing him at a tournament in seven years of covering tennis. He *had* written a Connors column that week, sort of the predictable aging hero/lion in winter type of column.

I wasn't so much angry about them deciding to choose Bob over me—although I certainly wasn't happy about it—as I was *really* angry that they'd deceived me. There had been no talk of a tryout. They had said, "If we do a tennis segment we'd like you to come on." When I pointed that out to the guy, he said, "What I said was, 'If we do a segment, would you be available to come on?'"

I told the guy to *never* call me again and said a number of very impolite things to him. That night, because I'm a masochist, I turned on *Nightline*.

This is how Ted Koppel opened the segment: "What James Scott Connors has done at the United States Open tennis championships for the last two weeks is defy mortality. That is certainly something with which all of us can identify."

Oh my God. The guy had not only cut me, he had stolen my line! Beyond that, at the end of the year, when *Sports Illustrated* compiled its ten best lines of the year, guess what line was number one. You got it.

I have never once done a pre-interview since that day. I've had shows say to me, "We don't book guests without a pre-interview." I tell them, "Fine, I don't do pre-interviews, and if you want to know why I'll tell you." Most back down—because most of the time when national shows call me it is when there's some kind of breaking news, *not* when I have a book out—but occasionally I've not done shows over the pre-interview issue. If I say something worth repeating, I'm going to say it publicly, I'm not going to be Ted Koppel's unpaid researcher.

All of that said, the success of *Hard Courts* was important to me because it proved that I could write a successful book on a sport other than basketball. And when Peter Gethers—then my editor it Villard Books, which is a Random House imprint—asked me what I wanted to do next, the answer was easy: baseball.

As much as I always wanted to cover tennis, as much as I still love college basketball and golf, there's no doubt my favorite sport is baseball. In 1969, the year of the Miracle Mets, I went to sixty-six games at Shea Stadium. I also went to twenty-five at Yankee Stadium. My buddy Marc Posnock and I would buy general admission tickets in the upper deck and, when we could, sneak downstairs. By September that year, the Mets were selling out and sneaking downstairs wasn't possible. That was okay. We were *there*.

To this day, there are few things I enjoy more in life than sitting in a ballpark watching a game and keeping score. I am psychologically incapable of being at a baseball game without keeping score. There is no tangible reason for me to do it, I just do. For years I kept score when I watched games at home, but the arrival of children in my life and the advent of the remote have pretty much ended that. Can I sit and watch a baseball game for nine innings on TV? Absolutely. Do I do it very often anymore? No.

I have always seen spring training as nirvana. For as long as I can remember, every year as soon as the World Series ends I begin counting the days until pitchers and catchers report. I always know the day the first exhibition games will be played—and God bless baseball for still calling them exhibitions, unlike other sports that stick the "preseason" euphemism on them—and, of course, I always know when Opening Day will finally arrive.

When I was young, spring training always began the same way: The Yankees would play their opening exhibition game against the Washington Senators in Pompano Beach on the first Thursday in March. The Mets, who shared Al Lang Field in St. Petersburg with the St. Louis Cardinals, would play Saturday–Sunday against the Cardinals. The Mets-Cardinals first weekend was always on TV—I watched. Sometimes I watched the Mets while listening to the Yankees—who usually played the Orioles that first weekend—on the radio.

I never went to spring training as a kid. There was always school, and even during spring break, I usually had something going on. Plus, my dad was working anyway. Even after I first went to work for the *Post* I didn't go because I was always smack in the middle of the basketball tournament in March.

After the success of *Hard Courts,* I wanted to do baseball. I wanted to go to spring training and spend a year traveling from ballpark to ballpark. I didn't have children yet but was hoping that would change in the near future. That meant this was the time. Peter Gethers, who I have forgiven for being one of the founders of fantasy league baseball, loved the idea.

So in the spring of 1992 when pitchers and catchers reported, so did I. Which was great. The only problem for me was that very few people in baseball had any idea who I was. I had gone to the winter meetings in December to try to meet as many general managers and managers as possible and had found it a largely frustrating experience. Baseball is a very closed sort of world. Those who are in it look at those they consider outsiders with a great deal of suspicion.

There were some people who went out of their way to be helpful from the start: Pat Gillick, who was then the general manager in Toronto, seemed to grasp what I was doing right away and said he'd be glad to spend time with me. So did Joe McIlvaine, who was the GM in San Diego, and Bud Selig, who was then the owner of the Milwaukee Brewers. Phyllis Merhige, who was the PR person for the American League, went out of her way to tell me she'd give me any help and guidance she could—and has been as good as her word for almost twenty years now. Katy Feeney, her counterpart at the National League back then, not so much.

I also learned a great lesson during that week from Jeff Torborg, who had just become manager of my beloved Mets. Since he was managing the Mets and since I had been told he was a bright, outgoing guy, I sought Torborg out almost right away. He was always friendly, although clearly guarded—I guessed because he didn't really know me.

One afternoon during a luncheon for managers and the media, word was passed that the Mets were holding a two o'clock press conference to announce a trade. Rumors had been swirling all week that the Mets were going to make a big deal before the meetings were over. Walking out, I saw Torborg.

"Is this the big trade?" I asked.

He smiled. "It is for the guys involved."

It was said almost as a joke—and to let me know it was a minor deal—but when I thought about the comment, it occurred to me that Torborg was right. To the guys involved it *was* a big deal. I try to remember that no matter what I'm covering or who I'm dealing with: to the people involved, it is *always* a big deal.

My most interesting encounter during those winter meetings was with Bobby Valentine, who was managing the Texas Rangers. I approached Valentine pretty much the same way I was approaching everyone else: introduction and explanation that I was working on a book on a season in baseball and that I hoped we might sit down and talk, perhaps during spring training.

Valentine and I were standing in the lobby of the Fontainebleau Hotel in Miami Beach, which was where the winter meetings were being held that year. Valentine looked at me and sat down on top of a nearby table.

"How long would this take?" Valentine said, one foot on the floor, the other dangling in midair.

That was a fair question and fairly typical. "Honestly, Bobby, I don't know," I said. "Everybody's different. It really depends a lot on you."

"Uh-huh. And what do I get out of it?"

That brought me up short. (This was before Barry Bonds had asked me directly for money, so this was new to me.)

"I guess nothing a lot different than what you get out of talking to newspaper guys or TV or radio guys," I said. "The difference is that instead of talking in short bursts every day, you might talk in longer bursts a couple of times over the course of the season."

"Yeah, but you're a big-time book writer, aren't you?"

"I write books, yes."

"So why should I help you with your book?"

I'd had enough. Bobby Valentine wasn't exactly Tony LaRussa or Tom Kelly or Bobby Cox.

"You shouldn't, Bobby," I said. "There's no need. Listen, thanks for your time."

A lot of guys were a lot more polite, just saying, "Come see me when you get to spring training."

Which is what I did with most people.

All the myths that surround spring training aren't myths—they're true. The warm weather in Florida and Arizona at that time of year is intoxicating. Spring training isn't nearly as relaxed as it used to be, and it has become a big moneymaker for the owners. But from a reporting standpoint, it is still about as relaxed an atmosphere as you can find in professional sports.

On my first full day in Florida, I did long sit-downs with Doug Melvin, then the assistant GM of the Baltimore Orioles (now the GM of the Milwaukee Brewers), and with Johnny Oates, the Orioles manager. The next day I spent almost two hours with Joe Torre, and the day after that I talked at length to Tom Glavine, who had just won his first Cy Young Award the previous season, and to Bobby Cox. The spring training pass I had been provided, thanks to being put on the Orioles media list by their PR director, Rick Vaughn, was a magic wand—it got me everywhere I needed to go.

I hit it off with Bobby Cox and Joe Torre right away. Torre, who was managing the Cardinals then, is a basketball fan and he knew who I was. In fact, when I introduced myself to him, his first comment was, "What are you doing down here in the middle of basketball season?" Cox didn't know me but was still more than willing to sit in his office and talk for most of a morning in the old West Palm Beach clubhouse, where the Braves trained.

Cox was the classic throwback baseball guy. He'd had a brief Major League career, playing third base for the Yankees for two years when they were struggling in the late 1960s. Like a lot of not-great players, he had developed a keen understanding of the game that made him a good manager. It wasn't just his knowledge of the game though: Bobby Cox was the manager everyone wanted to play for. He was the uncle every kid loves to have come over to the house. He knew a lot, he could teach a lot, and he always managed to make it seem like fun.

Torre was the same way. He had been an excellent player, a one-time MVP (1969), and was a borderline Hall of Famer long before he locked up his spot in Cooperstown during his tenure as the Yankees manager. He loved to tell stories about his pal Bob Gibson and about coming up to a Braves team that had Henry Aaron, Eddie Mathews, and Warren Spahn on it.

It wasn't surprising that the managers were more of a natural fit for me to talk to than the players. They were older, more experienced, and had seen and done more than most of the players. Jim Leyland and Tony LaRussa—who were in Pittsburgh and Oakland then, and were best friends—became two of my main characters. Buck Showalter, a rookie manager with the Yankees, also proved to be a wonderful story, even though the Yankees weren't very good.

And then there was Bobby Valentine.

Early in the season I tore my Achilles tendon. I was on crutches for a month, which didn't exactly make going into clubhouses or moving around ballparks easy. But I dealt with it, and most people were sympathetic. The only person I remember who wasn't sympathetic was Jody Reed, who was playing second base for the Red Sox at the time.

I was in the visiting clubhouse in Baltimore one afternoon, waiting to talk to Roger Clemens, who could not have been more accommodating to me throughout that entire season. My crutches were propped up against the wall. Reed walked past me, looked at the crutches, and said, "Make sure those things don't fall over. Someone might trip on them and hurt themselves."

Sure, Jody, I'll be real careful.

During the crutches period, I did a lot of my work from Baltimore since it was only forty-five minutes from my house. As luck would have it, the Rangers came to town and I went up to talk to Nolan Ryan and watch him pitch. Ryan was forty-five and nearing the end of his remarkable career. I'd spent an afternoon with him in spring training during which he had spoken eloquently about dreading the day when he wouldn't be a baseball player anymore.

"You can get an idea what it's going to be like when you're hurt and on the disabled list," he said. "You can be here in the clubhouse, talking to the guys, but you're not here. You're invisible. You can't help them win that day so, to them, you're not there. When I retire the thing I'll miss most is being one of the guys, being a part of a clubhouse. I know no matter what I do, I'll be invisible. You aren't in uniform, you're invisible."

Fifteen years later, Mike Mussina put it more succinctly: "I'll miss not having a locker. When you don't have a locker in here you really don't belong anymore."

Ryan is now the president of the Rangers. That's about as close to not being invisible as you can be without being in uniform or having a locker.

On the afternoon that he pitched in Baltimore early in the 1992 season, I hobbled into the clubhouse on my crutches—making sure not to drop them lest I hurt someone—and found Bobby Valentine standing right outside the manager's office. To get to the main area of the visiting clubhouse in Camden Yards, you walk (or hobble) right past the manager's office.

"What happened to you?" he said as if I were an old friend.

"Torn Achilles," I said.

"Did you have surgery?"

"No. I should be off these things in a couple weeks."

"Why don't you come into my office and sit down."

I had no idea if he remembered me from the winter meetings at all, but I accepted the offer. As soon as I sat down, Valentine looked at me and said, "How's the book project going?"

He *did* remember me.

"So far so good. The crutches have been a bit of a pain, but people have been really nice overall."

"Do you still want to talk to me?"

"Um, sure, if you have any time along the way..."

"How about right now? I'm not doing anything until we go out to stretch."

The great thing about covering baseball is the pregame access to the clubhouses. Again, it isn't as good as it once was: in 1992 clubhouses were open to the media three and a half hours before game time and stayed open until forty-five minutes before the first pitch. The three-and-a-half-hour rule was rarely enforced. You could usually walk into a clubhouse as early as you wanted and either meet someone or try to find someone. Baseball people get to work early. Only twice during that 1992 season did anyone enforce the three-and-a-half-hour rule on me: Lou Piniella did it one day in Cincinnati when he was in a bad mood (and apologized the next day), and a snarky clubhouse guy in Pittsburgh did it once. That was it.

And so Valentine sat and talked for almost two hours. He was funny and smart and likeable. I wondered if it was the crutches.

THE ENTIRE SEASON — crutches aside — was a joyride for me. I spent time hanging out with umpires, with owners and GMs, with the Phillie Phanatic and with commissioner Fay Vincent. In fact, I was with Vincent, who I really liked, three days before the owners forced him out and made Selig acting commissioner — for life, apparently, as he's still commissioner almost twenty years later.

Vincent, who had replaced his good friend Bart Giamatti under the worst possible circumstances in 1989, when Giamatti died suddenly of a heart attack, was trying desperately to convince the owners that going to war with the players again was a bad idea. As early as spring training, he could see disaster looming.

"If we have another work stoppage [the sport had endured seven of them dating to 1972], the public is going to see it as a battle between a group of greedy millionaires and a group of greedy billionaires," he said. "And they will be correct."

The owners had hired a guy named Richard Ravitch as their labor negotiator before the start of the season. Ravitch had a rep as a union buster and had told the owners he could break the baseball union, which has been the strongest in sports dating back to the days when Marvin Miller first took over and led the players out on strike in the spring of 1972, causing a brief delay to the start of the season.

Since that time, every single negotiation — seven in all — had ended with some kind of work stoppage and with the players "winning," for the simple reason that Miller and Don Fehr, his successor, were smarter than whoever represented the owners each time. Now the owners had hired tough-guy Ravitch and were girding for a fight.

Vincent was pleading with them not to do it. "If there is a strike, it will be a long one," he predicted. "And it will damage the game, regardless of the outcome."

Vincent spent most of the 1992 season trying to broker a peace that simply wasn't going to happen. By the end of the summer, Ravitch and the owners had come to see him as a stumbling block in the way of the war they intended to start. They asked for his resignation. Initially he refused. But when he realized the owners had the votes to fire him after they had voted 18–9 to express "no confidence" in his leadership—he changed his mind and resigned on Labor Day, an irony no doubt not lost on him.

I had lunch with him in his office in New York three days prior to that. Vincent had fallen off a roof and down four stories while in college trying to escape from a dorm room he had been locked in as part of a prank. He had recovered from his injuries, after being told he would never walk again, to the point where he walked slowly with the help of a cane. Most days though, rather than deal with going out to a restaurant, he ate lunch in his office with Rich Levin, who had come to Major League Baseball as the director of public relations when Peter Ueberroth became commissioner in 1985, and ended up staying until 2011.

Vincent and Levin would eat lunch and then light up a cigar. I turned down the cigar—they've always given me a headache.

"They believe Ravitch," Vincent said that day as he puffed on his cigar. "They're making a big mistake, but he's got them convinced this is the way to go. The irony is that Bart and I talked when he was commissioner about the fact that one of the most important things we needed to do was improve the relationships between the owners and the players. When I tried to do that during the lockout [spring training 1990], a lot of the owners saw me as a traitor."

I liked Vincent. We argued about politics all the time, but I thought he was 100 percent right in his views on what was going on in baseball. One of the reasons I gave my book *Play Ball* the subtitle *The Life and Troubled Times of Major League Baseball* was because I believed Vincent was right that there was serious trouble ahead. A couple of reviewers called me an alarmist—although the book actually got very good reviews, considerably better overall than the tennis book.

In August of 1994 the players went on strike because the owners were trying to unilaterally invoke a new collective bargaining agreement (CBA). The World Series was canceled and spring training began in 1995 with "replacement players"—scabs in big league training camps. It was only after future Supreme Court justice Sonia Sotomayor—then a Federal Court judge in Minnesota—ruled that the owners could not unilaterally impose a new CBA and that the players could return to work under the terms of the old one that the strike finally ended.

Just as Vincent had predicted, baseball took a huge hit because the owners decided to buy into Ravitch's notion that they could break the union. Ravitch was fired soon after the strike ended, but the damage had been done: a lost World Series, one-third of a season lost, and most important, many fans lost.

On a number of occasions during the strike, politicians got involved, including President Clinton asking both sides to meet with him at the White House. I was actually asked to testify before a congressional subcommittee that was looking into the possibility of revoking baseball's antitrust exemption. Believing all along that the owners were wrong, I sat in front of the committee and explained why. The person testifying at the same time was Bud Selig.

I had gotten to know Selig well during the 1992 season. In those days he would wander through the press box in old Milwaukee County Stadium each night and trade barbs with the local media. He worked out of a tiny, cluttered office, and when he talked about how much he loved baseball and how much it had meant to him to bring it back to Milwaukee five years after the Braves had fled to Atlanta, you could absolutely feel his sincerity.

That said, Bud was no different than any other owner: he wanted to weaken the union and, in his dreams, he wanted a salary cap—

which still hasn't happened in baseball, unlike in the three other major sports.

Not long after Vincent had been ousted by the owners, I was on Chet Coppock's radio show in Chicago discussing the situation. Most people I knew in the game believed that the overthrow of Vincent had been initiated and led by White Sox owner Jerry Reinsdorf. Jokingly I said, "If you look very carefully when Bud Selig's talking you can see Jerry Reinsdorf pulling on the strings."

It was a throwaway line designed to make the point that Reinsdorf was wielding most of the power back then, even if Selig had the acting commissioner title. I finished the interview, hung up the phone, and thirty seconds later the phone rang. I figured it was Mark Gentzkow, the show's producer, who always called to thank me after I made an appearance.

It wasn't Mark. It was Bud Selig. He was a regular Coppock listener up in Milwaukee, and he'd been listening.

"How can you say that about me, John? It's just not true," he said.

I was genuinely caught off guard. Needless to say, I was surprised that Bud would even care enough to pick up the phone and call, but I heard what sounded like genuine hurt in his voice.

"Bud, I'm sorry, I was exaggerating to make a point," I said. "I'm not exactly the only person who thinks Reinsdorf was the driving force behind Fay getting dumped."

We got into a lengthy debate on the subject. There was no shouting; in fact it was very valuable for me to hear in detail what Bud thought. We hung up with no hard feelings.

A little more than two years later, with Bud still the acting commissioner—he wasn't officially named commissioner until 1998, after he'd been on the job for six years—we were face-to-face, or at least side-by-side, in a congressional hearing room. At one point as I was explaining to the committee why I thought the owners were to blame for the work stoppage and had in fact hired Ravitch specifically to go to war with the players, Bud sat back in his chair, put his hand on the microphone, and said, "Do you *really* believe that? You can't believe that!"

I sat back, put *my* hand on the microphone and said, "Absolutely, I believe it."

After we were finished testifying, Bud and I engaged in another debate, this one in the hallway outside the hearing room. David Cone was standing there as we talked but didn't say a word. The commissioner arguing with me was about as newsy as February coming after January. One of the leaders of the players union arguing with the commissioner would have been entirely different.

When we finally decided to agree to disagree, Bud put out his hand and said, "Let's get together sometime soon for dinner."

Okay, seriously, how can you not like a guy like that? We had just almost screamed at each other while testifying before Congress and his parting shot is "let's get together for dinner." It wasn't a matter of Bud trying to court someone in the media; it was just who Bud was, and is — just as the phone call when his feelings were genuinely hurt was who Bud was.

Almost seventeen years after we had testified before Congress, Bud and I had a long talk about his stewardship as commissioner. To say that a lot had happened in those intervening years is a vast understatement. Bud had successfully pushed for expansion of the playoffs to include two wild-card teams. He had successfully pushed for interleague play. Both were notions that horrified baseball purists but were major steps forward for the sport and added to its popularity.

He had also overseen the entirety of the "steroids era," from the 1998 home run barrage led by Mark McGwire and Sammy Sosa — both outed later as steroid users — to the Mitchell Report to (finally) a comprehensive drug-testing policy. He had stood, literally, with his hands in his pockets and watched Barry Bonds trot around the bases after tying Henry Aaron's record as the all-time home run king. He wasn't there a few nights later when Bonds broke the record, leaving arguably the greatest record in sports in tatters, tainted by steroids.

"Sometimes I get genuinely angry when people say we stood by and did nothing about steroids," he said. "It isn't as simple as people think. You have to get the union to agree to drug testing, and I think even the union would now admit that they dragged their feet. We moved as quickly as we could when we could. When it was clear that things had gotten out of hand, I went to my good friend Senator [George] Mitchell and asked him to undertake an investigation, and he did it. Remember, the union wouldn't cooperate with him at all. He did an absolutely marvelous job."

At seventy-seven, Bud still has boundless enthusiasm. He still loves the game. He still refers to almost everyone whose name he brings up as his "good friend." John Fetzer, the former owner of the Detroit Tigers, was not only his good friend but his "mentor and teacher" when he first owned the Brewers in the 1970s. Bud has only good things to say about people—with one notable exception: Fay Vincent.

I asked him if he and Vincent had ever made up after Selig and the other owners had overthrown him. Vincent has written books about what went wrong with baseball and has been outspoken for years about the mistakes made by Selig and the other owners.

"No, I never did," Selig said. "I know Fay loves the game, and he has a lot of opinions on the game, but.... Let me just say this: it's my belief that an ex-commissioner should be like an ex-president. He should step aside and let whoever has succeeded him try to do the best job they can. I really don't think I should say much more than that."

That said, it is impossible not to tease Bud about the six years he spent as "acting commissioner" and the fact that he has now been on the job for almost twenty years. Stan Kasten, the former president of the Braves and Nationals, likes to joke that Bud will remain commissioner even in the afterlife.

"I know, I know," he said, laughing. "The day after we voted and the other owners asked me to take the acting job, I flew home to Milwaukee from St. Louis and my wife picked me up at the airport.

As soon as I got in the car, the first thing she said was, 'Buddy, what is this and how long is it going to go on?' I said, 'It'll just be a few months — tops.' She was skeptical and I guess you'd have to say with good reason.

"But look, when I took over I think the game was stagnating. We had labor issues, obviously, and the strike [of 1994 and 1995] and the lost World Series [1994] is still one of my most painful memories. It was a terrible thing for everyone. I remember testifying that day in Congress and feeling sick, just sick about the whole thing.

"But look at the progress we've made. The wild card has worked wonders. Interleague play has been great. The steroid thing was awful, but we've got the strongest drug-testing program in sports now. We're breaking attendance records. We've got great energy in the game again. I'm proud of what we've done."

His current term as commissioner is due to end in 2012. Will that finally be it? "I'll be almost eighty," he said. "I feel great but I have lots of things I want to do. I thought I'd be in the job a few months. It'll be twenty years. I know a lot of people don't believe me when I say it, but, yes, I'm going to retire."

Really?

"Really," he said. "Of course my wife doesn't believe me either, so if you don't, I'll understand."

It was fifteen years after *Play Ball* before I got around to writing another baseball book (*Living on the Black*), but I still spent a lot of time around ballparks — in part to write columns for various publications, in part because I never stopped enjoying it.

The two guys I always tried to go and see when I had the chance were Joe Torre and Bobby Cox. When Torre took over the Yankees in 1996, in spite of my lifelong affection for the Mets, I couldn't help but pull for him — and, thus, for his team. I was actually torn during the 1996 World Series because part of me wanted to see Cox and the Braves win back-to-back but part of me wanted to see Torre win, since it was his first shot at a World Series as either a player or a manager and I had no idea at the time that he was going to win four of the next five.

What Torre and Cox had in common, besides being great story-tellers, was their honesty. Both had been around the game so long that they didn't worry about saying the wrong thing. They would tell you who they thought was good and who they didn't think was good. When Torre pulled Mike Mussina out of the starting rotation in 2007, Mussina was upset with the way it came down. Torre walked into a small room off the main area of the clubhouse where Mussina was sitting about fifteen minutes before a game began and said, "We're going to have [Phil] Hughes take your start on Saturday."

Stunned, Mussina said, "Is this a one-shot deal?"

Torre shook his head. "Right now I'd say no."

Mussina thought he deserved more than the ninety seconds Torre spent with him to learn he would be skipped for the first time in a sixteen-year Major League career.

"He was right," Torre said when I asked him about it. "It happened fast. We had a meeting in which we made the decision to go with the kid [Hughes], and I had to get onto the field. I didn't want to take a chance that one of my guys [coaches] might say something to the media after the game and Moose would end up hearing it from a reporter.

"But I screwed up. I should have made time and talked it through with him so he understood. I have a feeling he still wouldn't have liked it, but there's no doubt I could have handled it a lot better."

Both Torre and Cox had decided that 2010 was going to be their last season. Torre was turning seventy on July 18 and was wisely concerned about the future of his last team, the Dodgers, because of the chaotic and expensive divorce the team's owners, Frank and Jamie McCourt, were going through. Cox, who is ten months younger than Torre, had simply decided it was time. He had been managing almost nonstop since 1971, starting in the Yankees' minor league system before managing the Braves, the Blue Jays, and the Braves again—for almost twenty-one years the second time. He had announced at the end of the 2009 season that 2010 would be his last. Torre waited until two weeks prior to the end of the season to make his exit official.

But Torre knew all along he was going to leave. "Unless something drastic happens that I can't think of right now, this will be it," he said to me on a Sunday morning in late April. His team was in Washington for a weekend series with the Nationals, and Torre, not being your typical jock, had spent the early part of the day watching the taping of *Meet the Press.*

We had started out talking about being an older father. I was about to become one, he had become one fourteen years earlier. "Here's the hardest thing," he said, sitting down in an armchair. "When they're old enough to roll a ball but not throw a ball, you're going to want to sit in the chair and roll the ball with them. But after a while you're going to hear, 'Daddy, sit on the floor with me.' That's really not so bad until your legs start to lock up and go to sleep.

"But what's *really* bad is when you have to try to stand up."

Torre had left the Yankees in the fall of 2007 after taking the team to the playoffs for twelve straight seasons and going to six World Series, winning four of them. He had written a book with Tom Verducci that chronicled in detail his relationship with George Steinbrenner, the Steinbrenner family, and general manager Brian Cashman. The book was extremely well done because Verducci is very good at what he does and because Torre allowed him to write it in the third person, meaning he could do a lot of reporting independent of Torre.

The book had been a major bestseller, but some in New York had sniped at Torre, saying he shouldn't have burned his bridges with the Yankees. Torre sighed.

"I knew that would come up, but I just told the truth about what happened and how I felt," he said. "If you read it, I didn't kill any-body, I just told Tom how I felt about the whole thing. Walking into that room in Tampa [the day he had his last meeting with the Stein-brenners and Cashman] was one of the toughest things I ever did in my life. After five minutes, I knew it was over."

In fact, Torre said, midway through that season he told his assis-tant to start quietly packing up things in his Yankee Stadium office. He didn't want to have to go back there when the end came and he was convinced the end was coming at the conclusion of the season. He had signed on to manage the Dodgers about fifteen minutes after leaving the Yankees—an interesting final twist for a kid who had grown up as a Giants fan in Brooklyn when the Dodgers were still there. In 2008 and 2009 the Dodgers had extended Torre's post-season streak to fourteen years (matching Cox's mark with the Braves), losing to the Philadelphia Phillies in the National League Championship Series both years.

But with the McCourts' divorce putting the team in a financial bind and injuries making life on the field difficult, Torre had decided enough was enough even though he hadn't made it public yet. His coaches, including Don Mattingly, his handpicked successor, knew. So did his wife, Ali, who had been pushing him to give it up for a number of years.

"I'd come home upset about something or frustrated, and she'd just look at me and say, 'Let's just go to Hawaii,'" he said. "The thought crossed my mind, especially those last few years in New York. Now though, I'm ready."

He had no plans to return to broadcasting, which is what he had done for five years after being fired in Atlanta before getting the managing job in St. Louis. "I liked it," he said. "But if I'm going to travel like that, why wouldn't I just keep managing?"

Managing the Dodgers—having success with the Dodgers—was important to Torre. There are always going to be people who will claim he won with the Yankees because of an unlimited budget.

The fact that the Yankees hadn't won a World Series since 1978, before he became the manager in 1996, is just coincidence, they will tell you. Those who know better will point out that Torre was a very good manager in Atlanta—where he won a division title after succeeding Cox in 1982, the Braves' first postseason appearance in thirteen years—and in St. Louis. The Yankees certainly had more assets. Torre made the most of them.

"Managing George [Steinbrenner] was a big part of what I did," he said. "It never pissed me off when he'd call and rant or come into my office and rant. I just figured it was his team, he had the right to do that whenever he wanted. But after he was through, my job was to talk him off the ledge. Most of the time I'd just tell him, 'George, we're going to be okay.'"

In the end, the irony of Torre's leaving the Yankees was that it happened because Steinbrenner, the renowned manager killer, had to give up control of the team to his sons and to Cashman because of health issues. For all his complaining and threatening, Steinbrenner clearly knew deep down that Torre was the best manager he had ever had. The sons didn't get that. They thought their money made the Yankees successful. So they offered Torre a one-year contract for 2008, knowing he had too much pride to accept it.

Torre went to the Dodgers and the Yankees hired Joe Girardi. A year later the Dodgers were in postseason and the Yankees weren't—for the first time since 1993 (there were no playoffs in 1994). The Yankees bounced back to win the World Series a year later, but lost the 2010 ALCS to Texas and headed into 2011 with almost as many questions on their pitching staff as the Mets had about their finances.

I asked Torre on that bright Sunday morning in Washington if this was truly it and if he would walk away when the season was over and not look back. He laughed. "I never say never," he said. "But that's certainly the plan. I've been promising Ali and [daughter] Andrea this for a long time. I've been in the game pretty much nonstop for more than fifty years. I'll still be around, still do some consulting or something. But I think the days in uniform are over."

As the season wound down, even before Torre formally announced his retirement from the Dodgers, there were all sorts of rumors about his future: The Mets needed a manager, maybe he would go back to where his managing career began and try to stick the needle into the Yankees' side from across the Triborough Bridge. The Cubs had lots of money, maybe he would go there.

There was even one rumor that started inside the Yankee organization that had Girardi going home to Chicago to manage the Cubs and the Yankees coming on bended knee to Torre saying, "All is forgiven, come home."

None of that happened. On October 3, Torre won his 2,236th game as a manager—a 3–1 win in Dodger Stadium over the Arizona Diamondbacks—and headed to Hawaii as he had been promising to do for so many years. Four months later he was back in baseball: Selig named him executive vice president of MLB and put him in charge of umpires and discipline. A lifer, in the end, is a lifer.

In the back of my mind, I had always thought Torre would be a great book subject. But he'd done his book—with Verducci—so I settled for his involvement as the manager of the Yankees in *Living on the Black*.

The first time we talked that season was on a windy, almost cold Saturday morning in Tampa, a few hours before Mussina's first start of the exhibition season. We were sitting alone in the Yankee dugout when my cell phone rang. It was my son, Danny, who I had been trying to reach all morning. I had the phone on vibrate but had it sitting on the dugout bench next to my tape recorder.

"I think you've got a call," Torre said.

I looked at the number. Torre read the look on my face. "Take it," he said. "It's one of your kids, right?"

"I'm really sorry," I said. I talked to Danny for a couple of moments, found out what he was up to, and hung up.

"I just like to check in when I'm away for a while," I said as I hung up.

Torre has four children in all. "Don't worry about it," he said. Then he smiled. "I'm old enough now that I can pick up in mid-anecdote if I'm interrupted."

Now that is a reporter's dream. Joe Torre was always exactly that.

So was Bobby Cox.

He had been a career minor leaguer until he'd managed to scrape out those two years with the Yankees—when the Yankees were lousy—in 1968 and 1969. He had hit .225 for his career with a total of nine home runs and 58 runs batted in. Contrast that with Torre: seventeen big league seasons, .297 batting average, 252 home runs—many as a catcher—and 1,185 RBIs.

At the end of my first session with Cox during spring training in 1992, he said to me, "It's too bad you aren't going to be around more, I actually enjoyed that." Even though my book was about a season in baseball, the Braves became one of my focus teams. They were good and they had a clubhouse full of personalities—from Cox to Tom Glavine, John Smoltz and Charlie Leibrandt (a truly bright and thoughtful guy) to Terry Pendleton, and David Justice (not a good guy but a smart one) to Deion Sanders.

Sanders was playing two sports at the time, playing for both the Braves and the Atlanta Falcons. He was about as gifted an athlete as anyone alive, but was known as much for his mouth and his show-boating as for his ability. When I started the project Sanders wasn't on my wish list of people I wanted to talk to. In fact, one of the best interviews I did early on was with Carlton Fisk, whose career was winding down in Chicago. Fisk had been involved in an incident at Yankee Stadium with Sanders a couple of years earlier when Sanders was playing for the Yankees.

When Sanders didn't run out a roller in front of the plate, Fisk yelled at him, chasing him down the first base line to do so. He was offended because he didn't think Sanders was showing respect for the game. "I could feel the ghosts of Ruth and Gehrig and DiMaggio and Mantle," he said to me. "I just thought it was wrong, and I told him that."

Sanders later implied that Fisk's comments were racial, which was silly. Fisk probably would have yelled at his own brother in that situation. He was one of the more passionate people I've met.

But as I spent time with the Braves, I kept hearing from guys I had come to respect—Cox, Glavine, Smoltz, Pendleton—that there was a lot more to Sanders than bluster and blinding speed. They encouraged me to talk to him, to get to know him. "If you don't talk to him," Pendleton said, "you'll be missing out."

Pendleton was the Braves' unquestioned leader. I had come to trust what he told me implicitly. So I decided to take a shot at talking to Sanders. Of course, by that point Sanders wasn't speaking to the media. Or at least the Atlanta media. I don't remember what the dispute was over. I knew if I just walked up to him in the clubhouse and introduced myself I was going to get nowhere. So I went to Cox for advice.

"Talk to Acree," he said. "I don't want to do it because I'm the manager and he might think I'm trying to give him an order even if I say I'm not. If Bill tells him to do it, he'll do it."

Bill Acree is one of those people in sports whose name almost never appears in print anywhere but who is as important to his team as just about any great player can be. He had been with the Braves since his days as a teenage clubhouse kid in the mid-1960s, and at that point was the only man in the sport who was both his team's traveling secretary and clubhouse manager. Either job was difficult by itself. Acree did both and made it look easy. He was also Cox's number one confidant.

I had first met him during the winter meetings. A longtime friend of mine, Terry Hanson, had told me I should meet him. Hanson had once worked for Ted Turner and had gotten to know Acree then. "He's one of those guys who knows everyone and everything," Hanson said. "Plus, he's a good guy."

Hanson was right on the money. Acree had quickly become a friend and someone who was always willing to help me whenever he could. Now I went to him about Sanders.

"I'll talk to him," Bill said. "I don't think it will be a problem."

The next day I was in Cincinnati for a Reds-Dodgers series. Bill called. "When are you seeing us next?" he asked.

The answer was in New York in a couple of weeks. "Deion will talk to you then," he said. "Just remind him you're the guy I told him about."

I did exactly that. Deion and I sat in the visiting clubhouse at Shea Stadium for a couple of hours while he proved to me that his teammates had been right. He was smart, he was funny, and he was honest. When I asked him how close he had come to getting his degree from Florida State, he laughed. "Not close," he said. "Hard to get a degree if you aren't going to class very often. I wasn't there to get a degree."

He did say one thing to me that I couldn't resist repeating to people. When I asked him about his continuing boycott of the Atlanta media, he said, "They had a privilege, they abused the privilege, they lost the privilege."

Okay, so he *did* have an ego.

Because I have a big mouth, that line circulated in the baseball media. During the playoffs, the *Atlanta Journal-Constitution*'s Terrence Moore was writing a Sanders column. By then, Deion had become even more controversial because he had made plans to fly from game four of the National League Championship Series in Pittsburgh on Saturday night to Tampa Bay to play for the Falcons on Sunday afternoon, and then fly back to Pittsburgh for game five on Sunday night.

Most saw this as a publicity stunt, including Sanders's

teammates, who were disappointed that he would do something like this when they were trying to get to the World Series. Moore called me about the "privilege" line. I probably should have asked him not to use it if only because one should save good lines for one's own writing. But I've never been good at saying no to other reporters because I know how I feel when I see my colleagues blow people off. So I repeated the line. He wrote it.

If the Sanders baseball/football/baseball weekend was a publicity stunt, it worked. Among other things, he was being trailed by a Pat O'Brien–led CBS crew that was chronicling his journey. The Braves won game four, thanks in large part to John Smoltz's heroics at the plate. I was standing with several other people talking to Smoltz when I saw Sanders coming in my direction with the camera crew, O'Brien and several bright lights right behind him. Off to the side, I noticed David Justice pointing at me.

"Him, right?" Sanders said, pointing a finger in my direction.

"Yeah, him," Justice said.

Apparently I hadn't made too much of an impression on Deion during our midseason talk because he wasn't exactly sure who I was. Now, aided by Justice, who was looking at me with a smirk on his face, he came right at me — the lights and the camera in my face.

"I went out of my way to talk to you and you told that guy [Moore] what I said and made me look bad. What the hell is that about?" he shouted. "I gave you all that time and that's what I get in return?"

I looked at the cameras and the lights.

"Deion, you want to talk, that's fine, but I'm not doing it on camera," I said. "We'll go off alone and talk."

"We'll talk right here, right now."

Of course by now the entire clubhouse had stopped and I knew everyone was looking at Deion, at me, and at the rolling cameras. A reporter's worst nightmare. It had happened to me one other time in a baseball clubhouse, during the 1979 World Series. I had been the *Post*'s sidebar guy and had gone to the Orioles clubhouse to write about Jim Palmer. Even though he had pitched well, the Pirates had won game six, 2–1, Willie Stargell hitting the home run off Palmer that decided the ball game. It was close to midnight, but no one really wanted to approach Palmer when he walked to his locker. I had been hoping someone who knew him would get him started talking. When no one went near him, knowing I had to file in about forty-five minutes, I walked over.

"Jim, John Feinstein from the *Washington Post,*" I said, putting out my hand.

"What do you want?" he said, glaring at me.

In those situations you always start with the easiest possible question. You do *not* begin by saying, "So what kind of pitch did Stargell hit?" I went for a complete softball. Since he had pitched well, I said, "How did you feel out there tonight?"

The answer I was looking for was something like, "I felt good, I thought I had good command, I just made the one mistake to Stargell and it cost me."

That, I hoped, would get him started. It was not the answer I got.

"How do I feel? How do I feel? Did you really just ask me how I feel?" Palmer screamed. "I just lost game six of the World Series and you come in here and ask me how I feel?"

I was trying to tell him that was *not* what I had asked him, but he wasn't listening. Everyone else in the clubhouse had stopped and was staring at Palmer and the moron who had asked him how he felt after losing game six of the World Series.

"My God, how do people like this get in here?" Palmer said before stalking off to the training room, leaving me standing there looking for a deep hole I could climb into.

"Don't worry," said Doug DeCinces, then the Orioles third baseman, who never was a big Palmer fan because of Palmer's tendency to glare at him when he made an error. "I heard what you asked him."

I appreciated that. I still wanted to find a hole to climb into. Years later, after Palmer retired and became a (very good) broadcaster for the Orioles, he and I became friendly, in large part because Palmer loves to talk about golf. My guess is he has no memory of that night in 1979. I do.

Now, thirteen years later in Pittsburgh, I was once again trapped with an entire clubhouse staring at me. If I didn't answer Deion's question with the cameras rolling, I'd look like a scared weasel. And yet, I really didn't want to be part of the Deion Sanders Over America Weekend Tour brought to you by Pat O'Brien and CBS Sports.

"You said it, Deion," I finally answered. "If you think you looked bad, I'm not the one who said it."

"Man, you quoted me out of context," he said. (Unlike a lot of athletes, Deion knew what context was.)

"No, I didn't. I explained the entire thing to Terry."

He was backing off a little bit by now. His voice softened.

"Let's go talk for a minute," he said, pointing toward a corner of the clubhouse. He turned to the camera people and said, "Give us a minute."

We walked off. "People are killing me with this," he said.

I knew—I'd known it when I first repeated the line to Moore— that I had been wrong. I would use the line in the book but it *would* be in context. With one thousand words and other points to make, it was tougher for Terry to put it in context.

"You know what, Deion, I'm really sorry," I said. "I shouldn't have opened my big mouth. I should have just saved the line for the book."

Deion put out his hand. "Don't sweat it, man," he said. "I can handle it."

The little on-camera discussion didn't make O'Brien's piece. As luck would have it, twelve years later when I was doing a book on the Baltimore Ravens, Sanders made a late-career comeback and joined the team. When he showed up for the Ravens' last exhibition game, Corey Fuller, one of the Ravens defensive backs, introduced us.

"John and I know each other," Deion said.

"Atlanta '92," I said.

He smiled. There was no one I enjoyed working with more that season in Baltimore than Deion Sanders.

ON SEPTEMBER 25, 2010, Bobby Cox won his 2,500th game as a Major League manager. It was in Washington, a Saturday afternoon game against the Nationals on a surprisingly hot, humid day for the first week of fall. Having managed in Atlanta for so many years, Cox hardly noticed the heat.

He did notice the win. The Braves were hanging on for dear life to the National League wild card, and Cox badly wanted to make the postseason one more time before hanging up his uniform. After making it to the postseason for fourteen straight seasons from 1991 to 2005 (again, no postseason in 1994), the Braves hadn't been back. Cox wanted his last game, whenever it came, to be in the postseason. The Braves had led the National League East for a large chunk of the season, but had been overtaken by the onrushing Philadelphia Phillies in September. Now they were locked in a battle with the San Francisco Giants and the San Diego Padres for the wild card. One of the western teams would get in as the winner in the National League West. The other would be the Braves' opposition for the wild card.

An afternoon game on the road on a non-travel day is rare in baseball. Most afternoon games are played on the last day of a series — getaway day — and teams head straight for the airport after the last out. In September, when the weather is cooler (normally), teams are more apt to schedule Saturday afternoon games. This being one of those days, Bill Acree had put together a postgame dinner at a Ruth's Chris restaurant not far from the Braves' hotel for Cox and several friends, one of them being pitching coach Roger McDowell.

Since I had told Cox I wanted to spend some time with him before the end of the season, I was invited along. "If necessary,

Bobby will just tell everyone to shut up so you guys can talk and everyone will shut up," Acree said.

It didn't prove to be necessary. Cox was in a good mood, in part because of the win that afternoon, in part because he was enjoying the race for the postseason, but also because he had made peace with his retirement.

"I've had all season to kind of ease into it and, for me, that was the right way to do it," he said. "I got to go to all the places I really like, see the people I like one more time. People have been really nice. I mean, who ever thought I'd get cheered in New York?"

Even Mets fans, who Cox had tormented for so many years, had cheered Cox warmly after his final game there. Everywhere he'd gone there had been standing ovations, people showing their respect for his remarkable record. "I'm glad they're having the ceremony in Atlanta on Saturday," he said, talking about the day planned in his honor for the last weekend of the regular season. "I think it would be too much for me if they did it on Sunday—especially if the game means something."

He took a sip of the red wine he had ordered for the table. "I'm hoping I mess everything up by delaying my last game for a little while."

It seemed apparent to me that even though he was at peace with the end of his managing career, Cox wasn't completely comfortable with it.

"No, it's time," he said. "I'm going to be seventy. I want to get good at golf, I really do. I'll still be at spring training; I'll still see the guys. I'm not going to be someone who just disappears. I like baseball too much to do that. I've really enjoyed this year. We've had injuries [notably to Chipper Jones] and we've hung in there with a lot of young guys. I'm really proud of this group regardless of how this turns out."

The conversation turned to memorable moments. Cox, who had always had a curiosity about people that is rare among those in sports, asked me if I had one baseball memory that stood out.

"Well, the whole '69 season," I said.

"That's right, I forgot," he said. "You're a New York kid."

"True. In fact, Roger"—I gestured at McDowell—"was involved in one of my all-time favorite games."

"Game six in Houston?" McDowell said.

I nodded. Cox laughed. "I forgot you were in that game," he said. "All I remember is [Jesse] Orosco hanging on for dear life at the end."

"Roger pitched five shutout innings in that game," I said.

Cox was genuinely amazed. "Seriously, Roger? I didn't remember that. How many hits did you give up?"

"One," McDowell said.

Cox raised his glass again. "Well here's to you for that. Nice going."

McDowell then told a story about his appearance years earlier on an episode of *Seinfeld*. Keith Hernandez, his Mets teammate, had guest starred in a two-part episode in which Jerry and Elaine had "fought" for his attention.

In real life, Seinfeld is such a huge Mets fan that he was mentioned as a potential investor when the Wilpon family fell into financial disarray in the winter of 2011 because of their involvement with Bernie Madoff.

McDowell had appeared on the show in a cameo role as the "second spitter," in a scenario in which Kramer and Newman had accused Hernandez of spitting on them after a game. Acting in the role of Oliver Stone, Jerry had theorized that, based on the angle of the saliva that had winged Newman and Kramer (yes, both of them), there had to be a second spitter. It turned out to be McDowell, hiding in the bushes.

"We taped the scene over and over so many times I ran out of saliva," McDowell said. "So they had to change it to just show me in the bushes, not doing the actual spitting."

Cox had been avoiding the question McDowell and I had already answered about a memory—not necessarily a game, but a moment. "Yeah, I've got one," he finally said. "You remember Pete Sheehy?"

I'd never met Pete Sheehy, but like anyone who followed baseball, I knew who he was. He had worked for the Yankees from 1927 to 1985 and had been their clubhouse manager until his death. The Yankees clubhouse is named for him, and he was famous for having known all the great Yankees from Ruth and Gehrig through DiMaggio, Mantle, and Berra to Jackson, Mattingly, and Guidry.

"When I played for the team I tried to talk to Pete whenever I could," Cox said. "He didn't talk a lot, but I knew he knew all the stories. Whenever I was with him, I'd say, 'Pete, who was the greatest Yankee? Was there one guy who stood out from all the rest?' He'd just look at me and say, 'I'll never tell.'

"When I was managing in the minors, I'd be in spring training every year and I'd actually help Pete with the laundry. I liked hanging out with him. I kept after him, 'Come on, tell me, who's the greatest Yankee?'

"Still no answer. Finally, one year near the end of his life I was back for an Old-Timers' Game. I saw Pete in the clubhouse before the game, and he kind of crooked a finger at me and waved me over to him. I went over and he pulled me close and whispered in my ear, 'It was DiMaggio. The greatest Yankee was DiMaggio.' That was one of the last times I ever saw him."

As it turned out, Cox did get to make his exit in the postseason. The Braves managed to beat the Phillies 8–7 (after leading 8–2) on the last day of the regular season, allowing them to beat the Padres by one game for the wild-card spot. After the final out, Cox came out of the Braves dugout to congratulate his players but also because he knew the fans wanted the chance to give him one last ovation after a win—since there was no guarantee at all his last game in Atlanta during the postseason would be a win. (It was, in fact, a loss in game four of the Division Series to the Giants, who would go on to win the World Series.)

Cox waved his cap and shook hands not only with his players but with the Phillies. That didn't surprise me. What *did* surprise me was seeing all four umpires walk over to shake hands with Cox. No manager in baseball history was ever ejected as often as Cox. His 158 ejections blew past the previous record of 132 held by the Giants' John McGraw. Torre, who also ranks in the all-time top ten, had 65. Seeing the umpires lined up to congratulate Cox, I thought back to something he had said the previous Saturday at dinner.

"I think the umps always knew it wasn't personal. I stood up for my guys. I think that's an important part of the job, letting the guys know you're always going to stand up for them. I'll bet 156 of my ejections were for that reason. A couple times I really was just pissed. But that was it."

I remembered Dean Smith pointing out to me that every time we'd had a disagreement, it was because he was standing up for his players. The great ones all do that. One way or the other, they take the hit for their players. And, almost without fail, their players know that.

Which is why it isn't surprising that when the great ones retire, the thing they miss most isn't the winning or the glory or even the money. They miss "the guys," as Cox put it. And, almost without exception, the guys miss them too.

14

Mark Twain Was Wrong

As MUCH AS I enjoyed doing the reporting and writing that went into *Play Ball,* the book's sales were a little bit of a downer. The reviews were very good. But baseball is a tougher market than basketball or tennis. In the spring of 1993, there were a total of twenty-three baseball books from major publishing houses—higher than normal, but not that much higher.

According to the sales figures I was given, *Play Ball* sold the best of those twenty-three. But the others cut into its sales. Kirby Puckett and Cal Ripken both had autobiographies out. I had written about both in *Play Ball.* No doubt some of their fans opted for the book *just* about them rather than one that included them. Peter Gammons, the dean of all baseball writers in the country, had cowritten a book about the coming problems in the game. There were baseball fans who were going to buy a book just because Peter Gammons's name was on it. Heck, I was one of them.

In those days there was no extended *New York Times* bestseller list. Unlike today, where the top thirty-five books are at least noted on the internet, you were either in the top fifteen or not in the top fifteen. There were several weeks when my publisher, Villard, was told that the book was being "tracked" for the bestseller list, meaning it was at least in contention, but the book never made the actual list.

Which was a disappointment.

The question then became what to do next. I had now written three books that had followed a year or a season in a sport. *A Season Inside* had done well but had not been a huge bestseller. *Hard Courts* had been a major bestseller, and *Play Ball* had not been a bestseller at all.

So the question was whether I wanted to go back to tennis, where I'd had success (no); basketball, where I'd had lots of success (maybe); or look for a different sport. Esther Newberg and Peter Gethers thought basketball—again—might be a good idea, since I had written my previous two books on other sports.

I had another idea: golf.

I had come to the game relatively late and had never played it especially well. My excuse has always been that the pro who taught me the game, Bob DeStefano, suggested to my parents that since they didn't want to spend a lot of money ordering lefty clubs—you had to get them made for you back then—that I learn to play right-handed.

"Hogan was left-handed and played righty," he said. "He did all right."

Yeah, well, I'm not exactly Ben Hogan, am I?

So I learned to play righty (although I've always putted lefty) and just never became very good. Golf was never a priority sport for me: I was thirteen before I played at all, and during high school I spent a lot more time swimming than playing golf. My number two sport by then was baseball, which I played reasonably well in high school. There, being a lefty was an advantage.

I have kidded Bob DeStefano for forty years about how good a player I could have been if I'd learned to play lefty. The fact is, I would have been just as mediocre. But I did learn to love the game and respect those who could play it well, whether they were the guys at Gardiner's Bay Country Club (my younger brother among them) who regularly competed for the club championship, or the very good amateurs I played with on occasion, or, certainly, those who made it to the tour.

I was lucky early on to play with some guys who were good enough to at least think about a career on tour: DeStefano, who stayed at Gardiner's Bay for fifty years until he retired last summer, had dreamed of the tour as a young man. Instead, he had gone to Gardiner's Bay, a tiny club on a tiny place called Shelter Island, at the age of twenty-one and built an extraordinary junior program that produced a remarkable number of very good players.

The three best were Jay Sessa, Gary Blados, and Rick Southwick. All went to college dreaming of making it to the tour. Rick was good enough to beat Phil Mickelson in the U.S. Amateur in 1992. Having played with all three of them—and with Bob—I knew just how good they were. I also knew that none could come close to making it to the tour. As good as Rick's amateur career was, he never made it out of the first stage of PGA Tour Qualifying School. Imagine that—a guy that talented and he couldn't get out of first stage.

That's how good you have to be to make it to the tour at all, much less have success out there.

When I had dinner in New York in February of 1993 with Esther and Peter, that was what I pitched them on: people don't understand how hard it is to get to the tour and stay there. Sure, there's no Nicklaus or Palmer or Watson dominating right now (golf was in its "faceless clones" stage, which turned out to be one of the greatest misnomers I've ever encountered). But I still thought there would be stories to tell.

Peter and Esther were a little bit skeptical: the tennis book had involved names like McEnroe and Connors and Lendl and Evert and Capriati and Graf and Sabatini. Who would the golf book have for glamour? Greg Norman, who was known more for losing majors than for winning them? Nick Faldo, who seemed to have the personality of sandpaper? Were there even any American stars out there at all? Fred Couples? Maybe, but he'd won only one major. Davis Love III? He'd won no majors and no one had ever seen him smile. Payne Stewart? Okay, he'd won two majors, but he was best known for his clothes and for bristling at reporters. Curtis Strange? Interesting guy, but he also could be prickly and hadn't won anything in four years.

They weren't wrong. This was one of my gut-feeling books though, the way *Season on the Brink* had been before, the way *A Civil War* would be in the future. Peter finally nodded his head. "I think you can write a great book," he said. "I'm not sure it will sell like the tennis book did, but I think it can be great because you're passionate about it. Let's do it."

Peter was willing to let me follow my passion, although, understandably, he wasn't willing to pay me as much in the advance as he had paid for the previous two books. That really didn't bother me. If my experience with *Season on the Brink* had taught me one thing it was that if you didn't get paid up front, you'd get paid at the back end if the book was successful. What's more, the advance was still quite generous. And I was convinced, faceless clones or no faceless clones, that the book could sell.

EVEN THOUGH I HAD covered golf on occasion for the *Post,* I had never been out on tour on a regular basis. I knew a handful of players and, perhaps just as important, a few caddies—most notably Bruce Edwards, Tom Watson's caddy. Since Watson was going to be the Ryder Cup captain in 1993 and I wanted the book to begin at the Ryder Cup, the two of them would be an important starting point.

The rest was pretty much going on instinct and advice from people I knew who had been around the game. Dave Kindred recommended I talk to Davis Love: "He doesn't smile on the golf course very much, so people get the wrong idea about him," Kindred said. "He's a good guy and he may end up being a great player."

Chuck Adams, who I had known early in my career covering soccer, was working for the PGA Tour. He recommended Billy Andrade.

Later, Dave Lancer, another PGA Tour media official, took me to dinner one night with two rookies he thought I'd like, Brian Henninger and Jeff Cook.

I picked other guys based on having dealt with them in the past—Mike Donald, who had almost won the U.S. Open in 1990, and Paul Azinger, who had almost won the British Open I had covered in 1987. John Cook had a reputation as a good guy; Curtis Strange did not, but I thought he might be a good subject given the ups and downs he had been through.

I stood on the putting green one night at Baltusrol, two days before the U.S. Open began, and watched Jeff Sluman, the 1988 PGA champion, clown around with some friends—making every single putt he looked at while wearing street shoes and talking nonstop.

And then there was Paul Goydos, who ended up becoming the symbol of the book to many people and a symbol of the ups and downs of life on tour. I was at the Buick Open in August, still trying to get to know people. I'd had breakfast in the morning with Watson to do some background reporting prior to the Ryder Cup. I was supposed to have dinner with Billy Andrade after the first round of the tournament, and I was killing time late in the afternoon in the press tent.

Almost all of the leaders had played in the morning: Larry Mize had shot 64 to take the lead. I was about to leave to go back to my hotel to shower before dinner, so I wandered over to say good-bye to Chuck Adams and Mark Mitchell, who was also a tour PR official. Chuck and Mark were engaged in conversation when I walked over.

"Paul Goydos shot 66," Chuck was saying. "I'm wondering if we should bring him in [to the interview room]. Looks like he's the only guy going low this afternoon, but I'm guessing most people will be writing Mize and [Greg] Norman" (who was also on the leaderboard).

"You're probably right," Mark said. "But it's not a bad idea to give the rookies experience in here even if there are only five guys in the room."

Chuck nodded. "Do you know him? Can he handle it okay?"

Mitchell laughed. "I know him from the Nike Tour. He can handle it. His nickname out there was 'Sunshine.'"

That got my attention.

"Sunshine?" I said.

"Oh yeah," Mitchell said. "He can find a dark cloud in any silver lining."

At the very least I thought it was worth sticking around a few minutes to hear what "Sunshine" might have to say. I had plenty of time. So when Goydos came in, I wandered into the back of the interview room with the six or seven—maybe it was eight—others who walked in to listen to him.

The very first thing I heard Paul Goydos say was this: "I'm guessing most of you have never heard of me. There's a reason for that: I've never done anything."

At that moment I heard myself do something I almost never did in an interview room: laugh.

Chuck Adams asked him to go through his round. "The thing about me is I need to get my slice going to play well," Goydos said. "I know on the PGA Tour you're supposed to call it a fade, but when you hit a seven iron and it goes twenty yards to the right, that's a slice."

I had no idea if Paul Goydos could, as the players say, play dead. But I knew I wanted to know more about him. As he walked out of the room I introduced myself and told him that I was writing a book about life on tour and that I'd like to sit down with him at some point.

He shrugged. "I'll talk to you all you want. But believe me, you're wasting your time writing a book about the tour. No one's going to want to read it."

To this day Paul and I argue about that comment: not *if* he made it but *when* he made it. He says it was the first time we actually sat down, over breakfast at the Disney Tournament. In my memory it was that first day at the Buick because it was so classically *Paul*.

Or, more accurately, Sunshine.

"That nickname is unfair," he always says. "I'm actually an optimist. Which is probably why I get upset when things don't go as well as I expect them to. I'm really an upbeat person."

Paul always says this with a perfectly straight face.

There may not be a better-liked player on the PGA Tour than Goydos because he is smart, he is funny, and he is honest. That's why he's been elected to the Player Advisory Council (PAC) and, more recently, the tour's policy board. That's why Corey Pavin asked him to be an assistant captain on the 2010 Ryder Cup team even though he's never come close to making a Ryder Cup team. People like having him around because they respect what he has to say, and he makes you laugh even when he's disagreeing with you.

One night during a PAC meeting, commissioner Tim Finchem was talking about perhaps changing the rules for the Tournament of Champions to make champions from the previous two years eligible rather than champions from just the past year—to try to breathe some new life into the event. Goydos gave Finchem about fifty different reasons why that wasn't, in his opinion, the answer or even the problem.

A few minutes later, Finchem brought up another topic and turned to Goydos and said, "Do you want to tell me why I'm wrong about this one after I'm finished, or should we just save time and have you tell me right now?"

On another occasion Finchem said, "Why don't we all just agree with Goydos on everything so we can get out of here before midnight."

And what does Finchem say about Goydos? "I love the guy. I'm glad he's on the board. We *need* him on the board."

One night in 1994 I was supposed to go out to dinner with Goydos. This was during the tournament at Doral, and the late John Morris, who was then the tour's director of public relations, was organizing a dinner with a few writers and Tom Watson. He asked if

I wanted to come along. I did, but only if I could bring Goydos. John said that was fine.

That night during dinner, Watson was railing about the subject of welfare, saying welfare fraud was one of the biggest problems we had. Right or wrong, Watson is tough to argue with because he's smart and he's articulate and he comes right at you. Everyone kind of sat around listening while Watson went off on welfare cheats. Finally, Goydos, who was in awe of Watson, said quietly, "You know, Tom, I actually knew quite a few kids from welfare families when I was teaching in Long Beach. I can tell you very honestly that most of them were trying very hard to find jobs, that they didn't like being on welfare, and that they hated the idea that their kids were growing up on welfare.

"I'm not saying there aren't welfare cheats—of course there are. But I'm guessing there are a lot more guys working on Wall Street who break the rules to get rich than there are people on welfare who break the rules to try to be less poor."

Watson listened. He asked Goydos how he'd come to teach in Long Beach, and Paul explained how he hadn't thought he'd be able to turn pro after college because of an arthritic condition in his hands, so he'd taught in the inner city in Long Beach for a while.

Two years later, Goydos won at Bay Hill, his first of two victories on tour. I was there, walking with Paul most of the way on Sunday. That night I ran into Watson in a restaurant. "I was thinking about you today watching your boy [almost everyone on tour refers to Goydos as "my boy"] come up eighteen," he said. "I was thinking back to that dinner at Doral a couple of years ago. I'm glad he won. We need him out here."

Paul has managed to stay out on tour for nineteen years now. He's had to go back to Q School a couple of times, and he's been through personal traumas that have been well documented: his wife, Wendy, became addicted to methamphetamines while trying to deal with constant migraine headaches. Her addiction brought about their divorce. Because she was in and out of rehab, Paul got custody of their daughters. He basically dropped off the tour for a year so he could stay home with them. In January of 2009, Wendy died of an overdose. Paul has never once complained or said woe-is-me about anything that has happened because of Wendy's drug problems.

"People are always trying to make me into the hero somehow," he said one night. "I'm not a hero. I have kids, I'm responsible for those kids. Plus, I'm lucky that I still have Courtney and Chelsea and I've been able to make a living playing golf. I'm not the one who died at the age of forty-four because of something I couldn't control. Wendy is the one people should feel sympathy for, not me."

Not long after Paul and Wendy had divorced, he and I were having dinner at the Palm in Charlotte, two nights before the start of the tournament that is now played there at the Quail Hollow Club. As we were having coffee, Jeff Sluman came in with several Mercedes executives. At the time, Mercedes was one of Jeff's sponsors. Jeff stopped to say hello and introduced us to the Mercedes guys, one of whom wasn't a guy but an attractive woman.

"Can I join you two?" she asked Paul and me. "I've sort of had enough of that crowd for tonight."

That was certainly fine with us. It turned out her job was to provide the players with their cars for the week. She'd had a problem earlier in the day with a young player named Garrett Willis.

"Every player in the field gets a Mercedes," she said. "Which isn't exactly a bad deal, right? Not everyone gets the *same* Mercedes though. The bigger stars get a bigger car. That's the way it works. Well, this kid comes up at the same time as Nick Price. He starts demanding to know why Nick is getting a bigger model than his. I told him that if he didn't like the car we had for him, he could probably go down the street somewhere and *rent* a car."

"I'm betting he took the car you offered him," Goydos said.

She laughed.

We talked a little while longer. She asked if she could buy us an after-dinner drink. Sure she could. Not long after the drinks arrived, she looked at Paul and said, "Has anyone ever told you that you have beautiful eyes?"

I almost gagged on my drink.

"Beautiful eyes?" I said. "No one has ever *seen* his eyes!"

I wasn't far wrong. Outdoors, Paul always keeps his cap pulled so low on his head you have to take it on faith that he has eyes somewhere under there. Indoors, he has a tendency to squint when he looks at you. At that moment, if you had paid me to tell you what color his eyes were, I couldn't have done it.

"You're a guy," the Mercedes woman said. "Trust me, he has beautiful eyes."

I stood up. "I think it's time for me to go home."

The next day on the range I told Paul's best friend on tour, Kevin Sutherland, the story. Paul had once been asked who would play in his all-time dream foursome. "Ben Hogan, Bobby Jones, and Kevin Sutherland," he answered.

"Why Kevin Sutherland?" came the follow-up question.

"Because I need one guy out there who will put up with me for eighteen holes. No way Hogan and Jones would last."

That day, Sutherland and I came up with a new nickname for Goydos: "Angel Eyes."

A couple of weeks later Paul called me at home. "I need you to do me a favor," he said.

"Sure, what?"

"Call my mother and tell her the story about my eyes."

"Why do you want me to tell your mother?"

"Because she's the only person on the planet you haven't told!"

He had a point.

I've often wondered about exactly why people who read *A Good Walk Spoiled*, the book that came out of that first year I spent on tour, identified so closely with Paul. No doubt a lot of it had to do with his personality: honest, funny, always thinking out of the box. But it also had something to do with the fact that a lot of people looked at him and thought, "If he can play the tour, why can't I?" Paul is about 5 foot 9 and looks like he spends more time with a remote in his hand than any sort of training weights. His golf swing will never be used on a "how to lower your handicap" video, and he shuffles around the golf course as much as he walks around it. In short, he looks like the guy in the group in front of you on Saturday morning.

And then he hits the ball and you realize that if he played your home course on Saturday morning, he'd probably shoot about 64 — on a really bad putting day. This is, after all, a guy who is one of five players in history to shoot 59 in a PGA Tour event.

Over the years we became good friends. When Wendy died in January of 2009, I was one of Paul's earlier calls. He had flown back from Hawaii after missing the cut there to learn that Wendy had overdosed. I was doing a basketball game on TV at Bucknell when my phone buzzed twice. At a time-out, I checked to see who had called: one call was from Paul, the other from my son, Danny.

I figured Paul was calling to tell me he was now really and truly the worst player in the world after missing the cut at a tournament he had won two years earlier. That could wait until I was back in the car en route home. I called Danny right back during the break.

"You okay?" I asked. "I've only got about ninety seconds, tell me what's up."

"I'm fine," he said. "But Paul Goydos just called here and he sounded like something was wrong."

Danny is very good at reading people, but my guess was he was just hearing Paul being grumpy about his play and a red-eye flight home. When the game was over and I was in the car driving south on Route 15, I called Paul back. As soon as I heard him say hello, I knew Danny had been right. Paul almost never says hello. He usually says something like, "So what game were you doing?" Or, "If I never play golf again, you think anyone will notice?"

This was a straight hello. "Hey, I saw you called and Danny said you called the house. Everything okay?"

"No. Wendy died."

I remember gasping but I also remember not being completely stunned—if you can be not stunned by news like that. I knew Wendy hadn't been able to kick her drug habit and had been in and out of rehab for a long time. Paul filled me in on the details as he knew them at that point. They couldn't be sure yet that she had OD'd, but it seemed pretty likely.

Paul handled the whole thing exactly as I would have expected. His real concern was his daughters. Courtney was eighteen; Chelsea was sixteen. At one point his good friend Steve Flesch stopped him in the locker room and said, "Hey, are *you* okay? I mean *you*. I don't think you've paid enough attention to that."

Paul was okay—shocked and sad, but okay. The players in the locker room rallied around him because he's a guy who has never made an enemy on the tour. He's upset some people with his honesty, and he's had his battles with rules officials, marshals, and, occasionally, a pro-am partner here and there. But his peers have nothing but respect for him.

I'm just happy I stuck around that day at the Buick all those years ago.

15

A Good Walk Not Spoiled

As it turned out, I was wrong in thinking the golf book would sell as much as the tennis book. *A Good Walk Spoiled* not only blew the tennis book away, it outsold *A Season on the Brink*.

To this day, I'm not absolutely certain what made the book such a huge seller. I can look back at *Season on the Brink* and figure out pretty quickly that I had unprecedented access to a unique figure — for better or worse — and that access allowed me to give people an idea of exactly what the method behind all the madness was and how the people around him dealt with it.

A Good Walk Spoiled did not succeed because of Tiger mania. His name appears in the book once — a reference to the pressure he was about to be under as golf's next "Black Hope." I think the book's success was much simpler than that: people just didn't understand how *hard* it is to get to the tour, much less succeed on the tour. I think the cooperation I got from the guys who were at the top of the game at the time — Nick Faldo, Greg Norman, and Nick Price — certainly helped. But I think it was the stories of struggle — Curtis Strange trying to deal with his wife's chronic fatigue syndrome, Davis Love III still feeling overwhelmed at times by his father's death in a plane crash several years earlier, the rookies Brian Henninger, Jeff Cook, and Paul Goydos trying to find their niche in a tough world — that resonated with people.

The title helped too. It was perfect for this book because Mark Twain's description of golf sums up the way most who play often feel about it. My brother Bobby, with an assist from Twain and my uncle Peter and aunt Vivian, deserves the credit for the title. My aunt and uncle had sent me a book of famous quotations for Christmas in 1993, and my brother was paging through it on Christmas morning. (We always celebrated Christmas instead of Hanukkah when I was a kid because my dad rejected all organized religion as an adult and my mom thought Christmas was a better holiday for kids.)

"I've got the title for your book," he said, sitting on the floor surrounded by opened presents.

"What's that?" I said, skeptical since I had always come up with my own titles.

"Mark Twain," Bobby said. "Golf is a good walk spoiled."

It was almost exactly like the moment walking around in the snow in Minneapolis thinking how sick and tired I was of every day being on the brink of an explosion with Bob Knight.

"Mark Twain said that?" I said.

"It's right here," Bobby said, showing it to me.

"You're right," I said. "'A Good Walk Spoiled.' That's the title."

Traveling the tour as much as I did in 1994 for the second half of the research was difficult because Danny, my first child, was born in January. But being out there almost every week yielded huge reporting dividends. I didn't just get to know the players, I got to know almost everyone who was part of the traveling circus that makes up the tour.

When Fred Couples keeled over on the range on Sunday morning at Doral, writhing in back pain, I wasn't there—I was out on the golf course. But Jon Brendle, one of the rules officials I had become friends with, was there, and he later described the scene to me in detail. When Greg Norman angrily confronted John Daly on the putting green at Turnberry on the Monday of British Open week, I wasn't there. But Frank Williams, who was caddying for Davis Love at the time, and Jimmy Walker, who was working for Jeff Sluman, were both standing there. Later that day on the range they both told me I needed to talk to Norman about what had happened, which I did. I never would have known it happened if not for Frank and Jimmy.

Later in the year, Couples was the target of a guy who insisted he *had* to talk to him on Sunday at the Buick Open because he'd had a vision about him. Again, it was the rules guys who clued me in about what was going on.

Since the internet wasn't widely available back then, when I wasn't at an event, I would call the press room to check on the progress of "my guys." Marty Caffey, who was working PR at the time, started calling the group "Team Feinstein." We never had jackets made, but I did become pretty invested in the ups and downs of those seventeen players. I had started out thinking I would follow ten guys, but as the year went on, players I'd never heard of— notably Goydos, Henninger, and Cook—became part of the storyline because they had good stories to tell.

There are two ways to cover golf: one is to spend most of your time in the press room and wait for the leaders to come in and tell you about their rounds. Maybe you venture occasionally to the locker room or the practice range. A lot of guys involved in daily coverage have no choice but to stay close to the press room, because they need to see what the leaders are doing and the best way to do that is on TV. Others do it because, well, they're lazy.

I knew from the start I wasn't going to spend a lot of time around the press room. For one thing, all I'd get there was what everyone else was getting. I was fortunate to be in there the day I met Goydos, but that was mostly because play for the day was just about finished. Most of the time I was out on the golf course, in part because there was more to see and hear there, in part because it was a lot more fun.

What's more, the players really appreciated it. It was considered so unusual I had guys actually *thank* me for walking eighteen holes with them. I'm not claiming by any means that I'm the only guy who ever got out and walked. Len Shapiro from the *Washington Post* walked every minute he possibly could before he had to write each day. So did Larry Dorman from the *New York Times*. Doug Ferguson from the AP has probably seen Tiger Woods hit more shots than anyone this side of the caddy formerly known as Stevie Williams.

But because I didn't have any daily responsibilities, I could be out early and out late, which was what I liked doing best. The middle of the day, especially when it was really hot, was a good time to talk to guys who had played in the morning.

One Thursday morning at Doral, I was out early with a three-some of Jay Haas, Curtis Strange, and Billy Andrade. Back then the tour still claimed that all their Thursday–Friday pairings were purely computer generated, and yet, somehow, the three Wake Forest guys had ended up together.

I was standing on the back of a tee when the three players walked onto it and Haas stalked over to me looking angry. You really have to work to get Jay Haas angry, so I was a little bit surprised.

"You are *not* supposed to be here," Haas said pointedly, causing several marshals to scramble toward us, no doubt to lend him support.

"Whaa?" I said, totally baffled. "I've got my arm band [which lets the media inside the ropes]. What's the problem, Jay?"

"You are *not* supposed to be here, dammit," he said.

One of the marshals started to put an arm on me, at which point Jay started laughing. "You're *supposed* to be inside with all the other media eating breakfast right now."

I saw Andrade and Strange behind me laughing. The marshal looked totally confused.

"Don't worry, Jay, I already ate," I said.

"I don't doubt it," Jay said. "But it's nice that you're out here."

The players really did notice when you walked. A couple of years later I walked early one Saturday at Bay Hill with Colin Montgomerie, who might be as unpopular as any athlete that I've ever *liked*. I find Monty funny, charming, and—believe it or not—caring. I don't claim to know him well, but all my dealings with him have been very pleasant, in complete contrast to his public image. I'm not saying I haven't seen him snap at people—he does it all the time—but he's truly a Jekyll-Hyde character, and I've been exposed more often than not to Dr. Jekyll.

On this particular Saturday, Monty played well and moved up the leaderboard quite a ways. When he finished, many of the European media were waiting for him in the scoring area to talk to him about his round. He answered a few questions and then, when someone asked him where he felt the round really got going, he looked at me—I was standing off to the side—and said, "I'd say it was the second shot at six, wouldn't you, John? You chaps should really talk to John, you know; he was out there for all eighteen holes."

I loved that.

In the summer of 2010, when Montgomerie was Ryder Cup captain, he and U.S. captain Corey Pavin were brought to the interview room at Whistling Straits prior to the PGA Championship for a press conference. This was the press conference that gained infamy because it was where Pavin had his confrontation with Jim Gray about Gray's (accurate, I believe) report on the Golf Channel. Gray said Pavin had told him Tiger Woods was a lock to be a wild-card pick for the Ryder Cup team. To me, the whole thing was much ado about nothing: how was Pavin *not* going to pick Woods? But Pavin insisted he hadn't said anything to Gray about Woods, and Gray, not liking the fact that Pavin had basically called him a liar, went in to confront him about it after the press conference.

I saw Jim walking inside and I could tell by the look on his face he was angry. I wish now, in hindsight, I had stopped him. As a reporter, you can't win if you confront someone publicly. If you feel the need to do it, you do it in private.

The best example of this I can think of in my career—other than knowing to keep my mouth shut with Bob Knight unless we were alone—came after the publication of *A Good Walk Spoiled*. Paul Azinger had been a compelling figure in the book because late in 1993, not long after he had "signed on" to Team Feinstein, he was diagnosed with cancer. Several weeks before Paul learned he had cancer, he and I had done about a four-hour sitdown in the players dining area at the tournament in Las Vegas. Azinger, when rolling, is about as good a storyteller as there is in golf.

He was talking about his Christianity, but not in a preachy way. In fact, he was questioning himself. He talked about how he often felt like a hypocrite and specifically mentioned the cursing jag he had gone on that day walking off the sixteenth hole after making a double bogey.

"I do stuff like that all the time," he said. "And then I sit here a little later, like now, and I think to myself: Heather Farr would *love* to be out here making double bogey right now. Who are you to get so angry and behave that way about a bad hole? It's just *golf*. It's not life and death."

Heather Farr was a talented LPGA Tour player who was dying of cancer at the age of twenty-eight. Everyone on tour knew at that point that she was gravely ill. She would die a month later.

Azinger's quote about Farr chilled me when I heard about his diagnosis. Naturally, I used it in the book. By the time the book came out in the spring of 1995, Azinger was in the process of making a full recovery from the cancer that had cost him most of 1994, although he had managed to make it back in time that year to try to defend the PGA Championship he had won in 1993.

The book had reached number one on the *New York Times* best-seller list in June and was still very high on the list the week of the

1995 PGA Championship, which was held in Los Angeles that year at Riviera Country Club. Not long after I arrived I bumped into Jeff Sluman in the locker room.

"Hey, better watch out for 'Zinger," he said. "He's warpathing you."

In Sluman talk that meant Azinger was angry about something.

"'Zinger's mad at me?" I said. "About what?"

Sluman shrugged. "Something about Heather Farr."

I was on my way down the hill to the range when I bumped into Ben Crenshaw. Same thing. "Boy, John, 'Zinger's really looking for you."

"Yeah, I heard."

I got to the range and saw no sign of Azinger. I did see Tom Watson, who began quizzing me about how the book was selling. As we talked, Azinger appeared.

"Hey, Paul," I said. "I heard you were looking for me."

"You bet I am," he said. "I've got a major bone to pick with you."

"Uh-oh," Watson said. "Do I need to clear some space?"

He was smiling. Azinger was not. The range was packed with people. I did *not* want to engage in a shouting match with anyone in this setting, much less one of the best-liked players on tour. Plus, I *still* didn't know what it was about. At least when Deion Sanders had come at me in the Braves' clubhouse, I knew what the issue was.

"Do me a favor, Paul," I said. "Let's go talk in private."

Azinger nodded and we walked to a far corner of the range.

"What's this about?" I asked.

"The Heather Farr quote. There's no way I said that to you. There's no way I would say something like that about someone who was dying."

"Paul, do you think I would just make something like that up? Do you really think that?"

"I don't know what to think, to be honest with you."

The good news was I knew I still had the tapes of our conversation. The bad news was they were sitting at that moment in a box in my house three thousand miles away.

"Look, if you want, I will get you a copy of the tape," I said. "But this is what happened..."

I walked him through the conversation, how it had come up, the context, the double bogey at sixteen that day. The look on his face changed.

"Oh God, I remember it now," he said. "I remember she *was* on my mind that day because I did feel bad about losing my temper. I'm sorry. I don't actually remember the moment I said it, but I'm sure you're right."

He apologized again. I am completely convinced that if I had confronted him in front of the other guys it wouldn't have come out that way. Later that day I saw Sluman again.

"Hey, 'Zinger told me he got it wrong, not you," he said.

Give Azinger credit: he made a point of telling the people he had told he was angry at me that he was no longer angry at me.

Which brings me back to Montgomerie at the 2010 PGA. While Gray and Pavin were occupying most of the media, Monty slipped outside. I was standing talking to Brandel Chamblee, who is now my colleague at the Golf Channel. Seeing us, Monty walked over to shake hands and say hello. After a few pleasantries he looked at me and said, "How's your health?"

I was completely taken aback. It had never occurred to me that Monty even *knew* what had been going on with me—that I'd had open-heart surgery fourteen months earlier.

"It's fine," I said. "I just have to do a better job with my weight."

"Well, I can attest how hard that is," he said, laughing. "But you need to do it now. You exercising I hope?"

"Swimming."

"Good. Keep at it."

He glanced around and said, "Better make my escape while I still can."

He shook hands and walked off.

"Wow," I said to Brandel. "It never occurred to me for one second that he would have known—or cared—about my surgery."

"He is a *lot* better guy than people give him credit for," said Brandel, who is right about most things and was 100 percent right this time too.

THERE WERE TWO GUYS I knew I needed to write about in *A Good Walk Spoiled* who were not playing the tour regularly and were not going to be members of Team Feinstein: Arnold Palmer and Jack Nicklaus.

I didn't expect to break any new ground writing about the two of them, but if you are writing a book about golf, how can you not write about Palmer and Nicklaus? From the start, based on reputation, I didn't think getting time with Palmer would be that difficult. Nicklaus would be another story.

The first day I was at Bay Hill in 1994, I asked Doc Giffin if it would be possible to get some time with Palmer. Doc has been with Palmer for almost fifty years. He was a newspaper guy in Pittsburgh when Palmer was at his zenith in the early '60s, and Palmer asked him to come on board to help him field all the various media requests he was getting. That was in 1962. Doc, who is the same age as Palmer, is still doing it and is kept very busy, even though Palmer turned eighty-two in September of 2011.

You won't meet a nicer man than Doc Giffin. His answer when I asked about seeing Arnold was simple: "I'm sure we can arrange it. Let me get back to you."

The next morning when I walked in, Doc asked me if I would be available Sunday morning to go to Palmer's house (which is on the grounds at Bay Hill) and talk with him over coffee and bagels. "That way you'll have some time," Doc said.

I actually had a commitment for that morning: since there was an NCAA basketball tournament first- and second-round sub-regional in St. Petersburg that week, I was shuttling back and forth between Orlando and St. Pete. I had made arrangements with Mike Krzyzewski to meet him after his team's morning shootaround to talk (this was going on the assumption that Duke would win its first-round game against Texas Southern), so I would have an early column in my notebook if Duke won that afternoon and not be scrambling on deadline.

That was a convenience. It was nice of Krzyzewski to agree to do it. It was also something I could skip if something more important came up, like the birth of a child or the chance to talk to Arnold Palmer. My guess is Krzyzewski wasn't exactly heartbroken when I called him, although he gave me a hard time about it. "Golf?" he said. "Golf's not a sport."

"We can have this discussion another time," I said. "But when you break 70, let's talk."

"For nine holes?"

Krzyzewski hasn't played a lot more than nine holes in his life. Golf and swimming were two sports they didn't play a lot of when he was growing up on Chicago's South Side. I don't think he's passed his swimming test at West Point to this day. When I asked him once what happened to the brick he had to swim the length of the pool with as a plebe, he said, "F—ing thing is probably still at the bottom of that pool."

I told Doc that I would gladly blow off Krzyzewski for the chance to talk to Palmer. And so, on a bright Sunday, he escorted me to Palmer's house at about 8:30 in the morning. This would give me plenty of time to talk to Palmer and still make it to St. Pete for the basketball games that afternoon.

When we walked in, Doc told Palmer that I had canceled a meeting with Mike Krzyzewski to talk to him that morning.

Palmer looked at me quizzically. "Mike Krzyzewski?" he said. "Who's that?"

So Palmer wasn't a basketball fan. "Oh, he's the basketball coach at Duke," I said.

"Duke," he said. "Oh yeah, Duke. They're the ones whose butt we've been kicking the last couple of years. Like every single game. Is that the Duke you're talking about?"

He was grinning now, a big-time "gotcha" grin. He was right too: his alma mater, Wake Forest, was in the midst of what would become a nine-game winning streak against Duke, aided immeasurably by the presence of Tim Duncan at center.

Naturally, I cracked up when Palmer "remembered" Duke. In an instant, I understood the Palmer magic: within sixty seconds of meeting him, I felt completely at ease.

The next couple of hours were as enjoyable as any I've ever had as a reporter. Palmer was relaxed—my guess is he's *always* relaxed—and he told story after story about his father and about Ben Hogan making jokes about his swing and about his relationship with Nicklaus. He talked about trying to get other players to understand that being a celebrity isn't just about perks, it is also about responsibilities. No one ever understood that better than Palmer.

He talked about how money had changed his sport and all sports. "I think I was the first guy on tour to have my own plane," he said. "I bought mine after I won my *second* Masters. Nowadays, if guys finish in second place in *any* tournament they buy a plane."

Still, he liked the fact that players came to him for advice, even if they didn't always follow it. Peter Jacobsen had told me a story about the last time Palmer had made the cut at Bay Hill—in 1991 at the age of sixty-one, a pretty impressive feat. Jacobsen had gone out on Friday night and gotten a cake, and all the players had gathered in the locker room before play began to present the cake to Palmer. When I brought that up, Palmer became a little bit teary-eyed.

"It meant a lot," he said. "Because the message was that they still respected me and still thought of me as one of them. That was a big deal."

After about two hours I thought I had enough—more than enough—and I needed to get on the road to St. Petersburg in order to beat the basketball traffic. I thanked Palmer for the time.

"Have you got all you need?" he asked. "I'm going down to my workshop to work on some clubs if you need a few more minutes."

Okay, you don't turn down the chance to chat with Arnold Palmer in his workshop in order to beat traffic. So I went downstairs with him and we spent another hour. He worked on some clubs—he showed me what he was doing, but I couldn't begin to tell you what he was trying to accomplish—and told more stories. He told me that one of his goals was to get the corporate name off his tournament.

"We needed to do it for the money," he said. "And Nestle has been great. But it bothers me. Makes me feel like we're just another tournament. I'd like to do what Jack has been able to do: keep Bay Hill in the tournament name and have a presenting sponsor."

Two years later, Palmer got his wish and the tournament became the Bay Hill Invitational presented by a tire company. These days it is the Arnold Palmer Invitational presented by a credit card.

It was noon by the time I left Palmer's house. The traffic getting to the basketball game was horrific. It was more than worth it.

As everyone had predicted, trying to pin down Jack Nicklaus wasn't nearly as simple as asking his right-hand man when he might have some time.

For one thing, Nicklaus had more than one right-hand man. His version of Doc for years had been Larry O'Brien—known to one and all in golf as LOB. By 1994 LOB was semi-retired and handed a lot of his duties to his son Andy. Both O'Briens were good guys, and like everyone else who worked for him, they lived in fear of Jack. When I first started talking to them about getting some time with Jack, they reacted as if I had asked to be added to his will.

"We'll do our best," was the repeated refrain.

By the time the tour got to Jack's tournament, the Memorial, in late May, I had decided the only way to get to Jack was the direct route: just ask him myself. That's almost always the best way because it is much harder to say no directly to someone than having someone else do it for you. About the only time I go to an agent or a PR guy is if there's no way to talk to someone directly, or if it is someone who won't know me from Adam. Nicklaus was in the second category.

Every year at the Memorial, Nicklaus does a "state of the Memorial" press conference. This is in keeping with his desire to make the Memorial as much like the Masters as possible. He's even got guys walking around in green jackets.

Because the Masters doesn't let the media on the range, the Memorial doesn't let the media on the range—even though PGA Tour rules say the media is allowed on the range. Recently, the rule at the Memorial has changed: now a media member can be "invited" onto the range by a player. (The Masters gets away with the media ban because it is technically not a PGA Tour sponsored event. It is for that reason that the tour's rule against playing tournaments at clubs that discriminate—in Augusta's case, against women—doesn't come into play the second week in April.)

Even the players joke about how seriously the people at the Memorial take themselves. One year I was walking the first day of the tournament with Davis Love, Greg Norman, and Mike Reid. From the twelfth green at Muirfield Village, the players walk straight back through the woods to the thirteenth tee. There are no spectators allowed back there, and the caddies don't walk back either—they go ahead and forecaddie down the fairway.

I always liked to walk back to the tee in those situations because it was about as private a moment as you are likely to get on the golf course with the players. I have no doubt it was against the rules, but no one ever stopped me.

On this day, as we walked back to the tee, Norman decided to run to the Port-a-John in the woods. He tossed me his driver as he turned in that direction and said, "Don't want to risk getting it wet in there."

I walked onto the tee with Love and Reid. They both hit their drives and then we waited for Norman.

"I'll give you a hundred dollars if you tee up a ball and take a swing with that driver," Davis said, laughing.

"I'll need a lot more than that for bail money," I said.

We were laughing as Norman walked onto the tee.

"Hey Greg, Mike and I think John should pop one out there using your driver," Love said. "What do you think?"

"Great idea," Norman said and actually flipped a ball at me.

"Greg, I have no desire to go to jail," I said. "Those green coats would have me arrested before I took three steps off this tee" (not to mention that Norman would no doubt be DQ'd, but that wouldn't have been my problem).

"No, they wouldn't have you arrested," Norman said.

"What, are you nuts?"

"Not at all. Why arrest you when they've already had you shot?"

He had a point.

On this particular afternoon, when Nicklaus finished his press conference, I approached him as he was walking out. Several other writers were trying to get in postconference "scrum" questions, and Andy O'Brien was trying to keep Jack moving. Finally, when the other guys were finished, I introduced myself to Jack, who looked at me as if to say, *"and?"*

Andy jumped in, trying to help. "You remember LOB and I mentioned John to you, Jack. He's writing a book on the tour..."

"Why do you want to talk to me?" Jack said. "I'm not much of a player anymore."

I knew this was the part where I was supposed to tell him how great he still was, but I chose a different route. "Because you're Jack Nicklaus. You can't write a book about golf without talking to Jack Nicklaus."

He smiled when I said that. "So how much time do you need?"

"I don't know," I said, giving him my standard answer. "Maybe an hour or so."

Nicklaus burst out laughing as if I had just said the funniest thing he'd ever heard in his life. "An hour?" he said. "You want an hour? I don't think I've ever given anyone an hour in my entire life."

This was funny, especially since Nicklaus is famous for using up most of an hour at times to answer *one* question.

He was looking at poor Andy O'Brien as if Andy had allowed a streaker into the press room. Andy was pale.

"I think John meant that would be his *ideal*," Andy said. "He doesn't really expect you to give him a whole hour."

"An hour?" Nicklaus repeated, still sounding stunned.

"Look, Jack, no problem," I said. "Thanks for the time."

I turned and walked away.

"Hey, where are you going?" Nicklaus said.

"You said you'd never given anyone an hour in your life," I said.

"I didn't say no, did I?" he said.

"No, but I thought 'I've never given anyone an hour in my entire life' was a pretty clear answer."

"Not so. Talk to Andy. We'll get it set up."

So I went back to talking to Andy. I honestly believe he did everything he could to pin Jack down to a time and place, but by the time I got to the PGA Championship that summer—my last tournament before heading home to write the book—I still hadn't talked to Nicklaus. On Monday morning, I bumped into Ken Kennerly, then one of Nicklaus's agents, in the locker room. Ken, who had actually been a considerable help to me early in my research, was fully aware of my Quixotic quest to talk to Jack.

"Did it ever get done?" he asked.

"No, and I've pretty much given up," I said. "This is my last week before I go home to write."

"Let me see what I can do," Ken said.

The next day he told me Jack had agreed to talk to me—*if* I flew back to Palm Beach with him and did the interview on his plane.

"What if he misses the cut?" I said to Ken. "Worse, what if he plays early on Sunday and leaves before the tournament is over?"

"Either way, he'll go straight from here to the airport," Ken said. "Your call."

There really was no call to be made. It was Jack Nicklaus. It was a book on golf. I had to do it.

The PGA that year was at Southern Hills in Tulsa—a pleasant place in August, if you are preparing to deal with the fires of hell in the afterlife. I checked flights. It would actually be better for me if Nicklaus missed the cut, even though the only way to get back to Tulsa from Palm Beach was to get up at 4:30 the next morning to fly back with a stopover in Atlanta. At least that way I would be free and clear on Saturday and Sunday to focus on the tournament—if I didn't fall asleep.

Nicklaus played in the middle of the day on Thursday and shot 79, grinding over a four-foot putt on eighteen. "Didn't want the snowman [8, as in the first half of 80] on my card," he said later.

I called my travel agent and booked my flights for Saturday morning. Not long after Nicklaus finished, I was sitting in the locker room with Jeff Sluman, who had been in Nicklaus's group that day.

Slu had been a member of Team Feinstein and had become one of my favorite people on tour. He was smart, thoughtful, and funny, and an excellent storyteller. To this day we laugh about the fact that when I first asked him about being involved in the book, he said, "I'll do it if you want, but I'm worried I might be too vanilla for you."

Jeff's anything but vanilla.

I was telling him about flying to Palm Beach with Nicklaus and my planned 4:30 a.m. wake-up on Saturday. As luck would have it, Nicklaus walked up at that moment. Slu offered condolences on his round.

"Not my week, I guess," Nicklaus said. He wasn't talking just about his golf. Earlier in the week he had been involved in a controversy over a comment he had made previously that month at the opening of a golf course in Vancouver. Someone had asked why there were so few African-Americans on tour. At that moment, with Lee Elder, Calvin Peete, Charlie Sifford, and Pete Brown on the Senior Tour, only Jim Thorpe—who was forty-five—was left from the first generation of outstanding African-American players. Tiger Woods was eighteen and not yet on the tour.

Nicklaus had talked about environment, city versus suburbs, and had then said something about white muscles and black muscles. He believed that he had said kids growing up in the city environment, many of them black, learned to use different muscles—to play football, basketball, baseball—than suburban kids. He'd been quoted as saying black and white muscles were *different*. Publicly, he had been no-commenting the whole thing all week, releasing a statement saying that was *not* what he had said and had left it at that.

Sluman and I both nodded sympathetically when he talked about having a tough week.

"So I hear you're flying back to Palm Beach with us tomorrow," Nicklaus said to me.

"Well, if you miss the cut, yes," I said.

Nicklaus laughed. "What do you think, I'm going to shoot 79-59?" He put up a hand. "It's nice of you to say though, I appreciate it."

"Should I just find you after you sign your card tomorrow?" I asked.

"Yes. That should work."

He was about to turn away when Slu said to me, "So what time do you have to get up Saturday to fly back here?"

"At four thirty," I said.

Nicklaus turned back. "You have to come back here?" he said.

One should never underestimate the ability of an athlete to convince himself an event is over once he is no longer in it.

"Well, yeah, I have to come back for the last two days of the tournament."

Nicklaus knitted his brows. "In that case, wouldn't it be easier for you if we just did it here?"

"Um, yeah, it would be a *lot* easier."

"Why don't you just meet me at the house we're renting in an hour," he said. "It's about a mile from here."

"That would be perfect," I said.

As soon as he turned away, I said to Sluman, "Bless you, my son."

"You owe me big time," he said.

He was right.

I SPENT THREE HOURS with Nicklaus that day. He was candid, talking very honestly about how crushed he felt by people implying he was a racist. "Look, there's no tape of the press conference," he said. "I can't *swear* to you that I didn't misspeak, but I certainly wasn't saying what people are trying to say I was saying. I think my track record is pretty good."

In fact, when Nicklaus had built and opened Muirfield Village—the club that hosts the Memorial—he had made a point of actually recruiting minorities to be members when the club opened: blacks, Jews, women. "Could we all do more?" he said. "Yes. Absolutely."

I asked him about his nickname among the players: Carnac. It had come about because a lot of players thought of Nicklaus as a know-it-all (Tom Watson was Carnac Jr. in those days). Nicklaus thought it had started during a Ryder Cup match when he had started predicting what would happen before players hit shots. Maybe, but there was more to it than that.

At about seven o'clock, Jack's wife, Barbara—known on tour as the nice Nicklaus—came in.

"Jack, the people we rented the house from are here," she said. "You promised to take a picture with them, remember..."

"Oh yeah, I forgot," Nicklaus said. "Give us a few more minutes."

That's the thing about Nicklaus. Pinning him down is just about impossible—he now has a PR guy who doesn't return phone calls even to media members he knows unless you leave a reason why you're calling *him.* So I never call him. But if you do get time with Nicklaus, he's a great interview because he's almost disarmingly honest. He was then; he is now.

Another twenty minutes went by and Jack was still talking. I began to feel bad for the people waiting for him. "Jack, maybe you should go take this picture," I said finally.

"Are you okay?" he said. "You have enough?"

"Plenty."

"Now that I know you, anytime you need me, just call. It won't be nearly as hard to get me in the future. I promise."

We walked outside and Nicklaus said hello to about a dozen people who had come to meet him.

"Who here can break 79?" he said. "Maybe we can play tomorrow and you can give me shots."

He shot 71 the next day, grinding all the way even with no chance to make the cut. The great ones do that.

Three years later, when I was beginning my research for *The Majors,* I went directly to Jack (as instructed) to ask him if we could sit down and talk at some point.

"John," he said with a smile, "have I ever denied you anything?"

16

Tiger

THE VERY FIRST TIME I laid eyes on Tiger Woods was in March of 1994 at the Bay Hill Classic—or as it was called then, the Nestle Invitational. I was standing on the range on Wednesday afternoon—I remember it was Wednesday because the pro-am there is played on Tuesday and I'd spent most of the pro-am day chasing Greg Norman. I was talking to Peter Jacobsen, Davis Love, and Billy Andrade.

Billy pointed down the range at a skinny kid hitting balls. "You know who that is?" he said.

I had no idea, although the fact that he was African-American and clearly very young made him stand out.

"You should know," Billy continued. "That's Tiger Woods. He's the Next One."

I *did* know the name. I'd heard it a few times on tour—a phenom from California who was already unofficially under contract to IMG. In fact, his father, Earl, was on IMG's payroll as a "junior talent scout."

I hadn't paid that much attention. My focus was on the players who were on the tour at that moment, and I tended to be skeptical about Next Ones. I could still remember Brent Musburger comparing Jeff Lebo to Jerry West when Lebo was a freshman at North Carolina. I had already seen what being the Next One had done to Jennifer Capriati, and I remembered reading a Rick Reilly piece in

Sports Illustrated a couple of years earlier on how Love and Fred Couples were the Next Ones in golf.

"I thought you and Fred were the Next Ones," I said to Love.

"Not like this kid," Love said. "At least that's what people are saying."

I shrugged, still skeptical. A few minutes later, I walked off the range. As luck would have it, Woods was walking a few steps in front of me. As he headed—I presumed to the first tee to play a few holes—a small cadre of maybe fifteen to twenty kids standing behind the ropes pushed programs and pieces of paper in his direction for autographs. Some knew him by name, others didn't. Woods put his head down, looked in neither direction, and walked right past them without slowing for a second.

Most players will stop when leaving the range on practice days. Walking to the first tee for an actual round is different. In that situation most guys will say "after the round" or "gotta go to work." But this was a practice day, and this was before Woods had become such a big star that stopping to sign autographs could turn into an all-day affair.

Watching him put his head down and keep on going, I distinctly remember thinking to myself, "Just who the hell does that kid think he is?"

Of course the answer, as it turned out, was simple: he thought he was Tiger Woods.

Woods won his first U.S. Amateur that summer and played in his first Masters the following April. That was the first time—in seven attempts—that he made a cut in a professional tournament, finishing tied for fifty-second. Even so, when he withdrew from the U.S. Open at Shinnecock that summer after hurting his wrist while making a swing in thick rough, I thought, "Oh yeah, Next One all right. He's not yet twenty and he's already getting hurt."

Of course, by the time he turned pro in the summer of 1996 after winning the Amateur for a third straight time, Woods had become a phenomenon, in part because he was so good, in part because he was African-American, in part because IMG and Nike were marketing him before he hit his first tee shot as a pro in Milwaukee, which came soon after that third victory in the Amateur.

It was after the tournament in Milwaukee that I first ran afoul of Team Tiger. I had been asked by *Newsweek* to do a story on Tiger mania. I wrote pretty much the same story as everyone else, talking about his vast potential, about how important it was for golf to finally have an African-American star, and about how the marketing machine was in motion already, playing on his status as a minority — remember his first line in his first press conference as a pro? "Hello, world. Are you ready for me?"

I also mentioned that Earl Woods had already developed a reputation in golf as a pushy father and that his avid pursuit of publicity for himself and every dollar possible reminded some (me) of Stefano Capriati. That wasn't a compliment. Earl Woods knew it and so did his son. The *Newsweek* people got several angry phone calls from Hughes Norton, who was then Tiger's agent. How *dare* he compare Earl Woods to Stefano Capriati.

Looking back, maybe I was unfair — to Stefano.

HAVING GOTTEN OFF TO a bad start with Team Tiger, I proceeded to make things worse in the fall of 1996. After finishing tied for sixtieth in Milwaukee, Tiger took off. He had a chance to win his third time out, in Moline, but got off to a bad start Sunday and finished tied for fifth. The winner that week was Ed Fiori, a roly-poly tour lifer who was known for years as the only man to *ever* catch Woods from behind on a Sunday. "I should write a book called *How to Beat Tiger on Sunday,*" he said once. "Probably sell a million copies."

At least.

Woods followed that performance with a tie for third at the B.C. Open. His goal when he turned pro was to earn enough money in seven tournaments—the maximum number a non-tour member could play in one year on sponsor exemptions—to avoid going to Q School in the fall. After the fifth and the third he had all but wrapped that up. And so, even though he had a sponsor's exemption to play the next week in the Southern Open, he decided to go home and get some rest.

Which sounds fine. Except it wasn't. To begin with, when you accept a sponsor's exemption, you are expected to show up and play unless you are deathly ill or something catastrophic prevents you from appearing. When you are the game's Next One and you know your presence in a tournament has been promoted you *really* should show up. And when the sponsors of a major college golf award have scheduled their awards dinner to suit *you* at a time and place where you have told them you will be, you don't blow off the dinner and go home.

That's what Tiger did. The dinner, scheduled around his schedule, was held without him. So was the golf tournament. A week later in Las Vegas, Woods won his first tournament, which Hughes Norton deemed proof he had done the right thing. I didn't agree and said so. Then, two weeks later, Woods won again—at Disney. The finish was controversial because Tiger actually tied with a guy named Taylor Smith and should have been in a playoff. But it turned out Smith was playing with an illegal putter (unknowingly, but that didn't matter) and he was disqualified. If winning that way bothered Tiger, he never said so in his press conference and, in fact, ducked questions about it when asked.

Press conference over, he headed back to the locker room. As frequently happens at the end of a tournament, several reporters followed the champion back, hoping to get a few more quotes that weren't quite as banal as what they'd just heard in the press conference. Players understand this and, especially right after a win, are more than willing to talk while they clean out their locker.

Not Tiger. As he walked in, he told the security guards he didn't want any media in the locker room, so the guys trying to get in were told the locker room was closed. Except it wasn't—not under PGA Tour rules, just under Tiger's rules. I was actually sitting in the media room—I was writing about guys trying to keep their playing privileges for the following year at the last full field event of the fall, so I wasn't that interested in Tiger—when someone came in to say the locker room had been closed, apparently by Tiger.

Wes Seeley was in charge of PR for the tour on site. He walked straight to the locker room (I followed, curious to see how all this would unfold) and told the security guards the locker room was open to the media. "The tour makes the rules, not this kid," Wes said. "Regardless of what he and his people may think, he's not the fifth Beatle."

Wes is a good friend who now works for a company that publishes books on the performing arts. Every now and then I remind him of that day. "Turns out you were right," I say. "The kid wasn't the fifth Beatle. He's John Lennon."

Of course, Wes was right to do what he did, and if more people in golf had stood up to Tiger and his people early, maybe things wouldn't have turned out the way they did. Or maybe they would have anyway. We'll never know.

While there was plenty to question in Woods's behavior, there was nothing to question in his golf. Paul Goydos played in a group directly behind Tiger the first three days that week at Disney. Walking into the locker room one day, he spotted me and said, "You know how you guys [the media] are always trying to figure out who the best player in the world is who hasn't won a major yet? I'm telling you right now it's Tiger Woods. You want to know why? Because he's the best player in the world—*period*."

He wasn't yet twenty-one. Tiger was such a phenom that *Sports Illustrated* named him Sportsman of the Year before he'd won a major. "First time they've ever given that award out on spec," said Mike Lupica, the *New York Daily News* columnist and my (then) colleague on *The Sports Reporters*.

Woods was so good that when he won the Masters the following April—the first major he had played in as a pro—no one was that shocked. The twelve stroke margin—*twelve strokes!*—was a shock, but the fact that he won shocked few people. The real surprise was when he didn't seriously contend at any of the remaining three majors that year.

It was at that Masters that I had my first face-to-face confrontation with Tiger's people. After I had written a column in *Golf Magazine* about Tiger's blowoff of the Southern Open and the college dinner, and about the scene at Disney, George Peper, the editor of the magazine, had gotten a call from Hughes Norton demanding a meeting with me. I had no problem meeting with Norton and his deputy, a guy named Clarke Jones. (Jones was furious when I referred to him later as "someone named Clarke Jones" because he thought he was a really important person in golf. Sorry, Clarke.)

And so Peper, Mike Purkey—who was my editor at the magazine—and I met with Norton and Jones over breakfast at the Masters. There were two highlights to what turned out to be a short meeting. The first was when Jones, apparently the designated bad cop, demanded to know who my sources were on several things I had written. I looked at him and said, "Clarke, if I wanted you to know that, I'd have used their names in the magazine."

"Well, I want to know, right now!"

"Can't have everything you want in life, Clarke."

Norton, the designated good cop, jumped in to say in what he no doubt thought was a soothing voice that he really didn't want to see Tiger's anger at me result in him deciding not to sign a contract with *Golf* as a "playing editor." At that moment, both *Golf* and *Golf Digest* were trying to get Tiger under contract. In fact, *Golf* had no chance because *Golf Digest* had a bigger circulation and it had Pete McDaniel—who wrote Earl Woods's first book. But Norton was using *Golf* to up the ante in his negotiations with *Golf Digest*.

I knew from talking to Peper that he was holding out hope they could somehow get Tiger, and I also knew it would be a big deal for *Golf*.

As soon as Norton started into his "I'd hate to see Tiger being upset with John affect our negotiations with *Golf*" speech, I stood up.

"Is *that* what this meeting is about?" I said. "So you can blackmail George?"

I turned to Peper. "Listen, if you need to fire me to get this deal done with Tiger, go ahead. My guess is *Digest* will hire me tomorrow. So it's fine, although I don't think for a second they're going to sign with you. In fact, I'll bet the deal's already done. But you do what you have to do.

"Meanwhile, I have things to take care of. If you want to stay and eat with these two assholes, go ahead. But I have better things to do than listen to this crap."

I stalked out. The month after the Masters, *Golf Digest* proudly announced it had signed a long-term deal to make Tiger Woods a playing editor. My guess is the deal was already in place when we met that morning.

Norton and I did talk again before the week was over. We bumped into each other under the famous tree outside the clubhouse where about half the business that is done at the Masters takes place. I apologized for calling him an asshole. He apologized for his tactics.

"How about if you and I just make a deal," he said. "Tiger does something you think is wrong, you call me. I'll tell you his side of it."

"How about if you get *Tiger* to tell me his side of it?" I said.

"Can't promise that. But I can promise some kind of answer every time you call."

"Done."

A week later I was on the phone to Norton. After winning the Masters, Woods had been invited by President Clinton to participate with him and Rachel Robinson in a ceremony in New York commemorating the fiftieth anniversary of Jackie Robinson breaking baseball's color line.

He turned down the invitation saying he was going on vacation with friends.

"Are you kidding me?" I said to Norton, who instantly took my phone call as he had promised.

"He's tired," Norton said.

"He's *always* tired," I said, referring to the blow offs at the Southern Open the previous fall. "This is the president of the United States and Jackie Robinson's widow. You *go*."

"He doesn't see it that way. He sees it as a last-second invitation, and he had plans."

"Last second? He only won the Masters on Sunday. Were they supposed to know in advance he was going to win?"

"You and I both predicted it in advance."

"Very funny."

So I ripped Tiger again, this time for turning down the president and Rachel Robinson.

Which is why I was very surprised a few months later at the PGA Championship at Winged Foot when Lee Patterson, another of the tour's PR guys, said to me, "How would you feel about sitting down with Tiger?"

"What?"

"He told me that if you'd do it, he would like to sit down and talk to you."

I was stunned. "Well, of course I'd do it," I said. "But why in the world does he want to talk to me?"

"I'm not sure. All I know is he asked me the other day what I thought about you. I told him I liked you and I thought you were honest. That's when he asked me if I thought you would talk to him. I told him I was pretty sure you would, but I'd check."

It was later that I found out more about what had led to Tiger talking to Patterson. One thing about Tiger is that he watches TV all the time and he reads about golf all the time. He sees, hears, and reads every word said about him. He'd been furious about what I had said about his father in the *Newsweek* story—"I wanted to kill you when I read that," he told me—and was baffled by the fact that I seemed to be the only person who covered golf on a regular basis who ever took him on for his behavior.

He also knew that I got along well with a lot of players and that they trusted me. So he asked several guys why they liked me.

"I told him he should sit down and talk to you," Jeff Sluman told me later. "I said, 'Here's the deal with John: if you're honest with him, he'll be honest with you. If he thinks you're trying to BS him, he's not going to accept it. But if he thinks you're being fair to him, he'll be fair to you.'"

Tiger had that conversation, or something like it, with several guys. That's why he decided to talk to Patterson—whose judgment he trusted.

I give Tiger all the credit in the world for making that effort. God knows he didn't need to do it. He was about as bulletproof at that point in his life as an athlete can be. I first suspected something might be happening when I was standing on the putting green at Winged Foot talking to Bruce Edwards. Tiger had just finished his pretournament press conference in the interview room and was crossing the putting green en route to the range, trailed by his usual coterie of security, photographers, shoe reps, agents, and hangers-on.

As he crossed the green he veered in my direction. "Uh-oh," Bruce said. "He's coming after you."

"Will you defend me?" I asked.

"Absolutely not," he answered.

I didn't need defending. Tiger walked over, hand extended. "John, how's it going?" he said.

"Good, Tiger, how about you?" I said.

"Find out Thursday," he said, continuing his walk in the direction of the range.

"What do you think that was about?" Bruce asked as the group trailed after Tiger.

"No idea," I said.

It was the next day that Patterson told me Tiger might want to talk to me.

It took almost six months to set up the meeting. I was starting work on *The Majors* early in 1998 and was going to San Diego to do some of the early interviews, specifically with David Duval, Steve Stricker, and Fred Couples. Just before I flew west on Monday evening, I got a call from Woods's assistant. Could I meet Tiger for an early dinner at his tournament hotel on Wednesday night?

I told her I'd be there.

The hotel was one of those boutiques right on the ocean. I walked into the lobby five minutes early and found Tiger sitting in a chair waiting for me.

"Couldn't wait to see me, huh?" I said as we shook hands.

"Actually, I'm just hungry," he said, not quite picking up on my sarcasm. Or choosing to ignore it.

We walked into the hotel restaurant, which was small and elegant with a view of the sea. Tiger asked for a table in the corner. There were no hangers-on or agents in sight. It was just the two of us. There wasn't a lot of small talk.

I would love to report that the two of us really hit it off, that we bonded and came away with a better understanding of each other. I *do* think we understood each other better.

We talked at length about our disagreements. He was upset that I had criticized him for not accepting the invitation from President Clinton. "They didn't invite me until I won the Masters," he said. "Why didn't they invite me *before?* I win the Masters and all of a sudden they want me there."

"You're absolutely right," I said. "Because before you won the guy who should have been invited was Lee Elder. *He* broke the color line at Augusta, not you. But when you *won* you did something no minority had done before, and that put you in a different category, made you more of a symbol the way Jackie Robinson was a symbol—and is a symbol."

We argued that one for a while. I asked him if there was any truth to the rumor that his father hadn't wanted him to go because he didn't like the fact that President Clinton hadn't served in Vietnam. "No, that wasn't it at all," Tiger said. "It was my decision."

One thing I learned that night was that Tiger made almost all his own calls—for good and bad. In fact, looking back at how he has behaved since the accident that changed his image and his life forever, that night is instructional. People, including me, have said that he should fire everyone around him, and he probably should if only because new people might—*might*—be more willing to tell him when he's making a mistake. But in the end I'm not sure it would matter. No one tells Tiger Woods what to do.

We also talked at length about the things I'd written about his father. I told him why I'd made the comparison to Stefano Capriati.

"I really don't think your dad is different than any other pushy, grab-the-bucks father," I said. "Except for one thing: you're his son. So I give him some credit for your genes, because you're smart enough and tough enough to deal with everything he's pushed on you and still be a great player. Most kids aren't that way. I think you've succeeded in spite of your father, not because of your father."

If the comment bothered him, it didn't show in his face. He disagreed, which didn't surprise me, and objected when I pointed out that his father had written *books* bragging about how *he* had created Tiger.

"He just did that because so many people asked him, 'How did you do it?' He figured it was easier to write a book than try to answer the question a million times," Tiger said.

"Really?" I said. "Then why did he write the second book?"

Tiger looked at me for a second and laughed—probably for the first time all night. "Good one," he said, the closest he came to conceding a point during four hours of conversation.

My one regret about the evening is that I didn't tape it. I didn't take notes either, because I wanted Tiger to feel as if we were having a conversation, not conducting an interview. Later, after I was back in my car, I wrote down everything I could remember, which I think was most of it. Back then my memory was still very good.

We didn't drink, in part because Tiger had an early tee time the next day, in part because it wasn't a social occasion. But the conversation did loosen up after a while. We talked about other sports and how we felt about different people. Tiger felt comfortable enough to take some shots at people, and that was educational for me—in terms of both his attitude and some of the people in question.

He also brought up the Augusta breakfast when I had walked out on his agents.

"I have to admit you surprised them," he said. "I think they really figured going to your boss would get your attention."

I explained to him that George Peper was only one of my bosses, that I didn't work full-time for anyone, and that most of my income came from writing books. "I like writing for *Golf*," I said. "But if George had fired me that day, my guess is I'd have gotten another golf writing gig someplace, and if I didn't it wouldn't really have been that big a deal."

He sat back in his chair as if he had genuinely learned something at that moment. "So that's it," he said. "You really don't need any one job."

"No, I don't."

"Makes it tougher to intimidate you, doesn't it?" he said, smiling.

"I would think so."

This time he actually laughed. "Well good for you then," he said.

At the end of the evening we made an informal pact that wasn't that different than the deal I'd made with Norton at Augusta ten months earlier: if I needed to get in touch with him, I was to call not Norton, but Tiger's assistant. She could get in touch with him anytime, anyplace. He would then call me back as long as I let her know what I was calling about.

"If you don't hear from me you'll know I don't want to talk about it," he said.

I'd have preferred dealing with him directly, but I knew he wasn't going to do that—at least not yet—and at the end of the evening I said something to him that I really meant.

"I think this was good for both of us. But you deserve the credit for it. You don't need me to like you or write or say good things about you. You're Tiger F—ing Woods. I think it says a lot about you that you did this. And I learned a lot tonight, not just about why we disagree on things, but about who you are."

He looked at me and nodded his head. "Guys I respect like you," he said. "I can see why after this, even though we disagree on a lot of things. But what'd you learn about me?"

"That you're smarter than I thought you were," I said. "I knew you were bright. You're glib and you're quick, but I know now you're smart—very smart. It makes me look forward to disagreeing with you in the future, because I know you won't make it easy for me."

"Me too," he said.

I also told him that night that I had a minibook coming out in several weeks that was called *Tiger Woods: Master or Martyr.* It was one in a series of minibooks created by Peter Gethers, who had been my editor at Villard. The book probably wasn't more than ten thousand words long. It was, not surprisingly, very critical of Earl.

"I'll get you a copy as soon as I have one," I said. "It basically says the same things about your dad that we discussed tonight."

"I probably shouldn't read it then," he said.

"Probably not. But I don't want you blindsided by it. I'll stick it in your locker when I get it, and you can do whatever you want with it."

That was where we left it. For the next few months, Tiger and I were cordial—almost friendly—when we encountered each other. He started calling me "Johnny" because he is a big nickname guy. Sometimes I think he's a hockey player.

"Who you got today, Tiger?"

"I've got Maggs [Jeff Maggert] and Cookie [John Cook]."

His former caddy is "Stevie," his agent is "Steiny," his interim Caddy last summer was "B.," and his best friend on tour is "M.O." (Mark O'Meara). His favorite reporters are "Rosey" (Tim Rosaforte), "Verds" (Bob Verdi), and "Kell" (Kelly Tilghman). Like I said, it's a hockey thing: the nicknames aren't clever, they're just prevalent. So for a while I was "Johnny." My mother often called me Johnny, and so do Bob Woodward and David Maraniss. That's pretty much the list. And, for a little while, Tiger ("Tiggy" or "T-Dub" to his friends) Woods.

I'm often amused nowadays when I hear other members of the media talk about how well they know Tiger. Many start sentences by saying things like "The Tiger Woods that I know…" or "I think I know Tiger pretty well…"

Really? Did any of us know about the secret life Tiger was living? Answer: no. Do any of these guys think Tiger has ever really opened up to them, shared what he really thinks and believes? I would make the case that on that night in San Diego I came about as close to getting at least a sense of the real Tiger as anyone in the media ever has. The exception to that would be *Golf Digest*'s Jaime Diaz, who has known him since he was very young. I also wouldn't claim for a second that I "know" Tiger. I'm not sure Tiger knows Tiger, but I'm damn sure no one on the outside knows him.

Our truce actually lasted into the summer. I gave the book to Tiger at Doral. We continued to be cordial, often talking casually on the range when he was hitting balls after a round. (I rarely talk to players much before they tee off.) In fact, during the U.S. Open that year at Olympic, I talked to him about doing a sit-down at the end of the season to discuss his year in the majors for the next book I was writing, called, cleverly enough, *The Majors*.

"Can we do it in Atlanta?" he asked (the Tour Championship). "There's no pro-am so that's a good week for me."

"Perfect for me too," I said.

So we planned it.

In August I was sitting in the locker room at Sahalee during the PGA Championship talking to Payne Stewart. We were actually making plans for dinner that night so that I could talk to Payne about his loss to Lee Janzen at Olympic a couple of months earlier. While we were talking a guy I recognized as being one of Tiger's IMG walk-around guys—honestly, I don't know if I ever knew his name—came up and said, "John, there's no rush or anything, but Tiger wants to talk to you when you get a chance."

I remember Payne looking at me with his goofy wise-guy grin. "Have you been a bad boy?" he said.

"Probably," I said. I then asked the guy if Tiger was around.

"He's on the putting green," he said.

The putting green at Sahalee is right next to the first tee. Tiger was out there putting—this was Monday so things were pretty relaxed—when I found him.

"Heard you were looking for me," I said.

He stopped what he was doing and nodded. "Look, I'm sorry about this because I feel like I made a commitment, but I just can't do the thing with you in Atlanta for your book," he said.

"Okay," I said. "Is there a particular reason?"

"Yeah," he said. "I just can't get past what you've said and written about my father."

I was a little taken aback. If this had come up in March at Doral I wouldn't have been surprised. But this was almost five months later. My immediate thought was that Earl had told him not to do it. Of course that didn't really matter. So I just nodded.

"You know what, Tiger, I respect your feeling that way," I said. "He's your dad. My dad was a public figure not like your dad [he had just retired as director of the Washington Opera], but he's a public figure and I get pissed off when people criticize him. So I understand. I thought we had talked all that out in San Diego, but I understand."

"I thought we had too," he said. "But I just can't get past it."

To this day I believe Earl convinced Tiger he shouldn't talk to me. I could be wrong, but why wouldn't we have had that conversation right after I gave Tiger the minibook in March? It was three months later that I talked to him about sitting down with me in the fall, and his initial response was to do it, without any strings or any of the IMG ifs and buts that were usually attached to a one on one with Tiger.

I remembered something Pete McDaniel said to me. Earl had been holding court with some media members under the tree at Augusta, and Pete had walked over to where I was watching the scene, sitting on a bench just outside the locker room.

"You going to go over and say hi to your pal?" he said, jokingly.

"You know, actually I was thinking I would do that," I said—because I thought I should. I always believe in putting myself in front of those I've criticized. If they want to vent, let them vent. If they want to talk specifics, the way Tiger and I had done that night in San Diego, I think that's all good. If they want to turn their back, that's fine too—I give them their shot. I can't stand people in my business—many of them radio talk-show hosts and bloggers—who lob bombs at people they never have to face.

Pete looked at me for a second and, realizing I was serious, said, "Don't do it."

"Why not? I don't care if he yells at me. I'm a big boy."

"He might try to hit you. I mean it. He told me once if you ever tried to talk to him he'd punch you in the nose."

I laughed. "My guess is I'm quick enough to duck him." Earl already had health problems at that point and wasn't terribly mobile.

"Yeah, and then he'll hurt himself trying to hit you and you'll be the one in trouble. It'll look like you baited him. Don't do it."

Pete and I joked around a lot, especially about his friendship with Earl. I could see now he was completely serious.

"You think it's a mistake to just introduce myself?"

"A big one."

I took his advice, so I never found out if Earl was just talking about hitting me—which I suspect he was—or not. Either way, Pete's point was well taken. Earl would probably tell people I was baiting him. So I steered clear.

And so, on the putting green at Sahalee, I was completely convinced that Tiger had no problem talking to me. Earl had the problem. But it didn't matter. And as I had said, I understood Tiger standing by his father.

I put out my hand. "I just want to tell you that even though I'm sorry we won't be talking, I really appreciate you telling me this yourself and not sending someone to do it for you."

He returned the handshake. "I owed you that."

The funny thing is, I don't think I ever liked him more than at that moment. I really believed that with his smarts he was going to grow into someone truly worthy of being admired. Several years after our dinner, he *did* write a letter to Rachel Robinson, apologizing for not showing up that night in New York to honor her husband. The potential to do good was very much there.

I also thought at some point he would get past his anger about what I'd said and written about his father.

Sadly, I was wrong on both counts.

17

More Walks

THE WAY THE PUBLISHING industry works is, no doubt, much like any other industry: something works, everyone copies it. Jeff Neuman, who edited *A Season on the Brink,* has often told me that he received at least a couple of hundred proposals in subsequent years that began with the words "This is the next *Season on the Brink.*" Of course there was no next *Season on the Brink,* because there was no next Bob Knight.

After *A Good Walk Spoiled* ended up outselling *Season,* there was great clamoring from Esther Newberg and my new editors at Little, Brown for another golf book. The story of my move from Random House to Little, Brown could take up several chapters here, but for now suffice to say this: Peter Gethers, my editor at Random House, was heroic, and a number of people working at Random House at the time were not. I was lucky that Charlie Hayward, who was running Little, Brown, had always wanted me on his list, and I ended up moving from one publisher to another in the middle of a contract — unusual to say the least.

The move worked out well for Little, Brown and for me — not so well for the woman at Random House who decided that selling my contract was a smart move.

The question after *Good Walk Spoiled* wasn't whether to do golf again but what golf book to write next. To me, there were two choices: the majors or Q School. During my research on *Good Walk Spoiled,* the four majors and Q School had been the most riveting weeks I had gone through. The pressures were entirely different but equally draining. John Daly called Q School the fifth major. Almost everyone who played golf had a Q School story of some kind.

But there were also great stories surrounding the majors—they just took place on a more public stage, which would mean it would be more difficult to get the kind of inside stories that had made *Good Walk Spoiled* work. I was pretty confident by then I could pull that off. At the very least, I was now well connected in the golf world.

And Jack Nicklaus had never denied me anything.

So I decided on doing the majors and following a similar reporting format to *Good Walk Spoiled*: pick a mixed bag of players, ranging from stars to unknowns, and follow them through the four major tournaments of 1998. In a way, I would get some Q School thrown in since both the U.S. Open and the British Open had qualifiers and there would no doubt be fascinating stories to tell there.

As it turned out, none of the four players who won the four majors that year were on my original list: Mark O'Meara won the Masters and the British Open, Lee Janzen won the U.S. Open, and Vijay Singh won the PGA Championship. Janzen had been on Team Feinstein for *A Good Walk Spoiled,* so I had written extensively about him, and when he won at the Olympic Club he was more than happy to give me some more time. O'Meara was one of the more outgoing guys on tour. I hadn't picked him for my new group, not because I didn't like him, but because I had figured at forty-two his time to be a factor in majors had passed. I was fortunate, again, that Mark was willing to give me lots of time after his breakthrough wins. I didn't get much from Singh, but that just made me a lot like everyone else.

It was the runners-up though who had the best stories: Steve Stricker, who finished second to Singh at the PGA, was in the midst of a great comeback year after falling off the golf map in 1997; Brian Watts, who lost to O'Meara in a playoff at the British Open, had been playing in Japan because he couldn't make the U.S. Tour and was thrilled that his second place finish at Royal Birkdale allowed him to come home; Payne Stewart, who blew a four shot lead at the U.S. Open to lose to Janzen; and Fred Couples and David Duval, who finished a shot behind O'Meara at the Masters.

I first met Stricker in 1993 at Q School. Several people had told me to keep an eye on him, that he was a budding star, and I did. He and his wife, Nicki, who caddied for him, were classic Midwesterners — polite to a fault and always enjoyable to be around. Steve made it through Q School in 1993 and finished number four on the money list in 1996 after winning twice, but he made an equipment change in 1997 when offered a big contract, and it completely messed with his mind and swing and he had a disastrous year. Plus, he had to start 1998 with a new caddy because Nicki was pregnant with their first child.

"It's worse for me than for Steve," she said one day walking outside the ropes at San Diego. "At least he's still playing. All I can do is watch."

I had done my first sit-down with Steve that week, the "life story" interview. Basically, I ask the person to tell me his life story before I ask a single question about what is going on in the present day. In describing his parents, Steve had said, "If you think I'm a polite Midwesterner, you should meet my parents. They're as polite as anyone you'll ever meet: never a bad word to anyone. They're sort of the anti–New Yorkers of the world."

I laughed and told Steve I knew what he meant, having grown up in New York.

Steve went white. "Oh my God," he said. "I didn't mean to offend you. I don't think *all* New Yorkers are rude or anything like that."

"Steve, stop, it's fine," I said. "First of all, most New Yorkers *are* rude. Second, your description is perfect. Please don't worry about it."

Steve nodded and we continued talking. The next day when he went out to play his first round, I walked with his group. Something backed up play and there was a delay on one of the tees. Steve walked over to where I was standing.

"You know it's really been bothering me since we talked about what I said about New Yorkers," he said. "I feel like I owe you an apology."

"Steve, seriously, let me say this to you as a New Yorker: *Shut up.* Stop worrying about it. Worry about your golf."

He smiled. "What would a New Yorker say in response to that?" he asked.

"I can't tell you that," I said, "because there are women around."

To this day the first time I see Steve every year he says, "Uh-oh, here comes the rude New Yorker."

I point out the redundancy of putting *rude* in front of *New Yorker* and we go from there.

The person I probably least wanted to talk to who contended in a major that year was Payne Stewart. I had never had any issues with Payne the way some writers had, but that was at least in part because I had steered clear of him when I first started spending time on the tour.

Frankly, I thought he was aptly named. My first up-close experience with him was at the 1993 U.S. Open—which he almost won, finishing second to Janzen then too, just as he would do again in 1998—when he was paired with John Daly the first two days. On Friday, Daly had become the first player to ever hit the green in two at the 600-yard seventeenth hole at Baltustrol Golf Club. Nowadays, there are players who can probably reach it with a five-iron, but back then it was a remarkable feat. Dave Anderson of the *New York Times* wrote his entire column that day about Daly's first two shots at seventeen.

During his press conference, someone asked Stewart about Daly reaching the seventeenth in two.

"Did he reach it in two?" Stewart said sarcastically. "I didn't notice. I wasn't paying attention. I stay focused on my own game, not anybody else's game."

It was a smarmy, wise-guy answer, which was not atypical for Stewart at the time.

Stewart was a wonderful player, and a colorful one too—with his plus fours that were impossible to miss. But he was one of those guys who was charming when things went well, snappish when they didn't go well, and smart-alecky almost all the time. We *did* talk occasionally because Mike Hicks, his caddy, was a huge basketball fan—specifically a Duke fan—so he would often grab me on the range to talk hoops. Payne would frequently join in the conversation, so we had a cordial relationship even though I had never once asked him a one-on-one question about golf.

When he blew the four shot lead at the Olympic Club to lose to Janzen by one, I had no choice: you can't write a book on a year in the majors and not try to talk to a guy who threw away a four-shot Sunday lead at the U.S. Open.

So when I saw Payne and Hicks on the putting green on the Tuesday of British Open week, I figured this was as good a time as any to ask. After we had all exchanged handshakes and Hicks had asked if I had an update on Duke's recruiting, I told Payne I needed a favor.

"Name it," he said, rolling ten-footers at one of the holes while Mike stood behind it and rolled the balls back to him.

"I'm doing a book on the majors, focusing on this year," I said. "I know Olympic probably isn't your favorite subject at this point, but somewhere along the line I'd like to sit down and talk to you about the week. I promise to make it as painless as possible."

He stopped putting, stood up straight, and leaned on his putter. For a second I thought he was going to say something like, "You've never once asked to sit down and talk to me and now you want to talk to me about *this?*"

That's not what he said. "If you're doing this for a book, you're going to need some time, aren't you?"

"Well, yeah, whatever you could spare."

He shrugged. "You're going to be at Sahalee, right?"

"Of course."

"Why don't we just have dinner there one night? It'll be more relaxed that way."

"Yeah, sure, that'd be great," I said.

"Just find me when you get there and we'll figure out details."

I thanked him and walked away in semi-shock. Maybe I had misjudged the guy for five years.

It turned out I hadn't. The person who told me I hadn't misjudged Payne Stewart was Payne Stewart.

I got to Sahalee on Monday afternoon and found him sitting in the locker room having just played a practice round. Before I could even remind him about our talk at Birkdale, he said, "I'm glad you showed up. How's tonight for our talk? I'm staying at a house right down the street. I've got some guys coming over and we're going to grill steaks. Come over and eat, we'll talk afterward."

Which is exactly what I did. Payne cooked and after everyone had eaten, he and I sat on the back terrace and talked. We talked about the Open and how much he had wanted to win a second one.

He told a funny story about getting to the Western Open a couple of days after the U.S. Open and learning that he had been paired on Thursday and Friday with Lee Janzen.

"I love Lee to death," he said. "But the last guy I wanted to spend two days with right then was Lee, especially with all the questions we were both going to get about Olympic. What pissed me off was I knew they'd done it for TV, and of course the tour claims all the pairings are done by computer."

The rules official in charge of the pairings that week happened to be Jon Brendle, who was not only one of Stewart's closest friends but was his tenant—Jon and his wife, Martha, rented their house from Stewart and lived right next door to him.

"So I went to see Jon and I told him he better fess up or I was going to throw a fit," he said, laughing. "I told him I might even withdraw if he didn't tell me the truth.

"He finally said, 'Okay, okay, they asked me to do it [*they* being the tournament officials and TV]. You know there aren't a lot of glamour guys in the field this week because it's the week after the Open, and they needed a glamour group for TV. So I did it. Guilty.'"

Payne was laughing as he finished the story. "So I pointed my finger at him and I said, 'Okay, that's it then, you know what I'm going to do?'

"He got this terrified look on his face because he thought I was really angry and I was going to withdraw. So I said, 'I'm going to raise your rent!'

"He was so relieved because he knew I'd never do that—I like Martha too much."

Seeing an opening, I commented that once upon a time he *might* have thrown a fit over something like that. What had changed?

It was then that Payne told me the story, which I recounted in *The Majors*, about the 1996 incident at the Masters when a father and son had asked him for an autograph while he was storming to his car after missing the cut. He had not only refused but had yelled at the man, telling him he was breaking the rules by asking for an autograph. When he got into the car with his wife, Tracey, she had let him have it, pointing out that the man had *not* violated the rules, that autograph seeking on the parking lot side of the clubhouse was allowed, and how dare he yell like that in front of the man's son when *he* was the one who had missed the cut—not the autograph seeker.

"You need help," she had said finally. "I'm tired of having you embarrass me this way."

He had listened and gone to counseling and had come away from the experience with a new attitude and a new understanding of how fortunate he was to do what he was doing and make the money he was making, even on days when he missed a cut.

We went backward from there, talking about growing up in the game and about his father's death at the age of forty-seven from cancer. "People ask me sometimes what my best win was," he said very quietly. "I tell them it was the Hardees Classic in 1983. It was the only tournament my dad ever saw me win."

We talked late into the night. Eventually Payne did something athletes rarely do: he turned the tables and started asking me questions. I talked about my mother's death and how it had affected me, and we shared how much it hurt us both that his dad and my mom had never gotten to see their grandchildren. For some reason, I never turned off my tape recorder, even long after we had finished the actual interview portion of the conversation. I'm so glad I didn't.

Fourteen months after we had that talk, Payne was killed—along with five other people—when the private plane he was flying from his home in Orlando to Texas on the Monday of the 1999 Tour Championship crashed after something went wrong with the air-pressure system in the cabin and the cockpit. The tragedy occurred a little more than four months after Payne's dramatic victory over Phil Mickelson in that year's U.S. Open at Pinehurst.

Not long after Payne's death, I dug out the tapes from that night in Sahalee and popped them into the tape machine in my car during a long trip. Hearing his voice: the Midwestern twang, the high-pitched laugh, the corny jokes, and the heartfelt emotion—especially when he talked about taking his infant daughter to visit his father's grave—made me laugh and cry all at once.

"I felt so sad that he would never see her," Payne said that night. "It wasn't fair at all. But I felt better knowing that he'd seen me grow up and marry someone he truly loved and overcome a lot of the dumb things I did as a kid. That's the best thing about being a parent, isn't it? Seeing your kids figure life out. It's the thing I enjoy now more than anything else I do, watching my kids grow and figure things out."

He smiled that night when he said that, and then added, "I just hope they figure things out a lot quicker than their old man did."

On the day Payne died—October 25, 1999—his daughter, Chelsea, was thirteen; his son, Aaron, was ten.

I REALLY WASN'T SURE what I was going to get when I asked David Duval to be part of *The Majors.*

I'd known him since Q School in 1993—where he'd failed to make the four-round cut after a much-ballyhooed career at Georgia Tech—but I didn't know him well. My gut feeling was that he was a good guy: I had this abiding memory of him on the day Arnold Palmer played his last round at the British Open in 1995 that convinced me his was a good soul.

A lot of players came out of the clubhouse that day to watch Palmer make his last walk up the eighteenth fairway at St. Andrews. The two I remember most vividly are Nick Faldo, who said simply, "He's the Great Man after all, you can't miss this," and Duval.

Duval was a tour rookie but was already a young star. He not only came out to watch Palmer, he brought a camera. He took pictures and then waited patiently while Palmer did his postround TV interviews and went inside to sign his scorecard. Then and only then did he ask Palmer if he would pose for a picture with him.

I liked that about Duval, and I also liked the notion that behind the sunglasses and the sometimes snappish press conferences, there was a very thoughtful person waiting for someone—how about me?—to draw him out. When I first asked Duval about spending time with me for the book, he actually said, "I'm really flattered that you would ask."

Hardly the cocky kid people thought he was at that point. A lot of that image, as Duval has noted, went back to 1992, when he had played in the Bell South Classic as a twenty-year-old junior at Georgia Tech and had been the fifty-four-hole leader. When he was asked on TV after the third round if he thought he could compete on Sunday with Tom Kite, who was in second place at the time, he shrugged and said, "I have so far."

It came off cocky when in fact it was just David being matter-of-fact. He didn't win the next day, shooting 79 to drop back to a tie for thirteenth. No doubt if TV had interviewed him that day, he would have said something like "I wasn't good enough to beat any-body today, much less Tom Kite."

All that said, we didn't get off to the best start on the book. At the same tournament in San Diego where I had my lengthy dinner with Tiger Woods, Duval and I made plans to get together on Thurs-day afternoon. He was playing fairly early and suggested we meet on the putting green after he was through with his postround practice routine at four o'clock (golf is, as far as I know, the only sport where players almost always practice *after* they are finished competing on a given day).

I showed up on the putting green at four o'clock. No Duval. I went inside to check the locker room and then walked out to the range. I finally ran into someone who said they thought he had left the golf course for the day.

He had forgotten. I was a bit miffed, but people forget appoint-ments on occasion; God knows I've done it. The next day when I saw Duval, I said, "Hey, David, I was on the putting green at four o'clock."

Honestly, I expected him to smack himself on the forehead and say, "Oh God, I forgot." Instead, he said, "Yeah, I was kind of tired so I just went back to the hotel."

"So you just blew me off because you were tired?"

"Yeah, I guess I did."

"And?"

"And what?"

"How about, 'And I'm really sorry I did that and didn't at least take five minutes to come by the press room [which at San Diego back then was directly above the locker room] and tell you or leave you a message that I was blowing you off because I was tired.'"

Duval smiled. "How about if I say it this way: You're right, I'm an asshole."

"That's much better."

"And you know what?" he added. "I *am* an asshole. You're right. I apologize. If you still want to talk to me, how about if I buy you dinner tonight?"

All was forgiven. When we did have dinner and David told me about his boyhood, which included the death of his older brother after David had given him his bone marrow to try to save him, I thought I had a much better understanding of why he tended to keep to himself.

"Being alone was the only place I could find peace after Brent died," he said. "My family life was chaotic. My parents fought all the time. The one place in the world I was truly happy was alone at the golf course. I could spend hours—I mean hours—all alone in ninety-five-degree heat with my feet dug into a bunker practicing and enjoy every minute of it.

"I still do it."

Duval was so different from the image he had cultivated it was almost mind-blowing. With the sunglasses and his Southern accent, his penchant for chewing tobacco and the fact that he enjoyed hunting, I would have labeled him a redneck right away. God knows the tour has a few of them. Duval was about as thoughtful as anyone I'd met in any sport.

He found it laughable that some people had labeled him a tour intellectual because he had once quoted Ayn Rand during an interview. "*That* makes me an intellectual?" he joked. "Come to think of it, in a group that considers *USA Today* heavy reading, maybe I *am* an intellectual."

Duval almost won the Masters in 1998, losing by one shot to

Mark O'Meara when O'Meara rolled in a twenty-foot birdie putt on the eighteenth hole. By early in 1999 he had gone past Woods to become the number one ranked player in the world after shooting 59 on the final day of the Bob Hope to come from way behind and win. Woods took back the number one spot and began to completely dominate the game. For a while, Duval chased him: he finally won his first major at the 2001 British Open after finishing second to Woods at the Masters that year, when Woods was completing his Tiger Slam.

That British Open was his last truly great moment in the game. Not long after, he met his wife, Susie, got married, and adopted her three kids. Then they had two of their own children. He moved to the suburbs of Denver, became a very proficient skier, and all but disappeared off the golf map. In 2009, almost from out of nowhere, he finished tied for second at the U.S. Open at Bethpage Black. The oft-asked question that week was "Where has David Duval been for nine years?"

The answer was, in many ways, simple: he had been finding happiness. And once he found it, he didn't want anything, including golf, to take it away from him.

18

Special Kids and Brick Walls

I'VE ALWAYS ENJOYED SPENDING time with Larry Brown, the man who has coached everywhere at some point in his life. Larry was best described years ago by Tony Kornheiser, for whom he was once a camp counselor: "Larry is completely sincere in absolutely everything he says. Of course, the next day he will say something completely and totally contradictory and be just as sincere."

Back in 1988 when I was working on *A Season Inside,* Larry was at Kansas and Danny Manning was a senior. They were—thank God—a big part of the book right from the start, so I spent a lot of time that winter with Larry. Rumors were rife—and correct—that Walt Hazzard was about to get fired at UCLA, a job Larry had left to become coach of the New Jersey Nets in 1981.

"That was my dream job," Larry said one morning at breakfast. "I loved Mr. [J. D.] Morgan [the athletic director] and I loved Los Angeles. That's really where I should be coaching."

When I pointed out that the opportunity to do that again might come at the end of the season, Larry waved me off. "No way. They'd never bring me back."

Except that they would have. Kansas went from 12–8 and hoping for an NIT home game (I still remember sitting on the bus pulling out of Ames, Iowa, after a loss to Iowa State while Larry asked his coaches if he thought they could get a home game) to winning the national championship. The team was dubbed "Danny and the Miracles" after they stunned heavily favored Oklahoma in the championship game.

Two days later, Larry flew to UCLA to interview for his "dream job." When he got back, I called him to see how it had gone.

"The people were great," he said. "They offered me the job."

"So you're going to take it."

There was a deep sigh on the other end of the phone. "You know, it's kind of a no-win situation," he said. "I love Kansas, I love the people there, but I love UCLA too."

"Isn't that more like a no-lose situation?"

He laughed, turned down UCLA, and then a month later found the perfect solution: having turned down one place he loved to stay at another place he loved, he decided to become coach of the San Antonio Spurs.

That was Larry.

It was also Larry to call almost everyone he had ever met or worked with a "special kid." He called fifty-year-old men special kids. The only person I never heard him call a special kid was Dean Smith, whom he had played for in college. Like all Carolina people, Larry worshipped Coach Smith.

One year when he was coaching the Indiana Pacers, Larry held training camp in (where else?) Chapel Hill. Dean often came down to watch practice. One night a fight broke out and two players—one was Byron Scott, the other a rookie—really got into it. Multiple F-bombs were dropped before everyone was separated. Larry looked white as a ghost. When practice was over, he ran over to apologize to Dean for what he had heard. Dean waved a hand at him and laughed. "I've heard those words before," he said.

"I'm so humiliated," Larry said afterward. "I can't believe Coach Smith heard my players talking that way. I feel terrible."

He was completely sincere. And the players involved, F-bombs or not, were still special kids.

As much as I like Larry, I got to a point in my career where I got tired of hearing about special kids—especially in big-time college athletics, where the one thing that made most kids special was the ability to play. They could do just about anything else off the field or off the court and it didn't matter, as long as they could perform, as long as they could win championships, and as long as they were future number one draft picks.

I CAN'T REMEMBER EXACTLY when I knew I'd had enough of the so-called big time, but I can remember the exact moment when I knew I wanted to do a book on the Army-Navy rivalry.

It was at my first Army-Navy game in 1990. I had grown up a big Army football fan and always watched the game on TV. When I was a kid my parents took me up to West Point once every fall for a football game. We would arrive early, go over to the plain to watch the cadets march, and then have lunch before kickoff inside Michie Stadium. I loved everything about West Point: it was spectacular, especially during the fall, and the traditions awed me. What's more, Army was good.

The Cadets were especially good during a three-year period between 1966 and 1968, when I was just beginning to really understand sports. I was vaguely aware of the fact that Paul Dietzel was considered a big-time coach when he left Army (I would learn later that he had coached a national championship team at LSU).

Army went 8–2, 8–2, and 7–3 during those three seasons under Coach Tom Cahill, who was named to replace Dietzel at the last possible minute after attempts to hire another big-time coach had failed. Steve Lindell was Army's quarterback those three seasons, and they had a superb running back named Charlie Jarvis. In 1967 the Cadets were actually invited to the Sugar Bowl, but the Pentagon refused to let the team go because it was concerned about the image of cadets partying in the streets of New Orleans while there were soldiers dying in Vietnam. To this day that decision remains controversial, especially with that generation of Army graduates.

All I knew was I expected to watch Army in the Sugar Bowl and instead I found myself watching a three-loss LSU team.

Army football fell on hard times in the 1970s, in large part because of Vietnam. There weren't that many quality athletes who wanted to sign on at the service academies, knowing that they would face a five-year service commitment (up from four) and might very well find themselves in a guerrilla war not long after graduation.

Even though I had gone to Army games as a kid and watched the Army-Navy game on TV every year, I really didn't have any idea of the intense feelings players from the academies had for football until I was in college. Then it was a fluke incident that gave me my first clue.

In October of my junior year, Duke played at Army. Neither team was very good: Duke would finish the season 4–5–2 and Army would end up 2–9. The game was played on a raw, windy day at Michie Stadium, and Duke pulled away late to win, 21–10. I was covering the game not only for the *Chronicle* but for the *Durham Morning Herald,* so I had a lot of work to do once the game was over. And I had to do it fast: the *Herald* wanted a lead and a sidebar and, since I was traveling with the team, both had to be done before the Duke bus left to go back to the airport.

There was no press box elevator, so after writing the first few graphs of my lead to get a head start, I made my way through the stands and began looking for the Duke locker room. Someone pointed to a door underneath the stands and told me that was where I could find the players.

He was right. Except the players I found were from Army.

Until the building of the multimillion-dollar Kimsey Center in 2005, the Army players and coaches used what was called "the half-time room" to meet (cleverly enough) at halftime and right after games—because it was a little bit of a hike to get to the actual locker room. There was no guard on the door, so I just pulled it open, expecting to find Duke players and coaches.

Instead I found the entire Army team—many of the players in tears—with one of the players (probably either Al Staerkel or Scott Gillogly, who were the captains that season) standing in front of his teammates and giving a passionate speech. I don't remember exactly what he said, but here's the gist of it: "We *should* have won this game. We *deserved* to win this game. We were *better* prepared, we were ready, we took the fight to them. How could we lose? This is not right! We are an Army football team and Army football teams do *not* accept losing this way! Does everyone understand me?"

He went on in that same vein for several minutes while I stood transfixed at the door. No one even looked in my direction. It was, looking back, my first experience with being invisible as a reporter. Part of me was, to be honest, amused by what I was hearing. They had just lost a game to a mediocre team and their record at that moment was 2–3, en route to 2–9.

But hearing the passion in that voice and seeing the looks on the players' faces gave me an understanding of just how important playing football was to these cadets—none of whom would be pros, none of whom would ever play in a bowl game. It was a scene that stayed with me.

Two years later I found myself working at the *Washington Post*. Even though my first two years on staff were spent as a night police reporter, I still worked for the sports staff whenever I had free time, and my first experience covering a Navy football game came in 1978. I was actually on vacation early that fall on Shelter Island when George Solomon called me. Bob Fachet usually covered the Midshipmen, but he had another assignment and George wanted to know if I could make it to Connecticut to cover Navy-UConn that Saturday. "Call Tom Bates, he's the SID," George said. "He'll get you a credential and take care of you."

So I called Tom Bates, who would come to be a close friend over the years. Bates was a graduate of Notre Dame but *loved* Navy. He was very good at what he did and, to put it mildly, brought as much emotion to the job as the Midshipmen brought to the football field and the basketball court.

Bates told me he would leave me a credential and a parking pass at the team hotel on Friday night. I thanked him and was about to hang up when he said, "Hey, let me ask you a question. Just how old are you?"

I wasn't sure what the relevance of the question was, but I had gotten used to people expressing surprise that someone my age worked for the *Washington Post*. In fact, at the end of my summer internship, when he didn't have any openings on his staff for me, George Solomon had put me in touch with Dave Smith, who was then the sports editor of the *Boston Globe*.

"He's got an opening for someone to cover colleges," George said. "I told him about you. He wants to bring you up there for an interview. I think he'll hire you."

That notion thrilled me. If I couldn't work for the *Post,* the *Globe* would be my next choice. (Remember, the *New York Times* sports section was pretty mediocre in those days.) I often bought the *Globe* while in college, especially on Sundays, when it had a massive sports section. I also loved Boston. I even knew a girl who lived there.

So I called Dave Smith.

"George is a big fan of yours," he said. "He sent me some of your clips. When do you think you can come up here so we can meet and talk?"

"Anytime," I said.

"Perfect. We'll set it up. By the way, where were you before the *Post*? He didn't tell me."

"Well, I worked on the student newspaper while I was in college."

"I know that. I mean since then."

"I just graduated in June and I've had this internship at the *Post* since then..."

"Wait a minute, how old are you?"

"I'm twenty-one."

"You're how old?"

"Twenty-one."

"George didn't tell me that. Listen, kid [yes, he said *kid*], get yourself about five years of experience and then call me back. I don't hire people at the *Globe* who don't have any experience."

With that he hung up. Not long afterward he became the sports editor at the *Washington Star.* By then I was working full-time at the *Post* and doing pretty well beating the *Star* to stories. Whenever I ran into Smith I was really tempted to say, "Gee, Dave, in another couple of years I might have enough experience to work for you."

Now, a little more than a year later, Tom Bates was asking me how old I was. When I told him, he almost gasped.

"What?" he said. "When did George Solomon start sending children to cover Navy football? Doesn't he know that we're *good?* What is he thinking?"

I was, of course, indignant. "Mr. Bates, I think I'm qualified to cover Navy football. I've covered some stories on the metro staff that were a little tougher than covering a football game."

"Okay, okay," he said. "But don't screw this up. This is *important.*"

I wasn't sure just how important a Navy-Connecticut football game was, but I told him I'd do the best I could. Years later, Tom and I would often joke about that first conversation because it was *so* Tom. I covered the game and Navy won 30–0 and went 9–3 that season, beating Brigham Young in the Holiday Bowl. So it *was* important. But I don't think I screwed up the game story. Or even the sidebar.

By the time I left the *Post* in 1988, I had covered Navy a lot in both football and basketball. I had covered the David Robinson basketball teams, which was a joy because they kept shocking big-time teams and their roster was packed with players who would fill your notebook in a heartbeat. The closest I think I've ever come to losing my cool and cheering on press row was the day Navy beat Syracuse in the Carrier Dome in 1986 in the second round of the NCAA Tournament. In fact, they blew them out of their own building. This was two days after Indiana had lost to Cleveland State and I was still riding a lot of adrenaline and mixed emotions about the end of my season with the Hoosiers. I'm not sure I was ever happier for a team than I was for Navy that day.

Five years later, when I was working for Frank Deford at the short-lived (sixteen months) *National Sports Daily,* I suggested doing a take-out piece on Army-Navy, focusing on what the rivalry meant to the players. Even then the scene I had witnessed in the halftime room fifteen years earlier was in the back of my mind.

I talked to a half-dozen players from Army and Navy before I wrote the piece. Two stood out, both seniors: one was Anthony Noto, who should have been too small to play linebacker for Army but played it quite well—even though he'd been through more surgeries than I can count. The other was Alton Grizzard, Navy's quarterback and captain. Grizzard had led a last-minute Navy drive in the rain a year earlier, hurdling two tacklers to pick up a fourth down and getting Navy into position for the game-winning field goal.

Navy's kicker that year was Frank Schenk—pronounced Shank—and Noto told me that he had spent the summer repeating Schenk's name to himself every time he got a little bit tired in the weight room. And Grizzard was exactly the kind of person you would expect to be a future Navy SEAL, which he turned out to be. He was tough and honest and was *angry* at the notion of going through a fourth straight losing season. The Mids were 5–5 and so were the Cadets.

"They're the same guys we are," Grizzard said. "They're tough, they're smart, they'll never give up. I respect the hell out of them. And I won't sleep for the next year if we don't beat them."

On the opening play of that game, Noto chased Grizzard out of the pocket and, lunging, brought him down.

"This is the way it's going to be all day, Alton," Noto said as he helped Grizzard up.

"This is the way it's going to be the rest of our lives, Anthony," Grizzard answered. "You got me this play. I'll get you the next."

The game was like that most of the afternoon. Army finally won, 30–20. When the game ended, the players congregated at midfield to exchange handshakes and hugs. Then, to my surprise, they walked together to the corner of the stadium where the Brigade of Midshipmen had stood throughout the game. I noticed that no one had left, that everyone in the stadium was on their feet. The Navy players lined up, standing at attention, and the Army players did the same.

"What's this?" I asked.

"Alma maters," someone answered.

Sure enough, the Navy band played "Blue and Gold."

As soon as the last notes died into the frigid late afternoon air, all the players turned and headed across the field to where the Corps of Cadets stood. Again, everyone stood at attention as the Army band played "Alma Mater."

The hair on my arms was standing at attention at that moment. All the years I had watched the game on television, I had never seen the playing of the alma maters. Whoever had the game—back then it was ABC—was usually rushing right to another game and didn't stick around to show the playing of the school songs.

Right then and right there I knew I wanted to do a book on Army-Navy. I wanted to get to know kids like Anthony Noto and Alton Grizzard better and to understand what made them tick, what made them put up with academy life, what football meant to them, and what the rivalry meant to them.

Of course, wanting to do the book and actually getting to do it were two different things.

As soon as I got back home, I called Jack Lengyel, the athletic director at Navy, someone I knew well because of my work at the *Post.* I asked if I could meet with him and with George Chaump, who had just finished his first season as football coach. I explained to them what I wanted to do: spend a season shuttling back and forth between Army and Navy, get to know the players well, get to know the traditions of the schools and what it was truly like to be a Midshipman or a Cadet. I needed access—complete access—during games and practices and meetings and to the academies themselves. I wanted to go to class, I wanted to be there for the pre-dawn wake ups, the whole thing.

Lengyel and Chaump said yes. They understood my respect for the academies and for the rivalry, and Jack knew me well. Plus, Tom Bates had told both of them this was a good idea. By then Tom and I were good friends. He trusted me not to screw it up.

Army, I knew, would be a tougher challenge. I knew Bob Kinney, the sports information director, and I knew Bob Beretta, his assistant. I had spent some time with Coach Jim Young while researching my piece for the *National,* but he had retired at the end of the season, replaced by his top assistant, Bob Sutton. I had talked to Sutton briefly in the locker room following Army-Navy, but hardly knew him. I had never met Al Vanderbush, the athletic director.

I called Kinney and told him what I wanted to do. Like the Navy people, he was very enthusiastic. He said he would set up a meeting for me with Vanderbush and Sutton.

Almost from the minute I walked into that meeting I knew it wasn't going to go well. I'm pretty good at picking up vibes. Kinney walked me upstairs to Vanderbush's office. In addition to Vanderbush and Sutton, there was someone else in uniform—I don't remember his name—but Army always has an assistant AD who is still active military. Vanderbush had been in the army but was retired.

I could almost feel the frost in the room when Kinney started introducing me to the others. Every question was skeptical. "But what if this happens...?" "What about that...?" "Why would we want to give an outsider so much inside access...?"

I tried to explain the exact moment when I wanted to do the book and how moved I had been by it. Blank stares. Kinney brought up the piece I'd written in the *National*.

"Best piece explaining why Army-Navy is unique I've seen in years," Kinney said.

"I read it," Sutton said. "It was very good."

A glimmer of hope. I pushed on, explaining I would do almost all my long interviews before the season began. After that, I'd pretty much just be observing until after the Army-Navy game was played.

"We'll be in touch," Vanderbush said at the conclusion of the meeting.

They were—in the form of a phone call from Sutton. He was very nice about it, but said that in his first season he just couldn't see dealing with a distraction like having a reporter around in places reporters weren't usually allowed. I tried briefly to explain—again— that after a while people would hardly notice me. He was firm. I wasn't going to convince him. I hung up, discouraged.

As it turned out, Sutton did me a favor. Navy was awful that season, 0–10 going into Army-Navy. Then the Mids turned around and won the game 24–3—no doubt a season saver, but hardly a dramatic game.

I moved on to other books—*Play Ball* and then *A Good Walk Spoiled*.

IN THE FALL OF 1994, I was starting the research on another basketball book. I was going to spend a season with three coaches—an NBA coach, a college coach, and a high school coach—so I could compare and contrast the pressures at each level of the game. My coaches were Larry Brown, who was coaching the Indiana Pacers,

Gary Williams at Maryland, and Mike McLeese, the coach at Dunbar, a public school in Washington, D.C., that often produced good college players.

Logistics certainly played a role in my picking McLeese and, to a lesser extent, Williams. In fact, my original idea had been to work with three coaches in the Washington, D.C., area, in part to show how different their lives were even though each lived within a few miles of the others, but also — again — because of logistics. Danny, my first child, had been born in January of 1994. Anything I could do to limit my travel was a bonus at that point.

But Jimmy Lynam, who had just become the coach of the Washington Bullets, turned me down. So I called Brown, who I had gotten to know extremely well during *A Season Inside*.

"I'd love to do it," Larry said. "I'd just think of you as another member of my staff. All we have to do is clear it with Donnie. I don't think that'll be a problem."

Donnie Walsh was then the general manager of the Pacers. He and Brown had been teammates at North Carolina in the 1960s and were good friends. Walsh was the perfect GM for Brown because he knew how to tune him out on those days when Brown wanted to trade his whole team, even the special kids among them.

On my way to the Western Open that June (I was still researching *A Good Walk Spoiled*), I stopped in Indianapolis and actually sat in on all of the Pacers' pre-draft meetings, which included a lengthy discussion on whether to accept a possible offer from the Bulls that would have brought them Scottie Pippen. During a lunch break the day before the draft, I met with Walsh and explained to him what I wanted to do.

"So it'll be like *Season on the Brink*," he said. "You'll hang out with our team from training camp through the playoffs."

"Yes — and no," I answered. I would be around quite a lot, but there were two other coaches involved so I wouldn't be there full-time.

"I loved *Season on the Brink*," Walsh said. "As far as I'm concerned, if Larry trusts you, I trust you." He smiled. "Even if you are a Duke guy." (The Carolina guys always have to say that.)

So I started the research at training camp, bouncing between the Pacers and Maryland and McLeese. My first sign of trouble came in November when McLeese informed me over lunch he had been hired to coach at Howard. Whoops. Okay, I needed to regroup, perhaps write about the transition from high school to college, pointing out that Howard was no more than five miles from Maryland as the crow flies but a world away in terms of basketball. Or I could find another high school coach.

In the meantime, I made a lengthy West Coast road trip with the Pacers. Things had gone well so far: the players seemed very comfortable with me around. Reggie Miller was the best player and the team leader, and he had accepted me right away. That paved the way with the other guys. And Larry had pretty much treated me like a member of the coaching staff since the beginning of training camp. He even called me "Coach." Of course Larry calls *everyone* Coach.

The Pacers were getting blitzed in the third quarter in Seattle when Larry got ejected. I'd always wondered what a coach did after being ejected, so I went with Larry to the locker room. There, we watched the rest of the game on TV. If getting tossed bothered Larry, it didn't show. No doubt he thought Jess Kersey, the ref who had ejected him, was a special kid.

The next day in Los Angeles, David Benner, the team's PR man, called me in my room.

"We better talk," he said. "You could have a problem."

I was baffled but went downstairs to see Benner, an ex-newspaper guy who had moved into PR. His brother Bill was still a columnist in Indianapolis in those days.

"Donnie called me this morning," Benner said. "He wanted to know if he saw you walking to the locker room with Larry while he was watching on TV last night."

"Why?" I asked.

"He said you aren't supposed to be in the locker room."

I laughed. This was no problem. I had already cleared my locker room/bench presence with the NBA, specifically with Brian McIntyre, the VP of public relations, who had checked with David Stern and said, "David says if the Pacers can put up with you, they're more than welcome to do so."

I explained this to Benner. He shook his head. "This isn't about the league. This is about Donnie. He says he didn't realize you were in the locker room during games."

I was stunned. We'd had a very specific conversation in June on the subject, including him saying, "Oh yeah, like *Season on the Brink.*" In fact, on a number of occasions after games, Donnie had walked into the locker room and said hello to me when I had already been in there with the team. Walsh was scheduled to fly out to LA to join the team for the rest of the trip. Benner suggested that I talk to him when he arrived.

I said I'd plan on it. In the meantime, I went to talk to Larry.

"John, I honestly don't know what's going on," he said. "I thought Donnie knew you were in the locker room from the beginning. I mean you sat in on our draft meetings and he was fine with that. I don't get it."

The next morning I went to shootaround with the team and returned to the hotel to find Walsh waiting in the lobby.

"I guess we should talk," he said.

Donnie got right to the point. "I can't have you in the locker room," he said. "I know how much Larry likes you, but you're a potential distraction."

I went through the chronology dating to June and pointed out that I'd been in meetings and in practice and the locker room since training camp. "The players hardly know I'm there," I said. "They're used to me now. I'm a piece of furniture to most of them."

Walsh shook his head. "Can't take a chance. We lose in the

playoffs and someone says it was because there was a reporter in the locker room, Larry and I are both in trouble."

I suspected someone had gotten to him—I was convinced of it but had no idea who it might be. I asked him if someone had convinced him that what he thought was a good idea before was now a bad idea.

"No," he said firmly. "I misunderstood you. I didn't know you were actually in the locker room until the other night. I'm sorry about the misunderstanding. You can go to practice but you can't go to meetings and you can't be in the locker room."

Practice was pretty much the least interesting thing on that menu. As with Bob Sutton, I knew I was in a brick-wall argument. I found Larry, told him what had happened, and said good-bye to Reggie Miller and Rik Smits, the two players I'd come to know best. They all expressed disappointment. There was no point in hanging around. I flew home on a red-eye that night.

In the end, like Bob Sutton, Donnie Walsh did me a favor. The night after I got home from LA—two days earlier than I would have if not for Walsh—Danny stood up and walked to me for the first time. I would have missed it if not for Walsh.

That said, I needed a new book idea. I decided it was time to try Army-Navy again.

19

Really Special Kids

IT HAD BEEN FOUR years since my first swing and miss with Army-Navy.

Navy had just fired George Chaump as coach and hired Charlie Weatherbie, who had been the coach at Utah State, to replace him. One of Weatherbie's selling points was that he'd been on Fisher DeBerry's staff at Air Force and Air Force had been dominating both Army and Navy for years.

I called Tom Bates and Jack Lengyel and told them I wanted to take another shot at doing the book. Once again, Jack set me up to meet with his coach. Over lunch, Weatherbie said to me, "If I call Bobby Knight and ask him if I should do this, what do you think he'll tell me?"

"He'll tell you not to do it—especially if you use a lot of profanity, which I suspect you don't," I said. (Weatherbie did say "Jesus Christ" quite a lot, but it was always while praying, which he did early and often every day.) "And if you listen to him, you'll be making a mistake."

Weatherbie told me he'd get back to me. Lengyel was fairly convinced he could assuage any doubts he had. The issue was the same as it had been the first time: Army and Bob Sutton.

On March 5, I went to the Patriot League basketball quarter-finals, which were played that year at West Point. I was there to write a column on Navy and then drive into New York to do *The Sports Reporters* on Sunday morning. Before I went up, I called Bob Kinney. Could I get a few minutes with Sutton?

Kinney said he could probably arrange it but he wasn't brimming with confidence. Sutton was going into the last year of his contract and his job was very much in the balance. In 1991 he hadn't wanted a reporter around because he was new to the job; now he probably wouldn't want one around because he was trying to save his job.

Sure enough, when I arrived for the basketball tournament, Kinney told me that Sutton was busy getting ready for spring practice and that his position on the book was pretty much the same as it had been. I was stymied. I went and watched the opening game of the tournament—Army upsetting Bucknell—and then found Kinney again.

"How about this," I said. "I'll come up during spring ball and just interview all the seniors and a couple of your key underclassmen. No special access. Just time with the players like you'd give me if I was coming up to write a story for the *Post*.

My thinking was simple: I'd start with the access I had to the Navy people and, at the same time, hope I could establish a rapport with the Army players without extra access early on. At the very least, if I did that, I could probably get players to fill me in on what went on inside the locker room as the season went on.

"I don't see why that should be a problem," Kinney said. I began interviewing players at Navy in April, and Kinney began setting up a schedule for me to come up for a week later in the month. In fact, I had made my plans to drive up on Sunday night to be ready to go early Monday morning when I got a call from Kinney on Friday afternoon. I could tell when I heard his voice that—as Miss Clavell might have said—something was not right.

"I don't even know what to say about this," he began, never an encouraging way to start a conversation. "Coach Sutton doesn't want you to talk to the players."

"Wait, I'm not asking for any special access."

"I know. I explained that to him. John, he's a good man, a really good man, but he's just got his mind set against *any* involvement in this. Believe me, I've tried to explain to him why this is a mistake. He's not listening."

I felt for Kinney. He was clearly caught in the middle. He believed the book was a good idea and clearly felt his bosses were going too far now. It was one thing to deny me special access, another to deny access that would normally be granted to any reporter. He kept apologizing, and I kept telling him I knew it wasn't his fault.

I was too far into the project now to turn back. Or maybe I was just tired of starting the research on a book and then having it yanked from underneath me. If Army wouldn't cooperate, I'd write the book from Navy's point of view. I had already started my interviews there and knew that my instinct that the players would be bright, admirable young men with stories to tell had been correct—it would be even more correct than I'd imagined.

I would do the best I could with Army. I'd still go to games—they couldn't deny me access to the players postgame could they?—but the focus would be on Navy. In some ways, Navy's story in 1995 was more intriguing anyway: new coach, three game losing streak to Army, each game decided in the final seconds. Plus, Navy had been dogged by unspeakable tragedy. In 1993 Alton Grizzard had come back for a game in Annapolis and spoken to his former team in the locker room before kickoff. The players still talked about his speech, how he had pleaded with them to please go out and end a five-game losing streak. They had done that.

A few weeks later, four days before the Army-Navy game, Chaump arrived on the practice field with tears in his eyes. He had to tell his players that Grizzard had been killed in a bizarre murder-suicide in Coronado, California. Grizzard had been talking to a friend, a young woman who had run cross-country at Navy, about her breakup with another SEAL, George Smith. Smith had burst into the room, shot and killed both of them, and then turned the gun on himself. To call Grizzard's death stunning was a vast understatement. It also provided a reminder of the uniqueness of the Army-Navy rivalry. When Bob Sutton got the call that Grizzard had died, he sat down and cried. He had met Grizzard at the Army-Navy pregame lunch three years earlier, but more than that he remembered what kind of a competitor Grizzard had been.

"I'm not sure I would have felt any worse if one of my own players had died," he said later.

The 1993 game was played in the Meadowlands that Saturday in a driving rainstorm. Army led 16–0, before Navy rallied in the fourth quarter to trail 16–14 and then drove the length of the field to set up a chip-shot eighteen-yard field goal in the final seconds. But Ryan Bucchianeri, a freshman kicker for the Midshipmen, let his kick drift wide right. It was a miss that would haunt Navy for years and Bucchianeri for the remainder of his time at the academy, even though he became something of a national hero for taking full responsibility for the miss.

That night, on the way home to Annapolis in the same awful rainstorm, three Midshipmen were killed when their car slid off the road within sight of the academy. They had just come over what the Mids call "oh shit hill"—because when you crest it, the academy comes into view and your first instinct is to say "oh shit."

There were plenty of storylines—some good, some bad, a couple horrific—at Navy. I would do the book that way.

THINGS BEGAN TO CHANGE that summer. Bob Kinney retired, but before he left he handed me over to his assistant, Bob Beretta, with instructions to "do anything you can to help him."

Together, the two Bobs came up with one more idea that they took to Sutton: Let the guy (me) at least talk to the captains. Let the captains report back on how the interviews went and then Sutton could decide whether to allow more players to talk. Sutton agreed. Beretta suggested I come up on the August day that culminated in the annual media barbecue.

"All the coaches will be there, the supe [superintendent] will be there too," he said. "You might get some informal time with Sutton, which can't hurt."

The only thing that hurt that day was the speeding ticket I got from a very humorless MP shortly after passing through the Stoney Lonesome Gate, which is at the very top of the army post that the academy is located on. After you pass through Stoney Lonesome you basically go straight downhill for a couple of miles. The speed limit is twenty-five. Unless you ride the brake hard, you can't help but go at least thirty-five. That's how fast I was going when I was pulled over by the MP, who had been lying in wait right outside the parking lot of the post exchange.

"What's your business here?" he asked.

"I'm a reporter going to interview members of the football team."

"Cadets?"

"Yes."

He nodded, took my information to his car, and handed me a ticket. "Next time obey the speed limit," he said, practically shoving the ticket through the window.

It was only later that I learned I should have told him I was a tourist, that I was a delivery boy, that I had taken a wrong turn and gotten lost—anything *but* saying I was there to talk to the football team.

"The MPs hate us," Jim Cantelupe told me. "They're all enlisted guys, and they see us as spoiled rich kid future officers. They call us Cad-idiots."

Lesson learned. Cantelupe was my first of four interviews that day. Beretta was sneaky fast: he had not only scheduled time for me with the two captains—Cantelupe, a defensive back; and Joel Davis, an offensive tackle—but with two other seniors, Al Roberts and Derek Klein.

"Let's get as much done as possible and go from there," he said.

Just as at Navy, I liked all four players instantly. Roberts said something that day that has stuck with me ever since: "Leadership is convincing people they can do things they shouldn't be able to do."

Given that Roberts was 6 foot 1 and 225 pounds and played defensive end, he knew what he was talking about. Most high school teams don't have defensive linemen that small.

Cantelupe and Klein spent as much time questioning me as I did questioning them. Klein knew my work well because he was a big golf fan. How much would I be around, they asked. I told them what had been going on.

"We'll talk to Coach Sutton," Cantelupe said. "We'll bring him around. This is too good an idea to let the Navy guys have all the fun."

I liked his attitude and his self-confidence (no one on earth has more self-confidence than Cantelupe). But I was, to put it mildly, skeptical.

That night at the barbecue, I met several people who would become close friends: Tim Kelly, the trainer, and Andy Smith, his assistant; Dick Hall, the equipment manager; and Bob Arciero, the team doctor.

"I hate Duke," was the first thing Arciero said to me. "They ran up the score on us last year."

I told him I hoped he wouldn't hold me responsible for that. Apparently, he didn't. Ten years later when I needed shoulder surgery, Arciero was my doctor.

At the end of the evening, I spent some time with Sutton. Much to my surprise, before I could say anything about it, he said, "The players you talked to today really enjoyed it."

"So did I," I said. "I'd really like to talk to more of them."

Sutton nodded. "How about this," he said. "We've got a bye week in mid-September. Come on up and talk to as many as you can then."

"Can I talk to you too?" I said, figuring this was the time to push my luck.

"Yeah, I think we can arrange that."

All I had to do then was get off the post without getting another ticket and the day would be well worth the thirty-five-dollar fine for my morning transgression.

BOB ARCIERO HATED DUKE even more after the second week of the season. The Blue Devils came into Michie Stadium and kicked a field goal at the buzzer after a horrid call by an official allowed them to retain possession on what would have been a game-ending fumble on their final drive.

I was there on the sideline, but not in the locker room until after the game. That was okay though; I was biding my time. Plus, my new friends Arciero, Kelly, Smith, Hall, and the four players were more than willing to fill me in on what I'd missed.

The next week I came up to do the interviews Sutton had agreed to let me do. One by one I sat and got to know the players the way I now knew the Navy players. Even though I was considerably older than each of them, I felt connected to them right away. After Navy had opened the season with a stunning 33–2 win at Southern Methodist, Andrew Thompson, Cantelupe's counterpart as defensive captain, had put his arm around me walking off the field and said, "I'm so glad you're part of this."

I was too.

The key to the week at Army was the lunch I had with Sutton. It was a miserable, rainy day, and we met at the Hotel Thayer, which sits just inside the main gate (both named for academy founder Sylvanus Thayer) of the academy. The dining room has a magnificent view of the Hudson River, even on a day shrouded by rain and fog.

Somewhere over lunch, Sutton and I finally connected. I think he sensed—at last—that the reason I wanted to do the book was the genuine respect I had for the academies and the feelings I had for the rivalry and the players. I never brought up any more access while we ate; I stuck to letting him tell stories about the players and the twelve Army-Navy games (eight as an assistant, four as head coach) he had taken part in.

After lunch, I gave him a ride back to his office. When we pulled up I took my best shot.

"Would you consider this?" I said. "Would you consider asking the players how they feel about having me around?"

Having now talked to just about all the seniors and the key underclassmen, I felt confident I had most, if not all, in my corner.

"I'll do that," Sutton said. "I think that's a fair request. If they want to do it—especially the firsties [seniors]—I think I should be willing to go along with them."

We shook hands and I thanked him. The next day he called me.

"You're in," he said. "Just let us know when you want to come up."

AS IT TURNED OUT, I missed one of the most dramatic games Army played that season. The one place the schedule had done me wrong was in putting Air Force–Navy on the same day as Army–Notre Dame. Knowing how important the Air Force game was to both Army and Navy, I felt I had to be in Annapolis that day. Plus, being honest, I figured that game would be more competitive than the one taking place in the Meadowlands.

I was wrong.

Air Force won fairly easily, 30–20. Notre Dame won 28–27 only when Army tight end Ron Leshinski was tackled a foot short of the goal line on what would have been a winning two-point conversion attempt in the final seconds. Army had been down 28–7 and had rallied to come that close to winning. This was a year before college football adopted overtime. Sutton could have kicked a routine point-after-touchdown and been at least a semi-hero for pulling out a tie against Notre Dame. He never considered it.

"The players never would have forgiven me," he said. "They didn't want to tie Notre Dame, they wanted to *beat* Notre Dame."

I spent a good deal of time at West Point the next week getting players to re-create the game for me. Then I went to Boston College with the team. Game day was rainy, windy, and miserable (my abiding memory of that season is bad weather). The Army players loved it: they were convinced that this was their kind of weather.

They were right. From the very beginning, Army dominated. By halftime the score was an astonishing 42–0. The score was so remarkable that when it was announced in the press box at Navy, a number of writers asked Tom Bates if it was the other way around: Boston College having the 42.

"I didn't blame them for asking," Bates said. "I double-checked it myself. I didn't *think* Army would be down by that much but there was *no way* they'd be up by that much."

Except there was a way. The final was 49–7 only because Sutton played everyone on the sideline except me. My only concern all weekend had been that if the team played badly, Sutton might somehow think my presence was a distraction. That wasn't a concern anymore.

"You are in, all the way in," Sutton said in the locker room afterward just in case I had any lingering doubts.

The rest of the season was pretty much a joyride for me—even Army's bitter loss at Air Force—because the people at both schools had grown to be completely comfortable with my presence. I went to class with Cadets and Midshipmen, hung out with them in their dorms, and basically saw and heard just about everything there was to see and hear.

One of the highlights for me was a day I spent with Cantelupe, meeting him for morning reveille at 6:15 a.m. and staying until he needed to get some studying done that night. We went to breakfast and then his first-period class. Since he had no second-period class, we went back to the barracks to spend time in his room (at Navy the dorm is called "The Hall," short for Bancroft Hall; at Army it is just the barracks).

Jim introduced me to Kevin Norman, his roommate. Norman was bright, engaging, and funny. He had been a punter but had given up football as a senior to focus on his studies. He would become a pilot who would be killed overseas in 2003. That was one of the realities of doing a book on Army and Navy: some of the people you met were going to put their lives on the line not long after graduation. It makes you stop and think a little bit about athletes who are deemed "courageous" for going for a green protected by water, or coaches who are called "brave" for going for it on fourth and two.

Norman was sitting on his bed, polishing some boots, when we walked in. Cantelupe sat down at his desk and I sat on Jim's bed. We were talking about life at West Point when there was a knock on the door and another cadet walked in, grabbed a clipboard off the back of the door, and began walking around the room taking notes.

"MRI," Cantelupe explained—morning room inspection.

I looked around the room. It was spotless. And yet the guy was scribbling away on the clipboard. That didn't seem to bother Cantelupe or Norman at all. Finally, he left, sticking the clipboard back on the door. I walked over to look at it to see what he possibly could have found wrong.

Plenty.

"Uniforms not spaced properly, Cadet Cantelupe's closet," he had written. "Too many civilian [aka family] photos, Cadet Norman's desk." And then there was one other note: "Unknown object, Cadet Cantelupe's bed."

The unknown object was me. I sat down and told Jim and Kevin I'd come a long way in ten years. "Once I was a pimp and a whore," I said. "Now I'm an unknown object."

THROUGH THE YEARS I'VE been fortunate enough to cover more major—and not-so-major—sporting events than I can possibly count. The one I remember most vividly and most emotionally is that year's Army-Navy game, played on a cold, clear day (no rain or snow, amazingly enough) on December 2 in Veteran's Stadium in Philadelphia.

Both teams had a lot to play for in addition to what is always played for in Army-Navy. The Midshipmen were 5–5 and trying to wrap up their first winning season since 1982. Charlie Weatherbie, aided immeasurably by his two coordinators, Paul Johnson and Dick Bumpas, had gotten Navy turned around in the right direction. This was their chance to end the streak of losing seasons and the three game string of heartbreaking losses to Army.

For the Cadets it was an even bigger deal: they were trying to save their coach's job. Everyone had known all season that Sutton's job was at stake and the loss at Air Force—after Army had led 14–0—had made it clear that Sutton's only chance to survive was to beat Navy. The players liked Sutton. The seniors, who had played for him for four years, believed he had grown into the job after adjusting to being the guy who makes decisions rather than suggestions—which is the toughest adjustment for anyone going from top assistant to boss.

For game day, I had lined up lots of help so it would appear that I was everywhere. Doug Pavek, an ex–Army defensive back who was now an OR (officer-representative) at Army, was carrying a tape recorder for me to turn on during those moments when I wasn't in the Army locker room. Kent Owens, who had the same job at Navy (they were called "officer-reps" rather than OR's in Annapolis), was doing the same thing in the Navy locker room. And my friend Wes Seeley, the guy who would declare a year later that Tiger Woods was *not* the fifth Beatle, had the week off from his golf job and had come to Philly for the game. When I was on one sideline, he was on the other.

So, in a sense, I was everywhere. The tension in the locker rooms was like nothing I had ever felt, except perhaps before I first swam a 200-yard butterfly in high school. My knees still shake when I think about that.

Neither team was going to a bowl so this was *it* for the seniors. All of them were going to feel a great sense of loss at the end of the day, regardless of the outcome. Football had been so important to them all their lives and they knew they would never play it again when it meant so much to them — and to so many others.

That feeling had been best expressed in a note Joel Davis, Army's offensive captain, had read to his fellow seniors a couple of weeks earlier, prior to the Air Force game. Davis had played at the Army prep school for a year, where his coach had been Anthony Noto — the same Anthony Noto who had been my first interview at Army in 1990 and had gone on to be a hotshot on Wall Street. Later he would become the CFO of the NFL before deciding Roger Goodell was going to be commissioner for a long time and returning to Wall Street.

Noto had written to Davis to remind him to treasure his last few days as a college football player. "The hardest thing in life is not rising to fight the battle," he had written. "It's rising with no battle to fight."

For all the seniors this would be their last battle in a football uniform.

I came down the tunnel before the game with Army for the simple reason that I found their pregame ritual more meaningful than Navy's. Weatherbie was a born-again Christian who believed in lots of prayer and lots of slogans. On game day he led his players and coaches in prayer no fewer than six times: before pregame meal, before the coaches met in the hotel, before the team met in the hotel, before the game, after the game on the field, and after the game in the locker room.

I have no problem with prayer, although I prefer it to be private rather than public. Those who choose to do it in public certainly have that right, but six times in a day—especially when Weatherbie would literally ask God for things like "great pad level" and "the ability to turn it all loose on the field"—was a bit much for me. Some of the players felt the same way but went along.

"If it helps us win I'll pray twenty times a day," Brian Grana, the only Jewish player on the team, had said to me early in the season.

Most football teams have some kind of sign posted above the locker room door. It has a quote or saying on it, like "Winners never quit" or "Play like a champion." Traditionally, as the players leave the locker room, they slap the sign on their way through the door to remind themselves that they are ready to play.

Weatherbie's said: "How do you spell fun? W-I-N!"

The players kind of rolled their eyes when he would bring that up in his pregame talks, but they dealt with it because they knew Weatherbie had hired a good staff and they desperately wanted to win after all the years of losing. Most of them had his pregame speech memorized because it was the same every week.

The Army locker room was a lot different. You never knew what Sutton was going to say to his players before a game. On this day he said very little other than reminding them what he always said about Army-Navy: "The most desperate team wins."

The sign on the door of the Army locker room was a little bit more inspired than the one in the Navy locker room. It was a centuries-old quote from the British poet John Dryden. It said simply, "I lay me down for to bleed a while but I will rise to fight with you again."

I still get chills when I type those words and when I picture in my mind's eye Dick Hall—who had fought in Vietnam before becoming Army's equipment manager in 1971—standing by the door as each player went out, giving each a firm handshake or hug and saying quietly, "Touch the sign, let's go," as each went by.

It was quiet, it was simple, and it was inspiring. There wasn't even a tiny bit of fake emotion in it.

And then, after you touched the sign, you were in the tunnel and Springsteen's "Born in the USA" was blaring in your ears (chosen by the seniors), and at the bottom of the tunnel the noise was even louder as you went from the darkness of the tunnel to the glare of the sunshine and the noise of the crowd, which was coming at you on all sides. No wonder many players on both teams had said the toughest thing about Army-Navy is getting your emotions under control before kickoff.

And then came the game.

Navy's biggest question mark going in was who was going to be the kicker. They had tried three different kickers during the season without much success. Ryan Bucchianeri, now a junior, wasn't even in uniform. He was standing with the rest of the Midshipmen, still believing he was the team's best kicker — and perhaps being correct given the performance of the others who had been given his old job.

After much debate among the coaches and a week of informal "tryouts," the Navy coaches had decided to risk going with a plebe who had never been in a college football game: Tom Vanderhorst, a quietly confident kid who had been the best kicker in practice all week. Twice, Vanderhorst trotted out to try field goals with everyone on the Navy sideline holding their breath. Twice, he was perfect.

Navy led 13–7 early in the fourth quarter and seemed to have the game in hand when it drove to the Army one-yard line. On third down it looked as if Navy quarterback Chris McCoy had an open lane to the goal line to score, but Cantelupe somehow closed on him fast enough to bring him down on the one.

Fourth down. The game clock was under nine minutes. Army had scored once all day. Logic said Navy should take the chip-shot field goal and make it a two-score margin at 16–7. Charlie Weatherbie wasn't sure. In the press box, Paul Johnson was telling him, "If you want to go for it, I've got a play we'll score on."

Gary Patterson, the defensive backs coach, who has since gone on to huge success as the head coach at Texas Christian, was screaming at Weatherbie to kick the field goal. Weatherbie decided to go for it. The play Johnson sent in was, in fact, wide open: a fake to the fullback followed by McCoy quickly throwing to slotback Cory Schemm in the end zone. But the ball slipped just a little coming out of McCoy's hands. Not used to throwing the ball very often, especially at such an important moment, he rushed it a little. The ball came up short and Schemm's dive was futile. The ball rolled to the turf while the Army bench celebrated as if it had just won the game.

In fact, I distinctly remember Jim Cantelupe turning to Derek Klein and saying, "We just won the game. We just won the f—ing game." In the book, I changed *f—ing* to *damn* so Jim's mom wouldn't get mad at him. She got mad at him anyway, so I can now reveal the truth. Jim has since given her two grandchildren, so I think she'll forgive him.

Army took over with 8:43 left and put together one of the most amazing drives I've ever seen—going ninety-nine yards and converting a fourth and twenty-four along the way when quarterback Ronnie McAda hit a streaking John Graves on the one-yard line to set up what proved to be the winning touchdown.

John Conroy, who is now a Chicago cop at least in part because asthma made it impossible for him to be sworn in as an army officer, scored the winning touchdown. The game ended with Al Roberts—"leadership is convincing people they can do things they shouldn't be able to do"—knocking Navy quarterback Ben Fay (in the game to try to pass the football) down just as he released a Hail Mary pass to the end zone. It was intercepted by Donnie Augustus, an extra defensive back put in the game just for that play.

Lying on the ground, neither Roberts nor Fay could see what happened, but when they heard the roar come from the Army side of the field, they both knew. Roberts jumped up, put his hand out, and helped Fay up. Then he gave him a hug.

As the teams came together for the playing of the alma maters, I found most of the seniors. I congratulated the Army guys, offered condolences to the Navy guys. I'd been torn the entire day: I didn't want the Navy seniors to go out without a win over Army. I also wanted Sutton, who I had come to genuinely like once he'd let me inside the circle, to keep his job.

The only person I couldn't find was Thompson. After the last notes of the Army alma mater had been played, I heard someone calling my name. I turned around and saw Thompson. Tears were rolling down his face. When I walked over to him, he buried his head on my shoulder.

"I can't believe they did it to us again," he said between sobs.

At that moment I said perhaps the corniest thing I've ever said to someone in my life, but I meant it: "Don't ever think you're anything but a winner."

Phil Hoffmann, who has been Navy's photographer for more than twenty-five years, happened to be standing nearby, and he took a picture of us as I was saying that. He sent it to me. It is the only photo of an athlete I have hanging on the wall in my office.

Thompson was still crying when Gary Patterson, his position coach, walked over. He was jelly-legged from the emotion, so Patterson and I each took him by an arm and walked him up the tunnel. When we got into the locker room, everyone else was in there, already kneeling for Weatherbie's postgame prayer. I knelt between Patterson and Thompson.

Just as I did, a security guard, who had followed us inside, put a hand on my shoulder. For obvious reasons I was dressed in neutral colors, so I looked different than anyone else in the locker room.

"Come on, pal, you don't belong in here," he said.

Before I could turn to show him the two passes—one for the Army sideline, one for the Navy sideline—looped around my belt, Thompson turned and pointed a finger menacingly in the guard's face. "He's with us. *You* get away from him."

The guard didn't argue for a second. He might have wanted to mess with me at that moment, but he did not want to mess with Thompson.

Weatherbie broke down midway through his prayer, blaming himself for the loss. It was one of the most intensely emotional scenes I've ever witnessed.

Once the players had stood from the prayer and started quietly making their way to lockers, I slipped out and raced down the hall to the Army locker room. The celebration was just beginning. Cantelupe and Joel Davis made a point of presenting the game ball to Sutton—trying to send a message to, as Davis put it, "all the stars" (army generals) in the room.

Once the speeches were finished, Cantelupe—still in uniform—went down the hall to find Thompson and console him. The two are still close friends to this day, as are many of the players on both teams.

Cantelupe left the army two years later during a downsizing of the military that allowed a number of graduates to get out before their five-year requirement was over. He's now a very successful money manager in Chicago.

Thompson is a major in the marines and about to become lieutenant colonel. He deployed to Iraq for a year in 2008 and came back in one piece. In the summer of 2011, after fifteen years of service around the world, he got the assignment he had always dreamed about getting: being sent back to Annapolis as the marine corps rep to the football team.

"Maybe now," he joked, "I'll get to be part of a win over Army."

20

"Can't You Just Write a Magazine Story?"

THE SUCCESS OF *A Civil War*, the book that came from my year following Army-Navy, was about as gratifying to me as seeing *A Season on the Brink* and *A Good Walk Spoiled* each reach number one on the bestseller list. *A Civil War* never climbed that high, but it was a bestseller and, to this day, still sells in paperback.

When people ask me what I think my best book was, I always say *A Civil War*.

What made the book for me—and I think for readers—was the quality of the people I was writing about. You just can't play football at Army or Navy without being a remarkable person. It's too hard. Just going to an academy is difficult. Going to an academy and playing football is pretty close to impossible. That's why, almost without fail, more than one hundred plebes show up each summer wanting to play football—many recruited, many not recruited—and somewhere between twenty and twenty-five are still around as first-classmen.

Having spent a year with Army and Navy football players, I had been spoiled. I got accustomed to walking into scheduled meetings a few minutes early and finding the player there waiting for me. If I had a frustration in dealing with the players, it was in getting them to call me John instead of "Mr. Feinstein," or "sir." I went to graduation at both schools that year and felt like a proud older brother as each of the young men I had come to know so well received his degree.

At the end of the season, I took each group of seniors out to dinner to thank them for all the time they had given me during the fall. There are not a lot of eating options in the West Point neighborhood, and the "Fat Men," as the Army offensive linemen called themselves, wanted to go to a Ponderosa because almost everything on the menu was all-you-can-eat.

So we went to Ponderosa.

One of the more amazing stories among the seniors that season had been that of a defensive lineman named Adrian Calame. He'd undergone knee surgery early in the year and had been told he wouldn't play again. Not surprisingly, Calame didn't accept that diagnosis. He kept working out and kept rehabbing and vowed he would play again.

I still remember the morning of the Boston College game when the team went for its morning pregame walk around the parking lot at the hotel. It was raining and no one really wanted to be out there, but this was part of the pregame ritual. Calame, on crutches, walked with his teammates. He was part of the team, he took part in the pregame walk.

And he did come back to play the last two weeks, including the Army-Navy game.

Calame was quiet and shy, one of the group I simply couldn't get to stop calling me Mr. Feinstein.

When we walked into the Ponderosa for dinner, the Fat Men jumped to the front to order their food so they could get started going back for more as soon as possible. Calame was near the back along with Jim Cantelupe, Derek Klein, Abby Muhammad (another defensive back), and me. When it was his turn to order, he said quietly to the cashier, "I'd like two of the all-you-can-eat shrimp dinners."

Cantelupe screamed in pain. "Adrian, you're a senior at the

United States Military Academy and you just ordered *two* all-you-can-eat dinners?"

"What's wrong?" Calame said innocently. "I'm hungry."

Then he realized what he'd said and everyone cracked up. It was one of those moments bound to come up at reunions years later.

Army and Navy both went to bowl games in 1996. Sutton had saved his job and proceeded to go 10–2 and win national coach-of-the-year awards. Navy was 9–3. The difference in their records was Army's 28–24 win in a driving rainstorm in Philadelphia. Eight times in the final two minutes of the game, Navy snapped the ball from inside the ten-yard line trying to score the go-ahead touchdown. Eight times Army stopped them.

The last Navy fourth down came with five seconds to play. After Ronnie McAda had taken a knee to end the game, Sutton said to me, "What a rout. We had the game won with five seconds left."

President Clinton was there to present the commander-in-chief's trophy, which was not going to Air Force for the first time since 1988. Soaked to the bone and shivering, the Army players stood in line to shake the president's hand after he presented the trophy. I was freezing. I'm not sure any of them felt the cold or the rain at all. They were that happy.

MY NEXT PROJECT WAS one that, in theory at least, should have been great fun: I would chronicle a season in the ACC, focusing on the nine coaches and the pressures they felt. Seven of the nine coaches gave me total access to their programs throughout the season. The two who didn't were Herb Sendek, who was in his first season at NC State and didn't know me very well, and Dean Smith, who was in his thirty-sixth season at North Carolina and *did* know me very well.

I wasn't that concerned with Sendek. For one thing, even though he was clearly a good coach, he wasn't all that interesting. For another, he gave me a lot of time and a lot of access. The only thing he didn't let me do was come into his locker room during games. I didn't feel as if I was missing that much.

Of course, I would have *loved* to be inside Dean Smith's locker room. But I knew that wasn't going to happen. Dean had made that clear to me when I was working on *A Season on the Brink* with his "I wouldn't let my mother in the locker room" line.

But I still had to try.

And so, after I had spoken to seven of the league's other coaches, I went to see Dean in the spring of 1996. As always, we talked politics—"Doesn't it bother you that Mike [Krzyzewski] is a Republican?" he would always say. We talked about how frustrating the previous season had been for him: for only the second time in sixteen seasons, Carolina had failed to make at least the Sweet Sixteen, and I had the feeling Dean was not in love with some of his players.

Then I came to the point. I told him I was doing a book, that the focus was the coaches (and I knew he thought I should focus on the players), and that I wanted complete access to his team whenever I was around throughout the coming season.

"What do you mean by 'complete access'?" he asked.

I told him.

He was, as I knew he would be, shaking his head before I was finished.

"You know I'm not going to do that," he said. "We've had this conversation before."

"I understand, Dean, but you should know that all the other coaches [Sendek had just arrived at NC State and I had not yet talked to him] have agreed to give me total access."

"Well, I figured Mike would do it [always the Duke thing], but the others have too? Gary [Williams]? Dave [Odom]? Bobby [Cremins]?"

"Yes. All of them. Not just Mike."

Dean leaned forward in his chair, clearly not pleased.

"Look, this really isn't fair," he said. "You know we don't let *anyone* in our locker room who isn't part of the team. We don't even let the managers come in at halftime. That's been our tradition for as long as I've been here."

"I know that, Dean," I said. "But you know slavery was a tradition once upon a time too."

Dean leaned forward in his seat, smiling just a little bit.

"You aren't really trying to compare slavery to me allowing you in my locker room, are you?"

As usual, he had me. "It was worth a try," I said.

Dean didn't let me in his locker room. But I think I can honestly say he was about as open with me as he's ever been. I was allowed to come to practice whenever I asked. I was allowed to sit near the Carolina bench, though not on it. Dean gave me all the interview time I asked for before, during, and after the season. And when I asked him about the various rituals—for example, exactly how did halftime work?—he answered.

One of our sessions came over lunch on Election Day. I voted early, drove to Chapel Hill, and met Dean in his office. As we walked to his car to go to the faculty club, where he liked to eat, I told *him* that he was driving a BMW because one of his first managers ran a BMW dealership.

"We really have known each other too long," he said, laughing.

After we had finished, I drove over to Durham to watch Duke practice. When I walked in, Krzyzewski asked me if I had just gotten to town.

"No, I was over in Chapel Hill," I said. "I had lunch with Dean. We were talking about how pleased we both are that Clinton's going to win tonight."

Krzyzewski smiled. "Oh yeah, I forgot about you and Dean bonding through your politics. You two bleeding-heart liberals deserve one another."

"Yes, we do," I answered.

The only time Dean balked at a question during the season was when I asked him what sort of pregame prayer, if any, his team said before a game.

"That's personal," he said. "I'm not going to answer that."

I didn't push it, in part because I didn't think he'd answer me, but also because I thought I could get the answer from someone else.

A couple of weeks later, when Carolina played at Clemson, I was standing in the hallway outside the visitors' locker room just after the teams had gone on the floor to warm up. Dean was one of the few big-time coaches (Dave Odom was another) who went onto the floor during warm-ups. He liked to sit on the bench and watch the opponent and see if he could pick anything up.

When he walked outside, he spotted me and waved me over. "We say a nondenominational prayer in the locker room before each game," he said.

"Thanks," I said. "Why did you decide to tell me?"

"I figured you'd find out one way or the other."

Spending time with Dean—any time—was always instructional. When Carolina went to play at Virginia in January, I found him pacing the hallway outside his team's locker room about an hour before the game.

"I don't like coming up here," he said. "They always play us well and I always get a speeding ticket on the way home."

"Seriously?"

He nodded his head. "Seriously. I think it's the same guy every time. He finds a spot and when he sees my [North Carolina] plates, he pulls me over. Last time we lost up here he pulled me over and said, 'Tough loss tonight, Coach. License and registration, please.'"

"Maybe you should slow down."

"Maybe we should win the game. Then I wouldn't mind the ticket."

As we talked, an old usher walked up to say hello to Dean. As he always did, even with people he barely knew, Dean remembered his name and greeted him like a long-lost friend. "Now here's someone you should talk to," he said to me—largely, I suspected, because it might mean I'd stop talking to him. "How long have you been an usher here?"

Back then, when Virginia was still playing in old University Hall, I don't think there was an usher working in the building under the age of eighty. The man pulled himself up straight, stuck his chest out, and said, "Twenty-eight years."

"Did you hear that?" Dean said. "He's been coming to this place for twenty-eight years. Isn't that amazing?"

"Amazing," I said. The man walked away, no doubt feeling as if he was only slightly less important (maybe) than the president of the United States.

"Dean," I said. "You realize that *you* have been coming to this place for thirty-six years, right?"

"Yeah, but let's not talk about that," Dean said.

I ENJOYED THAT SEASON, but not as much as my year doing *A Civil War*. The access I had made it fun, and I enjoyed a number of the players I got to know, notably Tim Duncan, who had decided to stick around for his senior year at Wake Forest even though he could have been the number one pick in the NBA draft had he come out after his junior year. Duncan liked college, and he liked being around his teammates.

I would say it worked out pretty well for him.

I can't say it surprised me to learn that just about every scholarship player in the ACC wanted to play professional basketball. What did surprise me was how *convinced* they all were they would play pro ball—if not in the NBA, then overseas. Many of them did. But the number of players who left ACC schools totally unprepared for Life After Hoops was a little bit of a shock to my system.

After *A March to Madness,* the ACC book, I wrote *The Majors.* I wasn't sure what I wanted to do next until a hot summer day in July of 1999. I told the story of that afternoon in the introduction to *The Last Amateurs.* What happened, in a nutshell, was I got to the point where I needed a break from the big time. I had written nine nonfiction books, and eight of them had focused on athletes and coaches who could be described as big-time.

On that July day I was at one of those summer camps sponsored by a sneaker company where the elite high school basketball players come to show off their skills to the elite college coaches. The gym at Fairleigh Dickinson that was used for the camp was packed. It would be in this same camp that I would first lay eyes on LeBron James a few years later.

I remember I was sitting with several top coaches: Jim Calhoun, who had just won his first national championship that March; Mike Krzyzewski, who had lost that championship game; Jim Boeheim, who would win his first four years later; and Gary Williams, who would win a national title in 2002. Only Williams isn't in the Hall of Fame at the moment, and he should be.

There were plenty of other coaches and media types sitting around us, but I remember those four because they were the ones who responded each time I asked about a player on the court. Each had an issue: SATs or grades, a couple had been at three different high schools, a couple more had a street agent, many played for AAU coaches who were asking for money or a job. Something inside me exploded. I needed to get away from all this.

I walked outside looking to get some fresh air. That's when I ran into Don DeVoe, the coach at Navy, and Emmett Davis, his former assistant, who had just finished his first year at Colgate. To be honest, I was surprised to see either of them in a camp like this one. They told me they were looking for kids who might not be quite as good as they thought they were but who had good grades.

As Don and Emmett were talking about some of their players, I remembered something DeVoe had said to me shortly after arriving at Navy: "The best thing about coaching here [as opposed to his previous jobs at Virginia Tech, Wyoming, Tennessee, and Florida] is that when I go to bed at night, I'm ninety-nine percent sure my players are in bed too."

It had been four years since I'd spent my year at Army and Navy. I still spent time at both places—especially Navy, which had asked me to become the color commentator on its radio network in 1997. I didn't do all the games, skipping the long plane trips because it meant giving up two days with my family (I now had two children). But I still made it up to Army at least once or twice a year and watched from the sidelines. When Danny was five and asked me which team we rooted for when Army played Navy, my answer was the truth: whoever is behind. It is one of the few rivalries in which I'm truly unbiased.

It took me about five minutes after leaving Davis and DeVoe that afternoon to formulate the seeds of a book idea: Navy and Colgate were both in the Patriot League, which at that moment consisted of seven teams (Army, Bucknell, Lehigh, Lafayette, and Holy Cross were the other five; American joined the league in 2001).

The Patriot League was known for three things: David Robinson, who had played at Navy before the league was formed in 1990; Adonal Foyle, who had played at Colgate for three years (because his guardians taught there) before becoming a number one pick in the NBA draft; and the fact that the league had been formed on the Ivy League model of not giving athletic scholarships—recruited athletes were given a wider swath by admissions than non-athletes, but they had to go through the same process to apply for financial aid as anybody else.

If I could do a book on ACC basketball, why couldn't I do one on Patriot League basketball? The Ivy League had more tradition; it played better basketball at the time and it was, well, the Ivy League. But in the end, the last was the reason not to do it: playing in the Ivy

League gave you a special kind of cachet the Patriot League kids wouldn't have. Plus, I thought the presence of Army and Navy would make for better storytelling based on my *Civil War* experience.

One of the ways I know I have hit on a good book idea is that I can't get it out of my mind, can't wait to get started on it. This was one of those moments. I called Esther from the camp and told her I was less than an hour from New York and wanted to come see her about an idea. I drove into the city the next day and told her what I wanted to do.

"Tell me the schools again?" she said.

When I told her she looked at me blankly.

"Is there anybody famous from there?" she asked.

"You mean besides people like Dwight Eisenhower and Ulysses S. Grant and Robert E. Lee?" I said.

"Basketball players," she said, giving me her disgusted look.

"Bob Cousy played at Holy Cross. David Robinson played at Navy. Bob Knight and Mike Krzyzewski coached at Army."

"Uck, I knew you'd find a book with Krzyzewski in it."

"Please put aside your biases for *one* minute. You [Connecticut] just beat Duke to win the national championship. You need to get over Christian Laettner."

"I think Michael [Pietsch, my editor at Little, Brown, who had played a key role in making *Good Walk Spoiled* such a success] will hate it."

"Michael hated the idea for *A Civil War.*"

"True. He'll let you do it, but he won't pay you."

She didn't actually mean he wouldn't *pay* me, she meant he wouldn't pay me nearly as much as I had gotten for *A March to Madness* or *The Majors.* I knew that. In fact, Michael offered more than he had paid up front on *A Civil War* based on that book's success. That meant I was paid (in advance) about 15 percent of what I had been paid for *The Majors,* and 25 percent of what I had been paid for *A March to Madness.*

I didn't care. I was already looking forward to Lafayette-Colgate on a cold winter night in Hamilton, New York. Of course, adding *cold* to *winter night* in Hamilton—or almost any night—is a redundancy.

Shortly after I had signed the contract for the book, I had lunch with Bob Woodward, which is always educational. I respect Bob's instincts as a reporter completely and unconditionally. When I told him what I was doing, he gave me a funny look. "Can't you just write a good, solid magazine story?" he said. "A book, a whole book?"

So maybe I don't trust his reporting instincts unconditionally. Or maybe I'm just very stubborn.

I began calling the league's coaches, whose responses when I told them I wanted to spend a season chronicling their basketball teams wasn't all that different from Woodward's. Fran O'Hanlon at Lafayette asked me if I was joking. Emmett Davis, knowing my aversion to snow, explained very carefully to me exactly where Colgate was located. Pat Harris from Army started to laugh. "When I told you [after he had gotten the job] to call me if you ever needed anything, I didn't think you were going to take me quite so literally," he said.

The funniest call was with Carolyn Femovich, who had just come on board as the league's executive director. This is Patriot/Ivy-speak for commissioner. Femovich was a lifelong administrator who I suspect didn't know me from Adam and who generally likes to check a rulebook or call a meeting to decide if lunch should follow breakfast.

I called her as a courtesy, since I knew I'd be seeing her during the course of the season. I explained to her what I was doing and that all the coaches—none of them had "Deaned" me—were on board. There was a long pause on the other end of the phone.

"Well," she said finally, "the most important thing, of course, is making sure you don't do anything that will jeopardize the eligibility of our student-athletes."

I hadn't actually realized that was the most important thing.

"Carolyn," I said, "are there any rules against being interviewed?"

"Well, no."

"Then I think we'll be okay."

I BEGAN MY TOUR of the Patriot League in September, spending a couple of days at each school so I could get to know as many players as possible and spend time with each coach. As with Army-Navy, I knew I'd made a good decision right away. One player after another—without jeopardizing his eligibility—came in and told warm, funny stories about realizing he wasn't going to play in the NBA and what it was like to play on the road against the power teams, which all the Patriot League teams did to make money for the athletic department budgets.

Devin Tuohey at Colgate talked about his first college basketball game at Syracuse, when he had turned the ball over the first two times he had touched it, which led to thunderous dunks. The third time he turned it over he had taken one of the Syracuse players down going to the basket to avoid another dunk and had been booed by about thirty thousand people in the Carrier Dome. The worst part had been when he had come out of the game and found his roommate, another freshman, named Jim Detmer, laughing uncontrollably on the bench.

"He said, 'I'm really sorry, Devin, but that's the funniest thing I've ever seen,'" Tuohey said, able to laugh at himself a year later.

That was the best thing about the Patriot League kids: they could laugh at themselves. This was completely different than what I'd experienced in the ACC. It wasn't that they wanted to win any less; they just understood where they fell in the basketball pantheon and made a point of enjoying themselves along the way. You weren't likely to catch them sneaking looks into the stands to see how many NBA scouts were watching. Most nights they knew the answer was a round number.

Much to my surprise, the best story turned out to be at Holy Cross. The best teams were Navy and Lafayette; Holy Cross was the best story. It had more basketball tradition—by far—than any other Patriot League school: Cousy, Tom Heinsohn, Togo Palazzi, not to mention a national title in 1947 and an NIT title (back when it meant something) in 1954.

When the Big East was forming in the late 1970s, commissioner Dave Gavitt had approached Father John Brooks, then the university president, about joining. It was a natural fit since Boston College was Holy Cross's number one rival and the school was close to both Providence and Connecticut. Father Brooks said no, believing that the *Big* in Big East was literal—as in big-time—and he didn't want Holy Cross going down that road. To this day, many Holy Cross alums revile Father Brooks because they believe Holy Cross could have been a factor nationally had it joined the Big East.

Instead, Father Brooks was very much involved in the formation of the Patriot League, which was about as far from the Big East as you could get with its no-scholarship rules. But cracks in that foundation began to form early: Fordham, one of the charter league members, wanted to start giving basketball scholarships again. When the league said no, Fordham bolted for the Atlantic 10, where it has now languished in or near the basement for most of two decades.

Holy Cross was next. Sick of losing—the Crusaders won the league in 1993, but when longtime coach George Blaney left for Seton Hall, they skidded to the bottom—the alumni pressured Father Brooks's successor to start giving basketball scholarships again. This time the league couldn't say no because if Holy Cross left, it would be down to six teams and would not be eligible for an automatic NCAA bid. Without that bid, the league would lose all viability—not to mention a lot of money.

So Holy Cross was again giving scholarships. Lehigh was next. By the mid-2000s, all the civilian schools (at Army and Navy everyone in the school is on a government scholarship) would be giving scholarships again.

During the transition from non-scholarship players to scholarship players, Holy Cross had hired Ralph Willard as its new coach. Willard had graduated from Holy Cross in 1967 but had been in the big time for a while. He'd been an assistant to Jim Boeheim at Syracuse and then to Rick Pitino with the Knicks and at Kentucky. He had become the head coach at Western Kentucky and had taken the Hilltoppers to the Sweet Sixteen in 1993, which led to his getting the Pittsburgh job.

But Pitt hadn't worked out for Willard. He'd taken some players he probably shouldn't have, been victimized by some untimely injuries, and had been fired after four seasons. That brought him full circle back to his alma mater, the Patriot League—and me.

Willard was the only coach in the conference I had any concerns about in terms of cooperation. My reasoning was simple: he was close friends with Rick Pitino, I was not.

I think Pitino is a great coach, and I've thought that since his days at Providence, when he was the first coach to really understand the impact of the three-point shot after it first came into existence in 1986. His understanding of how to take advantage of the shot had been the key to Providence reaching the Final Four in 1987.

I still remember watching Pitino do a clinic in the summer of 1986. Several players were demonstrating—under Pitino's guidance— how to run a secondary fast break. When one of them caught the ball on the wing, took one dribble, and fired an eighteen-foot jumper from just inside the new three-point line, Pitino screamed, "No—stop!"

The gym went quiet. "That's the *worst* shot in college basketball beginning this fall," Pitino said. "You do *not* catch the ball and take one step inside that line and shoot. You either catch it and shoot the three or go all the way to the basket."

If you are a basketball fan at all you will understand that, in that moment, Pitino described what college basketball has become: a game of catching and shooting behind the line or driving all the way to the goal. The mid-range jump shot has, for all intents and purposes, ceased to exist.

As much as I admired Pitino's coaching, his ego made me crazy. *All* coaches have huge egos—I'd spent a year with perhaps the biggest one in history—but Pitino had a way of saying things that made you cringe.

While he was coaching the Knicks he wrote a book modestly titled *Born to Coach*. Then, after the 1992 season, he cowrote a book with my pal Dick ("Hoops") Weiss in which he took none of the blame for failing to guard the inbounds pass on the fateful play that led to Christian Laettner's game-winning jump shot in the 1992 East Region final.

A year later, when Kentucky did make the Final Four but lost to Michigan, the lead on my *Washington Post* column was this: "For Rick Pitino, the numbers remain the same: two autobiographies, zero championships."

Okay, a tad harsh.

A year later I was convinced the lead hadn't been harsh enough. Kentucky played Marquette in a second-round tournament game that season in St. Petersburg. (It was, in fact, on the day I blew off Krzyzewski to go see Arnold Palmer.) Marquette had a little guard named Tony Smith who wasn't much of a shooter and wasn't especially dangerous in a half-court offense. But in the open court, he was a jet.

Pitino, as always, played ninety-four feet of pressure defense the whole game. For Tony Smith, this was a little bit like telling Tom Brady he could play quarterback all day with no one rushing the passer. Smith shredded Kentucky's defense and set up his teammates for easy baskets all day. Marquette won the game.

Pitino walked into his press conference that day with his three seniors—who were, understandably, brokenhearted that their careers had ended with such a surprising loss to a team they no doubt thought they would beat with ease. Instead of questioning himself, as almost everyone in the room not bleeding Kentucky blue was doing at that moment, Pitino said, "This was a Kentucky team that lacked leadership, lacked chemistry, and lacked talent."

Kentucky had finished 28–7. In one sentence Pitino had thrown his players, especially the seniors, so far under the bus they couldn't even see the wheels as they rolled over them.

I coached good, they played bad.

There's nothing that bothers me more than coaches who do that—especially on the college level. Knight had a tendency to do it, but more often it was in private and not in public. You would no more hear Dean Smith or Mike Krzyzewski do that than you would hear a Tea Party member praise President Obama.

After that I really was done with Pitino and ripped him at every turn, even when his team won the national championship in 1996. I gave him very little credit, which was no doubt unfair of me. Shortly after Kentucky won that title, Dave Kindred sent me a clip from something called *The Cats Pause*, which is, as you might imagine, a publication devoted strictly to all things Kentucky. There was a lengthy Q and A in it with Pitino, and he was asked if he was going to write another book in the wake of Kentucky's championship.

"You know, I've said for a long time that I wasn't going to write another book until we won a championship, because I wasn't going to give people like John Feinstein the chance to rip me again for writing one, even though a lot of people have told me I should write again. But now that we've won, I'm going to do another one."

Kindred had circled the quote and written, "Your fault." Kindred had been asked by the *Lexington Herald-Leader* to review the book that Hoops had ghosted for Pitino. Trying mightily not to criticize Hoops, Kindred had said of Pitino, "Someone stop this man before he writes again."

Even though the shot was directed at Pitino, Hoops took it

personally, and he and Kindred—two of the nicest men in my profession—barely spoke for years after that. Which is one of many reasons I don't write book reviews. Generally speaking, knowing how much it hurts when someone criticizes me (unfairly at all times, of course), I don't want to be in a position where, if I don't like a book, I have to rip it. I assume others who write books put as much into their work as I put into mine, and I just don't want to do it.

So now, a little more than three years later, I found myself in a seafood restaurant near the Holy Cross campus with Ralph Willard. Right from the start, I knew his Pitino background wasn't going to be a problem. We bonded right away—as New Yorkers, as basketball junkies, as cynics. When I brought up Pitino, just to get the issue on the table, Ralph waved his hand.

"Someday I'll get the two of you in a room and you'll be friends," he said. "Your problem is you're too much alike. You're both ball busters."

True to his word, Ralph sat me down with Rick a few years later at the same basketball camp where I had first come up with the idea for *The Last Amateurs,* and we talked at length. Since then we've gotten along fine—Rick's even played in the charity golf tournament I put on in Bruce Edwards's name. We're not best friends by any stretch, but we're cordial and Rick returns my phone calls. We have no plans to do a book together at any point in the future.

THERE WERE SO MANY good stories at Holy Cross I wasn't sure which one to work on first. Two seniors had been cut from the team because Willard only wanted guys who *really* wanted to play. One other had made the team, realized he didn't *really* want to play, and quit. Another quit, came back, and then quit again at midseason.

And then there was Chris Spitler.

There was no doubt Spitler wanted to play. The question was *could* he play? Willard kept thinking he should cut him, but couldn't bring himself to do it because it was tough to cut a guy who worked harder than anyone in practice.

I have told and retold Spitler's story more times than I can remember. He was completely unrecruited as a high school senior in Buffalo, where he averaged seven points a game. He went to Holy Cross on an academic scholarship and played JV ball as a freshman. He asked then coach Bill Raynor if he could try out as a sophomore, and Raynor told him he could—but that he had no chance to make the team.

He made the team—about 99 percent on attitude, the rest on grade point average (yes, even at Holy Cross they like high-GPA kids for the end of the bench). It was on an endless bus trip home from a loss at Colgate that Spitler famously (at least in my life's sphere) picked up the basketball magazine that ranked the thirty-one Division I conferences and noticed the Patriot League was ranked number thirty-one. It was then that he made his calculation that being the worst player on the worst team in the worst conference made him the worst Division I player in the entire country.

Quite a distinction.

By season's end, Raynor was starting him. He played thirty-nine minutes at Bucknell and scored 11 points and had 5 assists. He fouled out diving for a loose ball. Raynor made him try out again as a junior. He made the team *again* as the twelfth man on a twelve-man team and was *again* a starter by season's end. Willard arrived, told his coaches that Spitler *had* to be cut, and, of course, ended up starting him before the season was over.

Frank Mastrandrea, who was then the SID at Holy Cross and now has some associate AD title I can't figure out, called this "the three phases of Spitler": you can't possibly be on the team, you're on the team but you'll never play, you're the starting point guard.

My favorite Willard-Spitler exchange took place at Yale, when Spitler came into the game late in the first half and promptly launched a badly missed jumper with ten seconds left—when Holy

Cross was playing for the last shot. Walking off the court, Willard said, "Spitler, I thought the one good thing about you was that you were a smart player!"

"Oh no, not me, Coach," Spitler said. "You've got the wrong guy."

The first time I met Spitler I knew I had the right guy. After I finished my first interview with him, I went and found Mastrandrea, who remains to this day a close friend.

"You realize don't you that this kid *is* this book?" I said.

"I know," Frank said. "I didn't want to introduce you to him right away because I wasn't sure he was going to be on the team."

One thing about Spitler, he always found a way to make the team.

SINCE ELEVEN YEARS HAVE passed, I can now reveal that for all the complaining I've done throughout my adult life about game times being changed for TV, I was responsible for a game time being changed while I was researching *The Last Amateurs*.

The toughest thing about that season was figuring out where to be each night. It wasn't so much that I didn't want to miss the games, it was that I didn't want to miss the locker room moments, the time with the players and coaches—just the general "scene" of the league. I still remember one Saturday when I went to see Holy Cross play at Lafayette in Kirby Arena in the afternoon, then jumped in my car to drive the fifteen miles over to Stabler Arena to see Colgate play Lehigh.

Neither game was remarkable in any way (except for Lehigh coach Sal Mentesana saying to a referee who failed to call an obvious foul late in the game with Colgate up twenty-five, "Look, no one wants to get this over with more than me, but we *both* have to do our jobs. *That* was a foul"). But I remember as I raced into Stabler to join Lehigh in the locker room for their pregame talk thinking how much I was going to miss all of this the following season. I had only been to a handful of so-called big-time games all year and hadn't missed it for one second.

Each week I would sit down on Sunday night and plan my schedule for the next week. It would be based on who was playing whom, logistics (a day like the one where I could see two games back-to-back was an obvious choice), and whomever I hadn't seen in a while. I was driving everywhere, knew the hotels cold by midseason, and didn't even really need my credentials since everyone working in all seven buildings knew me by then.

Looking ahead to the last weekend of the season, I saw a problem. Army and Navy were closing out their regular season at Army at noon on Saturday. That was a game I needed to see because it was Army-Navy, because it was the last home game for the Army seniors, and because Navy needed to win to keep pace with Lafayette in the race to finish first. The highest-seeded team hosted the championship game and, given that each had beaten the other at home, that figured to be critical. Lafayette would be at Bucknell on Sunday to close out the season, so there was no problem getting there.

The problem was Chris Spitler.

Had it been early in the season, Lehigh at Holy Cross, scheduled for Saturday at two o'clock, would hardly look like a game I needed to attend. And at this point, both teams were in the bottom half of the league. But Spitler had become a central figure in the book and it was his last home game. Not only that but he was the *only* Holy Cross senior left and there was certainly something symbolic in that.

There was no way I could be at West Point for a noon game and then at Holy Cross—about two-and-a-half hours away—for a two o'clock game.

I called Mastrandrea. "I know this is crazy," I said, "but do you think there's any way you could play your game that day at seven instead of two?"

Frank thought for a minute. "Logistically, I don't see why not," he said. "There's no TV involved. We could easily get word to our season ticket holders [of whom there were *at most* three hundred at that point] and our students. As long as Ralph and Sal don't object, I don't see why not."

Neither Ralph nor Sal objected. In fact, they were glad to help me out. It would mean Lehigh would get home much later, but it was a Saturday, so the players could sleep in on Sunday. No one bothered to check with the league office because there would have been such paralysis in making a decision we might still be waiting for an answer right now.

So the game was changed to a seven o'clock tip. The only complaint I heard was from one of the women's assistant coaches at Lehigh. In those days the men and women played doubleheaders in the Patriot League, and the women's tipoff was moved from 12:00 to 4:30. When the women's coaches asked why—a reasonable question—they were told it was to accommodate me.

I guess they didn't like that and one of them decided to tell me so. "You should be ashamed of what you did," she said to me in the hallway of the Hart Center when I walked in at about five o'clock. The women's game was at halftime and Holy Cross, which back then had the best team in the league, was winning easily. Apparently that was because of the time change.

I wasn't ashamed and it was well worth the effort. Spitler made a couple of key free throws and Holy Cross won the game. Even the Lehigh people seemed to have a sense of appreciation for Spitler. Mentesana brought his team out from the locker room to applaud Spitler during the Senior Night (or Spitler Night) ceremony. "In a lot of ways he's what our league is supposed to be about," he said later. "I was glad to do it."

Lafayette won the conference tournament after getting home-court advantage for the final based on a slightly higher RPI (computer ranking) than Navy. Every other tiebreaker had failed after the teams finished 11–1, so that was all that was left. It was a shame to decide something so crucial based on something so inexact. But that was the way it was done.

The Leopards were sent to Buffalo by the NCAA to play Temple: a two seed versus a fifteen seed. This was one of those "coincidental" matchups that often pop up in the bracket. Lafayette coach Fran O'Hanlon was a dyed-in-the-wool Philly guy who had worked for Temple coach John Chaney earlier in his career. They were still good friends. So, somehow, of all the two–fifteen matchups available, Lafayette drew Temple.

I had no illusions about what was going to happen in the game. Lafayette was a good Patriot League team and it played a very good matchup zone defense. But O'Hanlon had learned the defense from Chaney, who played it with bigger, quicker athletes. A lot of people saw Temple as a potential Final Four team. I knew miracles happened, but I certainly wasn't counting on it.

One thing I wanted to be sure of was that I didn't get shut out of the Lafayette locker room after having had complete access all season. This was a potential headache because of the rule the NCAA had put in place after *A Season Inside*. Dave Cawood, then the NCAA's PR guy, had gone out of his way to enforce it in 1997 when I was working on *A March to Madness*.

I was able to write around not being in the locker rooms fairly well that year since, as with other books, the coaches and their assistants willingly told me what had been said. But I know I missed something not being in there, and it was all because of Cawood.

Now, in 2000, Jim Marchiony, someone I knew and liked, had Cawood's job. Even though Jim and I were friends, I knew in NCAA-world he would be almost obligated to try to keep me out of the Lafayette locker room. Of course, what he didn't know couldn't hurt him — or me.

So I applied for a media credential as if planning to cover the subregional in Buffalo like everyone else. Then I got Lafayette to put me on their team list at the last possible moment. I was fortunate that the committee representative in Buffalo was a close friend, Jack Kvancz, the athletic director at George Washington. I told Jack my plan so that if anyone asked him what my name was doing on the Lafayette team list, he could just say, "That's just so he can get into their practices without any problem."

Everything went well until halftime of the Temple-Lafayette game. I'd had no problems before the game or at halftime. In fact, when Fran O'Hanlon and I had walked out to the court together to watch the overtime of the Seton Hall–Oregon game, which opened the afternoon program, *Fran* had been stopped by a security guard because he'd left his jacket with his lapel pin in the locker room. I had to vouch for him.

When I came back out of the locker room with the team at halftime — Temple was winning the game in a romp — Kvancz was waiting for me.

"We've got a problem," he said. "Marchiony's here and he's onto you."

At that point it was obvious that all I needed was to be in the Lafayette locker room after the game. The Leopards would not be playing again on Sunday.

"Hold him off," I said.

Jack nodded. "I'm going to tell him you aren't going in after the game," he said. "You go in, then afterward he can yell at both of us."

That's exactly what happened. I went in and witnessed O'Hanlon's very emotional final talk to his team. When the locker room opened to the media, I walked into the hallway and found Marchiony waiting.

"I *knew* you were in there," he said. "I knew Jack was covering for you."

"Jack's my friend," I said.

"You shouldn't have done that," Jim said. "It was wrong."

"No, Jim," I said. "It was absolutely right."

———

Even after Lafayette got pummeled that day, I knew I had a very good book. Whether anyone would read a book about kids playing basketball in a league that had never won an NCAA Tournament game since its formation, I didn't know. Woodward's words about the magazine piece were still rattling around in my head somewhere.

The early reviews were very good. I did book signings at the schools, which almost brought back memories of that first day in Indiana with *Season on the Brink*. I went to a Princeton-Lafayette game to do a pregame book signing and never saw a minute of the game because people were still lined up through the entire game — which included overtime.

Patriot League people would buy the book. But would anyone else?

On a night in early December I was in Boston promoting the book. My last stop was at Harvard, where I had been asked to speak to a student forum. I told the story that night about the argument between my father and me about where I should go to college. Dad was teaching a graduate-level course at Yale at the time, and having gone to CCNY because he had grades but his family had no money, it had always been his dream to see his kids go to Ivy League schools. My sister came the closest, going to Wesleyan.

After my visit to Duke in January of my senior year, there was no doubt in my mind I wanted to go there. The campus was beautiful. It was 65 degrees and there were girls walking around in halter tops and shorts. The swimming pool was brand-new with giant windows that made you feel as if you were swimming outdoors. Even though the basketball team was lousy, the atmosphere in Cameron Indoor Stadium was amazing, and I happened to visit on a weekend when the team upset number two–ranked Maryland, 73–69. At Yale it had been snowing, everyone was bundled up, the basketball team was awful, and the pool in Payne Whitney gym felt like it was a hundred years old, even if Don Schollander *had* worked out in that pool en route to his four Olympic gold medals in 1964.

To me it was a no-brainer. Dad, of course, disagreed. I finally said to him, "Dad, I need to go to college where I want to go, not where you want me to go."

"Well," he said, "you didn't even apply where I really wanted you to go."

"What are you talking about?" I said. "I applied to Yale."

"I didn't want you to go to Yale. I wanted you to go to Harvard."

"You never said a word about Harvard!"

"I know. I *knew* you couldn't get in there."

The audience loved that story. Afterward, several students came up to thank me.

"Oh, it was my pleasure, I enjoyed it," I said.

"We're not talking about the speech," one of them said. "We're talking about not going to Yale."

That was funny. The people who sponsored the speech had a really nice dinner for me and then I headed down the road toward Hartford, where I was stopping to do several interviews for the book the next morning before going on to New York. It was snowing, but not hard, and I pulled off the road at the Mass Turnpike rest stop just before I-84 to get some gas and go to the bathroom. I also wanted to check my messages at home. I had a separate phone line that only rang in the basement, where my office was, so I knew I could check messages without waking my family.

The last message was from Esther. It was, as always, direct.

"Number fourteen," she said. "Congratulations."

I knew exactly what the message meant, but I stared at the phone for a second and then pressed replay just to be sure. The three words were the same the second time as the first.

I can remember where I was and how I heard the news every

time I've had a bestseller. Needless to say, the two times I've had books get to number one are especially vivid.

The first was in a Holiday Inn in Evanston, Illinois. I had wrapped up some book-promo stuff for *Season on the Brink* in Chicago and had driven up to Evanston to do a column on Bill Foster, who had been the coach at Duke when I was an undergraduate and was then coaching at Northwestern. I had gone for a walk during the afternoon, because it was an unseasonably nice day, and had wandered into a bookstore, where I was unable to find a single copy of *A Season on the Brink*.

Even with Macmillan going back for new printings constantly, this had been a problem for two months: the stores just couldn't keep enough copies on the shelves. It was a nice problem to have, but still frustrating.

I called Esther from the hotel to tell her we needed to bang on Macmillan some more about distribution. The book had gotten to number two on the *New York Times* bestseller list the week before behind Bill Cosby's book *Fatherhood,* which had been number one for a year. When I had called my dad to tell him the book had jumped from number eleven on the list to number two, he had said, "Why isn't it number one?"

"Dad, it's behind *Bill Cosby.* This is as good as it's going to get."

While I was talking to Esther, she suddenly interrupted and said, "Hang on, Jeff Neuman is on the other line. He says he has news."

I held my breath. I wasn't going to let myself believe that the news could be that I had gone past Cosby.

Esther was back on a moment later, almost breathless.

"This is just unbelievable," she said. "This just doesn't happen."

"What?" I screamed.

"You're number one."

It was an extraordinary moment in my life. I called my mom first and then my dad. Mom was Mom: proud, happy, wanting to know when I was coming home from my trip. Dad was, well, not Dad. *"You're kidding?"* he said. "You went past Cosby? I thought you said that couldn't happen? Linda, Judy [his two assistants], come in here right now. John's number one on the bestseller list! He beat Cosby!"

Other than when I called to tell him he was a grandfather, I don't think I ever heard my father so happy.

Not everyone in the world was that impressed that I had gone by Cosby. When Bob DeStefano, my longtime boss at Gardiner's Bay on Shelter Island, called the publisher of the Island's weekly newspaper, *The Reporter,* to tell her she should write something about the success of the book, she balked.

"I really don't like to do stories on Island authors," she said. "We have so many that if I do something on one of them, the others get upset." (A lot of writers *do* have places on Shelter Island, including, back then, people like Leon Uris, Robert Hughes, and Harold Schonberg, the Pulitzer Prize–winning music critic of the *New York Times.*)

"But John grew up here summers," Bob said. "He *wrote* the book out here. He went past *Bill Cosby* to get to number one on the bestseller list!"

There was a pause, and then the publisher said, "Okay, start at the beginning. Tell me who this Cosby fellow is."

By the time I got through making phone calls after hearing the news that day in Evanston, the only place I had time to eat my celebration dinner was McDonald's. That was just fine with me.

The second time I got to number one, I was in California the week after Father's Day. *A Good Walk Spoiled* had hit the list the week before at number eleven, and with Father's Day sales I thought it *might* crack the top five—but I wasn't counting on it. I had just finished an interview at a radio station in Pasadena. I had a little time before my next interview and found a pay phone in the lobby of the building where the radio station was to call home and see how things were going.

My wife, Mary—we have since divorced—answered the phone sounding very emotional about something. "Is Danny all right?" I asked, immediately concerned something might be wrong with my son, who was eighteen months old.

"Danny's fine," she said. "Have you talked to Esther?"

"No. Why?"

"Because I think she wanted you to know that a book you dedicated to your mother and your son [my mom had died on Mother's Day two years earlier, a few months before Danny was born] is number one on the *New York Times* bestseller list."

There was a chair right next to the phone. I remember feeling my knees semi-buckle and falling into the chair in disbelief. Thinking about my mom at that moment and how much she loved golf, I started to cry.

After I did my last interview in Los Angeles that evening, I had to drive to San Diego. I pulled off of I-5 to eat and celebrate at—you guessed it—a McDonald's.

Five years later, hearing Esther's message saying that *The Last Amateurs* was number fourteen on the *Times*'s list, I let out a whoop in the mostly empty rest stop. A couple of people glanced at me but kept going. The book no one wanted me to write was a bestseller. The book Bob Woodward thought should be a magazine story. When I hung up the phone I threw my arms into the air and shook a fist à la Tiger Woods.

It was almost midnight. I had eaten dinner but I had to celebrate.

Fortunately, the rest stop had a McDonald's.

21

Back to the Future

JUST UNDER TEN YEARS after my celebration at the Mass Pike rest stop, I walked up Eighth Avenue from Madison Square Garden—where I had parked my car—to meet Christopher G. Spitler, attorney at law (yes, that Chris Spitler), at the John's Pizzeria near Times Square, a few yards down from the entrance to Sardi's.

Both places brought back boyhood memories. Because of my dad's theater connections, my Bar Mitzvah party had been held at Sardi's. The John's where I was meeting Spitler didn't exist in those days, but the original John's of Bleecker Street—on Bleecker Street—did exist. Frequently, we would get in the car on Sunday night and drive down there for dinner. It was usually that or Chinese food.

I loved John's pizza then; I love it now. One of the great pleasures of doing *Sports Reporters* was walking down the street on Saturday night from the hotel where we stayed, picking up a John's pizza, and taking it back to my room.

On this particular day—November 18, 2010—I was very much looking forward to meeting Spitler, though not looking forward so much to the task that faced me after Spitler and I had finished eating pizza: trying to talk to Bob Knight.

When I first began researching this book, I knew I was going to try to go back and talk to many of the major characters from my first ten nonfiction books. Ten seemed like a good number to me for two reasons: it represented exactly half the nonfiction books I had written and it made sense to me to perhaps wait a little longer before I thought about going back to talk to people I had worked with in recent years.

I knew the book would begin with Knight, and believed it should end with Knight. I didn't expect for one second that Knight was going to sit down and talk to me at length, but I had to make the attempt.

Knight was working for ESPN that night, doing color on the Maryland-Pittsburgh game at Madison Square Garden. I was planning to arrive early to make sure I got a clean shot at speaking to him — one way or the other.

Before that though, I met Spitler at John's.

He walked in looking very much like the lawyer he had become. It was relatively warm out, so his suit jacket was draped over his shoulder. He had come from Grand Central Station, since his office was in Connecticut — even though he and his wife, Jodi, live on the West Side of Manhattan. He had left the law firm he had worked at for more than six years to work as legal counsel for an investment firm that was connected to the Royal Bank of Scotland.

"I like the people there," he said. "It's always been important to me to work someplace where I like the people. I remember when I graduated from law school I had two interviews the same day. One was at lunch, and the guys from the firm used a fork and a knife to cut the bread that was put on the table. I remember thinking, 'This isn't for me.' Then I went to dinner with the guys from this other firm and we had wings, chicken fingers, and ribs. I figured they were the right guys for me."

That was a firm called Cahill Gordon & Reindel. He had met Jodi in law school, and they had dated for a long time before deciding to get married. His three brothers — who all played college basketball as walk-ons just like Chris — were his best men.

He was thirty-two now, very much the successful young lawyer.

He and Jodi had bought a house in upstate New York, and they rode the train from Manhattan almost every Friday, picked up their car at the train station, and went to their favorite Italian restaurant for dinner. And yet he still described things as "awesome" and "excellent"—the Italian restaurant was both awesome *and* excellent—and sounded, to me, like the kid I'd met in November of 1999 whose work-study job was at the security desk in the Hart Center at night.

"I guard the building better than I guard other players," he had joked back then.

We had stayed in sporadic touch since the book. I had talked to him when I had done an epilogue for the paperback version, and he had told me a funny story about getting an e-mail from someone who had read the book inviting him to play pickup basketball with his team. "We suck," the e-mail had read. "But from what I've read, you suck too."

Spitler had agreed to join the team. "First time in a while I didn't have to go through tryouts," he'd told me. The twist to the story was where the team played: P.S. 87 on 78th Street between Amsterdam and Columbus Avenues. Henry Winkler—"Fonzie"—was a graduate. So was Don Adams, the original Maxwell Smart. So was I, fifth-grade class of 1966.

I asked Spitler if he still played basketball.

"Absolutely," he said. "In fact, when I leave you I'm headed downtown for a game. It's a local men's league. We play all over the city in different gyms one or two nights a week. It's a blast. You pay a hundred bucks to play ten games, plus playoffs. My team was 5–5, but we made the playoffs. Back in college, especially my senior year, I shuddered whenever I shot the ball because I was *never* the first option. Now I shoot all the time. I'm still not all that good, but God do I have fun.

"At Holy Cross when we lost, everyone took it so hard, which I understood because we all put a lot of time into it. Now it's totally different. We had one game this year where a guy came down court with the game tied and drilled a three right in my face at the buzzer. Honestly, by the time the ball hit the floor I was over it. I didn't want him to make the shot, but when it was over it was 'No big deal, I had fun tonight.' That's what I'm out there for."

What was interesting about Spitler was that he loved to play basketball but didn't often watch it. He had a vague idea of how Holy Cross was doing each winter, and he knew that Willard had left for Louisville two summers earlier to go work for his friend Rick Pitino. Spitler asked me why Willard had left.

"He convinced himself he was unhappy at Holy Cross," I said. "Which was too bad because people loved him there. Plus, Pitino was in trouble and really needed a friend at Louisville."

Not surprisingly, Spitler knew nothing about Rick Pitino's off-court troubles.

Spitler and Willard had never developed a warm, fuzzy relationship. For one thing, Ralph wasn't a warm, fuzzy guy most of the time. For another, even though he respected Spitler's work ethic and his willingness to do anything for the team, it absolutely killed him that he was coaching a team that actually *needed* Spitler.

"Poor Ralph," Spitler said. "Imagine, he went from coaching Pitt to coaching Spit. That had to be tough."

Willard had never named a team captain during Spitler's senior season. Spitler was the only senior and Willard just couldn't bring himself to name him the captain. Several years later, Frank Mastrandrea had tried to convince Willard to retroactively name him captain—at least in the media guide. Willard thought about it and then came back and told Mastrandrea, "You know, I really love the kid. But I just can't do it."

Spitler didn't mind. "I'll tell you one thing about Willard," he said. "He is one hell of a basketball coach. He wasn't easy to play for, but he was a great coach. All you have to do is look at what he did there to know that."

For all their differences, Willard understood Spitler. He kept him on the team because he knew having him around was a good thing. But he understood that Spitler was never going to be someone who lived and breathed basketball and that when he played his last college game he would walk away without turning back.

"We opened that year at Providence," Spitler remembered. "I got a call that week from Goldman Sachs saying they wanted me to come to New York on Saturday morning for an interview. Now it wasn't as if I was the leading scorer or anything, but a lot of coaches would not have been thrilled with a guy coming to them saying, 'I have to go to New York the morning of our opener. I'll try to meet you at the game.'

"I actually was going to tell Ralph that I'd try to postpone the meeting. He shook his head and said, 'Spit, this is your future. It's more important. Go.' So I went. Then I drove back to Providence and actually got there early. I couldn't find anyone who would let me into the arena so I had to wait outside until the team showed up."

I told Spitler that whenever I spoke I told his story as an example of someone without a lot of talent who stuck with it and made himself into a decent player. "Decent player is generous," he said, laughing. "You were very generous to me in the book."

The book still came up in his life on occasion: people would recognize his name and ask him if he was the guy who had identified himself as the worst Division I player in the country.

"Actually, my boss bought the book," Spitler said. "He went on eBay and bought it in hardcover for a penny."

A penny?

"Yup. I told him I hoped when he finished it he felt as if he'd gotten his money's worth."

I hope so too.

SPITLER WASN'T THE ONLY person I'd written about in *The Last Amateurs* and stayed in touch with. Chris Spatola, who had been

Army's leading scorer when I did the book, had been dating Jamie Krzyzewski, youngest daughter of Mike Krzyzewski. Shortly after Jamie graduated from Duke, they got married. Not long after that, Chris deployed to Iraq for a year.

When he came back, he went to work for his father-in-law (not a bad person to know if you want to coach) and now has one national championship ring and a son—who was born four months before Duke won the 2010 national championship. There's a photo in Chris's office at Duke of him with his wife and son that was taken while the nets were being cut down in Indianapolis. The same photo is in his father-in-law's office one floor up.

Two years after the book came out, I was approached by a friend of mine named Billy Stone, who at the time was an independent TV producer. Billy had put together a package of Ivy League basketball games that were televised on Friday nights on DirecTV. The package had been successful, at least in part because so few college games are played on Fridays. Billy wondered if I would be interested in doing color on a similar package of Patriot League games.

I will not waste a lot of time here on my various run-ins with TV people—most from ESPN, but not all. Billy told me DirecTV would only do the package if I would do the color. I was flattered and said yes. The games have wandered all over the TV landscape for the last nine years, from DirecTV to CBS College to ESPNU and back to CBS College. I've enjoyed being part of the package because it has allowed me to stay in touch on a regular basis with people in the league—coaches, athletic directors, and to a lesser extent, players. Obviously I don't know the players now the way I did when I was practically living with them eleven winters ago.

My style is, to put it mildly, a little bit different than most color commentators. I don't have pet sayings and I try not to raise my voice unless I'm genuinely excited. I prefer to tell stories about the people involved in the games rather than telestrate ball reversals. That can be difficult at times because there is always a very important promo to read about an upcoming hockey game or women's basketball game or a crucial sponsor drop-in that has to be taken care of before we talk about, well, the game.

In all though, I have enjoyed it. The Patriot League has come a long way since 2000. All the schools are still giving scholarships, although they still keep a close eye on the AIs (Academic Indexes) of the players each of them is recruiting. When Emmett Davis was fired by Colgate last spring, it meant that only Fran O'Hanlon was left from the coaches I had worked with on the book.

I still see many of those who have moved on. Pat Harris has a son who has followed in his footsteps to play at Army. Pat Flannery still works in development at Bucknell, and I try to get together with him whenever I'm up there for a game.

Ralph Willard is with Pitino, and it has not been a smooth ride. Not long after Ralph moved to Louisville, the story broke about Pitino's one-night stand with a woman in a Louisville restaurant. That was followed by the woman being charged (and later convicted) with trying to blackmail Pitino while claiming he had gotten her pregnant. Pitino ended up having to testify at the trial. None of it was pretty.

Louisville played in the first round of the 2010 NCAA Tournament in Jacksonville, which happened to be the first- and second-round site where I was working that year. On the practice day I went to find Ralph, and we spent some time chatting, leaning against a wall in the hall outside the Louisville locker room. Pitino came down the hall and stopped to say hello.

"Did he tell you that I promised him we'd have a good time?" Rick said, smiling. "Have we had nothing but a good time since you got here, Ralph?"

"Nothing but grins and wins," Ralph answered, deadpan as always.

Louisville didn't grin or win the next night, losing to California. A year later, after a surprisingly good regular season, the Cardinals were upset in the first round of the tournament by thirteenth-seeded Morehead State, becoming the highest seed to lose in the first round.

Meanwhile, back at Holy Cross, Sean Doherty, hired to replace Willard, went 9–22 after the Crusaders were picked in preseason to win the league. Athletic director Dick Regan decided he'd made a mistake and fired Doherty after one season — shocking the coaching world. Coaches don't get fired at *Kentucky* after one season much less at Holy Cross. The case can be made that if Dean Smith or Mike Krzyzewski had been judged on their first year — or, for that matter, their first *three* years — they never would have become Dean Smith or Mike Krzyzewski.

Milan Brown was hired to replace Doherty and, after an awful start, managed to go 7–7 in league play last winter. Still, it was another twenty-loss season in Worcester. Not a lot of grins or wins there or in Louisville.

The most remarkable story in the Patriot League since the book's publication was the one written by Bucknell in 2005 and 2006. After years of solid teams and near misses, Pat Flannery finally won a league title, upsetting Holy Cross at Holy Cross in the championship game, and made it to the NCAA Tournament in 2005. The Crusaders had come a long way from the "Spitler Era." They had won three straight titles from 2001 to 2003 and had come painfully close to winning first-round NCAA Tournament games against Kentucky, Kansas, and Marquette. The last two had gone on to the Final Four.

Still, the Patriot League had an NCAA tournament record of 0–13 when Bucknell, a number fourteen seed, went to play third-seeded Kansas in a first-round game in Oklahoma City. Bucknell won the game. After leading most of the night, the Bison got nervous and the Jayhawks roared back to take the lead, 62–61, with 24 seconds left. Just when it looked as if the game was going to be another close-but-no-cigar for the Patriot League, Bucknell center Chris McNaughton made a shot in the lane with 10.5 seconds to go and Kansas's Wayne Simien back-rimmed an open fifteen-footer at the buzzer.

I wasn't there that night but I was in a Patriot League town—Worcester—where a first- and second-round subregional was being held. I had just watched another stunning upset, Vermont over Syracuse, and was sitting down to write when someone told me Bucknell was still leading Kansas with five minutes to play.

Afraid to watch, I started writing my Vermont column. But the shouts coming from the TV area were too much to resist, and I walked over to watch the final few minutes. When Simien's shot was long, I actually felt my knees buckle slightly. I was *so* happy for everyone in the league.

"Hey, John, you gonna write another book?" someone shouted while we watched the Bucknell players celebrate.

No. But I'm awfully glad I wrote the first one.

I NEVER WROTE A book or tried to sell a movie on Steve Kerr's life, but I honestly believe it could have been done. Even if you just look at it in a basketball sense, Kerr's story is remarkable: he went from an unrecruited high school senior to the starting point guard on a Final Four team. Then he went from what looked like it would be a brief—at best—NBA career to spending fourteen seasons in the league, winning five NBA titles along the way, including one that climaxed with Michael Jordan throwing him the ball for the clinching three-point jumper in the NBA Finals.

That's not a movie?

Kerr laughed when I brought it up again on a snowy night in New York last winter. He was in town to do the Knicks and Heat the next night on TNT. I was en route to Worcester to do the just-as-glamorous Colgate–Holy Cross game. We met at one of my favorite New York steakhouses, Smith & Wollensky. Kerr walked in with snow in his hair.

"This is just from getting out of the cab," he said. "It's coming down out there in buckets."

He didn't look a lot different at forty-five than he had looked when I first met him shortly before he turned twenty. He had the same easy smile and the straw-colored hair and Tom Sawyer look. But he had traveled a lot of miles in twenty-five years.

"I still think about my dad all the time, as you might imagine," he said. "It happens more now in life situations. I look at his grandchildren and know how much he would have enjoyed them. But I always thought about him when I had my successes as a player because I think he would have been amused by it. I got my wise-guy sense of humor from him. I can almost hear him saying to me, 'Steve, you just aren't *that* good,' when everything happened, and he would have been right. When I was younger he'd say, 'You're a modest guy with much to be modest about.'"

It's a good line, but Kerr has spent most of his life disproving it. Even though his shooting ability was the key to his surviving fourteen years in the NBA, there had to be more to it than that.

"I think there was," he said. "But I also think you have to go all the way back to my senior year of high school to see how events conspired to get me where I eventually got. Lute [Olson] gets the Arizona job that spring and he loses five players to academics or transfers before the end of the school year. He's desperate and then he sees me. If I had been a senior when his program was established, I'd have never gotten recruited and *never* gotten in the rotation. But we were so bad I had to play right away. That helped me build my confidence and gave me a chance to see what I needed to work on. Then we got [future NBA star] Sean Elliott and all of a sudden I'm the point guard on what's now a very good team.

"When I got to the NBA, my shooting kept me in the league early. But I really kept working because I knew I wasn't as talented as other guys. I actually got to be a reasonably good defender. It *hurt* to play defense, physically hurt, because I wasn't very big or very strong and I had to fight through screens all the time and I got knocked around. But I have a pretty good pain threshold, so I was able to deal with it.

"Then I ended up with the Bulls on a team with Jordan and later on the Spurs with David [Robinson] and Tim [Duncan]. I played a role in those championships, but I think those guys might have played a slightly larger role."

Kerr vividly remembers the aftermath of his first title in 1996. That was the year Jordan had returned to the Bulls following the murder of his father a couple of years earlier. After the Bulls won, Jordan took the championship trophy and collapsed on the floor of the locker room, hugging the trophy, tears running down his face. Only one person in the room could really understand how Jordan felt—Kerr, whose father had been murdered twelve years before.

"It was Father's Day," Kerr said. "So that made it especially poignant, I'm sure for Michael and I know for me. Father's Day is still a little bit tough for me every year. Michael's dad had been by his side for every other great moment in his basketball career, so I have no doubt that's what he was feeling that night—his absence. I can certainly relate to that feeling."

Every championship was special, but the game Kerr remembers most wasn't an NBA game—not even the one in '97 when he made the clinching shot.

"There's only one game in my basketball career that I still think about all the time, and that's our Final Four game against Oklahoma," he said. "I still remember it like yesterday. My first couple of shots that night felt good coming out of my hand, and they both rimmed out. Then the next one was way off, and I just never found my rhythm after that. I wanted to win that game and win the national championship *so* much, and I probably was trying too hard. You see it happen every year with guys in the tournament. That's the beauty of it and the pain of it—one and done and if you don't get it done you *are* done. It hurts.

"It still hurts today. Honestly, I'd give back three of my NBA championship rings right now to have that one NCAA title. But that's not how it works."

Kerr is a natural at television: he understands the game, he's articulate, and he has a good sense of humor. In a way, he's the perfect partner on TNT for Marv Albert, whose off-the-wall sense of humor can make the most humorless analyst appear funny. With Kerr, Albert doesn't have to work to get his partner to spar with him. Of course, in 2011 Kerr also did the NCAA Tournament, working with Albert but also with Jim Nantz and Clark Kellogg during the Final Four.

Even though CBS's telecasts tend to be quite rigid and formal — because that's the way the NCAA wants them — Kerr lightened things up with his presence.

"I like doing it. I especially like now having a chance to do college games," he said. "I still love the college game, and next year my son [Nic] will be playing college ball himself [at the University of San Diego], so it's a perfect fit."

Does Nic have his dad's shooting touch? "He does — that's the good news. The bad news is he also has my quickness."

Kerr spent three seasons running the Phoenix Suns before returning to TV a year ago, in large part because the travel got to be too difficult. His wife, Margot, and their three children stayed in San Diego, and Steve rented a place in Phoenix. "I actually got home a lot," he said. "There were nights I'd leave our office at five, get to a Southwest flight at six, be home [with the time change] by dinnertime, and then get up early the next morning and go back to work. Not the easiest commute, but I had it down."

Someday he might return to the NBA or even to college coaching. The youngest of his three kids, Matthew, is now thirteen. "Once they're all out, I could see getting into coaching or going back to the front office," he said. "But we'll see. Maybe Margot and I will just travel and I'll keep doing the TV. It's certainly an easier lifestyle."

The chances are, whatever he decides to do, Kerr will be successful. He's already beaten the odds his whole life anyway.

And maybe, one day, someone will make that movie. I'm certainly available.

———

When I sat down to make the list of people I wanted to track down for this book, there was one person on it I had never interviewed or, for that matter, ever met.

Michal Pivonka.

It was Pivonka whose mother I had been interviewing in Kladno when the Czechoslovakian KGB had shown up at the front door. The last I had seen of her, the men from the KGB had been "taking her back to her job" as we all left her apartment following their lengthy interrogation of me that day.

I had checked with the Capitals after getting home and had been told that Pivonka had not reported any problems with his family back home. I had read stories subsequently in which Pivonka had talked about his parents and sister visiting him after he had gotten settled in the United States. So as far as I knew, Magdalena Pivonka had not been subjected to any further interrogation after I had left. Pivonka went on to a solid career in Washington, playing on very good teams, although he was injured during the playoffs the one year (1998) that the Caps made the Stanley Cup Finals.

I never introduced myself to him — in part because I only occasionally covered hockey, in part because the rare occasions when I did it was during postseason, when the locker rooms were a little too crowded to just wander up to someone and say, "Gee, I hope I didn't get your mom in trouble with the Czech KGB back in 1986." Now though, I figured, was as good a time as any to try and find out what, if anything, had happened.

I tracked him down with the help of then Caps PR director Nate Ewell. Pivonka still kept in some touch with his old team even though he had moved to Saddlebrook, Florida, after retiring. His two teenage daughters were talented tennis players and his ten-year-old son was a hockey player. I sent an e-mail first, telling Pivonka who I was and about my encounter with his mother, how gracious she had been, how guilty I'd felt all these years that I had never talked to him about the incident.

He wrote back quickly. He knew who I was because he is a big golf fan. His mother had never mentioned a problem with the Czech secret police. She had died, he said, three years earlier. Cancer. I hadn't seen Magdalena Pivonka in twenty-four years and had known her for about three hours. Somehow though, I felt a sense of loss when I read those words.

A few days later, Pivonka and I talked. He told me the story about his defection.

"It took a while to get everything organized," he said. "The Caps drafted me in 1984. David Poile was the general manager and Jack Button was the scouting director. The go-between in those days was a guy name Jiri Crha—he was a goalie who had defected to Toronto in, I think, 1979. He'd been at the end of his career and he kind of became an agent for players behind the Iron Curtain after he stopped playing. He would come and see our teams play and he would ask me if I was interested in going to play in the NHL.

"I was interested, although I didn't know all that much about the league. Nothing was really on TV or the newspapers about it. I knew who Wayne Gretzky was and that the Oilers were *the* team. That was pretty much it. But there had been other guys who had gone over there. I was certainly intrigued by it all."

Finally, in the spring of 1986, Pivonka decided he was ready to go. A plan was hatched—one he didn't tell his parents about because he knew they would not be at all happy about the idea of him leaving home, perhaps for good.

"The plan was for Renata [then his girlfriend, now his wife] and me to go to Yugoslavia on vacation," he said. "Yugoslavia wasn't quite as strict as Czechoslovakia, and, of course, we weren't nearly as strict as the Soviet Union. I remember when we traveled there to play in junior tournaments, we'd say to one another, 'God, it would be awful to live *here*.' It was all relative, I guess.

"Renata and I were told that after we got to this resort in Yugoslavia we were to wait until we were contacted by a guide. He was Canadian, I remember that, a guy who did these things more for the adventure than anything else. I think to us, that's what it all was—an adventure. We were a couple of twenty-year-old kids, we didn't know any better. When we left, my thought was we might go through with it if the guide contacted us. I wasn't completely sure until the last minute if we were going to do it."

The guide contacted them on a Saturday. It was go or no-go then. A decision had to be made. Michal and Renata decided to go for it. They got a little more than they bargained for when they met their guide the next morning.

"He walked us to the edge of the woods. There was a clearing of about three hundred yards from there to the border, and there was a guard tower right there on the border. He wanted us to be there right at noon because that's when the guards changed and there would be a couple of minutes when no one was really paying that much attention—one group leaving, the other one just arriving.

"He told me to bring a camera and wear it around my neck. If we got caught, we'd just say we were tourists—which we were—and that we got lost and didn't realize we were that close to the border. He also told us there was a chance they wouldn't ask questions if they saw us heading in the direction of the border and that they might just shoot us."

Just as noon struck, Michal and Renata walked into the clearing and, casually as possible, walked in the direction of the border—hearts pounding, to say the least. No one stopped them. When they cleared the border and reached the woods on the other side, Jack Button was waiting for them.

"We had to go to Rome from there to get visas," Pivonka said. "Jack told us to be sure to tell the people at the embassy that we were defecting for political reasons, not so I could play hockey. That was not considered a legitimate reason to ask for political asylum."

It was from Italy that Pivonka called his parents. "At first they said, 'Oh, you decided to go sightseeing there?' And I said, 'No. I'm not coming home.' That was very hard. Then they had to go tell Renata's parents. That was worse. I was the bad guy. I had lured their daughter to go with me and leave her family behind. There was some tension between the two families for a while."

It all worked out in the end, and the Pivonkas were allowed to visit the United States—especially after the communist governments fell in Eastern Europe in 1989 and 1990. "The whole world changed then," Pivonka said. "Renata and I were able to go home, and our families came over to see us a couple of times a year."

When I asked Pivonka if he was surprised his mother had never mentioned my visit, he laughed. "I'm sure at first she didn't want to worry me," he said. "There wasn't all that much fallout when I left, although my dad got demoted from his job as a head [hockey] coach to an assistant. Plus, I'm pretty sure nothing did happen after you left. One thing I learned after I got here is that propaganda here was just about as bad as the propaganda about the U.S. was in Czechoslovakia. It wasn't as bad over there as people here made it out to be."

Pivonka and I talked for a while, almost like old friends. He talked about coaching his son's hockey team and about going out each year to watch the golf tournament when the PGA Tour came to Tampa.

I told him what his mother had said that day in Kladno when she had picked up his sunglasses.

He laughed. "I packed light," he said. "I didn't want to tip anyone off that I was leaving for a while. Not even my parents."

It all worked out in the end for everyone. I was glad to know that—even if it took me twenty-four years to finally find out for certain.

22

Tennis, We Hardly Knew Ya

In March of 1994, while in the midst of researching *A Good Walk Spoiled,* I veered off course for a couple of days to go to the Lipton Tennis Championships in Key Biscayne, Florida. I was there for two reasons: to see if I could get Pete Sampras to give me some time for my *Tennis Magazine* column and to see some of my friends in tennis. I would stay two days and then drive to Orlando for Arnold Palmer's tournament at Bay Hill.

At that point in my life, I was "keeping my hand" in the sport with the column in *Tennis* and occasional other assignments. Even though *Hard Courts* had often been frustrating to research, I always figured I would write another tennis book at some point if only because the first one had done well.

Sampras was playing a second-round match early on Monday. After years of political battles, Butch Buchholz, the tournament's founder, had finally gotten the stadium he had always wanted, and it was quite impressive. I drove to Crandon Park that morning with Sally Jenkins, and she led me to the new press box. From there we watched Sampras play. When the match was over, I wanted to grab a cup of coffee, so I told Sally I'd find her in the interview room.

When I got downstairs, I realized I had no idea where the interview room was located. I asked a security guard if he could point me in the right direction. "Oh sure," he said. "It's right down there, just past the locker room and around that corner."

I thanked him and started walking in that direction until he gently put his hand on my arm and said, "I'm sorry, you can't go that way."

"But you just said . . ."

"I know. I'm sorry. But you'll have to walk around the other way. Media isn't allowed in the locker room area."

Honestly, I didn't know whether to laugh or cry. Now media wasn't allowed to walk *past* the locker room much less go *in* the locker room. Welcome back to tennis.

By then I had become completely spoiled by the easy access I had found in golf. The number of occasions when I had been told I couldn't go somewhere during my time on the golf tour could be counted on one hand—with a couple of fingers to spare.

There had been an incident in Los Angeles when the people in charge of security had tried to tell Larry Dorman of the *New York Times* and I that we couldn't walk inside the ropes without a camera, even though we were wearing armbands that said, "media—inside the ropes access." We had straightened it out thanks to Marty Caffey of the PGA Tour, but the security people had gone way out of their way to make life unpleasant for us the rest of the day.

I had ended up telling the guy in charge that he and his men were a bunch of "brown-shirted Gestapo stormtroopers." Apparently something got lost in the translation because he came into the media center later that day looking for me. I'd already left, so he found Caffey and complained that I had called him a cocksucker.

"I just want him to know," he told Caffey, "that I am *not* a cocksucker!"

The kicker to the story came a year later when, in the acknowledgments of *A Good Walk Spoiled,* I mentioned Caffey and thanked him for a number of things, including coming to Dorman's and my defense in dealing with the "boorish security thugs at the LA Open."

The PGA Championship was played at Riviera Country Club that year, the same place where the LA Open is played every year. On Sunday afternoon, as I was preparing to leave, a man approached me and asked if I could sign a copy of the book for him.

"Sure," I said, and opened to the page where I normally signed.

"Actually, could you sign it on a different page?" he asked. "Could you sign it on the page where you mentioned us?"

"Us?" I asked. "Who is us?"

"Oh, I was one of the security people here at the LA Open last year."

"You weren't the guy who kept telling my friend and I we needed cameras to be inside the ropes were you?"

"No, no. That was my boss."

"You know I called you guys a bunch of boorish thugs?" I said.

"Yeah, I know," he said. "We just appreciated being mentioned."

I laughed and signed where he asked me to sign.

My friend Wes Seeley, who still worked for the tour at the time and was very familiar with the story, heard most of the exchange.

"Was that the cocksucker?" he asked.

"No," I answered. "That was the cocksucker's assistant."

Beyond that, there were very few hassles in golf. We had access — without cameras — inside the ropes, inside the locker rooms, on the driving range (except at Augusta and the Memorial), and on the putting greens (same two exceptions). Players were easily approachable. I had become spoiled.

Now I was back at a tennis tournament and within two hours had been told I couldn't walk *past* a locker room.

I did the only thing that made sense: I *ran* back to golf. And for the most part, stayed right there.

I still make brief appearances at the U.S. Open each year, mostly so I can see Bud Collins and Mary Carillo and Patrick McEnroe and, if I'm lucky, Jim Courier. I still follow the sport because I love *watching* it, and I'm saddened by its spectacular drop in popularity in this country. Occasionally when I write about it, I still make tennis people angry.

Not long after that cameo appearance at Lipton (Sampras did sit down and talk to me for my column once I circled the building to get to the interview room), I wrote a column saying that the best way to fix tennis was to put everyone involved in the sport in a room and blow the room up. I proposed leaving Sampras, Patrick McEnroe, Steffi Graf, Collins, and Carillo out of the room.

"I picked up the magazine [*Inside Sports*] and started reading the story in an airport," Patrick McEnroe told me. "I was getting angrier and angrier with you. Then I saw that you left me out of the room and I said, 'Pretty good piece.'"

Others were not quite as pleased. Once upon a time Jim Courier would have been a lock to be left out of the room, but he had—in my mind—changed considerably after winning the French Open in 1991 and going on to become the number one player in the world, winning four major titles along the way. After he had beaten Andre Agassi in Paris in '91 in a classic five-set match, he walked into the interview room, pointed his finger at me, and said, "You owe me big-time."

He was referring to the fact that *Hard Courts* was about to come out and having one of the major characters win his first major title probably wasn't going to hurt sales. I figured he was joking and I laughed, but he really wasn't. Later Jim told me he didn't read the book because he was afraid I had ripped him. Even when his mother read it and told him there was nothing in it that would bother him, he still didn't read it.

That same summer, after the Lipton incident, I wrote a piece in *Tennis* saying that the sport should give the media the same access as golf did, if only so tennis fans would have the same chance to know and understand the players that golf fans were afforded.

A couple of weeks after the story appeared, I was walking out the player/media gate at the U.S. Open when I heard a familiar voice calling my name. I looked up and saw Courier, walking with José

Higueras, his coach. In all the time I'd known Jim, he had always called me John. Now he was shouting, "Hey, Feinstein!" until he got my attention.

I walked over with my hand out to say hello. He ignored it and began pointing his finger at me.

"You stay out of the locker room this week, you hear me?" he said. "Go hang out in a golf locker room with your golf buddies."

This was when the locker rooms at the Open were still accessible to the media, unlike any other locker rooms in tennis.

"Hey, Jim, if I want to go up to the locker room, I'll go up there," I said. "Last I looked you're playing in the tournament not running it."

"You stay the hell out of there!" he yelled.

"Tell you what," I said. "How about I stay out until Friday when you'll be gone."

Cheap shot. Courier had not had a good summer. He took a step in my direction and I took a step in his. Fortunately, Higueras got in between us before I could get my ass kicked and Courier could get in trouble for kicking my ass.

"John, do me a favor and get the hell out of here," Higueras said. People were stopping and staring because they recognized Courier. I always liked Higueras.

"Jim, I don't know what's happened to you, but it's not good," I said—and walked away.

The funny thing is Courier loves golf. A few months later he ran into Davis Love somewhere and my name came up. "He said to me, 'Feinstein just likes you guys because you're nice to him,'" Davis told me later. "I said to him, 'Is that a bad thing?'"

My pariah status in tennis was further sealed a few years later when I wrote an Op-Ed piece in *USA Today* saying that the biggest problem with tennis was that no one in the sport would admit that it had problems. "I guarantee you," I wrote, "when I go out to the U.S. Open today, more people will be upset with me for writing this than with the state of their sport."

Sure enough, I wasn't five minutes inside the main gate when Pam Shriver, who I'd known for years, was pointing a finger at me saying, "How can you possibly say anything's wrong with the sport?"

Much funnier was my encounter that day with John McEnroe. I was standing in the long hallway under the stands of Arthur Ashe Stadium talking to Elise Burgin, who had been one of the main characters in *Hard Courts* and was doing TV commentary for Sky TV, a British outfit. (Every ex–tennis player alive is on TV someplace talking about the sport to several dozen avid listeners.)

McEnroe stalked by, glanced at me, and said nothing.

"Hey, John," I said as he headed down the hallway. "You don't say hello?"

McEnroe turned and walked back in our direction. "Why should I say hello?" he said. "The only reason you're out here is to destroy tennis."

"Actually tennis is doing a pretty good job on its own," I said. "I'm really out here to try to get you the job as Davis Cup captain" (McEnroe was campaigning for the job at that point).

He smiled and walked back to where Burgin and I were standing with his hand extended. "In that case," he said, "it's good to see you. Welcome back."

Even Peter Bodo, who was once my colleague at *Tennis Magazine* and a good friend, can barely bring himself to speak to me these days. Some of it is our extremely divergent political views, but beyond that Peter is genuinely angry with me for not giving today's players their due.

We did finally sit down and talk about it over coffee at last year's Open. "All you ever do is write and say that the politics of the game suck," he said. "You never give guys like [Roger] Federer or Rafa [Nadal] or the top women their due. They're good, really, really good."

"I don't disagree," I said. "But to sit here and just say 'all is well in the sport' when you can clearly see that politics have been killing it for years is ridiculous. You're old enough to remember when the Davis Cup was really a big deal in this country. Now it's on Tennis Channel, which last I looked reaches about fifty-five homes."

Bodo shook his head in disgust. "You decided you didn't like the people in tennis," he said. "That's all it comes down to."

Maybe he's right. Maybe that is what it comes down to. Certainly my boyhood memories of the sport are as warm, if not warmer, than those of any sport because of my parents' involvement. I still enjoy watching a really good match and still make a point when I am at the Open every year to find my way to the back courts to try to watch a match between a couple of unknowns from up close.

But then someone tells me I can't walk past a locker room or that they don't talk on practice days and I throw my arms in the air and sprint back to golf.

IF THERE IS ONE person I have *always* liked in tennis, it is Mary Carillo. To begin with, she is as bright, funny, and entertaining as anyone I've ever known. She is also a born reporter in an ex-jock's body, which is why it is almost remarkable that she has not only survived in television but thrived in it and on it.

She's much too honest for tennis and for TV. Especially ESPN, as she proved when she walked away from the network in the middle of the 2010 U.S. Open. "I had to do it," she said. "I couldn't sleep at night. That's not a healthy way to go through life."

The first time I heard of Carillo was during the 1977 French Open. I was just starting my summer internship at the *Washington Post* and Barry Lorge was covering the French. He kept filing notebook items about these two kids from Long Island, Mary Carillo and John McEnroe, who were making their way through the mixed doubles draw. McEnroe was eighteen, Carillo was twenty. Every day Barry had another story about their latest win, and it always had a funny quote from Carillo—clearly the spokesperson for the duo.

They ended up winning the tournament. A few weeks later, McEnroe exploded onto the tennis scene when he reached the Wimbledon semifinals as a qualifier and got into all sorts of trouble with umpires and line judges along the way. Lorge kept going back to Carillo throughout for McEnroe quotes.

Carillo ended up on the same plane home from London with John and his father, John Sr. She was in coach, the McEnroes in first class—John McEnroe Sr. was a big-shot New York lawyer. At one point Mary walked to the front of the plane to talk to John for a minute.

"He was asleep," she remembered. "His dad was sitting there with all the London tabloids on his lap, the ones that had headlines like 'McBrat' and 'Baby Mac' and 'Worse than Jimbo.' He was sitting there with tears pouring down his face. Regardless of how John Jr. behaved, it was his son they were talking about. I felt awful for him."

Having grown up with McEnroe, Mary saw a different side of him. Her memories of that Wimbledon didn't focus on him yelling at umpires but his reaction when Dennis Ralston hit her with a volley during the mixed doubles semifinals.

"John had just lost to Connors in the semis," she said. "We were playing Dennis and Martina [Navratilova] in the mixed semis. At 8-all in the third, Dennis hit me with a volley. John thought he'd done it on purpose and wanted to kill him. He tried to hit him back on several occasions. We ended up losing 12–10."

I first met Mary in 1980 when I was caddying for Lorge on the final weekend at the Open. Knee injuries had forced her to retire by then (she had been ranked as high as number thirty-four in the world in singles) and she was working for the USTA escorting players from the court to postmatch interviews.

"Who is *that?*" I asked Lorge when I first spotted her.

"Mary Carillo," Lorge said.

"*That's* Mary Carillo?" I said. "I didn't know she was that good-looking."

We became friends when I started covering tennis regularly in 1985. Here is why you had to love Mary. She had started on TV working for USA and had become the first woman to do commentary on men's matches for the simple reason that she was *better* than any of the men. In 1988 CBS finally realized this and hired her for the Open. When Frank Chirkinian, the great CBS golf producer, heard that Carillo was going to be working for him during the Open (he also did tennis back then), his comment was, "Mary Carillo? She's strictly cable."

Throughout that tournament Mary wore a badge that read "Mary Carillo... Strictly Cable." She had taped the last two words over the spot that originally read "CBS."

Mary has been a shooting star in television for years now. When HBO started its show *Real Sports with Bryant Gumbel,* Mary was one of the first hires as a correspondent. Dick Ebersol asked her to do long-form essays and features for NBC's Olympic coverage beginning in 2000, and added her to the network's Wimbledon coverage — much to McEnroe's dismay. John likes the spotlight squarely on *him.*

Often, players get angry with her because she's just too damn honest. When she criticized Andre Agassi for not playing Wimbledon in 1990, he refused to do postmatch interviews with her because she might, you know, ask him a real question. Others, including the Williams sisters, have gotten huffy with her because she refused to do the "we're all in tennis together" routine that most TV announcers, including both McEnroe brothers, tend toward.

It was Mary's honesty that led to her leaving ESPN. She simply couldn't take the pandering to the players anymore. It all came to a head on the third night of the 2010 Open. Mary was already upset because ESPN had refused to let her discuss the Serena Williams foot-fault controversy of 2009 in its Open preview show.

Serena had been playing Kim Clijsters in the semifinals when, serving down a set and 5–6, 15–30, she was called for a second serve foot fault. That pushed the score to 15–40 and match point.

Serena went ballistic. She walked menacingly in the direction of the woman who had called the foot fault, holding the ball she had not served in her hand.

"I swear I'm going to f—ing take this ball and shove it down your f—ing throat," she could be clearly heard saying to the woman. Appearing frightened, the woman walked to the chair umpire and reported what had been said. Brian Early, the tournament referee, was called on court, and after a further consultation, Serena was given a point penalty—since she had already been given a warning for smashing her racquet earlier in the match.

The point penalty ended the match, a bizarre and ugly way for the defending champion to bow out of any tournament, much less the U.S. Open. Afterward, Serena was less than contrite. She said her temper wasn't nearly as bad as it once had been and didn't think she owed anyone an apology since "lots of players yell at line judges and umpires."

The incident was, clearly, the story of the tournament. And so, in looking back at the 2009 tournament during ESPN's 2010 preview, Carillo thought it important that the incident be discussed. She had already ripped the Grand Slam Committee of the International Tennis Federation when it fined Serena but didn't suspend her in the aftermath of the incident and non-apology. (Serena ended up grudgingly issuing a written semi-apology later under severe pressure to do so.)

ESPN didn't want to touch the story. Carillo was convinced it was because they were negotiating with her and her various reps—including her idiotic agent, who had actually put a hand over a CBS camera moments after the Clijsters match had ended, making it look as if her client was doing some kind of perp-walk—to come on ESPN during the middle weekend since she was injured and not playing.

The end though came on the third night of the tournament. Carillo was in her hotel room watching the matches on TV when Andy Roddick was called for a foot fault.

"One thing about me is that I actually do watch tennis for fun," she said. "I still *love* the damn game. I like to watch doubles, I like to watch kids I've never heard of, I'll stop in a park to watch kids just having a hit. I love it that much.

"So I'm in bed, under the covers, watching the match because ESPN has so many people working for them that I'm not doing any night matches. It's John and Patrick. Roddick foot faults and *he* gets into it with the line judge. He's not as bad as Serena was, but he's very cranky because he's losing and he's being obnoxious.

"I'm waiting for them to show the tape of Serena because God knows that's the time to show it. Nothing. I mean not a word, nothing. Apparently it never happened. I'm not sure if I'm angry or if I'm stunned or both.

"The next morning I go in and I find the executive producer—a guy named Jamie Reynolds—and I say, 'What happened there, where was the Serena tape?' He says something about not being able to find it. Please. This is 2010. They could have gotten it up there in about ten seconds if they wanted to.

"I asked Patrick, who was doing play-by-play, why he didn't mention it at all. He said, 'It never crossed my mind.' I'm like, *whaaa?* The funniest thing though was when I saw John and I started ranting, 'How could they do this, this is outrageous.' On and on. John looked at me and said, 'You know, I just don't get as upset about these things as you do.'

"That's when I thought, 'This is what my life has come to? John McEnroe is the cool head?'

"I went back to the hotel that night and couldn't sleep. I finally got out of bed at three o'clock in the morning and wrote to my agent [Sandy Montag] and told him I was resigning, that I couldn't do this anymore. He called me at about seven o'clock and said I need to rethink this. I know that's what he's supposed to do as an agent. I also know he has a lot of other clients with ESPN and he didn't want to get into a pissing match with them. But I was done. I went in that day [Friday] and told them I would work that day on the matches I was assigned and that would be it.

"I was working for CBS on the weekend anyway, and the following weekend they had plenty of people—*hundreds* of people—to work the matches. So that was it. I was done."

What was amazing was that no one noticed, which is more a reflection on the fact that ESPN *does* employ hundreds of ex-players and on the fact that not that many people are watching all those ex-players. I mean, how do you not notice the absence of Mary Carillo if you're paying attention?

I wasn't really paying much attention until the men's final, which for a second straight year was delayed until Monday because of rain. CBS opted to start the match at four o'clock even though with Nadal playing Novak Djokovic (both back courters) there was an excellent chance the match would end up going head-to-head with the opening *Monday Night Football* game of the season at seven o'clock and a reasonable chance it would bleed over into prime time.

That had happened the year before and had brought about the embarrassing sight of newly crowned champion Juan Del Potro asking Dick Enberg during the awards ceremony if he could address the crowd in Spanish for a moment and initially being told no by Enberg because the truck was barking in his ear to get the car presented and get off the air.

Not having learned its lesson, CBS got burned again. There was a rain delay in the second set, meaning there was no way the match would end before eight o'clock. CBS decided during the delay to give up on the match rather than lose prime-time advertising for a tiny tennis audience, and they turned the match over to ESPN—actually ESPN2, because the football was on ESPN—when the match was resumed.

Shortly before play was to start again, CBS producer Bob Mansbach let his "talent"—Carillo, Enberg, and John McEnroe—know that the match would be on ESPN2 when play resumed.

"Manzy, I can't go on ESPN," Carillo told him from the booth. "I don't work for them anymore."

"That's right," Mansbach said. There was a pause. "Mary, you're excused for the night."

When the match came back on air I was flipping back and forth between it and the Ravens-Jets football game (in spite of what Peter Bodo thinks, I *do* still like to watch the game). Almost right away I noticed that Mary wasn't there. My first thought, knowing her, was that she had to be somewhere Tuesday and the rain delay had forced her to leave early. I already knew that the delay was making Enberg crazy because he was doing play-by-play for the San Diego Padres and the team had gone into a swoon as soon as he left town for the Open and he *had* to get to St. Louis to meet them there as soon as possible.

The next day I called Carillo and asked her if she had a plane to catch. That was when she told me the Serena story. It certainly wasn't the first time she had fought with ESPN over the difference between doing journalism and doing public relations for athletes. It was just the final straw.

"No one's called you?" I asked.

"Not a soul."

It wasn't until just before the Australian Open that ESPN finally announced that Mary was no longer working for them. It put out the usual statement about how great Mary was and how much the network valued her contributions. The only person in the media who smelled the ESPN rat was SI.com media reporter Richard Deitsch. Although Mary wouldn't comment, Deitsch, with the help of SI's talented tennis reporter Jon Wertheim, pieced the story together.

"It's well known," Deitsch wrote, "that Carillo thought most of ESPN's coverage of tennis came a lot closer to cheerleading than reporting."

What was upsetting to Carillo was to read quotes from an ESPN suit named Norby Williamson, who had gotten together with Sandy

Montag to create a mythical story about Mary leaving because she wanted to branch out and do other things. He claimed—and Montag went along—that during the summer he and Montag had started discussing Mary leaving a year before her contract was up (yeah, right smack in the middle of the U.S. Open). ESPN, according to this fable, had magnanimously allowed Carillo to leave because of all she had done for the network.

Please.

Anyone with an IQ over 50 wasn't going to buy that story.

Through it all, Carillo remains Carillo. She's a star on NBC and CBS and a star on HBO. Tennis Channel signed her up about thirty seconds after learning she had left ESPN. She hardly needs ESPN, which is a nice place for someone in sports television to be in life.

And she still loves, as she puts it, "my damn sport."

"Sometimes I feel like such an apologist," she said. "I tell people I know there are problems, and I wish people would acknowledge them and work to make them better. But the fact is, and I know a lot of people don't want to hear this, the guys are in better shape—much better shape—than the women right now. You have real stars and they *do* play one another.

"The only real stars in the women's game are Venus and Serena, and they are, at best, part-time players and they're both getting close to the end. What was it Arthur [Ashe] said about the men's game in the '80s? Where are the next Venus and Serena? Or anyone like them or even close to being like them?"

Of course ESPN wouldn't want Carillo to say that on the air. She'll say it though—just not on ESPN. Good for her.

I FIGURED I SHOULD go back and catch up with John McEnroe and Ivan Lendl for this book because they were such polar opposites when I was covering them.

McEnroe is now a TV star. You can't really turn on tennis without seeing John—unless it's a non-major, in which case you see younger brother Patrick. John is everywhere: he does very good, very funny commercials (most notably the one where he goes to the umpire's house and hugs him), and he wrote a book called *You Cannot Be Serious* several years ago that was very well done.

It was Carillo who first pointed out to John his penchant for using that phrase. She and McEnroe and, as Mary put it, "one of John's walk-around guys," were ordering room service in a hotel one night when John was still playing, and the food was slow in arriving.

"John tells the walk-around guy to call downstairs and find out what's going on," Mary explained. "I said to John, 'Should he give him the "you cannot be serious" line or save that for later?' He looked at me like he didn't know what I was talking about. I said, 'You say that *all* the time.'"

Now he markets it all the time.

When I see McEnroe today—the sport's most visible spokesman and pitchman—working with juniors at a clinic he has started in the shadow of the Triborough Bridge on Randall's Island, undoubtedly still the best-known person in the game with apologies to Federer and Nadal—I think back to a conversation I had years ago with Arthur Ashe.

Arthur had been diagnosed with AIDS and knew he was dying. Talking about it seemed to bother others more than it bothered Arthur. There wasn't any question that Arthur was the most respected person in the game at the time. He symbolized all that could be right about tennis and had worked hard to take the game to the inner city and to keep expanding the sport's base. He had set up a clinic in Newark, and I went up to watch him work. Afterward, we had lunch.

He was the one who brought up the fact that he was concerned about who would pick up the mantle when he was gone.

"Is there anyone who can do it?" I asked.

Arthur nodded. "Yeah, there is," he said. "John."

I can't say I was stunned to hear him say that because I knew that Arthur probably knew better than anyone the side of McEnroe he was talking about. McEnroe talked often about the need to get more minorities playing the game. "It's entirely possible that the greatest player in the history of tennis will never pick up a racquet," he said, a classic McEnroe sentence. "We've got to find a way to get a racquet in that guy's hands."

Don't misunderstand. Ashe was often horrified by McEnroe's behavior. He had once told him before a Davis Cup match that he was tired of his acting out while representing the U.S. and if he acted out that weekend he was going to walk to the umpire's chair and, as captain, say to the umpire, "The United States defaults."

McEnroe isn't Ashe—no one is and no one is likely to ever be Ashe. He was unique: a brilliant, quietly driven man who happened to have a genius for tennis. But McEnroe has tried to pick up the mantle—although he has made very good money along the way while doing it.

Andre Agassi and Steffi Graf have done good things with the school they started in Las Vegas, and there are others in tennis who have tried to do good things. But Ashe was right all those years ago. The person with the most potential was—and is—McEnroe.

Now if he can just get his childhood pal Carillo to control her temper...

WHILE MCENROE HAS CONTINUED to live a very public life since his retirement, Ivan Lendl went in the opposite direction. He was forced to quit the game after the 1994 U.S. Open because of recurring back problems. He was thirty-four and had won eight major titles and was quite wealthy. He retired to do two things: raise his family and play golf.

Lendl had become obsessed with golf during his tennis career. He much preferred talking about golf than tennis and would actually play as soon as he got to his home in Greenwich after matches at the U.S. Open.

"It relaxed me," he said. "Anything to not think about my next match was a good thing."

Lendl and his wife, Samantha, had their first daughter in May of 1990—just prior to Lendl's last all-out attempt to win Wimbledon. They went on to have four more children—all girls, a twist not without irony. When McEnroe returned to the tour after his six month hiatus brought on by losing to Brad Gilbert in January of 1986, he ran into Lendl who congratulated him on the birth of his first child, a boy named Kevin.

"It is good that you had a boy," Lendl told McEnroe. "You aren't really a man until you have a boy."

Lendl laughs at that memory now. "I guess God proved to me that she has sense of humor," he said.

When Lendl left tennis he really left it. His back problems made it hard to play, so he didn't play at all. He focused on golf and became very good—a plus-two handicap. He played in a lot of celebrity events but also in regional professional events in the Northeast in the summertime and in Florida during the winter. Turning fifty in the summer of 2010 was a joy for him. "I get to play senior tees," he said. "Gives me fifty extra yards. That helps a lot."

I went to meet Lendl on an August afternoon at a tennis club he owns in Connecticut. He also has a tennis academy in Florida. In yet another twist, all his daughters are golfers—very good ones, in fact, among the top juniors in the country. The two oldest girls now play at the University of Florida and number three is a freshman at Alabama.

The club was empty when I pulled up at about five o'clock because it was only open until three o'clock on weekday afternoons. There were indoor and outdoor courts, and Lendl was on one of the outdoor courts playing with a kid who looked to me like a college player. I was half right. His name was Christian Coley and he had just graduated from Marist, where he had played for four years.

"You're early," Lendl said, which was true. I had left myself extra time figuring to get lost, but his directions had been so pinpoint I had found the place with ease. "We're going to play one more set. That okay?"

"Fine with me," I said. "I'll just sit here and take notes like I used to."

Lendl was playing for the first time in years, getting in shape to play some exhibition matches overseas against Bjorn Borg, but also to play an exhibition against McEnroe in Madison Square Garden in February. Sampras and Agassi were going to play the feature match, with McEnroe and Lendl, the old men, playing a pro set — first player to eight games wins — as a warm-up.

"If I'm going to play John in public, I want to play well," Lendl said. "I don't care how old we are."

Sitting and watching Lendl, I felt like I had slipped into a time warp. He was a little heavier — "Actually, I've lost forty pounds since I started working out again," he told me later — but all the strokes and movement and quirks were still there. The pre-serve routine, minus the sawdust he always kept in his pocket to keep his hands dry, was the same. The little twitches were all there, and so was the heavy topspin forehand that had been his trademark.

There may not have been anyone watching the way there would be at the Garden in February, but this was a long way from hit-and-giggle tennis. Both players were trying, running down balls, getting frustrated by missed shots. Lendl won both sets they played. When they were done, the two made plans to play again on Sunday. Lendl's family had headed back to Florida earlier in the week, so he was alone for a few days and wanted to play as much as possible before loading up his SUV — which was filled with golf clubs for his girls and for him — and heading south.

"When I wasn't playing because of my back, I didn't miss it," he said. "Golf gave me competition I wanted and needed. I *do* need to compete. I think we all do in one way or another. But now that my back is good [he finally found a doctor who helped him ease the pain], it is fun to play again. I'm much better now than I was two months ago. I hope by February I'll be a lot better than this."

I asked him if he and McEnroe had ever developed any kind of friendship after their years of intense competition had ended. The two had never gotten along when they were at the top of the game, in part because that's the nature of competition, but also because they were so different. Lendl planned every minute of every day from wake-up until he went to bed. He had strict training regimens and diets and grinded as hard to get better as anyone who has ever played.

McEnroe was The Natural. He had a feel for the game no one has ever had, and he never had to work very hard at it. One year, during the season-ending championships in New York, Lendl spent twenty minutes explaining to the media postmatch how going on the Haas Diet had changed his game and his life. When McEnroe came in later he was asked if he would ever consider a special diet to get into better shape.

"I am on a special diet right now," he answered.

"Really?"

"Yeah, it's called the Häagen-Dazs diet."

"It isn't that we're enemies or anything," Lendl said. "I just don't see him very often. I haven't been around tennis. He is. I did run into him last year at Madison Square Garden though, when I was there with my youngest daughter."

"How'd that go?"

"Great, actually. We were getting off the elevator and John was getting on. I stopped and introduced her to John, and I said, 'Nikola, before you were born, Mr. McEnroe and I played against each other many times.' Nikola looked at John and her eyes went wide. She said to him, 'I know you. I saw my daddy hit you with a tennis ball on a video!'

"John just looked at her and said, 'Which time?'"

Years ago that wouldn't have been so funny. Now though, everyone can laugh about it. But some things never change. Lendl still looks like he's on the Haas Diet and McEnroe is probably still on the Häagen-Dazs diet.

Technically, Lendl won their match in New York. Leading 6–3, McEnroe, who had hurt himself warming up earlier in the day with Sampras, had to retire from the match. That didn't make him happy. It didn't make Lendl happy either.

"Too bad," Lendl wrote me in an e-mail. "We had a great crowd—sellout. I think it was good for tennis."

No doubt he was glad so many people showed up, but he would have preferred kicking McEnroe's butt.

Like I said, some things never change.

23

The Existentialist and the Buddhist

ON A PERFECT FALL evening in 2010, I walked into the clubhouse at the Seaside Course on Sea Island, Georgia, and found David Duval waiting for me. We had made plans a few weeks earlier to get together for dinner, and Duval was sitting in the dining area of the clubhouse, having arrived early, watching the start of what would turn out to be Roy Halladay's National League Division Series no-hitter on a large-screen TV.

"Didn't want to be late," he said when I walked up. "I know that makes you a little bit cranky."

"A little late is fine," I said, smiling. "Twenty-four hours late makes me cranky."

Actually, walking into the clubhouse that October evening was both difficult and emotional for me. No more than a few feet from where Duval sat was the bar where I had last seen Bruce Edwards alive, in November of 2003. I glanced over there as I walked to where Duval was sitting, and in my mind's eye I saw Bruce and Tom Watson sitting there, drinking a beer after what turned out to be the final round of golf in which Bruce would caddy for Watson.

That had been at a long-gone event called the UBS Cup, a pseudo–Ryder Cup knockoff put together by IMG for players over forty. It shocked me to think it had been almost seven years since that melancholy afternoon. I had only been to Sea Island once since then, to give a speech, and that dinner had been on the other side of the island. This was the first time I'd been back inside the clubhouse, and I had been steeling myself for the feelings I knew would wash over me when I walked inside.

It had been a long time since Duval and I had sat down and talked at any length. He had been an important character in *The Majors,* and just before its publication in April of 1999, he had ascended to the number one ranking in the world, not long after shooting his historic 59 (13 under par) on the final day of the Bob Hope Desert Classic. He'd hit a five-iron second shot to within five feet on the par-5 eighteenth hole to set up a closing eagle.

At that moment it seemed likely that the next great rivalry in golf would be Duval and Tiger Woods. Duval was four years older, but he had just won for the ninth time on tour and had been achingly close to winning the Masters a year earlier. Woods had won the Masters in 1997 but hadn't won a major since then and Duval had wrested the number one ranking away from him.

"At that point in my life, I was completely convinced I could be a better player than Tiger," Duval said, sipping a glass of red wine that night on Sea Island. (He had suggested we eat there in the clubhouse. "Food's good, prices are okay, and no one will bother us," he reasoned—correctly.) "I thought my game was good enough physically and good enough mentally that I could beat him under the gun and over the long term.

"I wasn't thinking I would always beat him when we went head to head. But I thought I was good enough to compete with him on a regular basis."

He smiled. "Turns out I was wrong."

Duval never did anything the easy way in golf. In 1993, coming out of Georgia Tech as a four-time All-American, he didn't make the cut at Q School and had to play on the (then) Nike Tour for a year. When he made it to the tour a year later, he was instantly in the hunt at a number of tournaments, finishing second several times.

But it wasn't until October of 1997, at the end of his third year on tour, that he finally won. Then he won three times in a row.

The same proved to be true in his quest to win a major. He almost always seemed to be in contention but he couldn't break through. Finally, in the summer of 2001, he played a transcendent final round in the British Open, shooting 67 at Royal Lytham and St. Anne's, pulling away from the field to win by three shots. All of his dreams, dating to boyhood, had come true.

And then he stopped winning. In fact, he stopped contending. After a while he stopped playing golf altogether for long stretches of time.

"It's hard to explain because it's hard for me to understand," he said. "There was something existential going on. When I won at Lytham, the feeling was unbelievable. I felt satisfied and complete. I had done what I had worked my whole life to accomplish.

"And then, within a few weeks, I found myself thinking, 'Wait a minute, I worked my whole life, spent all those hours on driving ranges, in bunkers, out in the rain all by myself, for *this?*' Now, I can't even tell you exactly what *this* is, but I can tell you once the initial euphoria wore off, I felt kind of empty. I went to the PGA that year [at Atlanta Athletic Club] and was actually playing well enough that I could have won again. But there was no extra gear in me. I looked for it, tried to find it, but it wasn't there.

"To be fair, part of it was Tiger. At some point it occurred to me that I simply wasn't in his class as a golfer. I'm not being modest. I think I'm really, really good at golf—maybe even great at times. Phil [Mickelson] is great at golf and so are Ernie [Els] and Vijay [Singh] and a handful of other players. You know who they are because most are in the Hall of Fame or will be. I mean they're absolutely fantastic golfers. I've been, at times, in their league.

"But none of us—I mean none of us—are in Tiger's league. Comparing any of us to him is like comparing a very, very good painter to Van Gogh or Picasso. He just did things out there none of the rest of us could do. Period."

Like a lot of players, Duval knew for certain just how great Woods was during the 2000 U.S. Open at Pebble Beach. "Look back at the history of majors," Duval said. "Most are won by a shot or two or maybe in a playoff. I played the round of my life at Lytham and won by three. That was considered a runaway. He beat *everyone* in the field by an average of just under four shots *a day*. Think about that. The guys who finished second [Els and Miguel Ángel Jiménez] averaged what—72 shots a day? [71.75 to be exact]. He averaged 68 shots a round on a very hard golf course under U.S. Open pressure. That's simply ridiculous. Then he came back a few weeks later and won at St. Andrews by *eight*.

"So I accepted at some point along the way that I wasn't going to be as good as Tiger. That didn't mean I couldn't beat him—I did it at Lytham. But that was okay. Then, when I won the Open Championship [like almost everyone who has won the British, Duval refers to it the way they do in Great Britain, as "The Open Championship"], something definitely happened to me. It wasn't so much "Is that all there is?" I got plenty tangibly from winning. But none of it made me any more happy than I had been. I think I expected that it would, that I would feel some extra sense of fulfillment that would make me happier in my daily life.

"It didn't. What occurred to me then was that golf wasn't ever going to do that for me. It had to come from someplace else. Fortunately for me, it did."

A year after his win at the British, Duval and his longtime girlfriend, Julie McArthur, broke up. Most people in golf had assumed they would get married at some point since they had been together since Duval first came on tour. A year later, Duval and a friend were waiting for a table in a Denver restaurant during the International Tournament—another event that no longer exists—when they struck up a conversation with two women who were sitting at the bar. One was Susan Persichitte, and Duval was instantly smitten.

"I'm not usually the most outgoing guy with people I don't know," he said. "But for some reason I felt comfortable with Susie right away."

He managed to get her phone number that night and made up an excuse to come back to Denver so he could go out with her. Things moved quickly. They met in August; in November they were engaged. It wasn't long after he got engaged that Duval decided he needed a break from golf. He just had no desire to compete. He'd battled injuries throughout 2003 and had dropped to 211th on the money list. Because of his British Open win, he was exempt for five years — through 2006 — so he could afford to take time off and not lose his exempt status.

"At that point in my life I was just happier being at home with Susie and the kids [she had three when they got married, and they have had a boy and a girl together since then] than I was being away at golf tournaments," he said. "Part of it, no doubt, was that I wasn't playing well. But it was also that feeling I had after the British. Did I really want to work that hard to do something that didn't, in the end, mean *that* much to me?

"Don't get me wrong. I'm very proud of winning that championship—very proud. And now, at this point in my life, I'd like to win another. I'd like to win on tour again. But for a while it was hard to make any of that a priority."

As often happens with athletes when something they have taken for granted suddenly becomes jeopardized, Duval's desire to play began to come back at just about the same time that he couldn't necessarily just show up anyplace he wanted to and tee it up. He had finished 80th on the money list in 2002, but didn't come close to the top 125 the next four years. In 2007 he began the year playing on an exemption as one of the top 25 money winners of all time. He only played seven times before leaving the tour again for personal reasons: his mom was dying of cancer and Susie was having a very tough second pregnancy.

The tour ended up granting him a "major medical exemption" for 2008 under a newly created category: family crisis. Many players had been campaigning for this sort of exemption for years, among them Paul Goydos, who had asked for that sort of exemption when he had dropped off the tour in 2004 to take care of his daughters while Wendy was in and out of drug rehab. It had taken a while, but the tour had finally gotten around to it.

By 2009, Duval was down to his last exemption: he was still among the top fifty money winners of all time, so he was able to take a second exemption in the all-time money category. Early that year I ran into him on the putting green at the Honda Classic. In the midst of exchanging pleasantries about family and the usual talk about who was going to win the NCAA basketball tournament, David looked at me and said, "Remember that I said this: I'm going to win again soon. It's not that far away. I know it's close now."

Athletes say this all the time. But Duval had never said anything like that to me before. I remembered that comment a few months later when he almost won the U.S. Open at Bethpage—finishing tied for second, two shots behind Lucas Glover. To say that he came out of nowhere is putting it mildly: he had to go through qualifying to get into the field and began the tournament ranked 882nd in the world. He had gone from 1st to 882nd. People talk about Tiger Woods dropping like a stone since his "accident" in November of 2009. Going into the 2011 PGA Championship he was ranked number 21 in the world. That's a pretty fair distance from number 882.

If Duval had won it would have been one of the great comeback stories in the history of sports. As it was, it became his first top-ten finish on tour since 2002. He couldn't keep it going though and just missed finishing in the top 125 on the money list—finishing 130th. That meant, for the first time since 1994, he began a year without any kind of full exemption on tour.

"I've been forced to depend on the kindness of strangers," he said that night at dinner, definitely becoming the first golfer I had ever heard quote Tennessee Williams. "Right now, my goal is to avoid that next year."

Just as in 2009, he was fighting to make the top 125. He had started the year well, tying for second at Pebble Beach, but had dropped out of the top 100 with the year dwindling to a few weeks. And yet he wasn't at all discouraged.

"I still think I have a lot of good golf left in me," he said. "I wouldn't be out here if I didn't believe that. Every week when I leave my kids to come back out here it's tough and it isn't going to get any easier the next few years with Brady [age 5] and Sienna [age 2].

"But I want to win out here again, and I still honestly believe I have another major in me. If I had doubts about that, they went away at Bethpage. I can still play well enough to win in a major, and if I do I think I'll appreciate it more if only because I won't *expect* so much from it. I'll enjoy it. I want my kids to see me at my best because at my best I was pretty damn good."

One week after our dinner, Duval finished tied for sixth in the Frys.com Open and clinched his tour card for 2011. He ended up 106th on the money list, his highest finish since 2002. He still hasn't won since that British Open victory in 2001, and there's no way of knowing whether he will ever win again. He turned forty in November of 2011.

There's one thing though I'm pretty certain of: if Duval does win again, his reaction won't be existential. It will be ecstatic.

I DON'T THINK I would say the same thing about Tiger Woods.

I was watching a college basketball game on the day after Thanksgiving in 2009 when the first crawl came across the TV screen: "Tiger Woods was involved in a car accident early this morning. Reports are that it was 'not serious.'"

Most of me shrugged at the report. I understood that Tiger Woods going to the store for milk was news at that point in time. He had long ago surpassed Michael Jordan as the most famous person on earth. The three words that stayed with me as the crawl repeated itself were "early this morning."

Was that at seven o'clock in the morning while, perhaps, making a run to the Isleworth 7-Eleven? (I doubt that Isleworth has a 7-Eleven, but whatever.) Finally, when I needed to stand up for some reason, I went to my computer to see if there were details about the accident. That's when I saw the time and the place — 2:27 a.m., just outside his house — and the fact that it was a one-car accident.

Okay, now there were questions to be answered, the first one being, what was Tiger Woods doing coming in, or going out, at 2:27 a.m. on the morning after Thanksgiving? And what kind of one-car accident could he have gotten into a few yards from the front door of his house?

We all know the answers now, or at least some portion of the answers. Exactly why Woods fled *from* his house at that hour and whether he was on Ambien or painkillers that caused him to hit the now-famous fire hydrant have never been completely answered. What we do know are the basics: he was cheating on his wife and he got caught.

As the days and weeks went by we learned that he hadn't just cheated on his wife, he had *cheated* on her — over and over and over again. Whether he was addicted to the sex or the chase or even the danger — being the public figure he was — none of us will ever really know. And, in truth, it doesn't really matter.

His image will never be the same whether he never wins another golf tournament or wins thirty more golf tournaments and a half-dozen more majors. Woods worked just about as hard on cultivating his image — boy next door, husband, dad, all-around good guy — as he worked on his golf. There are some who believe, and I don't disagree, that getting married was another step in the Selling of Tiger.

He was closing in on thirty, it was time to marry a beautiful blonde and start having beautiful little children (and a dog) he could put up on his website and hug after victories.

That sounds so incredibly cynical the temptation is to not even write the words. But even though I don't "know" Tiger the way some of my colleagues claim to "know" him, it fits with what I've seen and heard through the years. Perhaps the most laughable part of a story that was decidedly unfunny was the notion that his father's death in 2006 somehow had set these events in motion.

Oh please.

Who do you think it was who set the example that Tiger followed? If anything, Tiger's issues—and he's got a boatload of them—almost certainly stem from his relationship with his father. That hardly makes him unusual; a lot of people are formed for good and bad by their relationships with their parents. But the idea that things might have been different if Earl had been alive is patently absurd.

Among the almost uncountable mistakes Tiger and his "team" have made since he plowed into the hydrant, the most inexplicable may have been that awful Nike commercial that was released the day before Tiger came back from his leave of absence to play in the 2010 Masters. Even putting aside the tastelessness of somehow bringing Earl back from beyond the grave to "talk" to Tiger, the whole idea that anyone might buy into the "sainted Earl" storyline anymore was flat-out stupid.

In the *Saturday Night Live* takeoff on the commercial, "Earl" says to "Tiger," "It goes without saying, I'm sure, that you would never use my voice to sell sneakers...in the wake of a sex scandal."

Yup, that's exactly what they were doing.

Raking Tiger over the coals again is pretty pointless. The only reason I come back to it is the extraordinary fiction that there might somehow be a "New Tiger" in the wake of all that has happened. There is no more a New Tiger than there was ever a New Nixon.

Tiger Woods and the people around him are sorry about one thing: that he got caught.

From day one they mishandled everything that could be mishandled, from refusing to talk to the police the first weekend to the pathetic Tiger-and-pony show they staged when he gave his mea culpa speech—only to interrupt himself to indignantly scold the media for hounding his wife and children. The fact that the golf media had fawned over him for years was apparently irrelevant. Even less important in Tigerworld was the fact that *his* behavior had brought about the harassment of his wife and his children by the tabloid media.

Honestly, having been asked the question several thousand times now, I have no idea whether Woods will come back and break Jack Nicklaus's record of eighteen major titles, and I honestly don't care. If he does, fine. If he doesn't, fine. Yes, he did great things for golf: sponsorships, TV ratings, purses all skyrocketed in the Tiger Era. But let's be honest. He didn't do any of these things on purpose. All he was trying to do was do good things for Tiger. There's nothing wrong with that; just don't sell yourself as something you're not and have no intention of becoming.

I feel sympathy for Tiger for one reason: much like Bob Knight, he is one of the least happy people I've ever met. For all his brilliance on the golf course, I never saw any real joy. Oh sure, there were the fist pumps after made putts, the momentary rush of happiness because he had won—or just as important—hadn't lost.

One story that sums Tiger up is told by Trey Holland, a former USGA president who was also the USGA's top rules official for many years. Holland was walking with Woods during the last round of the Open at Pebble Beach in 2000, arguably his greatest performance ever. On I believe the second hole, Tiger wanted a drop of some kind and asked Holland for a ruling. Holland didn't give him the drop, and Tiger ended up winning by fifteen shots instead of sixteen.

Walking off eighteen a few hours later, when Holland

congratulated him, Tiger looked at him and said, "I really wish you'd given me that drop."

Holland told the story later as an example of Tiger's competitiveness, which it certainly was. But it's also an example of the fact that in the *moment* of his greatest triumph he couldn't help but think about a minor incident that in no way affected his victory. My guess is when Tiger thinks of Trey Holland that's what he thinks about — not the fact that Holland was a witness to perhaps the greatest display of golf anyone has ever seen.

Great competitors are always looking ahead to the next challenge. I get that. But I'm not sure Tiger ever paused for more than a few minutes to enjoy anything he achieved. That's sad.

The saddest thing in all of this, other than what he did to his children, was that there was actually a chance for Woods to walk away from that accident a different person. Remember the last scene in *The Bridge Over the River Kwai,* when the realization hits Alec Guinness that he's been co-opted by the Japanese, and as he says, "Oh my God, what have I done?" he manages to fall on the detonator and blow up the bridge?

What if realization had somehow hit Tiger that morning? What if he'd walked out of the hospital and said, "Oh my God, what have I done?" What if he'd decided to stop doing everything just for himself and done a few things for others: played in a few tournaments not on his regular schedule, done charity work for something other than his self-promoting foundation, taken, say, a solid hour each day (Phil Mickelson takes forty-five minutes) to sign autographs at tournaments, and stopped trying to convince people that the minute he put on his bracelet engraved with words from Buddha he was transformed?

What if any of that had happened? Jockworld always forgives its heroes. Many people have forgiven Tiger anyway because he gave them so much enjoyment — far more than he ever gave himself — with his golf. That's fine.

Here's hoping, seriously, that at some point in his life he can find joy in something other than stepping on people's necks and filling his pockets with money. I don't think it is close to happening right now. And I never thought wearing that bracelet was going to make it happen either.

Apparently, he agrees. He no longer wears it.

24

Hoopsters

As MUCH AS I love covering golf and being around baseball and watching tennis and walking into the stadium on the morning of Army-Navy, I always seem to come back to college basketball—in spite of all its flaws.

I really don't like the NCAA and what it stands for, and I think it is fair to say the people in Indianapolis aren't my biggest fans. Every time I see one of those ridiculous "student-athlete" PSAs that they run nonstop during the NCAA basketball tournament, I want to throw a rock through the television set. When I see the chairman of the basketball committee—regardless of who it is from year to year—sanctimoniously refusing to answer simple questions about who got into the field and who didn't, I want to throw a rock at *him*.

The committee tends to bring out my violent side. Years ago, after they had completely screwed up the bracket and then defended everything they had done, I said on Tony Kornheiser's radio show that "everyone on the committee should be lined up against a wall and shot." Perhaps an overreaction. Tony pointed out to me that my good friend Jack Kvancz was on the committee. "Okay then, just shoot him in the leg," I answered. Jack told me later he was grateful I decided to spare him.

The NCAA Tournament games now start at sickeningly late hours and the commercials are endless—ten each game at three minutes apiece, plus a twenty-minute halftime and thirty-second timeouts that last between forty-five and sixty seconds so the network can squeeze in a couple of extra commercials. (The twenty-minute halftime was requested by CBS in 2003 so it could have time to update the war in Iraq, which had just started. Now, whenever I ask why we *still* have twenty-minute halftimes when there are no war updates, I'm told, "Well, in some buildings it takes teams a long time to get to the locker room." That, for the record, is a flat-out lie.)

I blame none of this on the networks. I blame it on the NCAA, which happily accepts an outrageous rights fee since men's basketball—*not* football—funds most of its other sports and the NCAA itself. It would not need to demand so much money in rights fees if it would simply start a football playoff and tell the BCS schools, "If you want to play in our basketball tournament, you *must* play in our football tournament."

But the NCAA won't do that. Instead it allows the self-righteous BCS presidents to yammer on about how a football playoff would hurt the "student-athletes" academically while they ignore the fact that most of the "student-athletes" who play basketball miss being in the classroom for almost the entire month of March. Last season when I walked into the Butler locker room after the Bulldogs had upset Pittsburgh in the second round of the NCAA Tournament, one of the first things I heard was, "Hey, no school for us this week."

Just to be sure, I asked if the upcoming week was spring break. No, that had been the previous week. "We leave on Tuesday for New Orleans," senior Zach Hahn said. "So we *might* make a class or two Monday, but that's it."

And Butler, unlike most top basketball schools, *does* graduate its players.

And yet, in spite of *all* that, I still love college basketball. I still love walking into a packed building, whether it seats 20,000 or 2,000, on a winter night. I still love making my Patriot League drives

468 • JOHN FEINSTEIN

back to Bucknell and Lafayette and Lehigh and even the seven hours to Holy Cross. Notice I didn't say Colgate. That's just a little *too* much back road driving in the snow.

It helps that I've been around the game so long that I know a lot of people and a lot of people know me. It certainly makes my job easier, and even now I love writing basketball columns for the *Washington Post*. I still get a buzz on deadline, especially after a game like Butler-Pittsburgh, even if I have under an hour to produce 1,200 words. The adrenaline flows and, most of the time, so do the words.

The list of people I've gotten to know through the years in college hoops is a lengthy one. When I began this book I wrote down the names of all those I wanted to go back and spend some time with. Sadly, I couldn't go back and see Jim Valvano. There were lots of others though, and I had to keep crossing names off the list because there were so many. I finally settled on five (other than Bob Knight) that I wanted to be absolutely certain I went and saw: Dean Smith, Mike Krzyzewski, Steve Kerr, Ron Felling, and Damon Bailey. I had a different purpose in going to see each one, but I knew I wanted to spend some time with them.

So that's what I did.

I ACTUALLY WENT TO see Dean Smith before I began this book. My hope at the time — May of 2009 — was that I would write his biography before writing the book you are reading now.

As I mentioned earlier, the first book I had ever proposed was one on Dean. That was in the spring of 1982. Since then, Dean had been a part of several other books I'd done: *A Season Inside, A March to Madness, Last Dance.* And he had been a continuing presence throughout my career.

The first time I had any clue that his memory might be slipping came when I went to talk to him during the research of *Last Dance,* my book on the Final Four. This was in February of 2005 and it was

Dean, while telling me stories from his college days, who brought up his memory issues to me.

"I just can't bring things back the way I used to," he said. "Before, everything stayed in my head. Now it's in and out."

I joked with him at the time that half his memory was better than all of most people's memories.

"Maybe," he said. "But it's frustrating, especially when you are used to doing most things by memory without having to think about it."

I didn't think that much of it at the time: Dean was seventy-four and even he was bound to have some memory slippage as he got older. I'd seen it in my father, who was ten years older, as he had gotten into his eighties. It wasn't that he didn't remember things — he just couldn't remember *everything*.

Then, over the next couple of years, I began to hear that Dean's memory had gone downhill quickly. I found it hard to believe. Dean Smith? Honestly, I didn't even want to contemplate it. It was at the ACC Tournament in 2009 that a couple of longtime friends from Carolina asked me if I was still giving any thought at all to doing a Dean biography. By then he'd been involved in a couple of books, including a really bad autobiography in 1999 that the publisher had brought Sally Jenkins in to try to rescue after the guy who had initially written it botched it so badly that he created a book that was completely unreadable.

Sally did the best she could, but Dean simply wouldn't open up to her — even for a book with his name on it. Because she had almost no time to try to rescue the book, Sally didn't have the chance to talk to others about Dean, which I knew was going to be the only way to *really* tell the story.

"I'd still like to do it," I said when the question came up. "But I'd need Dean to really cooperate, not just by talking to me but by telling everyone else that it's okay to talk to me."

"You should go see him — soon."

I took the hint. A little more than a month later, I drove from Charlotte, where I was covering a golf tournament, to see Dean in his office in the Dean Dome. He still went in a couple of days a week to answer mail and return phone calls and to spend some time with his old assistant Bill Guthridge, who had an office right around the corner from his.

It had been a while since I had seen Dean. When I walked into his office, he was standing next to his desk while his assistant, Linda Woods, was trying to fix something for him.

"Dean!" I said, genuinely glad to see him.

My exuberance must have surprised him. "John!" he said, mocking my enthusiasm the way he might have twenty years earlier. Maybe, I thought, things aren't as bad as I've heard.

When we sat down to talk, I quickly understood that things were not great. There were times when he was all there—every bit the Dean Smith I had always known. Then there were other times when I would bring up a name, one that should be familiar to him, and he'd look at me blankly. A couple of times when he was trying to remember things he got very frustrated, slamming his fist on the desk at one point because he couldn't bring back a name.

I finally told him why I had come. I told him I truly believed he was the most important person in college basketball in the last fifty years, not because of the games he'd won but because of the lives he had touched. More than touched—influenced.

"I honestly don't think there's been a book done that is worthy of the life you've led," I said. "I have enough ego to think I can write that book. I wouldn't even need *that* much time since we've spent a lot of time together through the years. What I need are phone numbers and the ability to say to people, 'Dean is cooperating on this book.'"

He was all there now. "My life hasn't been all that special," he said. "I'm just a basketball coach."

I knew he wasn't being falsely modest, that's not his way. "With all due respect, Dean, I disagree."

He finally said he'd think about it and get back to me. I went to see Rick Brewer as soon as I said good-bye to Dean. Rick has been Dean's PR person—officially and unofficially—for close to forty years. I told him what had happened.

"Talk to him," I said. "Time *is* an issue now."

"I know," he said. "You should try and get Roy [Williams] and Bill [Guthridge] to talk to him too."

Both were out of town. I left a message with Linda Woods for Bill and left one for Roy too. Roy actually called me back from vacation. I told him why I had called. "As soon as I get back, I'll go see him," he said. "I'll help you in any way I can." Bill said the same thing.

Before either of them could go see him, though, I got a call from Rick: "He said yes."

Honestly, I was stunned. I had expected a polite blow off.

"I went to see him and he said to me, 'Well, if I'm going to do something like this, John's the one I trust to do it.'"

"He didn't say, 'Even if he's a Duke guy'?" I asked.

Rick, who is as loyal to Carolina blue as anyone who has ever lived, laughed. "No," he said. "But I'm sure he thought it."

I WAS GOING TO spend the first week in July in Chapel Hill, but a health issue came up: not Dean's health, my health. I had to have open-heart surgery on June 29 after a routine stress test uncovered seven (not a typo) blockages in my arteries. I recovered well and rescheduled my trip for the second week in August. The first thing Dean said when I walked in was, "How's your heart? Are you sure you're okay to do this?"

I told him I was fine. Our sessions together went as well as I could have hoped. Again, there were good moments and bad. He remembered every detail about the night he met his first wife, Anne, at a graduation dance at the University of Kansas. That was good.

When I asked him to talk about Bob Spear, who had started Dean's college coaching career by hiring him as an assistant at the Air Force Academy, he looked at me blankly. "Tell me some things about him," he said. "Maybe it will come back." That was bad.

What I realized after we'd had three sessions over two days was that I was going to need two hours to get one hour of material most of the time. I didn't want to push him too hard in terms of time because I could see him getting tired after a couple of hours. Dean, being Dean, kept pausing and tapping his chest as we talked. "Your heart okay?" he would say.

He told Linda to give me any phone numbers I needed, and I began collecting them so I could start making calls. It was after I left Chapel Hill that the issues began to crop up. His family was concerned that the time he was spending with me might be too difficult for him. I understood, and as I said, I could see him getting tired at the end of our first session, so I had cut the next two short.

I talked to Linnea, his wife, and Scott, his son. (Dean also has four daughters. Scott and two of the girls are from his first marriage; the two younger girls are from his marriage to Linnea. All five are adults, and Scott referees basketball as a part-time job.) The short version of the story is simple: they were concerned about Dean's health. I understood, still thought the book could be done, but didn't feel I could argue with them at any great length because he was Linnea's husband and Scott's dad—not mine. Plus, they were around him more and had to know the situation better. Sadly, I decided to abandon the project.

The following summer the family went public with the fact that Dean was not in good health and struggling with memory issues. One thing that hasn't changed at all is the way I feel about his life: there still hasn't been a book worthy of who he was during those thirty-six years as North Carolina's basketball coach.

I hope someday that will change.

I HAVE TOLD THIS story often, and it came up again in December of 2010 when Mike Krzyzewski was about to win his 880th game — one more than Dean Smith won during his career.

It happened in March of 1993 on the same day that I last saw Jim Valvano alive. Duke, the two-time defending national champion, and North Carolina, which would win that year's national title, were closing out the regular season against each other in Chapel Hill.

They were ranked, I believe, number two (Carolina) and number five (Duke) in the country. Early in the game, both coaches were on the officials, each trying to get an edge for his team. Lenny Wirtz, a veteran referee who had worked a lot of Duke-Carolina games, finally called the two of them to the scorer's table.

"Look, fellas, I know it's a big game, I know you're both wound tight. But take it easy a little bit. Let us work the game."

Krzyzewski looked at Wirtz and, with a smile on his face, said, "Lenny, there are twenty-one thousand people in here who are all against me. You three guys are the only ones I can talk to."

Wirtz laughed. Smith did not. "Lenny, don't let him do that," he said. "He's trying to get you on his side."

Krzyzewski looked at Smith and waved his hand dismissively. "Come on, Dean, stop it. I was kidding. You're full of shit."

With that, the two men stalked to their benches. When Krzyzewski got to within earshot of his assistant coaches, he said, "If I ever start to act like him, don't ask any questions, just get a gun and shoot me."

The irony in the story is obvious: over the years Mike *did* act more and more like Dean. He succeeded Dean as the ACC's target coach and heard over and over how his team got all the calls, that there was a double standard for ACC officials — one for Duke and Krzyzewski, the other for the rest of the league. It was the exact same charge he had leveled against Dean and Carolina all those years earlier.

"I actually think it's tougher for Mike," Dean said to me in 2005.

"There's so much more media attention now, and the coaches are under such a microscope—especially him."

That comment is a pretty fair reflection of how the relationship between Krzyzewski and Smith changed after Dean retired in 1997. Nowadays, Krzyzewski and Roy Williams aren't exactly close friends, but Krzyzewski has nothing but nice things to say about Smith and their rivalry.

In fact, in 2010 amidst the spate of stories written in North Carolina as he was about to go past Dean's win total, Mike bristled when the "get a gun and shoot me" line came up.

"Whatever was said was said in private," he told Ken Tysiac from the *Charlotte Observer*. "I certainly always respected Dean."

I don't doubt that. But he repeated the comment to me right after that game. In fact, in the ensuing years when he would say or do something Deanlike, I would occasionally leave him a message saying simply, "We're rounding up the guns."

What Krzyzewski figured out as he got older was that more often than not, being like Dean was a *good* thing. That's not to say they aren't very different people: Mike has always been more blunt, more in-your-face than Dean, who was the master of the subtle shot (unless you knew him and realized the shot wasn't really that subtle).

Once, I asked Dean what he thought about Muggsy Bogues, the tiny (5 foot 3) Wake Forest point guard. "He does a great job of fouling you without getting caught," Dean said. "The refs miss it because he's so smart about using his size to foul down low where they don't see it."

Krzyzewski would have said the same thing only differently: "The refs let him get away with fouling because he's short."

They're both from the Midwest, but one grew up in a small town (Emporia, Kansas), the other in a big city (Chicago). They both served in the armed forces: Dean in the air force after graduating from Kansas, Krzyzewski in the army after going to West Point. No one I know has ever heard Dean curse. No one I know has ever heard Krzyzewski *not* curse. Dean's liberal on all issues: he marched in favor of a nuclear freeze, opposed the war in Vietnam, and can't remember ever voting for a Republican for president. Krzyzewski voted for Barack Obama in 2008—perhaps his first vote for a Democrat. He hosted fundraisers for Elizabeth Dole when she ran for the Senate in North Carolina and has photos of both Presidents Bush on the wall of his office. When President Clinton came into the Duke locker room after the national championship game in 1994, he posed for a photo with President Clinton. When it was sent to him, he put it in a drawer of his desk.

"He was an Arkansas fan anyway," he explained.

What they share—besides being great coaches and fierce competitors—is loyalty. Both take the same approach to their players that my mother took to her children: I can criticize them, but *you* can't. They are the same way with their friends, especially those they have known a long time.

I was covering the ACC when Krzyzewski first came into the league, and I witnessed a lot of his early struggles up close. That's why, even as he has become more and more insulated through the years, I can still call him directly and know I'll get a call back.

It's why I rode the bus that day going to Greensboro, en route to Krzyzewski's 880th win—much to Mike Cragg's shock.

We talked that day about his relationship with Bob Knight, which isn't nearly as lovey-dovey as it may appear now. "I love Coach Knight," Krzyzewski said that day. "I really do. But I also recognize him for what he is and for what he's not. I think once you do that, you can appreciate the good things he brings to the table in a friendship and not worry about the rest."

Knight had forgiven Krzyzewski for being "responsible" for *Season on the Brink* not long after the book came out. But he wasn't thrilled when the Krzyzewski coaching star kept rising—to the point where there were whispers that he just might surpass his old mentor at some point. When Alex Wolff, the superb *Sports Illustrated* basketball writer, did a long piece on Krzyzewski in 1992 calling him the best coach in college basketball, Knight wasn't happy.

A few weeks later when Duke beat Knight's last really good (as it turned out) Indiana team in the Final Four, Knight was even less happy. When the two men went to shake hands, Knight pulled the old "blow-by," not even slowing down as he went by Krzyzewski and barely shaking his hand. I watched that scene and laughed. Several people said, "What is that about?" My answer was simple: it was Knight being Knight.

A little while later, I walked out of the Duke locker room on my way back to press row to write my column. Someone grabbed my arm. It was Mickie Krzyzewski.

"Hey, Mickie, great win," I said.

She was shaking her head as if I was wrong. "You have to go talk to Mike," she said.

I was completely baffled. "Why?"

"Knight," was all she said.

I didn't ask for details. I walked back into the locker room, made my way through to the back, and knocked lightly on the door where Mickie had told me the coaches were located. Tommy Amaker, then one of Krzyzewski's assistants, opened it a crack and, seeing me, opened it so I could walk in.

If I hadn't known better, I would have thought I was walking into a room of coaches who had just lost the national championship game on a half-court shot at the buzzer (something that would almost happen to Duke eighteen years later).

The coaches were all sitting around in a circle: Pete Gaudet, Mike Brey, Jay Bilas, Amaker, and Krzyzewski. No one was talking. Someone brought over an extra chair and I sat next to Krzyzewski.

"What happened?" I asked.

"Nothing. It's no big deal."

"Then why did Mickie tell me I had to come back here?"

Krzyzewski smiled wanly. "Because Bob Knight is an asshole," he said.

"Film at eleven," I answered.

Here's what happened. The NCAA does everything it can to keep players and coaches from having to actually mingle with the media except in the locker room and the interview room. It had gone to the trouble of actually curtaining off an area leading to and from the interview room podium just in case someone might venture too close to a player or a coach. The losing team goes into the interview room first after games because the winning team has TV obligations that delay the beginning of their "cooling off" period. Knight and his players had just come off the podium and were walking into the curtained-off area as Krzyzewski and his players were arriving.

Knight stopped and shook hands with both Christian Laettner and Bobby Hurley as he passed them and wished them luck on Monday night. "Good," Krzyzewski thought, "he's over his little post-game funk now." He walked up to his old coach, hand extended, and was about to say something like "It was a hell of a game" when Knight put his head down, acted as if he didn't see him, and walked right past him.

Krzyzewski was crushed. No matter how well he understood Knight, he was hurt that Knight couldn't bring himself to be even a little bit gracious, to offer congratulations at all. When Krzyzewski finished the retelling, I shrugged my shoulders.

"Listen," I said. "F— him. You're playing for the national championship on Monday. You need to focus on that."

"I know that. I'll be fine."

He was, although several of his ex-coaches and players who went to see him that night and the next day said he was still disconsolate. He got himself together though and Duke blew out Michigan—the Fab Five—to win a second straight national title.

For most of the next ten years, Knight and Krzyzewski didn't speak. In 1996, when Duke and Indiana played in the preseason

NIT championship game in Madison Square Garden, Krzyzewski took one more shot at repairing the relationship.

I was there that night researching *A March to Madness*.

Shortly before the teams were going to be introduced, Krzyzewski walked down to the Indiana bench and shook hands with all the Indiana assistants. Then he waited for Knight, who, as usual, was taking his time coming out of the locker room. Krzyzewski just stood there waiting for Knight to arrive.

Finally, with about a minute left on the pregame clock, Knight walked out, accompanied by D. Wayne Lukas, the famous horse trainer. Knight almost always has *someone* with him, needing an audience at all times. I had been that audience for most of a year. On this night, it was Lukas.

As soon as Knight spotted Krzyzewski, he turned his back on him and began telling Lukas some kind of story. I was standing close enough that I could hear Knight saying, "And then I told the sumbitch..." My guess was I'd heard the story at some point.

The pregame clock hit zero. Krzyzewski shook his head and walked back to his bench. Only when he saw Krzyzewski walk to his bench did Knight stop talking to Lukas and make his way to the floor.

Afterward, I found myself with Krzyzewski and his coaches again. "That's the period on the end of the sentence," Krzyzewski said. "I'm done."

Except he wasn't done. Unlike his mentor, Krzyzewski *is* incredibly loyal to friends and doesn't hold grudges forever. When he was elected to the basketball Hall of Fame in 2001, Krzyzewski called Knight.

"Coach, I really don't care what's gone on between us," he said. "The one thing I know is life is short and we're both getting older. If I hadn't played for you and worked for you and known you, I wouldn't be in the Hall of Fame. I would really like it if you would give my induction speech."

Even Knight couldn't think of a smart-ass answer to that gesture. "Mike," he said, "I'd be honored."

Since then, they've been pals again. I'm glad because I know Knight means a lot to Krzyzewski, even though he understands and see his flaws. What's the old saying? A friend is someone you know well and you like them anyway.

I got caught between Knight and Krzyzewski once more in the fall of 2009 when Krzyzewski was being inducted into the Army Sports Hall of Fame. Kevin Anderson, who was then Army's athletic director, asked me to emcee the dinner. He said Knight was going to give Krzyzewski's induction speech. I told him I'd be glad to do it but only if my presence wouldn't cause any problems for Krzyzewski.

By then my relationship with Knight had thawed. It wasn't as if we were best friends or even friends, but I had interviewed him at length for my book on Red Auerbach (Knight loved Red) and when we saw each other, we were always polite. Still, I wanted to be sure. I called Krzyzewski. "If Knight says he won't do it if you're there, I'll just tell him he shouldn't come," Krzyzewski said. "But I don't think he'll do that."

He didn't. The dinner was black tie—except for Bob Knight, who showed up in a blue sweater. Personally, I thought that was out of line. It was a black tie dinner honoring not only Krzyzewski, but seven other West Pointers, including General Ray Murphy, who had been Knight's boss when he coached there. I honestly don't care if ESPN lets him get away with wearing a sweater on air (although I think it's ridiculous to put his partners in sweaters too; I mean, my God, how much can you pander to one person?), but for an occasion like this, someone should have said, "Bob, suck it up and get a tux."

Of course no one did.

I had the honor of introducing Knight. Here's what I said: "Please welcome college basketball's all-time winningest coach with 902 victories, a member of the Army Sports Hall of Fame, a member of the basketball Hall of Fame, but most important, the man who built my house . . . Bob Knight."

I'd used the line before and it cracked up the whole room. Except, of course, for Bob Knight.

As I walked off the podium and he walked onto it, we had to pass each other. He put his head down to do the same blow-by he had pulled on Krzyzewski seventeen years earlier in Minneapolis. I wasn't going to let him do it. I stood right in front of him and put out my hand.

Knight glared at me. Then he shook hands and talked about himself for the next fifteen minutes while introducing Krzyzewski.

Krzyzewski handled it all beautifully. First, he thanked Knight for loaning him his tuxedo. "You see, I forgot to bring mine tonight so Coach graciously gave me his and wore that sweater..."

I would have expected nothing less from Krzyzewski. You see, in the end, he *did* become Dean Smith, and never—thank God— became Bob Knight.

25

The Indiana Boys

In the twenty-five years since the publication of *A Season on the Brink,* I've been in touch with many of the players and coaches that I got to know during that remarkable winter.

On occasion I still see Joe Hillman, who works in Indianapolis, and Todd Meier, who went back to his hometown in Wisconsin, and backup forward Steve Eyl, who is now a successful businessman in California. I see Steve Alford every year at the Final Four and talk to him occasionally on the phone, and I have sporadic contact with Tim Garl, still the trainer at IU after all these years, and Larry Rink, who is still the team doctor.

Dan Dakich and I have remained friends throughout. We talked often when he was still on Bob Knight's staff and after he went to Bowling Green as the head coach. He even invited me to speak at his preseason banquet one season, which I was happy to go and do. Now Dan is a very successful radio talk-show host in Indianapolis and a rising star at ESPN. We talk on a semi-regular basis, and I occasionally appear on his radio show.

When I started working on this book, my first instinct was to track down at least a half-dozen people from that Indiana team and make them part of this book. Brian Sloan, who stood up for me to the security guard that day in Syracuse, is now a doctor in Chicago. Royce Waltman, who first delivered the news that "Coach" was pissed off about the book, had a very successful run as the head coach at Indiana State and now does color on the radio for IU.

In the end, though, not wanting the book to be even longer than it already is, I whittled my IU list to two people: Damon Bailey and Ron Felling. Both were important to *Season on the Brink*. Both were important to Bob Knight. And, unlike some of the others, they have been out of the public eye for a while now. Which made finding them and talking to them that much more intriguing to me.

Felling and I were good friends during my time in Bloomington. Even though he was the newest member of the staff, I always felt he was the one Knight leaned on the most. He was older than Royce and Kohn Smith and Joby Wright and, perhaps because he hadn't been around as long, was more likely than the others to tell Knight things he didn't want to hear.

He also stayed the longest. Royce and Kohn and Joby all went on to head coaching jobs within a couple of years of the 1987 national championship. Ron stayed, and whenever I was at an Indiana game, we'd spend a few minutes talking. When Indiana came to Washington to play in the first and second rounds of the NCAA Tournament in 1998, I asked Ron if he thought this was his last coaching stop.

"Yeah, I think so," he said. "I'm almost sixty and so is Coach. I imagine we'll just ride off into the sunset together."

As most people know, it didn't work out that way—for either man. Early in the 1999–2000 season, Indiana blew an eighteen-point lead against Notre Dame before recovering to win the game in overtime. The next day Dan Dakich called Felling from Bowling Green to check in—as he often did. When Dakich asked Felling how Knight had reacted to the blown lead, Felling told him the truth.

"I said he went ballistic, which he did," Felling said. "I described to Danny what he was like after the game. Heck, it wasn't anything that unusual. He just asked me how he was after the game and I told him."

There was one twist to the conversation this time though that made it different than others in the past: Knight, for some reason, had picked up the phone and was listening.

As soon as Felling finished telling Dakich what had happened, Knight broke in and said, "Dakich, I don't ever want to see you around here again. Felling, you're fired."

Knight firing coaches isn't unusual. Anyone who has ever worked for him has been fired on multiple occasions. It had happened to Felling before. Felling can't talk about what happened next because it is part of the testimony he gave by deposition in the lawsuit he filed against Knight and Indiana. As part of the settlement — Felling received $35,000 from Indiana and $25,000 from Knight according to several published reports — Felling isn't allowed to discuss his testimony or anything he knows about Knight's testimony.

"Honestly, John, I wouldn't want to talk about it even if I could," he said. "It was almost twelve years ago now. It's in the past. I have a lot of good memories of Indiana and the people I knew there. I'm happier leaving it at that. All I know is I told the truth."

Ron and I were sitting by a swimming pool in the condo development in Naples where he now spends his winters. He ran very successful shooting camps both when he coached high school and during his years with Knight, so he lives comfortably in retirement now. He spends most of the summer on his boat in Steamboat Springs, Arkansas, and he and his wife, Camie, still have a place in Bloomington. He's seventy-one now and looks like a Florida retiree, wearing shorts and sandals, walking more slowly than he used to. The sense of humor is still intact and so is the sense of sadness about the way his career at Indiana ended.

There's very little dispute about what happened in the minutes after Knight told Felling he was fired and hung up the phone. Felling went to the Cave — he'd been looking at tape on the other side of the building when Dakich called — and found Knight and assistant coaches Mike Davis (who later succeeded Knight), John Treloar, and Patrick Knight, who had joined the staff a year earlier, all there.

According to everyone in the room, Knight screamed at Felling, who defended himself by saying he had only told Dakich what had happened after the Notre Dame game, nothing more. At some juncture, while Felling was trying to talk, Knight charged at him and knocked him backward into the TV set that was right behind where Felling was standing.

Knight is 6 foot 5 and probably weighed about 250 pounds at the time. Felling was giving away about seven inches and probably 70 pounds. Mike Davis's testimony was eventually released through a Freedom of Information request made by an Indianapolis TV station. In it, he said he had his head down when Felling went flying, but was told later by Patrick Knight and Treloar that Knight had shoved Felling into the TV. As part of Knight's settlement, he admitted that he had "shoved Felling in anger."

Those words were part of a negotiation between the lawyers that appeared to be stalemated in September of 2002. Felling and his lawyer ended up walking out, telling Knight's attorney they would see them in court. A few minutes later, Knight's lawyer called Felling's lawyer and said a compromise could be reached.

"It was like in the schoolyard," Felling's lawyer told reporters. "We called their bluff and they backed down."

The money wasn't important to Felling. Getting Knight to admit he had done what he'd done was important. Clearly, he felt violated by the attack and by being fired the way he'd been fired. He was also angry when Indiana put out a statement that he had decided to retire in the middle of the season to spend more time with his family.

"That's the best they could come up with?" he said, laughing. "My youngest child was thirty-five at the time. Spend more time with my family? Who were they kidding?"

It was during that same season that former Indiana player Neil Reed went on CNN/SI and accused Knight of having grabbed him by the neck during a practice. Knight categorically denied that any such thing had happened and trotted out players and coaches to say they had never seen Knight lay hands on a player that way.

I didn't know Neil Reed, but when people began calling me and asking if I thought it was possible Reed was telling the truth, I said I had never seen Knight come close to doing anything like that during my year with him. Did he occasionally shove a player? Sure. Had Dakich told me the story about Knight throwing the ball in his face from about a foot away when he was a freshman? Yes. But choking—or anything close to it?

No. I'd never seen it.

Felling had.

"I used to take practice tapes home with me," he said. "I'd go through them, make notes, and talk to coaches and players about them the next day. When I heard Neil say what he said, I knew he was telling the truth. I remembered the practice and I was pretty sure I still had the tape."

He did. When he found it, he had someone mail it to CNN/SI, which had aired the original Reed interview. Since his lawsuit with Knight and Indiana was still pending at the time, Felling didn't want to be accused of leaking the tape. Even so, he was almost instantly fingered as the source when the tape leaked.

The tape is grainy, but it is clear on it that Knight charges in Reed's direction angrily and grabs him by the neck. When I first saw it I was truly surprised. The fact that Knight had lied didn't surprise me. In fact, based on my past history with him and stories others had told me, I wouldn't be surprised if Knight *thought* he was telling the truth. What really surprised me though was remembering Knight's press conference in Buffalo the day before what turned out to be his last game at Indiana—an embarrassing 77–57 loss to Pepperdine in a first-round NCAA Tournament game—in which he had trotted out players to insist that Neil Reed had to be lying.

That day was vintage Knight. He talked on and on about all the different things he had done to motivate players through the years. "This is basketball, not canasta," he said. "Kids get bloodied playing this game."

Someone brought up another ex-IU player who had defended Reed. Knight responded by saying the kid was an alcoholic. Seriously.

"I sent the tape to the TV station because I knew it had happened," Felling said. "I saw it happen. Coach just wasn't telling the truth. I've been consistent about all of this. I told Danny [Dakich] before I gave my deposition, 'All I'm going to do is tell the truth.' And that's all I did."

All these years later, Felling still calls Knight "Coach." Old habits are hard to break. He doesn't talk to many of the old gang anymore. When he ran into Royce Waltman a few years ago, Waltman told him he thought what he had done to Knight was wrong.

"I told Royce that was fine if he wanted to think that," Felling said. "But he wasn't there, was he?"

The hurt is still there in his voice as he talks.

"There was nothing I loved more than being out on that floor coaching," he said. "That was where I was most at home. I looked forward to practice every day because I felt like that was my time to shine. I was good at it.

"There was a time when I thought I'd get a chance to have my own team, but, honestly, I don't think Coach wanted me to leave. I'd hear that someone had been interested in me and he had told them I wasn't interested. In a way it was flattering because I knew he felt like he wanted me around, but I would have liked to have taken a shot. If there was one thing I was good at, it was coaching basketball."

He still has friends in Bloomington and was welcomed when he showed up one day at football practice in the summer of 2010 to see some of his old IU friends. "Tom Crean [currently the Indiana basketball coach] came down and walked me through all the new practice facilities, gave me a complete tour," Felling said. "We spent some time talking about what they're trying to do over there now. He couldn't have been any nicer."

The condo where Ron and Camie live is a couple of miles from the beach. Often they take their boat with friends and go into Naples to have lunch and then come back close to dinnertime. It is, for the most part, the sort of idyllic life one would hope for at the end of a successful career.

"I've got just about everything I want," Felling said. "My sons [who both still live in Indiana] are doing great. We spend Christmas up there so I can be with the [four] grandchildren. For the most part though, I stay wherever the weather is warm and I can be on a boat. Not a bad way to live at all."

No doubt. But as Felling sat in a seaside restaurant with a spectacular view of the Gulf of Mexico on a sparking early March day, there wasn't much doubt that, given a choice, he'd probably still rather be in a gym on a cold winter night doing what he loved to do.

"Remember," he says as we walked back to the car, "the night we all went to see Damon? How much fun was that?"

I remember. And it *was* fun.

Ah Damon. As Paul Simon might have sung, "Where have you gone, Damon Bailey? An entire state once turned its lonely eyes to you."

Actually, Damon has gone home. And he's very happy there.

Damon Bailey was the surprise star of *Season on the Brink*. He showed up on Knight's radar—and thus mine—sometime in January of 1986, an eighth grader who had already become a legendary figure playing middle school ball somewhere down along the back roads of southern Indiana. One night when I was in Indianapolis trying unsuccessfully to get Isiah Thomas to talk to me about Knight ("My mother always said if you don't have something nice to say, don't say anything at all" was his line), Knight and Bob Hammel drove down to Bedford to see the young legend play. The next morning Knight was like a teenager in love for the first time, describing everything Bailey did. He was insistent that Bailey—an eighth grader—was better than any guard Indiana had *right now*; not potentially better, better now. To say there was skepticism about this among the coaches is putting it mildly.

"We play Saturday so we can't go see him on the weekend," Knight said. "But next Tuesday, we're all going to see him."

A crusade was planned. Two cars would make the trip. Knight and three of his professor pals would go in one car; Royce, Felling, and I would go in the other car. "I don't think I want to ride back with you, Felling," Knight said. "I know you're going to find something bad to say about the kid."

Knight led the way with Royce driving the chase car. Felling was in the back literally waxing poetic as we headed down the darkened roads of southern Indiana. "A boy, a hoop, a dream, a dark winter night..."

I still remember walking into the tiny gym at Shawswick Junior High School, which seated about fifteen hundred. As I wrote in the book, if God had parachuted in through the roof, it would not have caused a bigger sensation than Knight walking in and standing by the door.

It was easy to pick Damon out once we sat down because he was bigger—at about 6'1" back then—than anyone on the opposing team, Oolitic Middle School, and because he had the ball most of the time when Shawswick was on offense. It wasn't long after we arrived when Royce asked Felling the question that brought about the answer that would be most repeated in future years by those of us who had spent any time with Knight.

"So, Ron, what do you think?"

"I think the mentor has slipped a cog."

Bobby Dwyer had first called Knight "the mentor" when he

arrived at Duke with Mike Krzyzewski in 1980. Keith Drum and I had picked up on it, and whenever we referred to Knight in Krzyzewski's presence, we called him "the mentor." *Never* "the general," that was someone else's cliché. For years after that night at Shawswick, whenever Knight began doing Knight things and I would be asked what the hell he was doing, I would just say, "To quote Ron Felling, the mentor has slipped a cog...again."

When we walked out of the gym that night with Knight rattling on about the wonders of Damon, it was Felling who wouldn't back down and declare Damon the next Jerry West. Knight asked both assistants what they thought. Royce, always the diplomat, said, "He's pretty good, Coach, very good." Felling just said, "I thought Jay Shidler was better in eighth grade."

Shidler had been a reasonably good player at Kentucky—nothing more—a few years earlier.

I wrote about Bailey in *Season on the Brink* as much to show how carried away Knight could get with a young player, literally *years* before he would go to college, as anything else. Alford, who was assigned to take Bailey out to eat one night after a game, asked me what I thought about him since I'd seen him play.

"It was hard to tell because there was virtually no opposition," I said. "He's very mature for a kid that age. I think he can be good, maybe even as good as you."

Alford laughed. "Come on, he's got to be *way* better than me. I can't guard anyone, remember?"

"That'll be true until Damon gets here," I said. "By then you'll be the toughest sumbitch Knight ever coached and poor Damon will be the worst player who ever lived."

Bailey's presence in the book helped add to his rapidly growing legend. High school basketball in Indiana is a huge deal under any circumstances. Being a white high school star makes you an even bigger deal. Having been anointed by Bob Knight—in a book that was a number one bestseller—helped create four years of Damon-mania.

"There were times I praised you for writing about me and times I cursed you," a thirty-eight-year-old Damon Bailey said, sitting in his comfortable office inside the Hawkins-Bailey Warehouse in Bedford. It was the morning of the 2010 NCAA title game, which would be played ninety minutes away in Indianapolis. I had driven down from Indy early that morning to spend some time with Bailey. "On the one hand, being treated as a star was a lot of fun. On the other hand, I couldn't just go to the mall with my girlfriend because people would recognize me and ask for autographs. I was a teenager. I didn't think it was right to big-time anyone."

He had dealt with the hype caused by Knight's comments about him the way almost everyone who ever crosses Knight's path deals with anything Knight says. "When I read it, my first thought was that it was Coach Knight being Coach Knight," he said. "I thought I was pretty good, but I knew I wasn't *that* good."

Bailey was never the type to big-time anyone. I first met him when he was a high school sophomore, when I went to one of his games as part of my research for *A Season Inside*. I had been asked, "How's Damon Bailey doing?" so often I thought I should go and try to answer the question.

The answer was quite well. Bailey was a great high school player, a four-time first team All-State player at Bedford–North Lawrence High School. As a senior, just like Alford, he was Mr. Basketball in Indiana, and he ended his high school career in absolute storybook fashion by scoring the last eleven points in the state championship game to bring BNL from six points down in the last two minutes to win in front of more than 41,000 people in the Indiana Hoosier Dome. The state championships had been moved to the Dome in large part because of Bailey's overwhelming popularity.

When I first introduced myself to him after that game in 1988, I told him I hoped the book hadn't caused him too many problems. "Nah, it's been fine," he said. Then he smiled. "Sometimes people do expect a lot of me though, after what Coach Knight said."

Bailey handled it all remarkably well. "What people sometimes didn't understand is that I had Coach Knight in my life before Coach Knight was in my life—that was my dad," he said. "He coached me until high school and he was always very tough on me. I never minded having demands put on me because I loved to play and I thought I always gave everything I had. So my dad getting on me didn't bother me most of the time, and Coach Knight getting on me didn't bother me most of the time.

"Both my parents were strong people in different ways. They both made sure I never got a big head. My dad was Coach Knight— always demanding more, getting on me. My mom was more like Dan Dakich [who was a full-time assistant during Bailey's years at Indiana], the one who talked quietly and told me not to get too upset about what my dad had said."

Wendell Bailey was the transportation director for the North Lawrence school district. Beverly Bailey was a bank teller. "I grew up dreaming of going to Indiana," Damon said. "To me Coach Knight *was* Indiana. If he had left before I got there, would I still have gone there?" He paused and nodded his head. "Probably."

He committed to Indiana as a junior, although he did give some thought to going to Louisville, which was about the same distance from home and wouldn't have involved carrying the hopes and expectations of an entire state—not to mention Knight—with him to college. But Indiana was his destiny, and to a large degree, he lived up to all the hype in college.

In his four seasons at Indiana, the *worst* the Hoosiers did was a trip to the Sweet Sixteen. From 1991 to 1994, Indiana went to the Sweet Sixteen, the Final Four, the Elite Eight, and the Sweet Sixteen again. The Final Four game in 1992 was the loss to Duke on the day that started the almost ten-year Knight-Krzyzewski freeze. Coincidence or not, in Knight's last six seasons at IU—after Bailey's graduation—Indiana never reached the Sweet Sixteen again.

It was during Damon's freshman year that his younger sister,

Courtney, was diagnosed with leukemia. Damon had been forced to leave a game at Michigan with a thigh bruise. On Monday, after getting treatment, Damon walked back into the locker room to get ready to join the rest of the team on the floor for practice and found his father and Knight waiting for him.

"Honestly, my first thought was that my dad was upset with me because I'd had to come out of the game," he said.

He wishes now that had been it. Instead, his father and Knight quietly explained to him that Courtney had leukemia. *"This happens to other people,"* was Damon's first thought. His second thought was, "This is my little sister. She's a high school freshman. This isn't right."

When he went to see her, he felt better. "She wasn't the least bit down," he said. "She said she was going to fight it and beat it—and she did."

A little more than three years later, Damon Bailey played his last home game at Indiana. He was going to graduate as the school's sixth all-time leading scorer, with 1,741 points. He had been a four-year starter on very good teams. In his office is the *Sports Illustrated* cover he was on in December of 1993 with the headline "Hoosier Hero."

He had been all of that for eight years.

Knight always insisted on holding Senior Day ceremonies after the last home game was over rather than before it began. He didn't want players getting too emotional before they played. This created some pressure because a loss could put a damper on those ceremonies. In 1985, after Indiana had lost to Michigan, Knight refused to take part in the ceremony for Dakich and Uwe Blab. "You're on your own," he told them.

Before the game, Damon told Knight that he wanted to recognize Courtney when it was his turn to speak. Knight said that was fine. Indiana won the game and Bailey spoke emotionally about his definition of courage. "I get cheered, I get all the hoopla because I can dribble a basketball and shoot a basketball," he said. "Courtney is the one who should be cheered. She's been through a lot more than I have."

It was warm and sweet—and a few minutes later it was largely shattered because Knight decided to read a poem when it was time for him to speak about the seniors. Actually it was a lyric from a rap song. Knight had been under a lot of pressure—again—that season for his behavior. He had head-butted one player and had appeared to kick his son Patrick, who, like Bailey, was a senior on that team.

And so, in response to all the (of course, unfair) criticism, Knight concluded his senior day speech by saying, "When my time on earth has gone, and my activities here are past, I want they bury me upside down, and my critics can kiss my ass."

Naturally, most of the crowd hooted and cheered when Knight was finished. Naturally, that was the clip shown a million times over the next week. Did it bother Bailey that Knight couldn't allow Senior Day to just be Senior Day and not step on his sister's moment?

"Like I said, it was Coach Knight being Coach Knight," he said. "That's a bittersweet day under any circumstances. I gave him everything I had for four years, I do believe that. I had played hurt that year, I had a torn muscle in my abdomen. What got me through it was reminding myself that my sister was dealing with a lot more pain than I was and that she wasn't complaining. I wanted to make that point."

He smiled. "I got to make my point."

Bailey's career ended with a round-of-sixteen loss to Boston College. I remember that game, played in Miami, because Patrick Knight was on the floor for the final couple of minutes. When the buzzer sounded, he made a point of walking over to press row to shake hands with me. It's a shame Texas Tech didn't work out for Patrick, but he'll do fine coaching at Lamar. I'd say he's a good kid, but he's forty years old now. I'm proud to have been his babysitter.

Not long after that game, Bailey saw a quote from his coach that really hurt him.

"Coach said, 'If there was ever a player I felt I failed with, it was Bailey,'" he said, able to recite it almost word for word sixteen years later. "He said he got less out of me than anyone he'd ever coached. All I knew about my career at Indiana was that I gave Coach Knight everything I had to give—whatever that was. That's what I said when I was asked about it because that was how I felt."

Of course, in Knightworld, the bad guy in that exchange was Bailey.

It was soon after he graduated that I crossed paths with Damon again. He had been drafted in the second round by the Indiana Pacers and was on injured reserve for the '94–95 season after he had torn a patella and ended up having to have surgery on both his knees. That was the fall of my aborted book involving Larry Brown, so I ended up sitting behind the Pacers bench with Damon on several occasions.

It was funny because I sensed a strange bond—not a closeness or even a friendship—but a bond because Damon knew that I understood what he'd been through. I had watched Steve Alford go through the almost identical experience: the difference being that Alford had ended his career on a national championship team, so Knight—after hammering him for most of four years—ended up talking about him as if he had invented basketball.

I reminded Damon, not even being aware at the time of what Knight had said about him, of something I had written in *Season on the Brink*. "It is a crisp October day in 1990. Damon Bailey, Indiana freshman, fails to help on defense. Knight stops practice. 'You know, Bailey, when we had Alford here he was so much tougher than you it wasn't even funny. Why, I never had to talk to him about playing defense even once in four years!'"

I didn't remember exactly what I wrote, but when I brought up the passage to Damon he laughed. "You had that one right," he said.

Bailey never played in the NBA. He sat out that first season, didn't make the Pacers the next year, and landed in Fort Wayne in the CBA. The good news was he was such a big star in Indiana that he single-handedly sold a lot of tickets for the team. He was paid far more than the typical CBA player because he sold a lot more tickets than the typical CBA player.

"There was no salary cap," he said. "So they could pay me as much as they thought I was worth."

He was in a couple of NBA camps and played briefly in Europe, but Fort Wayne was the best place for him. Then Isiah Thomas bought the league and put in a salary cap: $40,000, a fraction of what Bailey had been making. He was still fighting various injuries. One day in the fall of 1999 he went to Keith Smart—another former Indiana star—who was coaching the team and said simply, "It's time. I'm done."

He went home to Bedford and began working full-time at Hawkins-Bailey, a business he and a friend had launched soon after he graduated from college. "We sell preventive maintenance products to coal mines and limestone companies, and lubricants like Castrol for heavy machinery," he said. "My partner did most of the work while I was still playing. Now we've built the company to twenty-one people and—last year—eighteen million dollars in sales."

The economy hurt business, but not that much. "People still need to run furnaces," he said.

He has also had summer camps around the state for years, running as many as eighteen at one time. In Indiana, the name Damon Bailey is still magical. "What's changed is when we first started the camps, kids came because they knew my name," he said. "Now kids come because their *parents* know my name."

He still has the same boyish face as the kid Knight fell in love with back in 1986, but there are hints of gray now in his close-cropped hair. He married his high school sweetheart, Stacey, and they have three children—all basketball players—who are fourteen, twelve, and ten. "My oldest is very talented," he said. "She wants to play at either Connecticut or Tennessee. We'll see. You have to let kids choose their own path."

Bailey's path has led him back home. And like most who have been close to Knight and fallen out with him, there has been a rapprochement of sorts.

"Right after I stopped playing, I was home one morning and Stacey came in and said, 'Coach Knight is on the phone for you.' I was stunned. We hadn't spoken once since I graduated. I picked up the phone, and in that way of his, he just said, 'Bailey, I think it's time you reconnected with the program. We have practice at ten o'clock this morning. I'll see you then.'

"I hung up the phone, thinking, 'Who is he to just tell me to show up at practice like that?' Of course, I got in the car and went."

There is no doubt in my mind what bothered Knight most about Damon Bailey. It was the same thing that bothered him most about Steve Alford: both were more popular in Indiana than he was. As much of a hero as Knight was, he always had detractors because of his behavior. Neither Bailey nor Alford had any detractors.

"I think that's true," Bailey said. "Coach Knight has a pretty big ego, and I think that did bother him. Plus, Steve and I didn't need his help when we graduated. We didn't need him to get us a job or into law school or into coaching. We were both just fine."

He smiled. "The way I always looked at it was this: no matter how bad we had it as players, the coaches had it worse. I never could have worked for him. I respect the guys who did, a lot. I think all of us would say the same thing about Coach Knight: you learn a lot from him—some of it is what to do, some of it is what *not* to do.

"I watched what happened at Indiana when I graduated and then when he went to Texas Tech. In fact, when I coached the high school team here [for two years], I took my coaches down to see a game and watch practice for a couple of days. [Patrick Knight arranged the trip.] When we were going down, I said to my guys, 'I almost hope they lose so you can really get a sense of what it's like to be around him.' Well, they won and he went off anyway, so it worked out fine.

"People ask me if the game passed him by. Absolutely not. He knows the game as well as anyone who ever lived. But I do think people passed him by. Fair or unfair, today's players won't put up with what we put up with. And it's probably fair to say the guys before us put up with things we wouldn't put up with. I just think it got harder for him to get the quality of kid and of player that he had gotten in his glory years."

There are certain truths buried deep in Bob Knight's soul that he will probably never let escape. One is that *Season on the Brink* did exactly what it was supposed to do: give people some semblance of an answer to the question "Why do the players put up with him?"

And then there's this truth: there was almost no way for Damon Bailey to live up to the hype created by Knight's trips to Shawswick in the winter of 1986. And yet, he came about as close to it as was humanly possible.

A LITTLE MORE THAN five months after my meeting with Damon Bailey, and about an hour after my pizza at John's with Chris Spitler, I went in search of Bob Knight at Madison Square Garden.

As I've mentioned before, our relationship had thawed through the years to the point of civility, if not cordiality. I have often told the story about the first time we spoke after the book came out — eight years later. I was in Hawaii covering Maryland in the Maui Classic, and Indiana was also in the tournament. One night Gary Williams and I walked back into the hotel after a game and saw Knight and his old friend Bob Murray walking through the lobby on a direct path for us.

"Uh-oh," Gary said. "Here we go."

Knight and Murray stopped. To my surprise, Knight said, "Gary, John, how are you guys?" putting out his hand as if the last time any of us had talked had been at lunch earlier that day.

We all shook hands. Knight said something complimentary about Gary's team. He asked how things were going with me, what I was working on. We chatted casually the way you do for about seven or eight minutes, I would guess. The coaches wished each other luck the next day and off they went.

"Well, you just witnessed history," I said when they were gone.

Gary smiled. "After all the crap he said about you, why would you even talk to him?"

That was the first time I used the "built my house" line.

After that, when we saw each other, we would exchange hellos. And I had spoken to him for about two hours on the phone while researching my Red Auerbach book, *Let Me Tell You a Story.*

I had no illusions though about what our relationship was and would continue to be. He had spoken to me for the Red book because of his devotion to Red. I'd even said that to him as we wound up the conversation. "Bob, I know you did this for Red, but I want to thank you for doing it," I said.

"John, you actually did me a favor," he said. "You gave me a chance to do something for Red, and that's almost impossible to do."

He was right about that. Red was always doing things for everyone else, but doing something for him *was* almost impossible.

My last encounter with Knight had been at the Army Hall of Fame induction fourteen months earlier, when he had not been amused by the "built my house" line. When I told people I was going to New York to try to speak to him, they had all said, "He'll talk to you. It's been almost twenty-five years."

Sadly, I couldn't get anyone to put up the million dollars I was willing to bet that Knight would *not* talk to me. You see, this is who he is. By the very act of saying, "Bob, I'd like to talk to you," I would be putting him in the position he loves most in life: one of control.

Later that same season, when Knight agreed to do an interview with CBS College Sports (he was extremely available in February and March, largely because he was being paid to be a spokesman for a company promoting prostate cancer awareness), someone asked me if I would like to do the interview. I couldn't help but laugh.

"There's exactly one way to get Knight to do the interview with me," I said. "Tell him he can be interviewed by anyone who does work for the network *except* me. Tell him I won't do it. Then there's a *possibility* he might say, 'I'll only do it with Feinstein.'"

I was half joking. Maybe one-quarter joking, actually. My best approach to Knight that evening in the Garden would have been to say, "I'm writing a new book; you're in it, but I have no interest in talking to you for it because, frankly, I don't think you've got anything interesting to say at this point in your life."

It probably wouldn't have worked, but it would have had a better chance than just being straight up. Still, I knew I had to go with straight up.

I walked into the Garden at about five o'clock, trying to remember how much the building had meant to me as a kid. It's old now, and the rafters, which were once reserved *only* for Knicks and Rangers championship banners, are now filled with so many cheesy banners for anyone who has ever walked in the front door that you can't even pick out the ones that matter.

Still, it was the Garden, the place I had dreamed about getting the chance to work in as a kid. And I had work to do.

When I walked out to the floor area, Knight was standing in the entrance to the tunnel holding court with about ten people who were clearly hanging on his every word. I instantly thought back to 1996: Knight was standing on the exact spot where he had turned his back on Mike Krzyzewski to tell D. Wayne Lukas that story he just *had* to tell him at that moment.

I could see this would go on for a while, so I went in the back to see Gary Williams. Knowing I don't go to that many games anymore,

Gary asked me what had brought me to New York. When I told him, he laughed.

"What's the over-under on how long that conversation lasts?" he said.

"I've got about a minute in the pool," I said.

Fifteen minutes later, when I walked back out, the crowd had dwindled to Dick Groat, the baseball Hall of Famer who had been such a great athlete that he had played both Major League Baseball and in the NBA, and some kid from ESPN who was clearly there to get Knight over to the announcer table as soon as possible.

Okay, I thought, now or never.

I didn't want to interrupt Knight and Groat, but I didn't want Knight to escape. So I stood a few yards away and waited. Knight was telling Groat a story about Groat when I walked up.

"You see, I know more about you than ninety-nine percent of the people in the world," he said. "For example, I know that you were such a good softball player that Fred Zollner [the owner of the Fort Wayne Pistons in the 1950s] actually paid you to play softball for his team in the summertime."

Groat, who does color on the Pittsburgh radio network, shook his head. "No, he didn't," he said.

Knight was thrown off stride for an instant. "He didn't? I heard that he did."

"Not true," Groat said.

At that point Knight glanced up and saw me. He immediately launched into a story about Seth Greenberg, the coach at Virginia Tech, calling him for advice after he had done Tech's game against Kansas State a few days earlier. I wasn't really listening anymore. Knight was slow-playing me just as he had done with Krzyzewski on the same spot. I knew how this was going to turn out, but I had to play it to the end.

At some point as Knight was explaining to Groat how he had explained coaching to Greenberg, Groat looked up and saw me. "John," he said, breaking into Knight's monologue perhaps in the hopes of ending it. "How are you?" He turned in my direction and offered his hand.

"I'm fine, Dick, great to see you," I said shaking his hand. "Bob, how are you?"

"I'm fine, John."

Knight was looking out at the floor as if studying the midcourt logo. I took another shot.

"I was really sorry to hear about General Murphy. I know how much he meant to you."

Ray Murphy had been Knight's boss at Army. He had passed away a few months earlier.

"Yeah."

Groat now saw his chance to escape. "Bob, I have to go get ready," he said. "It was great to talk to you."

"Yeah, me too, Dick," Knight said.

As soon as Groat walked away, he turned and, moving quite well for someone who had just turned seventy, began walking back into the tunnel. I had seen this act before.

"Bob, have you got a minute?" I said, falling in next to him.

"No," he said, still not looking at me.

"Bob, I literally need to ask you one question which requires a yes or no answer," I said. I was telling the truth. My one question would be: "I'm doing a book. It's been twenty-five years since I wrote *Season on the Brink*. Is there some point this season when we can sit down and talk?"

Knight stopped and turned briefly in my direction, pointing a finger. "I told you no," he said. "Do you speak English, John? No."

He started to turn to walk away but I couldn't resist a parting shot (I never can). "Bob, if you don't like my next book, please don't complain about it to me. Thanks for the time."

I have no idea if he responded to that in any way. I had turned my back to walk away. To quote Krzyzewski, it was the period on the end of the sentence.

As I walked away, I couldn't help but smile and think back to that hotel room in Lexington twenty-five years earlier. You see, Krzyzewski had it right from the very beginning: I *was* insane to volunteer to spend a season with Bob Knight. Krzyzewski's advice was reasoned and sound.

But I'm very glad I didn't listen.

EPILOGUE

The Best and the Brightest

WHEN I BEGAN THIS book, I planned to end it with the period on the end of the Bob Knight sentence—whatever that period proved to be. But as I closed in on the finish line, it occurred to me that I didn't want the final scene of the book to involve Knight.

There's no doubt that *A Season on the Brink* was the beginning for me—but it certainly wasn't the end. As I wrote earlier, I don't question for a minute the significance it had in my life. That said, the book I enjoyed the most and the book that still resonates most with me is *A Civil War*.

I still have to catch myself when I refer to "the kids" I wrote about in that book. Like it or not, they are all men now, well into their thirties. Some are still in the military, some are not. They all remain special in my eyes.

Of course, the first time I wrote about athletes from Army and Navy in a book was when I wrote about David Robinson and Kevin Houston in *A Season Inside*.

David was the unlikely superstar, the gawky kid who had gone to Navy as a 6-foot-7-inch future engineer and had emerged four years later as a 7-foot-1 future NBA Hall of Famer. He had gone on to win three NBA titles playing for the San Antonio Spurs and had become the role model for how one could be a superstar athlete and still be a truly admirable human being.

Kevin Houston was as admirable, just not as rich or famous. As an Army senior he had led the nation in scoring as a 5'11", 165-pound shooting guard. While Robinson was the number one pick in the NBA draft when he graduated, even though the Spurs knew they would have to wait at least two years to get him in uniform, all Houston wanted was a decent shot to make the 1988 U.S. Olympic team. He was invited to the team's training camp in Colorado Springs, but was an early cut.

"John Thompson was the coach," Houston said. "He liked guards who were tall and quick, long and defensive-oriented—not shooters. I was none of those things. My chance was to make the team because he wanted at least one three-point shooter to bring in off the bench. He obviously didn't want that."

Houston was on night maneuvers in Fort Sill, Oklahoma, on the night the U.S. team lost to the Soviet Union in the Olympic semifinals. He listened to the game on a handheld radio. "All I remember is they couldn't make a jump shot," he said. "Believe me, it didn't make me feel any better about things."

Houston served in the Army until the downsizing in 1990. During his time in the military, he played with Robinson on the All Armed Services team. They knew each other from competing for four years, and there was great mutual respect between them. During their time as teammates, they became friends. After leaving the service, Robinson went to San Antonio; Houston had a couple of brief tryouts with NBA teams—first the New Jersey Nets, then the Washington Bullets.

He was a late cut both times and knew it was time to find a job. By then he had a family. He had married Liz, his high school sweetheart, right after graduation from West Point. Their daughter, Lauren, was born fourteen months later. Luke came along four years after that, and LeAnne came three years after Luke. Houston got a job working for Verizon in corporate security and has stayed with the company since then. Even after he settled into a real job, the basketball bug hadn't completely gone away. He continued to play on weekends for the Scranton Miners in the Eastern League, getting a hundred dollars a game to play with quite a few former Division I players. He also coached for six years at a private school near Pearl River, the town where he had grown up, only a few miles from West Point.

During those years I would often see Kevin because he came to most Army home games. By the time Luke was about six, he was going to games with his dad and already seemed to have inherited his sweet shooting stroke. Kevin was always upbeat, someone who was completely happy with his life and comfortable with what he had been as a basketball player.

He stayed in frequent touch with Robinson. "Whenever David would come to town to play the Knicks or the Nets, he would leave tickets for me," he said. "It was fun, especially when Luke got older because he loved going with me to the games. One night we met David afterward for dinner, and he brought Tim Duncan and Terry Porter. I think Luke was about seven and you can imagine how cool that was for him. David and Tim talked to him all night like he was a little brother."

He smiled. "The best part was when David kept telling him what a great player I had been. Luke couldn't believe that David Robinson was sitting there telling him that his *dad* was a great basketball player."

Robinson ended up playing for fourteen seasons in the NBA and was selected as one of the top fifty players in NBA history during the league's seventy-fifth anniversary celebration. He retired in San Antonio, where he has built and financed a school for the underprivileged. A lot of people would like to see him run for mayor.

"Not going to happen," he said early in 2011. "Why would I get into politics? I'm happy doing what I'm doing right now, and I don't need to ask anyone to vote for me for anything."

Robinson was walking, talking, and signing autographs all at once as he discussed his political nonambitions. He was back at Navy for an alumni game and a twenty-fifth reunion of the 1986 team that he had led to the Elite Eight.

His teammates had urged him to come back for the weekend largely because the school was planning to honor Paul Evans, the coach who had seen something in Robinson as a high school senior that made him believe he could be a good college player. "A 7'1" superstar? No, I never imagined that," Evans always said. "But a good college player—yes. He really didn't know how to play, but you could see the potential."

Robinson's growth spurt, along with the arrival of a tough little point guard named Doug Wojcik and the presence of talented, heady players like Kylor Whitaker and Vernon Butler—whose number is retired in the rafters at Alumni Hall right next to Robinson's—made Navy into a special team. The Mids went to three straight NCAA Tournaments, including that magical run to the Elite Eight.

Billy Lange, Navy's coach until the spring of 2011, had come up with the idea for an alumni game shortly after arriving in 2004. The first year nineteen players showed up. By 2011 the number was fifty. This was Robinson's first one back.

He didn't look a lot different in uniform than in his playing days, but this was hit-and-giggle hoops. He was content to walk up and down the floor, catch an occasional pass, and maybe—maybe— take a shot here and there. There was a lot more laughing going on than rebounding.

Then Robinson caught a pass inside and casually went up to shoot. An eager youngster named George O'Garro (class of 2006) flew through the air and blocked the shot. Robinson gave him a look as if to say, "What did you just do?"

But he never said a word. The next three possessions he called for the ball, made a quick move each time, and fired the feathery jumper that earned him the nickname "The Admiral." Swish. Swish. And swish. O'Garro and everyone else just watched and learned. If you want to play hit-and-giggle, fine. But if you want to *play*, you better be ready to duck.

When it was over, everyone went upstairs for dinner and speeches and presentations. Navy was opening conference play that night with a game against Bucknell, but the presence of the '86 team and *David Robinson* was the main draw for a crowd that was probably close to double what Navy might normally draw on a Saturday night.

Prior to the game, all the players from the '86 team sat at tables on the promenade upstairs and signed autographs. "We know the deal," joked Carl Liebert, who had been the team's sixth man. "They'll take our autographs, they *want* David's."

The game was scheduled to start at eight o'clock. The autograph party was supposed to end at 7:45. At 7:30 an announcement was made that the line was being cut off. No one paid any attention, in spite of the best efforts of several young Mids in uniform to tell people time was up. The game started. The autograph signing continued. Finally, just before halftime, having signed every single autograph, David Robinson and his kids were able to sit down and watch the game.

Once a hero, always a hero.

IT WAS DURING 2004 that Kevin Houston's world began to crash. Liz was diagnosed with a rare disease called scleroderma, which is a connective tissue disease that in a worst-case scenario can infect blood vessels, muscles, and internal organs. For a long time the disease made her weak and often made it difficult for her to function. It is degenerative and it kept getting worse. One can survive with scleroderma for a while if all goes well, but there is no cure.

"The doctors told us if we were lucky she could be around into her midfifties or so," Houston said. "We weren't that lucky."

During the Christmas holidays in 2008, with her immune system already weak because of the disease, Liz came down with pneumonia. She had been sick before and always bounced back. When she went to the hospital on December 30, the thinking was she would bounce back again. "I remember my mom saying, 'She always pulls through, she'll pull through again,'" Kevin said. "I think we all thought that, kids included. Liz even asked me to bring her laptop to the hospital so she could get some work done when she felt a little better."

That never happened. On New Year's Day, Kevin sat down with the children—who were then twenty, sixteen, and thirteen. "I don't think we're getting the miracle this time," he said. "I think we have to face up to the fact that we're going to lose Mom."

Two days later, Liz died. That night, Luke, who was then a high school sophomore, had a game. "We all decided he should play," Kevin said. "My brother [Jerry] coaches him. He told me he thought Luke could handle it. He hit his first two 3s that night. Had a career high.

"It's funny, all my life basketball was my bailout when other things weren't that good. At the moment of the worst tragedy of my life, basketball became my bailout again—only this time it was through Luke. His games became the place we could all escape to, at least for a little while."

Three years later, Kevin Houston is dating. He is forty-four now but still has the reddish hair and the freckled face he had when he was making Robinson's buddy Doug Wojcik look bad in front of his family, pouring in thirty-eight points on Robinson and Wojcik's Senior Night at Navy. He's still friends with Robinson—he was invited to his Hall of Fame induction along with most of Robinson's Navy teammates—and as is always the case when genuine tragedy strikes an Army or a Navy graduate, he has been aided immeasurably by his classmates and teammates being there to help.

"The old saying is that West Point isn't a great place to be, but it's a great place to be *from*," Kevin Houston said on a cold January morning in 2011, a few hours before an Army-Navy basketball game. "I'm proof of how true that is."

THEY'RE ALL PROOF OF that, the kids, now men, I got to know from Army and Navy. When I get phone calls or e-mails, they are usually updates on weddings or the arrival of kids or job changes. Sometimes they are about deployment, which is always scary. Andrew Thompson re-upped for the marines after ten years because they promised to send him to graduate school. They did, but first they sent him to Iraq for almost a year.

He survived. Kevin Norman, Jim Cantelupe's roommate, was not as lucky. Norman was an army pilot stationed in Korea shortly before the war in Iraq began. He was piloting a C-112 transport plane when something went wrong and the plane caught on fire. According to the reports of witnesses and the official army report, Norman and his copilot began to descend, with the plane in flames, toward a heavily populated area filled with apartment buildings. But before the plane hit the ground, Norman steered it away from that area and kept it in the air until he found an empty field. That's where the plane crashed. Norman and his copilot died. No one else did.

When I talked to Cantelupe, who was out of the army by then, he talked about how everyone who signs on at an academy feels about what they may face when they graduate.

"None of us want to die overseas fighting for our country," he said. "But every one of us who graduates from an academy or volunteers as an enlisted man knows he *might* die overseas fighting for our country. We're all willing to do that if we have to do that. Kevin always understood that he could die doing what he was doing. He didn't want to die, but he didn't fear it. And when that moment came, he saved countless lives, probably knowing that he was about to die himself."

That's courage—*real* courage. As Cantelupe put it, what made Kevin Norman a hero wasn't that he died for his country, but that he was *willing* to die for his country.

Every year at Army-Navy, several of us go to dinner the night before the game. The group varies from year to year depending on schedules, but often has included Cantelupe and Thompson—good friends who stay in touch all the time—in addition to Derek Klein and John Graves and Anthony Noto and Dave Lillefloren. The last two had already graduated from Army and Navy when I wrote *A Civil War.* Lillefloren was one of Alton Grizzard's closest friends, having played with him in both high school and college.

Lillefloren played on the offensive line; Noto was a linebacker. Every year Lillefloren brings up the pancake block he executed on Noto on the first series of the 1990 Army-Navy game. Every year Noto says the same thing: "It was the other linebacker, not me." Each keeps promising to bring a game tape the next year to prove his point.

After dinner, Noto and Lillefloren always go to a nearby Irish bar. It is an unspoken tradition that every year on Friday night, ex-players from Army and Navy gather at this bar to give one another a hard time and to share memories and tell old stories. Just before midnight, the ex–Army linebacker and the ex–Navy tackle slip off to a corner of the bar by themselves. They order a shot of Jack Daniel's and hold up their glasses just as midnight strikes.

"Alton," they say to each other. Then they hold their glasses up to the sky to honor their fallen friend. Army, Navy, it doesn't matter. In the end, they're all comrades.

ON THE NIGHT OF January 21, 2011, I got in my car not long after dark to drive from the Thayer Hotel to Loughran's, a truly great prime rib restaurant outside of Newburgh, New York, a place with sawdust on the floor and portions of food so big even I sometimes can't finish.

This was one of my favorite weekends of the winter. Navy was playing at Army the next day, and I was doing the game on CBS College Sports as part of the Patriot League basketball package I did during the past nine years. My routine was almost always the same: drive to West Point on Friday afternoon and check into the Thayer, one of my favorite hotels because it has fabulous views of the Hudson and absolutely reeks with tradition and history. Sitting in front of the lobby fireplace reading the newspaper on game morning, after I have walked from one end of the post to the other and back, is one of my favorite things to do in life.

Dinner at Loughran's on Friday was part of the tradition. Depending on who was around, I would meet anywhere from one to five people to eat there. On this night it would be just Bob Beretta, the former Army SID who had played such an important role in my being able to write *A Civil War*. Bob was now the number two man in the Army athletic department. Dicky Hall, the equipment manager, had the flu. Tim Kelly, the trainer, had a hockey game. Mike Vaccaro and Kevin Gleason, who had been covering Army when I wrote the book, were both in Pittsburgh covering the Jets in the AFC Championship game. So it was just Bob and me.

I was driving over the mountain on Route 9W, a very scenic but often treacherous piece of road, when my phone rang. I hit the button on my Bluetooth and answered. It was Jim Cantelupe—no big surprise. He would know I was at West Point for the weekend and would call to check in and see how things were at his alma mater.

"What's going on?" I asked. "Where are you?"

"I'm in Dallas," he said. "Just landed."

My first thought was that he was going to a game down there with someone famous and wanted me to know about it. Jim is a big-time money manager now and works with a number of famous people in jockworld, including LeBron James, Brian Urlacher, and Joe Girardi.

"What brings you down there?" I asked.

He took a deep breath, which was my first hint that something was wrong.

"I've got some bad news," he said in that way when you know the news is *very* bad. "Christina Klein died this morning."

I remember gasping and gripping the wheel tightly because I was afraid I might lose control of the car. All I could say—and I think I said it at least five times—was "Oh my God."

Christina Klein was Derek Klein's wife. I had first met her when she was Christina Wills at postgame tailgates during my *Civil War* season. She and Derek were high school sweethearts who had continued to date through college, even though Derek was at West Point and Christina was back home in Michigan going to Albion.

She was one of those people you like instantly: tall with dark hair and eyes that lit up when she smiled. Beyond that, she had a way of making everyone feel as if they were her best friend within five minutes of meeting her. She was, along with Cantelupe's mom, Tina, the mayor of the postgame tailgate. If someone didn't have a drink in one hand and food in the other, Christina was running around insisting on finding you a drink or more food.

When I made the standard jock joke to Derek about "How in the world did you convince her to date *you?*" I think I was only half joking. As Derek would say years later, "She was the role model for the girl all the guys wanted to marry."

Derek and Christina got engaged soon after the Army-Navy game in December of 1995 and were married a year later. Derek made Christina wear flats during the ceremony so she wouldn't be taller than he was when the photos were taken. After Derek got out of the army, they lived back home in Michigan for a while before Derek got a great job in sales and they moved to Dallas. By then they had three children—Caroline, Carson, and Michael—who are now eight, six, and three.

If there was ever an All-American family it was the Kleins. Most years they came to the Friday night, pre–Army-Navy dinner. Caroline and Carson also attended those dinners as infants.

It was Derek who one night proposed a toast to Andrew Thompson.

"What for?" Drew asked.

"For sacking [quarterback Ronnie] McAda to put us in fourth and twenty-four," Derek said. "If it weren't for you, we never would have pulled off one of the most dramatic plays in Army history."

I won't repeat Thompson's response, but you can probably guess.

Once I had stopped saying "Oh my God," I asked Jim what had happened. It turned out Christina had a history of depression in her family. She'd had a bad bout with it in 1998, but her doctors had gotten her on the right meds and for twelve years she was completely healthy.

But in 2010 the disease flared again. Derek and Christina went to three different doctors who tried different meds for both depression and insomnia. "The last six weeks, she didn't sleep at all," Derek said later. "She wasn't just in emotional pain, she was in physical pain too."

That morning, Derek had awakened at about 5:30. Christina wasn't in bed. Her battle with manic depression had just ended.

I have known Jim Cantelupe for sixteen years. When his college roommate died, he was stunned but in control. Now he was crying on the phone.

"I caught the first plane down," he said. "There are about five guys already here and there are more on the way. We'll find a way . . . somehow . . . to get Derek and the kids through this."

The guys he was talking about who were there or on the way were Derek's teammates. By nine o'clock that night no fewer than ten of his Army teammates were in his living room. "They just dropped everything in their lives and got down here to help me right away," Derek said. "They haven't stopped."

All the time in sports we hear athletes talk about their team-mates being family or how close they are. Most of the time you hear this talk in winning locker rooms. The closeness and the bonding are all tied to winning.

At the academies the bonds are far stronger than that. They have to do with shared experiences and with truly becoming family. No one would have more support in dealing with tragedy than Derek Klein. At the memorial service for Christina, twenty-two Army foot-ball players—Class of '96—were there. Cantelupe was designated to speak on their behalf.

"I remember I had my head down because I was trying not to lose it completely," Derek said. "I knew if I looked at Jim while he was talking about Christina, I was going to break down completely. But as he was winding down I looked up and there were twenty-one other guys standing up there with him. They had walked up there just to show their support for Christina—and for me. That memory has gotten me through a lot of tough days and nights since then."

So has Andy Person—also Class of '96, United States Naval Academy. Person was one of four brothers who played at Navy. In 2007 he lost his wife, Dottie, to cancer, leaving him to raise their five children. One of the people who reached out to try to help him back then was Derek Klein. And so, not long after Christina's death, Andy Person got in touch with Derek.

"You are in hell now," he told him. "I know, because I've been there. Slowly, it will get better."

They are in constant touch. "If you understand what Army-Navy is all about," Derek said, "then you understand that I know the Navy guys are going to be there for me too. We played football against each other a thousand years ago. We're brothers for life."

A couple of days after Christina's death, I talked to Derek on the phone. He was, as you would expect, in hell.

"Marrying her was the best thing I ever did in my life," he said. "What people don't understand is that she had a fatal disease. It killed her the way cancer kills people. It just happened differently, with the suddenness of a car accident. I've loved her since I was sixteen."

"And she loved you back," I said, knowing after all those years that it was true.

The next day Derek sent me an e-mail, basically thanking me for calling. The last line of the e-mail came straight from the John Dryden quote that had hung over the door to the Army football locker room.

"I lay me down for to bleed a while but I will rise to fight with you again."

I read that line over and over again, crying—just as I'm crying right now. And then I thought, as I am thinking right now, how very damn lucky I have been to have known the people I have known over the past twenty-five years.

Acknowledgments

In a sense, I have twenty-five years of people to thank for this book. I will attempt to get through all those who deserve mention in a little bit less time than that.

I'll begin with those who were gracious enough to give me time for this book, who sat and talked about the old days and the more recent days in their lives: Damon Bailey, Ron Felling, Dan Dakich, Dean Smith, Mike Krzyzewski, Gary Williams, Steve Kerr, Ivan Lendl, Mary Carillo, Paul Goydos, David Duval, Tom Watson, Davis Love, Joe Torre, Bobby Cox, Bud Selig, Andrew Thompson, Jim Cantelupe, Chris Spitler, Kevin Houston, David Robinson, and Michal Pivonka. Special thanks to Derek Klein, who was willing to talk about an unspeakable tragedy only a few weeks after it took place.

Thanks also to a bevy of people who helped me track people down: Bill Acree, Nate Ewell, Pat Courtney, Rich Levin, Scott Strasemeier, and Bob Beretta.

And, as always, the people I work with: Michael Pietsch, John Parsley, Eve Rabinovits, Heather Fain, and Marlena Bittner at Little, Brown, and my agent-for-life, Esther Newberg, and her staff at ICM—Kari Stuart, Lyle Morgan, Liz Farrell, and the always-thorough John Delaney.

And then there are my friends and colleagues: Keith and Barbie Drum; Jackson Diehl and Jean Halperin; Ed and Lois Brennan;

Rick Brewer; David and Linda Maraniss; Lexie Verdon and Steve Barr; Jill and Holland Mickle; Terry and Patti Hanson; Doug and Beth Doughty; Bob and Anne DeStefano; Bud Collins and Anita Claussen; Wes Seeley, Andy Dolich, Pete Alfano, and David Teel; Stan Kasten; John Dever; Eric Spitz; Gary Cohen; Beth "Shumway" Brown; Beth Sherry-Downes; Bob Socci; Pete Van Poppel; Omar Nelson; Frank DaVinney; Chet Gladchuk; Eric Ruden; Scott Straseemeier; Billy Stone; Mike Werteen; Chris Knoche; Phil Hoffmann; Joe Speed; Jack Hecker; Steve "Moose" Stirling; Tiffany Cantelupe; Anthony and Kristen Noto; Pete Teeley; Bob Zurfluh; Vivian Thompson; Phil Hochberg; Al Hunt; Wayne Zell; Mike and David Sanders; Eddie Evans; Bob Whitmore; Tony Kornheiser; Mark Maske; Ken and Nancy Denlinger; Matt Rennie; Matt Vita; Matt Bonesteel; Kathy Orton; Camille Powell; Chris Ryan; Harry Kantarian; Jim Rome; Travis Rodgers; Jason Stewart; Mike Purkey; Bob Edwards; Tom and Jane Goldman; Mike Gastineau; Tom Ross; David Stewart; Mary Bromley; Dick "Hoops" and Joanie "Hoops" Weiss; Jim O'Connell; Bob and Elaine Ryan; Frank Hannigan; Geoff Russell; Jerry Tarde; Mike O'Malley; Larry Dorman; Jeff D'Alessio; Marsha Edwards; Jay and Natalie Edwards; Len and Gwyn Edwards-Dieterle; Chris Edwards and John Cutcher; Aunt Joan and Neil Oxman; Bill Leahey; Andy North; Steve Bisciotti; Pam Lund; Kevin Byrne; Dick Cass; Mike Muehr; Martha Brendle; Joe Durant; Gary "Grits" Crandall; Drew Miceli; Bob Low; Steve Flesch; Brian Henninger; and Tom and Hilary Watson. And extra thanks to Jake Pleet.

Thanks also to the folks at the Golf Channel and at Comcast SportsNet who have actually made television fun the last couple of years: Tom Stathakes, Joe Riley, Dave Taylor, Kristi Setaro, Matt Hegarty, Eric Rutledge, Jon Steele, Scott Rude, Jeremy Davis, Tim Rosaforte, Frank Nobilo, Brandel Chamblee, Rich Lerner, Gary Williams, Eric Kuselias, Kelly Tilghman, Todd Lewis, Whit Watson, and Kraig Kann at the Golf Channel. And at Comcast: Joe Yasharoff, Larry Duvall, Manda Gross, Ivan Carter, Russ Thaler, Chick Hernandez, Julie Donaldson, and Brian Mitchell.

Also, the usual suspects in different sports. At the USGA: David Fay (ex-exec director), Mike Davis, Mike Butz, Mary Lopuszynski, Pete Kowalski, Amy Watters, and Craig Smith (still). Frank and Jaymie Bussey get their own category. At the PGA Tour: Marty Caffey, Henry Hughes (still), Sid Wilson, Joel Schuchmann, Todd Budnick, Dave Senko, Doug Milne, Chris Reimer, Colin Murray, John Bush, Chris Smith, Laura Hill, James Cramer, Joe Chemyz (pronounced Krzyzewski), and Phil Stambaugh. Thanks also to Dave Lancer and Ward Clayton for years of friendship, and special thanks as always to Denise Taylor and Guy Scheipers. At the PGA of America: Joe Steranka, Bob Denney, and Julius Mason.

And, of course, the rules guys: Mark Russell (and my favorite Republicans, Alex and Laura Russell), Jon Brendle, Steve Rintoul, Slugger White (*not* my favorite Republican), Robbie Ware, and Mike Shea. Special thanks to John Paramour, my wife's biggest fan.

Basketball people: David Stern, Tim Frank, Rick Barnes, Mike Brey, Jeff Jones, Lefty Driesell, Brad and Seth Greenberg, Fran Dunphy, Karl Hobbs, Jim Calhoun, Jim Boeheim, Brad Stevens, Billy Donovan, Larry Shyatt, Tom Brennan, Tommy Amaker, Dave Odom, Jim Larranaga, Mack McCarthy, Pat Flannery, Ralph Willard, Emmett Davis, Billy Lange, Fran O'Hanlon, (last coach standing), Zack Spiker, Dave Paulsen, Milan Brown, and Brett Reed. Frank Sullivan will always get his own sentence.

I can't forget my various medics—although sometimes I wish I could: Eddie McDevitt, Dean Taylor (I'm happier to remember Ann), Bob Arciero, and Gus Mazzocca, not to mention Tim Kelly, Steve Boyce (who, no offense, I hope to never see again), and Joe Vassallo.

Two guys who fit no category because they are unique: Howard Garfinkel and Tom Konchalski—yes, still the only honest man in the gym, as we learn firsthand more and more with each passing year and scandal.

The swimming knuckleheads: Jason Crist (aka the newlywed), Clay F. Britt, Paul Doremus, Danny Pick, Erik Osborne, John Craig, Doug Chestnut, Peter Ward, Penny Bates, Carole Kammel, Mary Dowling, Margot Pettijohn, Tom Denes, A. J. Block, Peter Lawler, and the still-missed Mike Fell. One other note: the two best moments of 2010 for me were the birth of my daughter and my wedding. Third on the list was swimming a relay with new dad Jeff Roddin, Mark Pugliese, and Wally Dicks. Each of us had undergone some kind of major surgery in the recent past. We swam the year's fastest 200-meter long course medley relay in our age group in the country. Yes, I'm bragging. Pretty good for a bunch of broken-down old men.

The China Doll/Shanghai Village Gang lives on: Aubre Jones, Rob Ades, Jack Kvancz, Chris Wallace, Arnie "The Horse" Heft, Stanley Copeland, Reid Collins, Harry Huang, George Solomon, Geoff Kaplan, Jeff Gemunder, and Murray Lieberman. Pete Dowling, Bob Campbell, Joe McKeown, Morgan Wootten, Ric McPherson, and Joe Greenberg remain members in absentia and make occasional cameos. Absent friends: Zang, Hymie, and, of course, Red. We now have a horse named for the group (thanks to Arnie): Red's Roundtable, who has won six of seven as this is written. You go, girl.

The Rio Gang celebrated in 2010, not so much in 2011, but what the heck: Tate Armstrong, Mark Alarie, Clay Buckley, and Terry Chili, better known these days as Alex's dad.

The Feinstein Advisory Board: Drummer, Frank Mastrandrea, Wes Seeley, and Dave Kindred. The loss of my friend and mentor Bill Brill leaves a void that cannot be filled.

Last, never least, my family—which grew in 2010: Bobby, Jennifer, Matthew, and Brian; Margaret, David, Ethan, and Ben; Marlynn and Cheryl. Those who deserve more credit than anyone are Christine, Danny, and Brigid, who are now joined by Jane Blythe Feinstein—born October 26, 2010—seventy years and one day after Bob Knight. Thank God for that one day.

Index